*f*P

What Co·u·n·t·s

How Every Brain

Is Hardwired

for Math

Brian Butterworth

THE FREE PRESS

*f*P

THE FREE PRESS
A Division of Simon & Schuster Inc.
1230 Avenue of the Americas
New York, NY 10020
Copyright © 1999 by Brian Butterworth
All rights reserved, including the right of reproduction
in whole or in part in any form.
THE FREE PRESS and colophon are trademarks of Simon & Schuster Inc.
Designed by Kim Llewellyn
Manufactured in the United States of America

1 3 5 7 9 10 8 6 4 2

Library of Congress Cataloging-in-Publication Data
Butterworth, Brian.
What counts : how every brain is hardwired for math / Brian Butterworth.
p.   cm.
Includes bibliographical references (p.   ) and index.
1. Number concept.   2. Mathematical ability.   3. Mathematics—
Psychological aspects.   I. Title.
QA141.5.B786   1999
510'.19—dc21   99-17314
CIP

ISBN 0-684-85417-1

For Amy, Anna, and Di, who count

CONTENTS

PREFACE

I am not a mathematician. In fact I am not particularly good at maths or calculation. But, like everyone else, I do use numbers every waking hour of every day. Numbers invade my dreams and fantasies, my hopes and anxieties. Perhaps because we see the world through numerical spectacles which we never take off, even in our sleep, it is hard for us to realize how utterly dependent we are on numbers. I am just looking at the front page of this morning's newspaper. It is fairly typical, I suspect.

The paper costs 45p, it is published on 12 June 1998; Sport is on page 28; the Chancellor of the Exchequer will sell £12 billion of public assets at £4 billion a year, local authorities expect to raise £2.75 billion, public sector salaries will rise by 2.25%, Government investment has fallen by 0.8% of GDP, net investment of infrastructure to 2002 will be £14 billion, public sector spending will rise by 2.75%, the Government will raise £1 billion a year from selling unused assets, leader comment is on page 19, financial analysis on page 21; Catherine Cookson dies at 91 years, 13 days before her 92nd birthday, she had 85 best-selling books at the rate of 2 a year since 1950, they had sold 100 million copies, earning her £14 million, she was the 17th richest woman in Britain, her husband Tom is 87, she gave £100,000 to a charity in 1996, her neighbour Gertrude Roberts is 78, the obituary is on page 20, and a notice of the death of writer Hammond Innes is on page 4; Stephen Lawrence aged 18 was murdered in 1993, his mother is 45, 5 men summonsed to give evidence are aged 21, 22, 21, 20, and 22; the maximum charge for Cable & Wireless telephone calls on Saturdays is fixed at 50p until the end of September, you can call 0800 056 8182 to find out more; there's a horrifying racist murder reported on page 3; the other sections in the paper run from Home on page 5, through pages 15, 17, 18, 20, 23, 24, and 29 to Radio schedules on page 31, and the newspaper's bar code is 9770261307354.

There are 51 separate numbers on just one page, which it took me less than five minutes to read over breakfast. I was keen to get to the sporting pages, with World Cup results and cricket scores—numbers by the bucketful. So in the half-hour it takes me to get through the paper, I probably see, and at least half attend to, about 300 visual numbers. Radio 4, 93.5 kHz, was on at the same time, and other numbers were going into my ears, occasionally making it all the way into my consciousness (which doesn't mean that the others were not processed at all). I had to check the numbers on my watch—two out of the twelve—to make sure I wasn't late cooking daughter Anna the approved number of bacon rashers—three. The two digital clocks on the kitchen appliances advanced by 35 minutes while I was reading and cooking. Anna's elder sister, Amy, needed £70 for a school trip. As I walked Anna to school, we passed 73 houses, each with a number, and many cars, also with numbers. All this before work, which of course involves lots more numbers.

At a very, very rough guess, I would say that I process about 1,000 numbers an hour, about 16,000 numbers per waking day, nearly 6 million a year. People whose jobs entail working with numbers, in supermarkets, banks, betting shops, schools, dealing rooms, will process many more than this.

Behind these numbers are vast systems of other numbers. The time now is set in relation to the 1,440 minutes of a 24-hour day. Today's date is set in relation to the number of days that have passed since 1 January, AD 1; people's ages at death depend on this numerical system. The Chancellor's statistics rest on other statistics of public accounts, economic growth, and so on, which rest on the daily, weekly, and monthly transactions of an enormous number of public bodies, private companies and individuals, including Mrs Cookson, her publisher, its printer, and her accountant and PR company.

Not all numbers are the same. On the front page of that newspaper there are whole numbers and decimal fractions. There are numbers to denote how many things there are in a collection; real visible things such as 5 men, invisible things like 91 years, or things that are potentially visible, I guess, like 50 pence, 100,000 pounds, or 14,000,000,000 pounds. There are also numbers used solely for ordering things in a sequence, for example, Cookson's 92nd year; the date 12 June falls into this category, as does the page number 15. And there are also numbers for which both their value and their position in a sequence are irrelevant: the telephone number and the bar code. These are no more than numerical labels.

I confess that I didn't focus on our dependence on numbers until, as part of my work as a neuropsychologist, I started to test people who couldn't use them. One of the most remarkable was an Italian hotelier, who kept the hotel's accounts until she suffered a stroke, after which she was blind and deaf to numbers above 4. This meant she couldn't shop or make phone calls or do innumerable other things she had previously taken for granted.

Then there was an intelligent young man with a degree and professional qualifications. He was even good at statistics, provided he could use a computer, yet he was unable to do even the simplest numerical things in a normal way. Arithmetic was a disaster area for him, but it went further than that. Most of us can tell how many things there are at a glance, without counting, as long there aren't more than about five. This young man had to count when there were just two things! This wasn't a failure of education—it was something of a very different order.

In the 1980s reports began to appear in the learned journals of experiments showing that newborn babies, who certainly hadn't learned to count, were able to do what this young man could not: recognize the number of things they saw at a glance. Naturally, I tried a version of one of these experiments on our first daughter, when she was just four weeks old. She was sat inside a large cardboard box in which industrial quantities of nappies were delivered, to watch one, two, three, or four light green rectangles appear and disappear on a dark green computer screen. Her response to what she saw was measured by how often she sucked on a rubber teat attached to a pressure transducer connected to the computer. The more she sucked, the more interested she was. We were getting very promising results until the subject decided that she wasn't going to suck the teat any more. She has remained averse to doing things she can't see the point of ever since.

It crossed my mind at the time, though without really registering, that if you are *born* with the ability to recognize the number of things you see, then maybe you could also be born with a handicap that prevented this ability from developing normally. I remember thinking that perhaps there is a numerical equivalent of colour blindness. Ten years later, I began to wonder whether this was what was wrong with people like the young man who needed to count two items. From this it was a relatively short conceptual step to wondering whether the human genome normally contained instructions for building circuits in the brain that are specialized for numbers. But were these circuits built for just this purpose, or had they evolved for some other purpose and been co-opted by the need to cope with numbers?

Colour vision is universal. Everyone, save those with particular identifiable genetic abnormalities, sees the world in colour. But does everyone see, or think about, the world in terms of numbers, save those with some genetic abnormality? If thinking in numbers is something that has to be taught, then there should be people who had not been taught and couldn't do it.

We, in our advanced technological, trading society, need to be able to use numbers, so numeracy has emerged as a key ingredient of our educational system. But what about 'stone-age' societies with little technology and little trade? Do they use numbers? Do they count? Is number ability really universal?

Finding out is by no means as easy as it might at first seem. Let me give an example. One way to tell whether a culture uses numbers is to see whether they have symbolic representations for numbers, either written or spoken. English has special words for numbers, and a syntax that allows us to name numbers as large as we like, but most indigenous Australian languages have words only for 'one', 'two', and 'many'. Users of these languages—particularly the Aborigines of the Central

Desert, who are traditional hunter-gatherers—have little to trade. Their technology, although exquisitely adapted to their way of life, is limited to a few implements such as boomerangs and bark shields and containers. If anyone is likely not to use numbers, not to think about the world in terms of numbers, it is they. The problem is how to tell. Nowadays, all Aborigines have encountered Western money culture, and the English language with its number words and written numerals. So the question turns into a historical one: before contact, did they use numbers? If they didn't, this would be one strike against the universality of a specialized number ability.

An obvious objection to this idea is that, even within a society, some people are really good with numbers while others approach numbers with fear and loathing. Surely, if we are all born with much the same brain circuitry for numbers then our abilities too should be much the same, just as almost all of us are born with nearly identical abilities to see colour, or to use language (also thought to depend on special genes, as yet unidentified). But perhaps that's like requiring everyone to show the same sense of colour in the colour coordination of their clothes, or the way they decorate and furnish their homes, or maintaining that we should all be equally good at putting words together to create narratives or poetry. It may turn out that there are basic capabilities that are indeed innate and universal, and that the differences in the level of adult performance will depend on experience and education.

Thinking along these lines, I began to wonder what these basic capabilities could be. The things that babies can do without instruction seemed to me a good place to start. How do babies think of the world? Do they see it in terms of numbers of things, just as they see it in terms of colour? Another line of attack was to see which numerical ideas seemed natural and easy to grasp. For example, I noticed in my own children that what I was taught to call 'proper fractions' ($\frac{1}{2}$, $\frac{3}{4}$, $\frac{7}{8}$) were easy, while 'improper fractions' ($\frac{3}{2}$, $\frac{5}{4}$, $\frac{8}{7}$) were hard. Most people find probabilities obscure. Can calculus be made easy? Are the ideas that seem natural and easy those we are born with, or are they just learned earlier, or taught better?

Certainly there is much anxiety about mathematics education. Children are distressed when they fail, as are their parents.

Governments worry that their working population is not properly equipped to compete in a highly technological, and therefore highly numerical, world. Could we improve how well we understand mathematical ideas if the education system were to base its teaching more firmly on the mathematical toolkit we are born with?

These are some of the questions that led to this book. They have led me into all kinds of fascinating subjects completely new to me: thermoluminescent dating of rock faces and the intricacies of Venetian house numbering, Aboriginal sign language and New Guinea body-counting, Ethiopian farming practices and ancient Indus Valley poetry, the origins of number words and the Venerable Bede's system of finger-counting. I have also had to rethink much of what I thought I knew about numbers and about the brain.

On the way I have had help from many people. I have been struck by how willing busy experts have been to answer naive and often stupid questions from a complete stranger. Among them are Jean Clottes, Gordon Conway, Les Hiatt, Deborah Howard, Rhys Jones, Karen McComb, Alexander Marshack, Bert Roberts, Robert Sharer, Stephen Shennan, and David Wilkins.

Over the years I have had the enormous benefit of working closely with brilliant and knowledgeable scientists on how the brain deals with numbers: Bob Audley, Lisa Cipolotti, Margarete Delazer, Franco Denes, Marcus Giaquinto, Luisa Girelli, Jonckheere, Carlo Semenza, Elizabeth Warrington, and Marco Zorzi. This work was generously supported by the Commission of the European Union and by the Wellcome Trust.

I have also benefited enormously from discussions with Mark Ashcraft, Peter Bryant, Jamie Campbell, Marinella Capelletti, Alfonso Caramazza, Laurent Cohen, Richard Cowan, Stanlislas Dehaene, Ann Dowker, Karen Fuson, Randy Gallistel, Rochel Gelman, Alessia Granà, Patrick Haggard, Thom Heyd, Jo-Anne LeFevre, Giuseppe Longo, Daniela Lucangeli, Mike McCloskey, George Mandler, Ference Marton, Marie-Pascale Noël, Terezinha Nunes, Mauro Pesenti, Manuela Piazza, Lauren Resnick, Sonia Sciama, Xavier Seron, Tim Shallice, David Skuse, Faraneh Varga-Khadem, John Whalen, Karen Wynn, and the late Neil O'Connor. Some of these discussions were held at a workshop on 'The Concept of Number and Simple

Arithmetic', sponsored by the Scuola Internazionale Superiore di Studi Avvanzati in Trieste, organized by Tim Shallice, the Director of Cognitive Science. Sean Hawkins and Martin Hill provided invaluable library research. My being Editor of the learned journal *Mathematical Cognition*, published by Psychology Press, has helped me keep in touch with the latest developments.

The philosopher Marcus Giaquinto inspired my approach, and he kindly read all the chapters and offered penetrating but helpful comments. Designer and film-maker Storm Thorgerson worked with me on adapting some of the ideas in the book for other media, and tried to ensure that the written material was as clear and gripping to the reader as it was to me. My daughters Amy and Anna were major inspirations, not just because they have been handy, and often unwitting, sources of data on how children construct numerical ideas, but also because their witting insights into their own mental processes have been invaluable. My partner, Diana Laurillard, contributed so much and in so many ways that it is now hard to identify her contributions, except negatively: the least sensible ideas are not hers.

Lisa Cipolotti, Margarete Delazer, and Norah Frederickson expertly scrutinized some of the chapters. My original editor at Macmillan, Clare Alexander, commissioned the book and provided perceptive comments on the first two chapters. Georgina Morley at Macmillan and Dr Michael Rodgers offered detailed advice on many aspects of the text. Stephen Morrow at my US publisher, The Free Press, offered strategic suggestions on the organization of the whole book, as well as detailed comments. John Woodruff scrupulously edited the whole text.

Probably none of this would have happened without Peter Robinson, my agent, whose faith that people would want to read a book with the word 'math' in the title reassured me, and persuaded my publishers, that it was a viable project.

For me, this has been a wonderful adventure into the history, anthropology, psychology, and neuroscience of the ideas that shaped how we all think about the world. I hope you find it so too.

1

THINKING BY NUMBERS

This grand book, the universe . . . cannot be understood unless one first learns to comprehend the language and read the letters in which it is composed. It is written in the language of mathematics.

GALILEO[1]

THE WORLD BY NUMBERS

Of all the many abilities that have raised us from cave-dwellers using stone tools to creators of great cities and modern science, one of the most important is the ability to use numbers. It is also among the least understood. Traditional studies of the role of numbers have been concerned largely with their contribution to the development of science.[2] However, numbers have affected almost all the aspects of our life which are most characteristically human. We have used numbers from the beginning of the historical record, and perhaps from way back in the prehistory of our species. This book is an attempt to explain why we all think about the world in terms of numbers.

Nowadays, we use numbers routinely. We use them to count things, to tell the time, as statistical data, to gamble, to buy and to sell. Even barter needs numbers: I'll give you six knives if you give me two pigs. We use them to rank competitors, in addresses (house numbers and postal codes), to grade examination candidates. Blood pressures, temperatures, and IQs are given numerical values. Cars and their engines, TV stations and telephone lines, all have their number labels. Goods in shops have bar codes. People have social security numbers, bank account numbers, and passport numbers. Your height, weight, and age are all denoted by some numerical multiple of a standard unit.

The importance of numbers lies not just in their obvious utility, but also in the way they have shaped how we think about the world. It is the language in which we formulate scientific theories. Numbers, as Einstein said, are the 'symbolic counterpart of the universe'; they are crucial to the measurements we take as the fundamental evidence for our theories. 'When you cannot measure ... your knowledge is of a meagre and unsatisfactory kind,'[3] to quote the great nineteenth-century scientist Lord Kelvin, who, not coincidentally, invented the scale for measuring absolute temperature.

To get some idea of just how fundamental numbers are, try to imagine our world without them. There would be no money, no counting, no income tax. Without numbers, trade would be restricted to face-to-face barter. I could see the knives you wished to trade, and you could see my pigs, but trade at a distance would be extraordinarily difficult: how could I convey the number of pigs I would be willing to trade for your knives, and the number of knives I would be willing to accept for my pigs?

Without numbers, there would be none of our familiar sports, such as football, baseball, and tennis, since they use numbers to define how many players may be in a team, and to keep the score. Many sports obsessively keep numerical records; thus athletics is a good example. Qualification for the Olympic Games depends on exceeding a numerical standard. This tradition goes back to the original Olympian Games, whose very period—the Olympiad—is a definite number of years, four. Numerical records were kept of some events. Phayllus of Croton was credited with a leap of 55 feet (16.8 metres),[4] which you might think raises the question of just how good the Greeks were at measurement. Some modern competitions, such as the heptathlon, are defined by the number of events in which the athletes take part, seven in this case.

Without numbers, we could not frame basic theories of physical nature, such as Kepler's laws of planetary motion, Newton's laws of motion, or Einstein's $E = mc^2$. Chemists would be at a distinct disadvantage without the numerically ordered periodic table of the elements. The study of human nature has also depended on numbers to quantify mental attributes such as intelligence, reading age, or degree of introversion.

The basic laws of perception are another good example of the use of numbers in the study of human nature. To see a bright light get brighter you need a bigger absolute increase in energy than to see a dim light get brighter; to hear a loud noise get louder you need a bigger absolute increase in energy than for a quiet noise. The scientist, with or without numbers, would ask whether there is some general law that will predict how big an increase is needed to make a noticeable difference to brightness or to loudness. It turns out that there is, and it was discovered in 1834 by Ernst Weber. The law states that a barely noticeable change in brightness depends on a proportional increase in energy, not an absolute increase. What is the value of the increase that yields a difference which is just detectable? Experimentation tells us that an increase of roughly 1% in energy gives us a noticeable difference in brightness and about 10% is needed for a noticeable difference in loudness.[5] Weber's law could not be formulated, perhaps not even thought about, without numbers.

Clearly, numbers are extraordinarily useful, but there is still the question of how we came to describe and represent our world in terms of numbers. Is there something about the world that would oblige us to invent numbers if we didn't have them already? Many useful but difficult inventions, such as the alphabet, double entry bookkeeping, or the printed circuit,[6] were invented just once and were diffused around the world. One possibility, then, is that there was one ancient Einstein who invented numbers. Once he had made the breakthrough, it became clear how valuable the idea was and so it was eagerly adopted by neighbours, and then neighbours of neighbours, and so on. This scenario implies that cultures distant from the inventor would get numbers later than those nearby, or perhaps not at all. This is what has happened with the alphabet, for example. Indeed, some Amazonian tribes still haven't learned to read or write.[7]

On the other hand, many inventions seem to have been less difficult, like plant domestication, pottery, and fire, and arose independently in many areas. Is the idea of numbers a relatively easy invention that many societies could have developed by themselves? But even easy inventions depend on local circumstances. The invention of settled agriculture with crops and domesticated animals has depended on having plants and animals that are suitable and easy to domesticate.[8] Although trading creates a *need* for numbering (as I discuss in Chapter 2), it is not clear what would make the invention of numbers harder or easier.

A third possibility is that the idea of numbers was not invented at all. Rather, they are something about us, an intrinsic part of human nature, like the ability to see colours, or *schadenfreude*.

Today using numbers for trading, ordering, and labelling seems very easy, convenient, and natural. In a way this is very surprising, since numbers are, in the words of Adam Smith, 'among the most abstract ideas which the human mind is capable of forming'. Numbers are not properties of objects. You cannot touch, see, or feel them. They are not like the properties of an orange. If an object is an orange it will have a characteristic colour, texture, size, shape, smell, and taste. You can check each of these properties to see whether a candidate object is an orange or, for example, a ball or a lemon. But a collection of five things doesn't possess characteristic colour, shape, or taste. What all such collections have in common is their fiveness, and this is abstract. To understand numbers—to understand, for example, the difference between five and four—is to understand something very abstract indeed.

To use numbers, therefore, we should require extensive training, as for other abstract concepts. Think how long it takes to learn and apply the principles of chemical reactions or the Linnaean taxonomic categories. This is not just a matter of acquiring the Latin names, since in traditional societies, which of course use the vernacular, learning to classify plants and animals is a very long job which starts in earliest childhood. And yet, as I show in Chapter 2, everyone can count or tally up small collections of objects, and can carry out simple arithmetical operations, whether they are Cambridge graduates or tribesmen in the remote fastnesses of the New Guinea highlands. Even cultures which have no words for numbers still count, calculate, and trade. Despite its abstractness, the idea of number seems to be universal. What is it about our brains that makes us all familiar with this idea?

THE UNIVERSALITY OF NUMBERS AND THE MATHEMATICAL BRAIN

The philosopher and psychologist Jerry Fodor divides cognitive abilities into two sorts: the highly specialized, which he calls 'cognitive modules', and the general purpose, which he calls 'central processes'.[9]

Cognitive modules extract just one type of information from the senses. For example, one module extracts information about the colour of objects, while another module works out the shape of an object. Fodor calls this property of modules 'domain specificity'. Because they are specialized, they can operate fast, but to do so their operation must be automatic. For example, you cannot see a red flower without processing the information about its colour—you cannot choose not to see its redness. These fast, automatic, domain-specific modules confer an adaptive advantage on the organism: seeing colours in this way speeds identification of prey and predators. Through our genes we inherit instructions for building these modules in the brain (and the nerve cells in the sense organs). The modules consist of distinct neural circuits, which in many cases will be ready to go as soon as the organism is born, or very soon after—as with colour vision in human infants. Since we are born with functioning colour vision circuits, we do not need to learn to see in colour. Fodor believes that key aspects of our linguistic abilities are modular in this sense. Of course it is true that we have to learn English (or French or Chinese), but the basic mechanisms for doing so are built into our brains at birth, and many of the operations are fast and automatic. For example, you cannot see the letter string RED without identifying the word and evoking its meaning.

Central processes are the converse of cognitive modules. They operate slowly; we can choose whether to operate them or not; we are not born with brain circuits specialized to do them; and they need learning. The ability I am exercising now—typing English words into my computer—falls into this category. Typing English depends on learning. It's not automatic: I don't do it if I don't want to. And the ability to type English is so recent that there has been no time for evolution to select brains that are particularly good at it. This means that we are not born with specialized typing circuits: we have to rely on training and practice to become proficient. Memory is another central process for Fodor. It is not domain-specific—we can remember anything, if we work at it. And reasoning, too, is central, since we can reason about anything.

So what is numerical ability, a cognitive module or a central process? Fodor is quite clear that it is a central process. Calculation is slow and effortful; reasoning seems to play an important role, unlike seeing the world in colour; it seems to depend on formal instruction;

it does not seem to be innate because there are very wide variations of numerical ability—as compared with the ability to see colours—and there may even be people who have been denied instruction who cannot use numbers at all. Finally, we do not appear to be born with specialized brain structures for numeracy.

The Number Module

I shall try to show that Fodor was wrong in every particular. I shall argue that the human genome—the full set of genes that make us what we are—contains instructions for building specialized circuits of the brain, which I call the Number Module (Figure 1.1). The job of the Number Module is to categorize the world in terms of numerosities—the number of things in a collection. It makes us, and other creatures who possess it, sensitive to the number of things in a collection. Compare seeing the world in terms of colour with seeing it in terms of number. Both processes operate automatically: we cannot help but see the cows in the field as brown and white, nor can we help seeing that there are three of them. Both processes fail to develop normally in some individuals. Just as there are people born colour-blind, there are also, as I argue in Chapter 7, people born with a kind of number-blindness.

What makes human numerical ability unique is the development and transmission of cultural tools for extending the capability of the Number Module. These tools include aids to counting, such as number words, finger-counting, and tallying, and also the accumulated inventions of mathematicians down the centuries—from numerals to calculating procedures, from counting-boards to theorems and their proofs.

Our Mathematical Brain, then, contains these two elements: a Number Module and our ability to use the mathematical tools supplied by our culture. This may seem obvious, but it is contentious. Another idea is that we possess an innate sensitivity to quantities, but not to numerosities. For example, Stanislas Dehaene, in his book *The Number Sense*,[10] following a twenty-year tradition of work with animals and infants, postulates a brain mechanism, called 'The Accumulator', which interprets numbers as approximate quantities, rather like the level of liquid in a bottle. Different numbers are represented by different levels. It works by recording events—a drop of liquid for each event. So the three cows in the field would first be coded as three

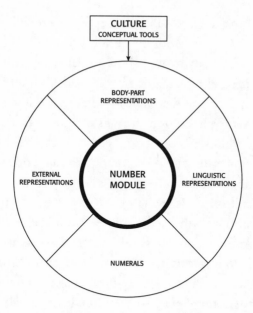

Figure 1.1 The Number Module is the innate core of our numerical abilities. It categorizes the world in terms of numerosities, up to about 4 or 5. To get beyond 5 we need to build onto the Number Module, using the conceptual tools provided by our culture. We add these to other items of our conceptual toolkit through learning from other people. The tools fall into four main categories, as we shall see in more detail in the following chapters: body-part representations (fingers, toes, etc.), linguistic representations (specialized counting words), numerals (specialized written symbols), and external representations (tallies, calculators, etc.).

events, and represented by the level of the total amount of the three drops of the imaginary liquid.

Another possibility is that numbers are just like anything else we learn, such as the periodic table, the capitals of African states, or how to use WordPerfect in DOS. Good numerical ability depends on just those capacities that make us good at school subjects: good teaching, high intelligence, hard work, and an excellent memory. There is nothing specialized about this ability.

Testing the Number Module. All scientific hypotheses are empirically testable. That, according to philosopher of science Karl Popper, is what distinguishes scientific hypotheses from the propositions of mysticism and religion. The sceptical reader has no doubt already formulated some tests that my hypothesis of a Number Module in everybody's brain will need to pass before it is accepted as credible.

First, if the Number Module is built into all our brains when we are born, then everybody should show evidence of being able to carry out tasks that depend on categorizing the world in terms of numbers of things—what I call numerosities—whether or not they have had the opportunity for instruction, formal or informal, in numbers and arithmetic. Everybody should be able to match the numerosities of collections of things on the basis of one-to-one correspondence between the members of the collections, and they should be able to tell which of two collections is the larger. Not much, you may think, but these two operations form the basis of everything else we know about numerosities. And we must be sure that the universality of the ability is not explainable in terms of the spread of an invention combined with the fact that humans are just about smart enough to learn how to use it. Compare numbers and the alphabet. The alphabet was invented just once, presumably after a lot of hard work by intelligent and dedicated scribes, in the Middle East around 1700 BC. Few probably have the capacity to invent an alphabet, but most of us are smart enough to learn how to use one.

Second, if specialized brain structures are in place when we are born, though of course they will mature and develop over time, then we should see evidence of capacities that depend on numerosity even in the infant.

Third, we should be able to locate these specialized structures in the brain. Certain localized brain damage could affect number skills only. Imaging of brain activity should show the same localized hotspots whenever the brain is calculating.

Fourth, if we have a Number Module, we should be able to find evidence that will satisfy Fodor's criteria for modules: fast and automatic numerical operations, at least for basic operations such as identifying or comparing numerosities.

Fifth, if this numerical capacity is part of all our brains, then we need to explain why some people are good or very good at arithmetic, while others are bad or hopeless.

Sixth, if we inherit a Number Module, then it is encoded in our genome, which in turn we inherited, with mutations, from our ancestors. Does this mean that there is a set of genes that code for the building of the specialized brain circuits? Does it mean that our near ancestors, in the last ice age, counted as well? What about our more distant ancestors, *Homo erectus*, or great apes, other mammals, birds, reptiles, worms?

Seventh, how does the way we talk about numbers and the way we write them affect the development of number skills that go beyond basic numerosity? Does the Mathematical Brain hypothesis have anything to say about how we can help our children learn more advanced arithmetic, or how we should design our education system?

Finally, there is something strange and emotive about numbers and counting. Many cultures from Africa to orthodox Jews forbid counting people. Some numbers are regarded as lucky or unlucky. Some people suffer anxiety at the thought, not to mention the practice, of arithmetic. Does this have anything to do with our Mathematical Brain?

The chapters that follow fully investigate all these issues.

TYPES OF NUMBER AND THEIR USES

The first step is to clarify what numbers can mean. Perhaps because we use number words and Arabic numerals all the time, we may unreflectingly think that each time we use, say, the number word 'five', we mean the same thing. After all, five is five: it is always half of ten and a tenth of fifty; it always comes after four and before six; it's the number of fingers on the average hand; it's the number of tanners in half a crown.

In fact, this is far from the case. The number word 'five' has many distinct and different meanings, just as the word 'orange' has distinct meanings—the fruit and the colour. Of course, the two are related, the colour meaning is derived from the (typical) colour of the thing, but the colour isn't the fruit: you cannot eat the colour. Languages sometimes distinguish explicitly at least some of the different number meanings. English and other European languages distinguish ordinal meanings by using the special terms *first, second, third, fourth,* and so on, rather than *one, two, three, four.*

Let me start by explaining how number terms—words and numerals—have different meanings. But fundamental to human thinking about numbers are the meanings that answer the question, 'How many?' These are numerosities. My hypothesized Number Module is a brain mechanism that identifies numerosities.

Numerosities

Think of a collection of things, any collection of any things. This collection will have a number, or what I prefer to call a 'numerosity'[11] to distinguish it from other meanings of number terms. Many of our familiar ideas of number are properties of numerosities, and the relations that hold among numerosities. For example, numerosities are completely ordered by the size of the collections that represent them. Let us call a collection of cups with the numerosity four, a four-collection, and a collection of saucers with the numerosity three, a three-collection. Four is larger than three, because you can take each cup, pair it with a saucer, and still have one cup left over. Another example is adding: the sum of two numbers means finding the numerosity of their collections combined. Since collections are simply combined (technically, we are forming the *union* of the two collections), it does not matter in which order the collections are taken: this is why $4 + 3 = 3 + 4$. Other numerical operations and properties can be built from these foundations.

One fundamental property is so obvious that it is frequently overlooked. Every numerosity, every number, is the sum of other numerosities: 2 is the sum of 1 and 1; 3 is the sum of 2 and 1; 4 is the sum of 2 and 2, and of 3 and 1; and so on. (In the simplest number system, 1 is not a sum.) This property—sometimes called *additive composition* because numbers can be added together to form other numbers—turns out to be critical in understanding how the child comes to understand numbers, as I show in Chapter 3.

Although numerosities depend on collections, they are properties of collections and cannot be defined in terms of them, rather as 'yellow' is a property of a banana but is not definable in terms of bananas. Of course, you can use a banana as a representative of yellow things. In the same way I can point to a particular collection, for example, the collection of fingers on my left hand, to illustrate what a collection with a numerosity of five is like.[12]

A numerosity is the number you get when you count a collection.

In this sense, counting means putting each thing in the collection in one-to-one correspondence with a number. In practice, this normally means putting each thing in one-to-one correspondence with a number word, where the last number word counted denotes numerosity of the collection of things counted: 'one, two, three, four, five: five pigs'. Counting is the key to numerosity. Children use counting practice to build a sense of numerosity into a full numerosity system. Counting also helps children discriminate among numerosities since collections that have different counts have different numerosities.

To understand numerosities, you need to have a grasp of two other ideas. First is the idea of an object—something that can be *individuated*. In most cultures, anything that can be individuated can form a collection that has a numerosity. They can be things that are clearly visible as individuals, such as pigs, wives, or handkerchiefs; they can be things which have a visible manifestation, but are rather more complicated, such as teams in the Premier League, or hops on one leg; they may be invisible yet distinct to the senses, such as notes in a bar, bars in a Blues; they may be abstract, such as days in my holiday or resolutions for the New Year. However, there are exceptions. For example, the language of the Hopi of New Mexico allows only collections of things you can see to have a numerosity, so you can say 'five dogs', 'five stones', or 'five brides', but you cannot say 'five days'. So instead of saying, 'I will be there in five days', you have to use a locution equivalent to the English sentence, 'I will be there on the fifth day'.[13] The Hopi language distinguishes grammatically, as do European languages, between numbers for numerosities and numbers purely to denote order, ordinal numbers, as we shall shortly see.

I have allowed myself a simplification when I talk of 'the idea of numerosity' as if possession of it is all-or-nothing. So, for example, if you possess the concept, then not only can you tell that two collections A and B have the same numerosity, but you can also tell whether A has a larger numerosity than C. What is more, the concept should apply to collections of any number of members. Yet, when we come to examine the abilities of animals and infants, we shall see that they might be able to tell whether two sets are the same, but not which of two sets is bigger, and animals and children can deal only with small numerosities. This raises the question of whether animals and children really do possess the concept, but are limited in applying it, or whether they possess some other concept.

Ordinal Numbers

Ordinal numbers are used for ordering things, like houses, placings in a competition, and so on. Unlike numerosities, the essential property of ordinal numbers is in the ordering, not in the size of the collection, though of course each ordinal corresponds to a numerosity. What is important is that there is a definite relation among the numbers: each number is either before or after any other number, so that all the numbers are completely ordered. Knowing the numbers of two houses in the same street means, usually, that we know their relative position in the street. A higher number is farther up (or farther down) the street than a lower number, though this will depend on the ordering principle: most streets in Britain have even numbers along one side and odd numbers along the other.

Some house numbering, incidentally, is completely useless as an address. In Venice, for example, buildings were renumbered in 1841, by district, called a *sestier* ('sixth'), not by street. The *sestier* of St Mark's begins with number 1 in St Mark's Square at the Doge's Palace and is numbered consecutively up to 5562 on the wall of the Fondaco dei Tedeschi (an important place in the history of arithmetic, as we shall discover in the next chapter) near the Rialto Bridge. There is no way of working this out—you just have to know it. To help, the Venetians put up a notice saying *Ultimo numero del Sestier de San Marco*, but you do not find this out until you get there. If you want to find an address, say San Marco 3832, you will have no idea where it is unless you buy Jonathan del Mar's *Indicatore Anagrafico di Venezia*,[14] which tells you in which street every number is. Should you not have this invaluable guidebook, and end up in Campo San Angelo, where you notice the number 3555 and decide to follow the numbers in ascending order to get to 3832, you will walk through the Calle de la Madona, via Rio Terà dei Assassini and several other side alleys, to Calle de la Verona, then on through the Calle de la Mandola, several other side streets, to the Rio terà de la Mandola, and several more side streets. Then, after a quarter of an hour of steady walking, you will find 3832 back in Campo San Angelo.

For ordering things, number words or numerals can be replaced by any set of symbols that are completely ordered, for example letters of the alphabet, provided the ordering principle is well defined and understood by the users. There is a curious ordering principle to be found in a street in the London suburb of Willesden. The original houses were given the names Belmont, Rayleigh, Overton, Newlyn, Delmore, Everon, Shirley, Beechcroft, Uplands, Rutland, Yelverton. The initial letters spelled out the word BRONDESBURY, the name of the street in which they were situated. The postman, the inhabitants, and their visitors understood the ordering principle, so there was no difficulty in finding the right house.

A striking feature of the terms for the names of the ordinals corresponding to one and two is that they have a quite different origin. The words for 'first' in English, French, Gothic, and Greek are derivations of the Indo-European preposition *pro-*, meaning 'before', which through historical sound change became *fr-* and then *fir-*. 'Second' comes from the Latin *secundus*, meaning 'following', from the verb *sequi* ('to follow'), while in the Gothic, as in Latin *alter*, the word for second means 'the other'. Similarly, Finnish and Basque, which are unrelated to other European languages, do not derive their words for first and second from the corresponding cardinals, the terms for the numerosities. All this suggests that the conceptual origin of ordering is separate from that of counting and numerosity.[15]

Numerical Labels

A very striking feature of the modern world is the need to label things, places, and people uniquely. Numerals are very convenient for this. First, there are enough of them for each thing labelled to have its own number. Second, there are only ten symbols, all of which are part of the standard repertory of symbols on keyboards all over the world. For historical reasons some labelling conventions still incorporate letters as well as numbers. Most national systems of car registration numbers, British National Insurance identifications, and British and Canadian postcodes all mix letters and numbers. Telephone systems in the USA and Britain used to have three-letter district codes followed by a four-digit number. My old telephone number was WIL 4025, which located me in Willesden. Numbers starting MAY indicated fashionable

Mayfair, though others were more obscure, such as AMB for Ambassador, which was never the name of a district of London. The letters have long since been replaced by numbers.

Numerical labels are not ordered by size. My telephone number is 4259 7461, but it is never read out as genuine numbers are read. When asked for my telephone number I never say, 'Forty-two million, five hundred and ninety-seven thousand, four hundred and sixty-one', and I do not claim that it larger than my friend David's, which is 'only' 2673 6579. In fact, labels are not ordered at all. For this reason, labelling can be done in other ways, provided each label is unique. Car registrations in California (and now in Britain) can be chosen by the user, as long as no one else is using the same registration. One linguist I know has the registration LINGUA, and a neurologist has BRAINS. TV channels used to be given names—BBC, ITV, NBC, CBS—and could still. It is just more convenient to give them numbers, because the ordering may help viewers find the desired channel, provided they can remember that BBC 1 is on Channel 31 on the remote control (unless you re-program it).

Although numerical labels are designed to be unique—no two people have the same telephone number nor the same National Insurance number—they are felt to be depersonalizing, in a way that names are not, even though names, such as John Smith, or even Brian Butterworth, are not unique. Number Six in the TV series 'The Prisoner' continually protested, 'I am not a number!'

Fractions

Fractions are ratios of two numerosities, two whole numbers. The most familiar even have special names, such as 'half' and 'quarter'. For some reason, other simple ratios use the words from the ordinal series—'third', 'fifth', 'sixth', and so on. In fact, even 'quarter' comes from the Latin word *quartus*, meaning 'fourth'. Fractions are often used for measures, but not all measures can be expressed as fractions, as we shall see.

Measure Numbers

Measure numbers answer questions like 'How much?', 'How long?', 'How heavy?', where there is an agreed scale or dimension. Historically, the dimension was divided into easily grasped chunks of every-day experience. For length, parts of the body formed the chunks. In Biblical times people used the width of the finger, of the palm, the span of the hand, the length of the forearm from the elbow to the tips of the fingers (the cubit), and so on. Of course, people differ in their dimensions, which would create unacceptable confusion today, but even in Renaissance Italy the *braccia* ('arm length') was standardized only city by city, so a Florentine *braccia* may have been shorter than a Milanese. Even British standardized Imperial measure was based on bodily chunks. The inch was the length from the tip to the knuckle of the thumb. The foot is self-explanatory, though a thousand years ago it was standardized on barleycorns as these were less variable than human feet: a foot was 36 barleycorns 'taken from the middle of the ear'. A yard was the length from King Edgar's nose to the tip of the middle finger of his outstretched arm.[16]

These convenient and readily visualized chunks meant that lengths for most practical purposes could be expressed as whole-number mul-tiples of these units. For example, the Turkish *kilim* in my study is 2 yards 1 foot 7 inches long. Today we would express this length as a multiple of a single standardized unit type that has no basis in the di-mensions of the human body—in this case 224 centimetres.

But even with chunks, some answers needed more precision than whole numbers could provide. Suppose a yard of timber cost four pennies; how much timber could you get for one penny? The solution was to use fractions of the smallest unit—one-half, one-quarter, two-sevenths, and so on. These fractions are the ratios of two whole num-bers, and are readily understood because they map neatly onto the numerosity concept. One can easily envisage a length divided into, say, four equal segments; that is, as a four-collection. It is then quite straightforward to think of a sub-collection of one or two or three segments. You may recall learning these as 'proper' fractions.

Pythagoras' theorem, for which Pythagoras is said to have sacri-ficed a hundred oxen to the gods, states that the square on the hypotenuse of a right-angled triangle is equal to the sum of the squares of the other two sides. This led directly to the problem of 'incommen-surables'—unmeasurables—whose discoverer was allegedly drowned by Pythagoreans for upsetting their philosophy that 'all is numbers'.

Here is the problem. If the sides of a right-angled triangle are equal to 1, then the square on the hypotenuse is equal to 2, and the length of the diagonal is thus $\sqrt{2}$, the square root of 2: a number not expressible as a ratio of two whole numbers. This means that measure numbers can be very different from the other numbers we have considered.

These measure numbers are familiar enough as 'decimals', that is, as whole numbers followed by more numbers after the decimal point, for example 2.50, 2.666, 3.141 592 62. They are ordered according to a different principle from the counting numbers 0, 1, 2, 3, . . . used for numerosities. For any two (different) whole numbers, one will be larger; and for any whole number there will be one and only one successor. For any two of the measure numbers, one will be the larger; however, there is no unique next number. After 2.50, there is 2.51, but between these two there is 2.501; and between 2.50 and 2.501 there is 2.5001, and so on. In fact, there are infinitely many 'next' numbers between, say, 2.50 and 2.51, or indeed between any two decimals.

The German mathematician Leopold Kronecker once said, 'God made the integers. All else is the work of man.' Of course, he was wrong on both counts, but he did articulate the idea that whole numbers are somehow different from other types of number.

Cyclical Numbers
There are also numbers that repeat in a regular cycle. The most familiar is clock time, where 4 is both before and after 5, and addition doesn't work in the usual way (11 o'clock and 5 o'clock add up to 4 o'clock—the sum is 'smaller' than the numbers you add together). It is possible to express the arithmetical rules of cyclical numbers in terms of ordinary arithmetic, by using the idea of the modulus. Clock time has a modulus of 12 (or 24 on a 24-hour clock), which means that you carry out your arithmetic operation—addition, subtraction, and so on—on the remainders of the numbers after you have divided them by 12 (or 24). So when 11 is divided by the modulus, 12, it leaves remainder 11, 5 leaves remainder 5, and their sum is 16, whose remainder after dividing by 12 is 4. So the arithmetic of cyclical numbers can be translated into the arithmetic of ordinary numerosities. However, they have the unusual property that there is a largest number, the modulus.

Days and dates are also cyclic. For us, days repeat in a seven-item cycle, and dates in a cycle of 365 or 366 days. It wasn't always quite so neat. The Chaucer scholar Paul Strohm[17] describes the situation at the end of 14th century:

> Rather than considering the present as a year in a sequence— 1399, for example—the medieval person would have dated the year in terms of the present king's reign; in this case, the twenty-third year of King Richard, second of that name since the conquest ... Weeks and days were normally measured by the liturgical calendar. Henry IV's deposition of Richard II occurred on Monday of the feast of St Michael the Archangel (rather than on 29 September).

Even the time of day followed a different rhythm:

> Clocks were a rarity, and most of those in existence were astrological, measuring the movements of the heavens rather than the hours of the day. Thus people were as likely to identify the time of day by an adjacent liturgical service, such as prime or lauds, as by a particular hour.

Infinite Numerosities

Over the centuries, mathematicians have found that other types of number can be constructed from the natural numbers. Some of these we already grasp intuitively, without needing mathematicians to construct them for us. One example is infinity (or, at least, the smallest infinity). We all know that there is no largest number. As children, we played a game in which one of us would name the biggest number they could think of, and another would try to top it. We quickly got bored with this game since it soon became clear that any number I came up with, for example 'quadzillion zillion zillion', you could always top it with 'and one'. Now, any number like this is finite. One way of expressing this finiteness is to say that you could count up to the number, starting from 1, in a finite time, albeit perhaps a very long time indeed. However, the collection of all numbers is not countable precisely because however many numbers you have counted, there is always that number 'and one'. Evidence from children as young as five suggests that they understand that there is no largest number,[18] and so they have at least the beginnings of a grasp of infinity. However, very few of us understand the properties of even this smallest infinity without specialist training.

There are many other types of number that have been described by mathematicians, but they take us well beyond the main argument of the book. I have focused on seven types of number familiar in everyday life. In Chapter 9, 'Hard numbers and easy numbers', I explain in more detail why some kinds of number problems are hard for us, and others easy. Essentially, those that can be expressed straightforwardly in terms of collections and their numerosities are easy, while those where the connection is more obscure we find difficult. So, for example, proper fractions such as ½ or ¾ are easy because ½ can be expressed as sub-collection of a collection with 2 members; while ¾ can be expressed as sub-collection of a collection with 4 members. Improper fractions, such as ½ or ⁵⁄₄, don't translate so readily into these concepts, and so even children doing maths at secondary school have trouble with them.[19] Decimals are also relatively difficult, both conceptually and practically, and these, as we have seen, have a quite different structure from the numerosities.

The argument I present in this book is a very simple one. We are born with brain circuits specialized for identifying small numerosities. I call these circuits the Number Module, which is the inner core of all our numerical abilities. Onto this inner core we build more advanced abilities, largely by learning from the culture around us what is already known about number and mathematics. This means that my numerical abilities, and yours, depend on three things: the innate inner core, the mathematical knowledge of the culture in which we live, and the extent to which we have acquired this knowledge, as was shown in Figure 1.1.

Had we been born into a culture with very little mathematical knowledge, our abilities would typically be much less than those we have the potential to acquire from our mathematically more advanced culture. Of course, with little opportunity or desire to acquire mathematics, our mathematical abilities would be less than if we had devoted much time to study under the guidance of skilled and dedicated teachers. But, I argue, even the most idle and uninterested person born into the least mathematical culture will still categorize the world in terms of numerosities. At the same time, my hypothesis implies that there will be people who are born without the Number Module—that is, without an innate ability to recognize small numerosities. This, I predict, will be a serious handicap to acquiring the cultural resources needed for good mathematical abilities.

Even if you are not convinced by anything else in this book, I hope that you will be convinced that our ability to use numbers is fundamental to the way we think about the world, that it is the basis of much of what we call civilization, and that to understand our common humanity we need to understand how we understand numbers.

2

EVERYBODY COUNTS

Many of us, poor at maths, blame our teachers. It is certainly true that for advanced concepts and fluent expertise, education is critical. But do the basic idea of number, the concept of numerosity, and our ability to categorize the world in terms of numerosities require special training? My hypothesis is that we are all born with a Mathematical Brain—a brain that contains a special Number Module that categorizes the world in terms of numerosities and forms the basis for our concept of numerosity. Our brains also contain the cultural resources that have extended the capacity of the Number Module, to an extent that depends on the resources available to us, and our mastery of them.

In this chapter I shall try to show that the use of numbers is so universal that it is reasonable to infer that everyone is born with a Number Module. I shall call this the Mathematical Brain hypothesis, in contrast with the invention–diffusion hypothesis, according to which the idea of number was invented and was then diffused around the world.

Many skills are really quite easy once you have been taught them, but you do need to be taught by someone who has previously mastered them. For any one skill, there was a time when no one possessed it, and someone had to come up with the idea of it. An example is reading an alphabetic script. The first such script was invented nearly four thousand years ago in the Near East. To use such a script you need to learn how to represent the spoken word in terms of written letters. I shall be arguing that the ability to categorize the world in terms of numerosities is not like the ability to read an alphabetic script. We don't have to learn it; we are born knowing how to do it: it is part of our Mathematical Brain. If I am right then everyone is able to count, in the sense of possessing the concept of numerosity, irrespective of their education or, more generally, of the cultural resources they have at their disposal. So, whether a culture has extensive trading or not, whether they are technologically advanced or not, whether they are literate or not, its members should be able to carry out tasks that depend on a grasp of numerosities. In the remote highlands of New Guinea, where until the 1970s some tribespeople had no contact with members of other tribes, still less with formal education or money culture, people should still be capable of demonstrating that they can count.

If, on the other hand, I am wrong, and acquiring the concept of numerosity depended on an ancient Einstein inventing numbers (or discovering them, if you prefer), then its possession should depend critically on access to the appropriate training. People raised in a culture to which this invention has not spread will not have access to the training and therefore should not be familiar with the concept. Our New Guinea tribes would have been cut off from all this and so should not be able to count. What is more, if all number systems—words and techniques for counting—are descended from the original invention, then they should all resemble one another, in the way, perhaps, that descendants of the earliest alphabets resemble one another. This resemblance should go beyond mere logic. Obviously, any linguistic representation of numbers will need one distinct word or phrase for each number. If our ancient Einstein, sitting cross-legged and shoeless in his mud hut in Ur, counted on his fingers, then his system and its descendants might also use a base of 5 or 10. Now, what is passed down to his descendants may not be the exact number of a base, but instead the principle or idea that the base should reflect visible digits. What his neighbours took away with them could have been the repeating number term, the base, or it could have been the digit technology that might express itself as a 20 base, to include also their visible toes. What would be unexpected in this 'invention then diffusion' hypothesis would be systems that had a base of 29 or 33, or perhaps no base at all.

There is a way in which the invention–diffusion and Mathematical Brain hypotheses could both be true. We may possess a latent and specialized numerical capacity that needs some kind of cultural trigger to get it working. However, if it could be shown that numbers were not invented at some 'civilized centre' and then diffused, but rather that they sprang up wherever there were people, then this would be positive evidence for the Mathematical Brain as the source of numbers, and negative evidence for invention–diffusion.

What we shall be looking for in this chapter is evidence for the use of numerosity across the world and back in time as far as the record permits to see whether everyone counted and whether they had to learn how to do it.

In her subtle and profound story 'The Masters', Ursula K. Le Guin imagines a world in which only those people able to do arithmetic are initiated into the rites and mysteries of The Lodge. Even then, they are instructed only in memorizing tables of basic facts. The 'gentiles', the non-initiates, may know some of these facts, though every business will a need Master, like the hero, Ganil, to help solve everyday numerical problems.

> 'XVI plus IXX,' Ganil said impatiently, 'what the devil, boy, can't you add?' The apprentice flushed. 'Isn't it XXXVI, then, Master Ganil?' he asked feebly.[1]

The apprentice was unable to 'compute' the answer and had to rely just on his shaky memory. Neither the apprentice nor the Master had been taught how to calculate, and indeed to do so, rather than retrieve a learned fact, was a 'Necromancer's' heresy, punishable by death.

In Le Guin's grey, rain-sodden world, a heretic Master, Mede, shows Ganil how to calculate by using a symbol for Nothing to create a numbering system with base ten. Along with the 0 for Nothing, Ganil learned about 'black numbers'—our familiar numerals. These tools opened up new possibilities.

> 'What's CXX times MCC?' Mede inquired.
> 'The tables don't go that high?'
> 'Watch.' Mede wrote on the slate:

$$\begin{array}{r} 1200 \\ \underline{120} \end{array}$$

and then, as Ganil watched,

$$\begin{array}{r} 0000 \\ 2400 \\ \underline{12000} \\ 144000 \end{array}$$

> Another long pause. 'Three Nothings ... XII times itself ... Give me the slate,' Ganil muttered. Then after a silence broken only by the patter of rain and the squeak of chalk on slate, 'What's the black number for VIII?'
> 'Numbers are the heart of knowledge, the language of it.'[2]

Many people behave as if manipulating numbers is a kind of black art whose adepts were fortunate, or unfortunate, enough to have been initiated into its mysteries. I once saw a broadcast by the then Secretary of State for Education, Kenneth Baker, going on, as Conservatives will, about the appalling standards of spelling, grammar, and numeracy among children today—at least those children condemned to the state educational system—the system for which he was responsible. He gave some examples of bad spelling and poor grammar, and then explained the errors and corrected them. When he came to a simple numerical problem involving one unknown, he smiled (I thought smugly) and said, 'I think we can leave that one to your teachers.' This attitude, that the black arts of arithmetic need adepts, but they will be the servants (working classes) not the masters, is typical of the English upper class's contempt for the sciences.

However, ignorant as Mr Baker may be of mathematics, arithmetic is no black art accessible only to initiates. Of course, this is not to claim that everyone's Number Module will enable them to grasp everything about numerosities. Of course, people have to learn from the cultural resources available to them, from the ways of representing numbers in words and in writing to techniques for calculating. The claim is that everybody counts, save those suffering from a specific disability.

The origins of our perceptions of number are shrouded in mystery. We have three sources of evidence. The first is language. If a language has words for numbers, we can be sure that the culture has counting practices and that at least some of its members understand numerosities. Since we know nothing of the earliest forms of language, we have no linguistic evidence as to whether our cave-dwelling ancestors had words for numbers. The converse, however, is not true: the fact that a language has no special words for numbers does not mean that its speakers cannot and do not count, as we shall see.

The farthest back we can confidently reconstruct languages is about 5,000 years ago for Indo-European, the precursor of most of the European languages and most of the languages of India and the near east, including Sanskrit and Persian (though not Hungarian, Finnish, Estonian, Basque, Turkish, or the Semitic languages of the Arabs and the Jews).

Our second source of evidence comes from tools and other artefacts inscribed with marks that may represent counting, including ancient paintings and engravings found on the walls of caves such as Lascaux and the recently discovered Grotte Chauvet, or on outdoor rock sites in the protectively dry climates of Australia and southern Africa. These tools and rock art show that number use is considerably older than 5,000 years, so we start by considering what we can learn from them.

BONE AND ROCK TALLIES:
THE EARLIEST KNOWN COUNTING

The prehistory of the Mathematical Brain turns out to be one of the most intriguing problems in what we may call 'cognitive archaeology'—trying to reconstruct the minds of prehistoric people. Numbers are simple, clear concepts, so how can we tell if a culture knew about numbers, if its members possessed the concept of numerosity? In our culture, when we apply the concept, we assign a numerosity to a collection. We have our special symbols for these numerosities, the so-called Arabic numerals[3]—for us, a vital cultural resource. If a culture uses these symbols, or their precursors, then it is a fair guess that it knows about numbers. When we can find the symbols in an appropriately numerical context, such as in trading accounts, record-keeping, or schoolbooks, we can be confident that the culture knows about numbers. What about cultures that did not use our numerals? If they had writing we can understand, and a reasonably systematic way of representing numbers, for example by letters, then the problem is easy to solve. It is thus uncontroversial that the biblical Hebrews, the Greeks and the Romans, and the ancient Chinese all used numbers.

Keeping Accounts: Trade and the Beginnings of Agriculture

When the cuneiform script was first deciphered in the nineteenth century, it became clear that the Sumerians and the Babylonians had had numerals from at least 3000 BC. Clay tablets have been found on which are inscribed tables of multiplications, tables of square roots (Figure 2.1), and even cube roots. One of the main applications of this ancient mathematics was to the keeping of records of business transactions. These included accounts of goods traded, and of the wages paid to workers. A tablet has been found which records the rates paid to field workers in standard units of wheat, a common currency in Uruk 5,000 years ago. Unsurprisingly, supervisors received much more than ordinary workers, and women received least, only two-fifths or four-fifths of the men's rate.[5]

Whereas we use 10 as a number base for most purposes, the Sumerians, the Babylonians, and their neighbours used 10 and 60 (base 60 survives in our measures of angle and time). These two bases and their common factors (2, 3, 5) made calculations in trading and

Figure 2.1 Cuneiform numerals impressed on a clay tablet found at Larsa in ancient Babylonia (about 1900 BC). This is a line from a table of squares and square roots discovered by Sir Henry Rawlinson in 1855. It reads, from left to right: '(58 × 60) + 1 [3,481] equals 59 squared'. The vertical wedge used to represent 1 can also mean 60 (the base of the Babylonian number system) or any power of 60, just as 1 can mean for us 10 or any power of 10, depending on its position. Rawlinson also discovered multiplication tables and tables of measures that seem to have been made by apprentice scribes, which would make them the oldest known school exercise books. (Adapted from Jöran Friberg[4])

accounts relatively simple. With our number system, the value of a numeral depends on its position in the number—in other words, it is a place-value system. The 3 in 300 is 3 × 100, a hundred times the value of 3 in 103. The Babylonians also used a partly positional notation, as we shall see later. Because we can interpret cuneiform as a system of numerals with a base, we can understand how it was used to add, subtract, multiply, and divide collections and measures. There is therefore no doubting that the users possessed the concept of numerosity, and indeed that they had developed it to an extent that formed the basis of Egyptian, Greek, and ultimately our own mathematics. But how did the Sumerian system arise?

We have an almost complete answer, thanks to the work of Denise Schmandt-Besserat, an archaeologist working at the University of Texas. The cuneiform inscriptions were impressed on clay tablets. Before the development of cuneiform, clay tablets were impressed with pictographs which were the precursors of the cuneiform characters. This transition, from pictures that are difficult to draw and have potentially idiosyncratic meanings, to simpler shapes with agreed meanings, is a natural and unsurprising development. This is what happened in the development of both Egyptian hieroglyphics and Chinese ideograms, traditions quite independent of cuneiform.

However, there is one set of pictographs that have a separate origin. For over 5,000 years, from about 8000 BC, traders in Mesopotamia used small tokens to represent and record goods traded. The practice spread as far afield as the Mediterranean, the Indus Valley, the Nile Valley, and the shores of the Caspian Sea. These tokens had simple shapes that could be made from soft clay using just the hands. Over the centuries more complex tokens came to be used, but the simple forms also remained in use. Each token seems to have stood for an item of trade: an animal, perhaps, or a measure of grain. To start with, tokens were sealed inside a clay envelope that bore two designs which seemed to be the seals or names of the parties to the deal. This system was in use for at least 2,000 years, but suffered from a major practical drawback: the deal could be checked only by breaking open the envelope to reveal the tokens within. The solution was to mark the outside of the envelope with pictographs depicting the contents.

Some of the pictographs stood for objects, either in realistic forms, such as the signs for vessel, oil, and granary, or in more abstract forms, such as the signs for legal decision, place, and perfume. The evolution from tokens to pictographs is quite clear. For example, a solid ovoid token with an indentation, meaning oil, and presumably depicting an oil jar, becomes an ovoid shape with a line through it at a position analogous to the indentation in the token. Other signs seem to have stood for numbers.[6] There are separate pictographs, and indeed tokens, that represent 1, 60, and 600 (Figure 2.2), as well as powers of 10. Interestingly, the token for 10^2 is the same as the token for 60^2. Schmandt-Besserat has argued more recently that some of the signs originally interpreted as numbers are actually measures, and only later became numbers abstracted away from what they are counting. The cone, 'which originally meant a small quantity of grain, now meant 1, a circle, which had represented a larger quantity, stood for 10, and a large wedge came to signify 60 and a large circle 360'.[8]

From about 10,000 years ago, the people of the Mesopotamian region were clearly able to use numbers for trading, keeping accounts, and measuring goods, produce, and land. They had developed a system of numbers based on 10 and 60 and were able to represent them permanently on clay tablets. We have been able to deduce this from the pictographs on the early clay tablets, the interpretations being developed and confirmed by relating the pictographs to the later cuneiform symbols. In the nineteenth century, Georg Friedrich Grote-

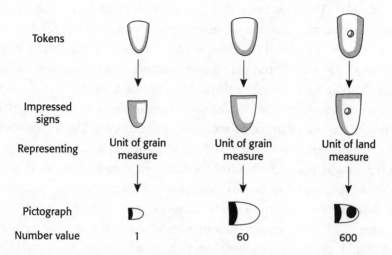

Tokens		
Impressed signs		
Representing	Unit of grain measure	Unit of grain measure	Unit of land measure
Pictograph			
Number value	1	60	600

Figure 2.2 From clay tokens to pictographs. Ten thousand years ago, traders in the Middle East used small clay tokens to represent quantities of goods traded. These tokens were sealed into clay envelopes, on the outside of which the tokens were first impressed so that the receiver knew how many tokens there should be inside. By the third millennium BC the signs alone were used, and these were later transformed into the cuneiform symbols. This figure shows how cone-shaped tokens representing measures of grain and land evolved into impressed signs, and thence into symbols representing the numbers 1, 60, and 600. (Adapted from Denise Schmandt-Besserat[7])

fend and Sir Henry Rawlinson were able to decipher cuneiform inscriptions (often termed 'epigraphs'), so subsequently the early tablets could be checked against texts that were relatively well understood. Schmandt-Besserat has suggested that the system of tokens and measures was a specific invention that spread throughout the Fertile Crescent, presumably having originated in one community and diffused by contact with other communities. Who invented it, and when, is lost in the mists of prehistory. The earliest tokens so far discovered, from around 10,000 to 11,000 years ago, have been found in southern Turkey, Iran, and Sudan. They must have originated further back in time for them to have spread over such a wide area.

The theory that numbers were an invention of some ancient Einstein, or perhaps some ancient firm of accountants—a Sumerian proto-Price Waterhouse, which spread from a single site in the Fertile Crescent to the rest of the world has also been advanced by the American scholar Abraham Seidenberg. His view was that the centre of invention developed a series of counting schemes, each better in some way than the last, and that these were diffused in successive waves around the world. Those places most remote from the invention site in the Middle East would be the last to use numbers.[9]

Broadly speaking, it is true that communities remote from the Middle East, for example in the Amazon rainforest, the highlands of New Guinea, and the deserts of central Australia, have historically shown much less use of numbers than the inhabitants of Europe, India, China, and North Africa. Seidenberg had a further argument. He thought that the first type of counting was what he called 'two-counting'. There were just two numbers: *one* and *two*. Larger numbers could be made by combining them thus: *one*, *two*, *two-one*, *two-two*, *two-two-one*, *two-two-two*, and so on. The trouble with two-counting is that when you want to count above about 7 or 8, you begin to lose track of just how many twos you have used.

Intriguingly, two-counting exactly on this model is found in remote hunter-gatherer cultures in Australia, South America, South Africa, and Papua New Guinea (Table 2.1). Variants of the model that include a few other number names or other ways of combining the number names, and which according to Seidenberg are later developments, can be found in slightly less remote cultures in Southeast Asia, North America, central Africa, and the Pacific. It certainly seems to be stretching the bounds of coincidence that these very widely separated groups should have hit upon exactly the same solution to the problem of counting. In this century we can observe how the familiar decimal system, along with Arabic numerals, has diffused to (perhaps more accurately, been imposed upon) remote groups. The mechanism is not hard to understand. However, Seidenberg's proposed explanation for the spread of counting and numbers is surprising. It was not imposed by a colonizing culture, nor was it exported along trade routes to lubricate trading practices. His explanation is that it spread on the back of a story, the story of the Creation, and the rituals that accompanied it. In the Creation myth (the origin of the familiar Bible story and the earlier epic of Gilgamesh) are found complementary pairs: heaven–earth, light–dark, earth–water, male–female: 'Counting was invented in a civilized center, in elaboration of the Creation ritual, as a

| Gumulgal | Bakairi | Bushman | Kiwai |
Australia	South America	South Africa	Papua New Guinea
urapon	tokale	xa	nu'a
ukasar	ahage	t'oa	netowa
uskasar-urapon	ahage-tokale	'quo ,	netowa n'au bi
ukasar-ukasar	ahage-ahage	t'oa-t'oa	netowa netowa
ukasar-ukasar-urapon	ahage-ahage-tokale	t'oa-t'oa-ta	netowa netowa n'ua
ukasar-ukasar-ukasar	ahage-ahage-ahage	t'oa-t'oa-t'oa	netowa netowa netowa

ble 2.1 'Two-counting' in the languages of some remote cultures.[10]

means of calling participants onto the ritual scene, once and only once, and then diffused.'[11] Seidenberg and those who incline towards his theory agree that the evidence for the ritual origin of counting is far from conclusive. Nevertheless, the theory as a whole raises interesting and difficult questions.

Now, if Seidenberg and other 'inventionists' are right, does this mean that the theory I am proposing here must be wrong? Not necessarily. There could be a latent specialized capacity that needs some appropriate cultural trigger to release it, to make it manifest itself. The spread of the story and the need to enact its ritual could be that trigger. Others have suggested that the need to keep accounts and to trade would provide the trigger. A third possibility is that the Mathematical Brain exploits available resources to handle numerosities. One resource is the human body. It is a handy collection of parts, shared by everybody, that can be used as a reference collection for counting. We shall see later in this chapter, and in more detail in Chapter 5, how body parts are used in counting and arithmetic. The simplest division of body parts is into left and right—for example, left arm and right arm, left leg and right leg. This could have been a basis for two-counting.

As I argued earlier, invention–diffusion and the Mathematical Brain hypothesis can in principle both be true, but if we can find evidence for counting that pre-dates both the Creation myth and the earliest trading, the two proposed triggers, then we can show that these versions of the invention–diffusion hypothesis are false.

Counting in Ice-Age Caves

Plants and animals were domesticated in the Fertile Crescent about 13,000 years ago, and trading of agricultural and manufactured surpluses was certain to have taken place, providing the practical impetus for the development of keeping accounts. So it would be very reasonable to interpret the early inscribed tablets as having numerical significance.

Let us go further back in time—before the invention of writing, before the invention of agriculture and settled farming communities, before the Creation myth, back to when our ancestors were hunter-gatherers, still using stone tools. Did these people possess a Mathematical Brain? Trading relations with neighbouring clans would certainly have been more basic than in later agricultural times. Trade probably consisted of face-to-face bartering of goods visible to both parties. Deals could be struck without the need to count: 'I'll give you this bag of flint knives if you give me that pile of beads'. The fact that many, most, or even all transactions would not have needed counting or the keeping of numerical accounts does not mean that counting was not carried out and that accounts were not kept. Better trading and resource management may have followed from the use of numbers.

How can we tell with confidence that numbers were used? We lack from this period any counterparts of the legible and comprehensible epigraphs that helped us to decipher the early Sumerian tokens and tablets. We also lack a description of the context: we have only the most indirect evidence of these people's beliefs and business. Most of our evidence is in the form of scratches on bones and dots on walls of caves. Can we make any reasonable inferences about the numerical capacities of the makers of these marks?

Imagine the prisoner in his cell keeping track of the days of his confinement by putting one mark on the wall for each day. Could we count this as conclusive evidence for his use of number? Keeping track of numerosities entails putting each member of a collection into one-to-one correspondence with a number. For us, this means putting each member in one-to-one correspondence with a number word.

However, our only evidence is marks on the wall: we do not know whether the prisoner can use number words. As we shall see, speakers of languages that lack number words can still count and have an awareness of numerosity, so being able to put number words in one-to-one correspondence with the marks on the wall is not critical. What does seem to be important is putting the marks into one-to-one correspondence with a collection of mental 'tokens' (see Chapter 3). It is not enough to treat each mark as a separate entity.

However, our prisoner is simply putting each day into one-to-one correspondence with marks on the wall, and although the ability to do this is needed if he is counting, it surely is not enough. We need to see some evidence that he understands about equivalence between collections, and whether one collection is larger or smaller than another. Suppose the prisoner scores through every group of, say, five marks. This will demonstrate that he grasps when collections have the same numerosity, and by implication when they do not. Presumably, he will be putting each mark in a group into one-to-one correspondence with a collection of five mental tokens, where the mental token could simply be the thought of the first group of five marks on the wall. A similarly orderly progression of groups of four or six marks, for example, or another systematic arrangement, would also be a good indication.

Let us go back to the last ice age, which ended about 12,000 years ago. This marks the end of the period known as the Palaeolithic—the Old Stone Age—and its cultures are defined by archaeologists in terms of the surviving artefacts. Most of what survives consists of stone and bone tools, but there is also art on the walls of caves, and 'portable' or 'mobile' art, mostly carved bones. There was probably extensive use of wood and animal fibre, animal hides worked into clothing or coverings, but almost none of this has survived. It is customary to divide the Palaeolithic into phases according to the characteristic types of tool produced. Lower and Middle Palaeolithic tools are simple, relatively easy to make, and produced not just by *Homo sapiens*, but also by our hominid ancestors *Homo erectus* and by our cousins and, for a while, our contemporaries, *Homo neanderthalensis*. The Upper Palaeolithic is generally taken to have started around 30,000 years ago.

The most recent Upper Palaeolithic culture is called Magdalenian, after the cave at La Madelaine in France in which beautifully made stone and bone tools have been found. It produced the great cave art of Altamira in Spain and Lascaux in France, and of many other sites in Western Europe. Here were people, physically modern, physically just like us, able to produce representations of the world around them of great accuracy and with great skill. They produced many examples of portable art, carvings in bone and stone, providing ample testimony to their sophistication. Many scholars have attempted to infer how they thought from these artefacts. Were they capable, for example, of abstract thought, of logical reasoning, of language? It is now generally agreed that these people had fully developed the capacity for language.[12] A mere 2,000 years later, in the Fertile Crescent and elsewhere, people were able to record transactions in tokens and pictographs, and were well on the way to writing.

However, although the Magdalenians produced realistic depictions of animals and people, this is no guarantee of either logical reasoning or abstract thought. On the walls of their caves and on their portable artefacts have been found strange markings of dots and lines, rectangles and triangles, that have intrigued and puzzled archaeologists since their first discovery. The pioneer nineteenth-century archaeologist Edouard Lartet suggested that the marks on some bones and antlers were 'hunting tallies' denoting the number of animals taken, which would certainly fit with a very early date for the Mathematical Brain.[13] A second and more influential approach has been to interpret them as sexual, triangles with an extra line representing the vulva. It is well established that this is a reduced form of the female body, as represented in wall art at, for example, La Madelaine,[14] where the same arrangement of lines is clearly the vulva. This symbol is found in pictures and on figurines from many other sites going back well before the Magdalenian (such as the famous Venus of Willendorf). The French archaeologist André Leroi-Gourhan has argued that most the symbols are connected with the great division in the metaphysics of the period between the male and the female principles. Wide symbols such as triangles and rectangles are female, while narrow symbols such as lines and dots are male.[15] These interpretations have had many critics, and even archaeologists sympathetic to the basic approach interpret the symbols in different, even opposite ways.[16]

Another possibility is that some of these marks, especially the dots and lines, could represent the results of counting. In some contemporary Stone Age cultures with a tradition of wall art, for example in northern Arnhem Land in Australia, tribal members say that dots are used to record the number of people attending an event.[17] One such people, the Gidjingarli, use this convention, and have only four terms for numbers—*one*, *two*, *one-two*, and *two-two*; beyond that is a term that means 'big mob'. Could the Magdalenians have used a similar convention to record people who turned up for a ritual, or for a party?

First, we must look for evidence that Magdalenians could count. As with our prisoner, systematic grouping of marks would be a good indication of this. In an exhibition about the Chauvet Cave in Vallon Pont d'Arc, Ardèche, France, there is a small Magdalenian bone from the nearby Grotte de Colombier. It has beautifully engraved lines, perfectly parallel in clearly defined groups: two groups of eight lines, and three groups of four lines, with a further group of four partially damaged. In Jean Clottes's fascinating and beautiful book, *Les Cavernes de Niaux*, about a well-researched Magdalenian cave system, there are some very clear pictures of large red dots that do not appear to have a decorative function, and may depict numbers of something. According to a doyen of French archaeology, Abbé Henri Breuil, in the picture shown in Figure 2.3 the circle of dots represents the hunters and the dot in the middle of the circle represents the bison. The realistically drawn bison to the left of this circle is vertical, rather than on his feet, indicating perhaps that he is dead. Needless to say, this interpretation has been challenged.[18] The important issue from my point of view is this: do the dots in the circle represent the number of men surrounding the bison, or indeed the number of anything?

On another wall of the cave is a pair of lines of 11 red dots, and to their left a third line of 11 red dots. Of course, this might be a coincidence. Clottes thinks not: the repetitions, he says, 'betray intention'. It might also be a matter of making a first line 11 dots and then making two new lines on the model of the first, though it is unclear why the maker should seek to get the collections of points to have the same numerosity without having a concept of numerosity in the first place. It seems more likely that the three lines were made deliberately to have the same number of elements, and that some form of count-

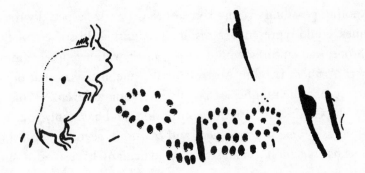

Figure 2.3 Figures from the Cavernes de Niaux, drawn about 15,000 years ago. This design has been interpreted as a dead bison with, to its right, a tally of the number of hunters who killed it—the circle of dots around a single central dot. The lines with bumps, called 'claviforms', have been interpreted as women. (Adapted from Clottes[19])

ing was used at least to get the leftmost line to have the same number of dots as the others. We cannot, of course, know for sure if this interpretation is correct, but I shall now present further evidence from earlier periods and from different regions to suggest that this kind of counting was very widespread, if not universal.

Out of Africa, and Australia

The bison drawings of Niaux are about 14,000 years old according to radiocarbon datings. Ten thousand years earlier, on the shore of Lake Edward in the Great Rift Valley on the border of Uganda and Zaire, a small bone less than 10 cm long was engraved at a fishing site now called Ishango. It has intrigued researchers ever since it was found in 1961 by Jean de Heinzelin.[20] You can see from Figure 2.4 that one face of the bone has the marks 11, 21, 19, 9 down one edge, and 11, 13, 17, 19 down the other. What could this mean? Could the first edge be 10 + 1, 20 + 1, 20 − 1, 10 − 1, showing evidence of counting in tens? If so, what about the second edge? These are the four prime numbers between 10 and 20. Does this indicate a knowledge of factors and primes? Then again, look at the other face of the bone: 3 and 6, 4 and 8, 10 and 5. Can this show knowledge of the idea of doubling? But what about the final pair, 5 and 7? De Heinzelin certainly thought that the bone was our earliest evidence of these num-

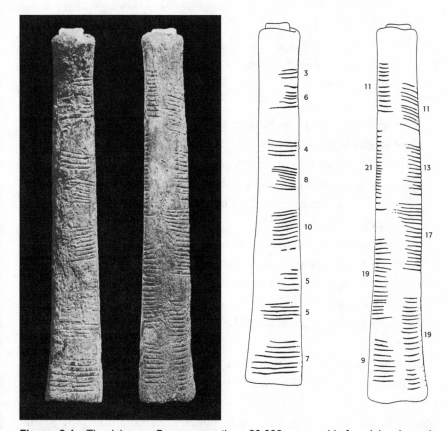

Figure 2.4 The Ishango Bone, more than 20,000 years old, found by Jean de Heinzelin in 1961 on the shore of a lake in central Africa. The two faces of the bone are redrawn for clarity. Along the right edge of the face shown on the left are three pairs of notches representing doubled numbers—3 and 6, 4 and 8, 10 and 5—suggesting that the hunting and fishing folk who lived by the water understood the idea of doubling a numerosity. On the other face of the bone there seem to be represented numbers related to 10: along the left edge, each group of notches is either one more or one less than 10. The total number of notches along each edge is 60, and they are grouped into pairs that add up to 30. It has been suggested that the bone not only indicates the use of a base-10 system, but also that it was used for calendrical calculations, 30 being the approximate number of days in a lunar month. (From de Heinzelin[21])

ber skills, which, if correct, would certainly be sufficient to establish a pre-Magdalenian date for counting and even arithmetic.

A different explanation of these marks has been offered by Alexander Marshack from the Peabody Museum at Harvard. He added the numbers in the lines along the two edges in Figure 2.4:

11 + 21 + 19 + 9 = 60; 11 +13 + 17 + 19 = 60. 'Could each line represent two months? Could the two lines together represent four months of lunar notation, one scratch representing one day?' Marshack had a fascinating speculation.

The sequence of 19 is broken down, for the eye, into 5 and 14. Could this separation have meaning? The next sequence of 17 has a swelling of some six scratches towards one end, and, of these, some seem to be higher and visually separated from the rest. Following it is a sequence of 13, and this seems to contain the smallest scratches in that line of 60 marks.

Could these differences be a clue? Could they have a meaning? Or were they the 'accidents' of a crude draftsman?

In the next series of scratches there is a sequence of 21 very small scratches. Could these smaller marks be significant? Could they be similar in concept to the lesser sequence of 13 in the previous line?

Let us assume . . . that these differences do have meaning, and that they represent, in some way, the phases or periods of the moon.

If you watch the sky each night and count the days of the waxing and waning moon, you will find that the number of days between one invisibility and the next is either 29 or 30 days. One cannot observe the astronomically precise 29.5 days. Instead there may be one, two, or three nights without a visible moon, with two as an average. The observer of this uneven visual month might mark it off as 28 or 31 days. But if he is off by one day here or there in his notation he will *always* be corrected in the next series of lunar phases. For the phases of the moon are accurate, though the observer and his notations may not be. . . .

Let us break the lunar month down further. From the day of invisibility to the full moon is approximately 15 days. If you make a mark on the day of invisibility and proceed to the day of full moon you should have 16 marks, representing the 15 days. But again, for the observer, this is not a precise count and he may mark 14, 15, or 16 days from invisibility to full. Once more these variations will always be corrected by the next phases of the moon.[22]

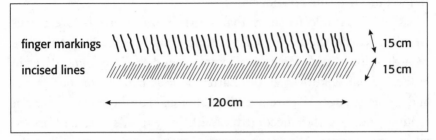

finger markings \\ 15 cm

incised lines /// 15 cm

← 120 cm →

Figure 2.5 A herringbone pattern added to a wall in Koonalda Cave, South Australia, 20,000 years ago. This ice-age site was mined for flint by the earliest inhabitants of southern Australia. The soft stone of the walls is covered with markings. In this pattern, the top row consists of thirty-seven finger marks, while in the bottom row there are exactly twice this number of marks, made most probably with a flint. This could be an example of a method for tallying that developed independently of European (or African) models. (After Maynard & Edwards[23])

Here, then, is an example of a culture outside Europe, probably unconnected with European cultures (though we do not really know), that seems to have invented a notation for recording the phases of the moon. Does this involve counting or other numerical skills? Marshack thinks not, since there is no evidence for arithmetical operation such as adding, or of a number *system*, just putting one mark down for each event observed—'observational counting' he calls it.

A second example, from about the same time, but on the other side of the world, can be found in a cave deep beneath the stifling Nullabor Plain in South Australia. Five hundred metres from the entrance and 60 metres below the surface, in pitch darkness, is a chamber whose walls are covered with markings. One, shown in Figure 2.5, is a neat herringbone pattern with parallel diagonal finger markings made in the soft surface of the wall, thirty-seven of them. Not a terribly interesting number, you may think. What is fascinating is that directly underneath is a diagonal row of incisions made with an implement, probably a piece of harder rock, and there are seventy-four of them. You can see that the incisions are not grouped in twos, two for each finger mark. So either it is just a coincidence that there are 37 finger marks, a prime number, and 2×37 incisions, or it is deliberate. It is not known what these markings mean, but my question is this: if the correspondence is deliberate, could they have been made if the maker or makers were unable to count?

In the Europe of the Neanderthals

Marshack was able to show that some 10,000 years before marks were incised on the Ishango Bone, early Cro-Magnon humans were recording lunar cycles in rock shelters around the Dordogne River in France. What is known as the Lartet Bone is marked on both faces and along its edges (Figure 2.6). It is obvious that these marks are not random, nor are they decorative. With his expert's eye, and armed with a microscope, Marshack says that 'You can see at once that the lines on each face are made in groups, by different points, at different angles, and with different pressures.'[24] He lines up the groups of points with the phases of the moon suggesting that the bone is recording six months—two whole seasons.

Do the marks on this bone show that people were counting 30,000 years ago? The marks are certainly grouped, and the groups are organized into larger patterns. Let us assume, with Marshack, that these marks do indeed represent phases of the moon. If each group had the same number of marks, then this would definitely suggest that the maker understood about equal numerosities and could make collections with the same number of marks. We would say to ourselves, 'Let's make six groups of seven marks each.' But we do not know whether these people had number words. As we shall see in Section 3, people can count efficiently without having number words in their language. However, it is possible to create equal collections without counting at all. When you lay the table, you can get equal numbers of plates, glasses, knives, and forks, simply by putting each in one-to-one correspondence with a chair marking the places at table. Now, while you have to understand one-to-one correspondence to understand numerosity, this in itself is not enough. Marshack argues that the makers of these marks could simply have been putting down a mark each night in one-to-one correspondence with their observation of the state of the moon—for example a small mark when the moon is crescent-shaped, a larger one when it is full.

In any case, the markers were not putting down equal groups of marks: on the faces of the Lartet Bone there are groups of from two to ten. The group size may reflect what the observer sees: for example, two nights with the moon obscured by cloud, to ten nights with the moon waxing. Of course, the notations may not have been made night

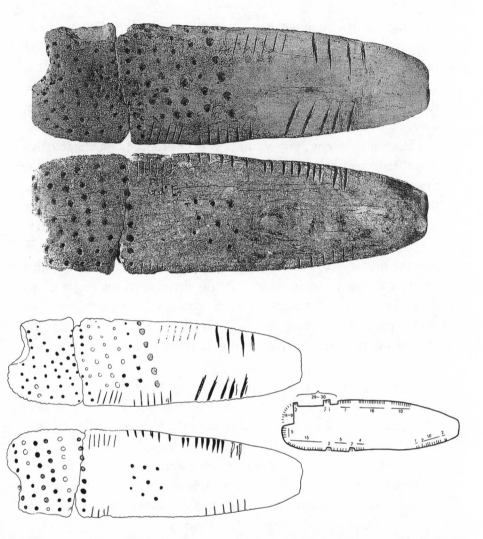

Figure 2.6 The Lartet Bone, found at Dordogne, France, is about 30,000 years old. According to Alexander Marshack of the Peabody Museum, Harvard University, the Cro-Magnon inhabitants of south-west France kept track of the phases of the moon by marking bones. In this example, distinct groups of marks are visible along the edges and on the faces of the bone. The bone's two faces are redrawn for clarity; the smaller drawing shows marking revealed by electron microscopy. (Adapted from Marshack[25])

by night. The maker may have kept track of the waxing phase, and, when the moon was full, inscribed ten marks corresponding to the ten waxing nights. If this happened, then so did counting! Ten mental marks—not necessarily words, though they might have been words—

must have been held in the memory until the incised marks were made. We shall see later that many traditional cultures count with body-part names, not special number words. Roughly it would be equivalent to counting like this: 'Little finger, ring finger, middle finger, index finger, thumb, wrist, forearm, elbow—elbow pigs [= eight pigs]'. Perhaps our ice-age moon-watcher did this; we cannot know.

There is, however, important new evidence. Many archaeologists have been skeptical of Marshack's claims: how can we tell whether these marks are notational, or simply decorative? In an attempt to find out, Francesco d'Errico, the leading authority on bone markings, has examined marks on bones like the Lartet Bone using a high-powered scanning electron microscope. This makes it possible to tell how the marks were made—with one stroke or more than one, with a blade or a pointed tool—as well as the direction of the incision and the order in which the marks were produced. In an examination of a Magdalenian bone from Spain, d'Errico found that distinct sets of marks were made by separate tools in different ways:

> Changing the tool, technique and direction of its movement for every set involved extra time and complicated the technological procedure ... This behaviour produced a less regular design than that which could have been made more rapidly and simply. Such behaviour, therefore, cannot be accounted for by decorative purposes alone. It seems more reasonable to assume that this behaviour had a utilitarian origin. The hypothesis that this engraving is a 'system of notation' should be considered.[26]

D'Errico does not speculate about what is notated, but from our point of view the fact that notational marks are grouped by tool and technique is consistent with the idea that the maker engraved a collection of marks in one go. Of particular interest is the finding that on one face of the bone there are two sets of marks oriented along parallel incisions, made in opposite directions, by different tools and using different techniques, and both sets contain eleven marks. On the other side there are two parallel sets, again differently made, with sixteen marks in each. We cannot know whether these sets are complete and as the maker intended, nor can we know whether the agreement between the numbers was intended. But, like the prisoner in his cell, when we see deliberate groups of marks with the same number, paired off like this, particularly when the number is larger than the number of fingers, we are entitled to entertain the hypothesis that this person could count.

Let us consider for a moment why our ice-age ancestors would record lunar cycles. Marshack gives relatively little attention to this issue; perhaps he feels we can never know. My first thought was that cave-dwellers didn't have much to do of an evening, and artificial lighting was poor and expensive (valuable animal fat would be used in lamps, or wood would have to be collected for the fire). As those who camp will tell you, the most enjoyable night-time occupations, indeed almost the only night-time occupations, are observing the heavens and sex. The heavens become a sphere for contemplation and speculation, and one notices changes night by night, especially of the largest and brightest nocturnal body. Moreover, in an uncertain world the phases of the moon can be predicted with complete confidence, which must have encouraged our ancestors to believe that there were some things they indeed could know.

My second thought was that the moon and sex go together. The menstrual cycles of women in small groups tend to become synchronized, and in traditional cultures, where people live together in small groups, the correspondence between the menstrual and lunar cycles is readily apparent. If the tribe can use the lunar cycle to predict the menstrual cycles then this would be a good way of controlling population, because fertile and non-fertile periods can be determined. If there is a fertility cult, it can be made more effective by ensuring that the rites take place at the most effective lunar–menstrual phase. However, there is a serious problem with the menstrual cycle theory. For women in hunter-gatherer societies, indeed in many traditional societies, the average menstrual cycle is actually four *years*! There is the nine months of pregnancy followed by two to three years of lactation, during which time the mother is infertile. This long period of breast-feeding is necessary where there is no animal milk available to use as a substitute. With normal rates of sexual activity women are likely to get pregnant again within about six months of the end of breast-feeding, and so menstruation will arrive every four years or so. Since the fertility of individual women within the group will vary, there will be little chance of synchronized menstrual cycles, and not much reason for counting lunar phases as a means of population regulation.

On the other hand, counting the lunar phases would be useful to the women themselves. It could help them decide whether they'd missed a period—i.e. whether they were pregnant—and could allow them to predict more accurately when the birth was due.[27] So it is at least possible that the first numerical recorders were women. This is not as far-fetched as it might seem. An Aurignacian female figurine from southwest France has incised marks on her breasts and upper body; and a female figurine from the East Gravettian culture of about the same period in Moravia, with breasts but no vulva, has marks in groups. These markings may indicate times of lactation.[28]

A knowledge of lunar cycles would be useful in hunter-gatherer societies, which these cultures were, because they could also be used to predict when there would be a full moon, and when, therefore, it would be best to get together to hunt nocturnal prey.

Now, if lunar cycle recording was used predictively—either for forecasting births or for timing the hunt—then counting and number are entailed. If the moon is invisible, you can predict that the full moon will be about fourteen days hence, and to do that you will need to count. Of course, we do not know how these forebears of ours might have counted. To predict over periods longer than half a month is complicated and needs more sophisticated numerical skills. This is because the lunar month is 29.5 days on average, so, by and large, on roughly alternate months you will count 29 nights, then 30 nights. If you always count 29 or always 30, you will get out of phase pretty quickly. Maybe this is why it was important to keep track of the lunar cycle, so that the tribe didn't get out of phase in its planning.

Even before these bones were engraved, at the time of the last of the Neanderthals, other people were decorating a cave in the Ardèche Gorge near the southern Rhone in France, called Grotte Chauvet after one of the speleologists who discovered it at the end of 1994. It contains beautiful and accurate pictures of hairy rhinoceroses, lions, bears, and bison; and of an owl, drawn in charcoal, painted in red ochre, and engraved. The pictures are by no means primitive in style, and bear comparison with the best pictures in the Lascaux caves, painted 15,000 years later. The members of the early Aurignacian culture were clearly sophisticated in their representation of animals, and may well have had complex social practices and rituals that went with the production of these pictures.[29] The cave also contains mysterious marks made in red ochre. These are not part of animal pictures, and do not seem to be decorations.

Since the cave was discovered, work has concentrated on its preservation. Archaeological research has not yet begun, so our interpretation of the iconography is even more speculative than is usual in this area. Do the arrangements of dots provide evidence that these people had mathematical brains? Figure 2.7 shows two rows of three dots and a row of three lines. Did the painter count three lines, and repro-

Figure 2.7 Are these mysterious marks in the Chauvet Cave the oldest known numbers? At the end of 1994, the oldest human drawings so far found were discovered on the walls of this cave in the Ardèche Gorge, France. The charcoal markings have been dated to 32,000 years ago. The markings shown here, painted probably in red ochre, consist of three rows of three marks. Was this a coincidence, or did the maker intend the same number of marks in each row? (From Chauvet et al.[30])

duce that number in the two rows of dots? What of the cloud of forty-six dots painted on a nearby hanging rock? Could these have recorded the number of people attending some event, in the same way that some Australian Aborigines record those present by marking a rock at the site? We do not know. However, these markings are consistent with our Aurignacian cave painters being able to count as well as paint.

At about the same time, in a different culture, there is very good evidence for counting on a wolf's bone found in Moravia dated to over 30,000 years ago. Its discoverer in 1937, Karl Absolon, wrote:

> An exceedingly valuable find was a radius of a young wolf, 18 cm long, engraved with fifty-five deeply incised notches. First come twenty-five notches, more or less equal in length, in groups of five, followed by a single notch, twice as long, which terminates the series; then starting from the next notch, also twice as long, a new series runs up to thirty. We know of several of these Diluvial objects with markings denoting the conception of five. This number corresponds to the fingers on each hand, which Diluvial man had before his eyes and which no doubt led him to think in terms of numbers. We have here direct proofs of reckoning by fossil man.[31]

What about the Neanderthal contemporaries of the Aurignacians? We are now sure that Neanderthals were not our ancestors, so the presence of a Mathematical Brain in them would suggest that it was inherited from a common ancestor to both *Homo sapiens neanderthalensis* and *Homo sapiens* proper. The Neanderthals seem to have shared come cultural characteristics with their *Homo sapiens* neighbours, perhaps through borrowing. Stone tools were similar, for example. But is there evidence that they made tally marks? What about our direct lineal ancestors, *Homo erectus*, whose brain capacity was 800 cm^3 compared with our 1,500 cm^3? Both the Neanderthals and *Homo erectus* were actually rather successful, perhaps more successful than we turn out to be. Neanderthals survived for about 250,000 years until about 30,000 years ago, and *Homo erectus* for 2 million years, spreading certainly throughout Asia and Africa, and perhaps reaching Australia.[32]

Here the evidence is scarce. A bone discovered in the grave of a Neanderthal child at La Ferrassie in France is scored with neat parallel lines, grouped as 4, 1, 2, 3, 3, 2, 5, 3, 9, 3.[33] The markings are clearly intentional, though their meaning is unknown. Parallel lines on bones from relatively recent *Homo erectus* sites in Germany have been reported.[34] Little has yet been suggested about the interpretation of these marks. As well as direct evidence from artefacts, there is indirect evidence. Michael Morwood, an Australian archaeologist, has dated a *Homo erectus* site on the island of Flores in Indonesia to about 1 million years ago.[35] What makes this remarkable is that the island has never been connected to the mainland of Asia, so its inhabitants must have sailed 30 km across the open sea to reach it. Is it possible to get together to build a seaworthy craft, to plan to sail to an unknown and invisible destination, without being able to count?

The Prehistoric Mathematical Brain
When we look back through the prehistory of the Mathematical Brain, we see that some kind of tallying can be traced back through the Babylonians and Sumerians, deep into the ice-age cave-painters and bone-engravers of the Magdalenian era 15,000 years ago, before plants and animals had been domesticated. That in itself is surprising enough, but 15,000 years before that we can find tally marks on bones and possibly on the walls of caves as well. We do not know what these people were counting, but physically they were people like us, as far as we can tell, and their brains were as our brains. So the capacity to count, the roots of the Mathematical Brain, go back to what has been called the Great Leap Forward or the Big Bang, when art was first produced and perhaps language, in something like its modern form, was first used. This certainly pushes the use of numbers back beyond an invention by an ancient Einstein in Ur 10,000 years ago. In itself, it does not rule out an invention, say, in France 32,000 years ago which spread quickly to other sites in France and eastwards to Moravia, and perhaps onwards to Asia. But against this invention–diffusion account we may cite the Ishango Bone and the Koonalda Cave herringbone pattern from cultures thought to have had no contact with Europe, yet the methods of marking seem remarkably similar.

If people in the depths of the ice age already possessed a Mathematical Brain, and the urge to count, and especially the urge to count the phases of the moon, it is perhaps not wholly surprising that they devised similar solutions to keeping track of their counts. If the Mathe-matical Brain is encoded in the genes of these fully human ancestors, we may still ask from whom they inherited it. Tantalizingly, there are glimpses beyond our own species to tallying in our cousins, the Nean-derthals, and our ancestors *Homo erectus* perhaps a million years ago.

NUMBER WORDS: FROM 'PENIS' TO 'THIRTY-THREE'

> Some *Americans* I have spoken with (who were otherwise of quick and rational parts enough) could not, as we do, by any means count to 1,000; nor had any distinct *idea* of that number, though they could reckon very well to 20.[36]

These are the words of John Locke, the British philosopher whose po-litical theory influenced the American constitution, writing in 1690. He was not condemning the numeracy of foolish Englishmen unfortu-nate enough to find themselves in the Thirteen Colonies. He was praising the Tououpinambos, a tribe from the depths of the Brazilian jungle, whose language lacked 'names for numbers above 5'. Despite this, they were able to do simple arithmetic with low numbers. If Locke's observations were accurate, then our ice-age ancestors, whose brains were no different from ours, may well have been able to do the same, despite lacking special words for numbers and for counting. Of course, we have no idea whether they had number names or not; we do not know for sure whether they had language, although it is gener-ally assumed that they did.

Locke noted that the Tououpinambos went beyond five 'by show-ing their fingers, and the fingers of others who were present'. Cave-men had fingers, and, if they were like these 'Americans', they could use other people's fingers as well when 'reckoning' to 20. The impor-tant thing for Locke was the ability to use some external aid to keep track of numbers: it could be special names for numbers, or it could be fingers. Words are better because you can get really big numbers by combining words, but with fingers you can only get up to the num-ber of fingers present. Even more importantly, we need these aids to keep separate the idea of each number in our minds—keep separate what I have called numerosities.

According to Locke, we construct the idea of each number from the idea of 'one'—'the most universal idea we have'. By repeating 'this idea in our minds and adding the repetitions together ... thus by adding [the idea of] one to [the idea of] one we have the complex idea of a couple'. When we have many repetitions of one, for example 90, we will need to refer to it by a special name so as to keep it separate in our minds from the idea of its immediate successor, 91, or its predecessor, 89, which will also require special names. He thought that number names were essential for acquiring the ideas of biggish numbers, since he observed that children, for 'want of names to mark the several progressions of numbers' can 'discourse and reason pretty well and have very clear conceptions of several other things, before they can tell twenty'. Locke believed that a *system* of number names 'conduce[s] to our well reckoning', and is essential for keeping in mind the ideas of the numerosities bigger than the set of handy fingers.

But is this true? Can we possess ideas of the exact sizes of large numbers without having the words to name the numbers? If the idea of numbers was invented by our ancient Einstein sitting in a mud hut in Ur, and the invention was passed on to others, able to understand but not to invent them, then some means of representing the ideas will be necessary, not just handy. It would mean that our cave-dwelling ancestors not only had language but had number names as part of it. Alternatively, those marks I have interpreted as numerical had some other significance for their makers. One way of testing Locke's hypothesis is to see what happens in cultures whose languages lack number names. Do these cultures use numbers? Do they have an alternative way of representing them, of keeping the idea of each number distinct?

Locke's informants were certainly right in that there are languages with very few words for numbers, typically just for 1 and 2, sometimes 3, and for numbers above that they just say 'many' or its equivalent. Speakers of these languages tend to be cut off from numerate cultures: by impenetrable jungle, such as Amazonia, by impassable mountains, such as the highlands of New Guinea, or by great empty deserts, such as the red centre of Australia. Traditionally, these people had little need for counting. Most were or are hunter-gatherers with little surplus to trade. Australian Aborigines of the Central Desert made few essentials—boomerangs, woven baskets, spears, personal adornments, digging sticks and knives—most of which could be made by the individuals or the groups that needed them, without the need to trade. Nevertheless, one could imagine that some tasks would need numbers. For example, it would be difficult to set a date for a corroboree (a tribal get-together) without counting. It seems that, when necessary, the number of days to a planned social event is indicated by points on the palm of the hand, a kind of sign language.[37] Now, if parts of the hand are used to indicate numbers, then this constitutes an external aid.

Aranda, an Aboriginal language from the desert south of Alice Springs, like other languages round there, has words only for 1 (*nyente*), 2 (*therre*), 3 or a few (*urrpetye*), and many (*atningke*). Do speakers of Aranda therefore lack the idea of numbers above those which they can name? They do not, as Australian anthropologist David Wilkins has discovered. He points out that Aranda has a special word for 'how many?': *nthakentye*, with a special suffix, *ngare'*, for 'how many times?' and distinct from the word for 'how much?' Not only that, it has a special word for 'this many, as many as indicated'. Speakers show how many is intended, not by saying something, but by drawing lines in the sand—a natural drawing board permanently at hand.[38] As far as I know, they are the only people to rely exclusively on non-linguistic means to represent numerosities.

Aboriginal groups in the Australian desert are generally multilingual and these days, of course, they all speak English and have been in contact for several generations with money culture, so it is difficult to determine precisely the cognitive impact of growing up with a language having only the words for 'one', 'two', and 'many'. However, there is one extraordinary natural laboratory where we can find many peoples with such languages: Papua New Guinea (PNG). The highlands are cut by steep valleys whose walls are cloaked with almost impenetrable forest. This has isolated small groups of people for centuries, perhaps millennia, with their own separate languages, virtually uncontaminated by outside languages. As a result there are about a thousand distinct, mutually unintelligible languages, grouped into some sixty different language families,[39] some with just a few remaining speakers, others with many thousands of speakers. It is only since about 1970 that many of these societies have been contacted for the first time by anyone from outside, including other tribes. Some may still be uncontacted.

Some languages in PNG have no specialized number words, others do; some cultures have quite extensive trading links with their neighbours, others do not; and children from some highland societies have begun to go to school in the last twenty or thirty years. We thus have an opportunity—perhaps the last ever opportunity—to study the effects of different types of language on people's mathematical capacities. Fortunately for us, anthropologists, linguists, and psychologists have been studying mathematical capacities, not just out of scientific curiosity but as a way of helping PNG move from the Stone Age into the modern age. Most of the material I shall be using comes from the Indigenous Mathematics Project sponsored by the PNG Department of Education, carried out between 1976 and 1982 by the psychologist and educationalist David Lancy and his colleagues on ten different societies in the highlands and coastal regions of PNG. It is summarized in Lancy's gripping book *Cross-Cultural Studies in Cognition and Mathematics*.[40] Their results show very clearly the impact of language, and the numerical capacities which the children bring with them when they start formal schooling.

Many cultures in PNG count not just on their fingers, as Europeans have done since at least Roman times, but on their toes and other body parts. The Oksapmin, for example, use a system with a counting limit of 29. Counting starts with the right thumb and continues up to the nose, which stands for 14, and on to the left little finger and beyond. The number names are the names of the parts of the body, so that to say 'eight', you use the term that means 'right elbow'. The Kewa, like the Oksapmin, live in a remote fastness of the highlands of PNG, and like them they have elaborate exchange rituals in which prestige is gained by giving things to a neighbouring tribe. The Kewa counting is nevertheless different from Oksapmin: 1 is the right little finger, 8 is the bottom of the palm, and the nose is 34, not 14. The whole system has a counting limit of 68. Even more extraordinary than these systems, is the one used by the Yupno (Figure 2.8). Unlike Kewa and Oksapmin, this system does not start on one side of the body and finish on the other, but alternates between the two. The order is left hand, right hand, left foot, right foot, left ear, right ear,

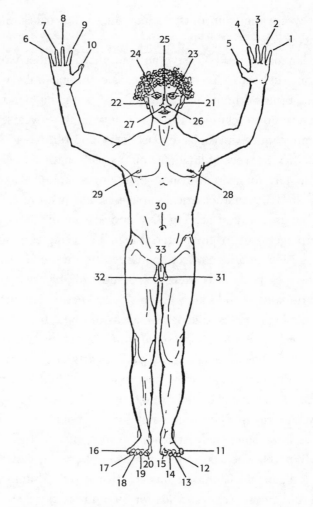

Figure 2.8 The Yupno people, like many of their neighbours in Papua New Guinea, have no special words for numbers, but use body parts and body-part names to count. It is thought that even modern European number words were derived from body-part names. The Yupno, unlike their neighbours, count back and forth across their body, ending up counting left testicle (31), right testicle (32), penis (33). (From Wassmann & Dasen[41])

left eye, right eye, nose, left nostril, right nostril, left breast, right breast, navel, left testicle, right testicle, and penis (= 33). (Women, by the way, do not count in public, and nothing is currently known about how or indeed if they do it at all.)

All body-part counting systems call the counting limit 'a man', or some version of this phrase, and it is possible to go beyond 'a man' to higher numbers. Like Locke's 'Americans', the PNG body-part counter uses other people's body-parts to continue the count. The Melpa, a tribe that counts in fours, 'pay little attention to quantitative aspects of the world' except when it comes to *moka*, a ritual exchange of pigs and shells. Then they 'count things often: they count in the absence of actual referents (items need not be present); they add, subtract, and multiply; and they have evolved procedures for counting to very large numbers by using two *or more* counters. One man keeps track of the ones, a second keeps track of the eights.'[42]

Adding two numbers can be achieved by using a version of the method of 'counting on from larger' which most children in literate cultures use when they cannot recall the answer immediately. For example, when asked to solve $3 + 5$ the child will say the word 'five', the name of the larger number, then hold up one finger and say 'six', hold up a second finger and say 'seven', and then a third finger and say 'eight'. The child will then look at the three fingers held up, and reason that since the three had been counted on from five, the last number counted, 'eight', would be the sum (see Chapter 3 for further details of children's addition methods). The Oksapmin, who have no number words, solve additions in an equivalent way, though they seem to count up to the larger number first. The psychologist Geoffrey Saxe observed a trade store owner adding 14 shillings and 7 shillings by first counting up to the nose for fourteen, then he named the left eye (15), the right thumb (1), the left ear (16), the first finger (2), and so on until he reached the left forearm. Ordinary arithmetic is a bit of a business for Oksapmin traders, but they manage by combining the use of body parts and of body-part names.[43]

What kinds of number capacities do these people have? One way of telling is to see how they manage at school. Are they handicapped compared with children who have number words in their language? Lancy identifies four kinds of counting system in PNG:[44]

Type I. Body counting, such as is used by the Oksapmin and the Kewa (the Yupno were not included in this study).

Type II. Tallying, using sticks or pebbles and a few number terms.

For example, the Kiwai just have words for 1 and 2, and count like this: *n'au* (1), *netowa* (2), *netowa n'au bi* (3: 1 + 2 with a special suffix), *netowa netowa* (4), *netowa netowa n'ua* (5).

Type III. This is a verbal system, where most of the words refer to body parts, usually based on the hand (5) and the man (20: two hands and two feet). The Kilenge, for example, have special words for 1 and 4, but 5 is 'hand', 10 is 'two hands', 15 is 'two hands and a foot', and 20 is 'a man'. They can count higher by combining terms, so that thirty is 'one man and one pair of hands'.

Type IV. This is a fully verbal system using a base of 10, usually with a word for 10 borrowed from an unrelated Austronesian language. The Ponam, an island fishing society, combine number words: 20 is 'two tens', 55 is 'five tens and five'; and they have a special word for 1,000.

One way of seeing whether the language makes a difference is to look at how quickly children can learn school mathematics and counting in English, the language of schooling. Lancy and his team looked at a range of other factors that might have made a difference to the maths tests, including years of schooling, region, nutrition, and teachers' own knowledge of maths.[45] Overall, the children were on average about two years behind their Western counterparts on most tests, but there was no systematic effect of language. Those with Type I languages counted in English just as readily and just as soon as those with the much more similar Type IV counting system.

According to the Mathematical Brain hypothesis, the capacity to think of numerosities is there in the brain, ready to be used whether the society possesses good counting tools or not, but the cultural resources provided by words and other signs can greatly enhance the utilization of this capacity. But why are there so many types of counting among the societies in PNG, which are relatively very homogeneous ethnically and culturally? The economic basis of these societies is a mix of hunting and gathering with tending gardens or stands of naturally occurring yams, so the demand for numbering things seems similar. Where there are differences in patterns of trade, and therefore in the apparent utility of numbering, these are not necessarily associated with the more advanced Type of number system. For example, while it is true that the coastal dwellers trade more than the highlanders, Type I and Type II counting is also found on the coast. Within one type, Type I for example, there are many variations, as we have seen, both in the counting limit and in the parts of the body used, though all use their fingers. (The significance of fingers is discussed at greater length in Chapter 5.)

The variety even of just body-counting is evidence against the diffusion of the invention of numbers from a single centre. If a body-counting system had been introduced at some place and time and then copied from one tribe to the next, then the basic patterns at least would have been preserved: either the same counting limit, or the pattern of counting, say starting at one side of the body and working across to the other. But counting limits range from 12 to 68, and some cultures alternate sides instead of counting across. It seems much more likely that these individual, very isolated groups independently came up with similar basic ideas for keeping track of their counting, using handy, portable, and easily distinguishable body parts.

The urge to count efficiently, as well as the capacity to do so, is reflected in the way people very quickly adopt new and better ways of doing it. A system of words with a regular base, such as 10, is more efficient than pointing to body parts or using body-part names. (We shall see in Chapter 3 how children in our culture progress naturally from finger-counting to verbal counting.) Reconstructing the historical development of PNG counting systems, one can trace progress from Type I to Type IV, from body-counting to verbal counting. This has to be a speculative reconstruction, since written records of pre-contact times are scarce. The Kiwai (Type II token-counting) are known to have used Type I counting in the past. However, the main evidence is from residues of earlier systems in societies that use the later systems. For example, the names used in Type III counting are clearly taken from body-part counting (e.g. 'hand'), and a Type IV society still uses Type I for the ritual counting of shell money, rather in the way that we still use base-12 counting for special purposes such as telling the time.

Unschooled traders as well as those with schooling use English number names—and, of course, Arabic numerals—in everyday numerical tasks. We find the same phenomena in many other cultures. The Zulu of southern Africa also have number words based on body-part counting (Table 2.2). It's easy to see the close connection between the number-name meaning and the finger gesture used to indicate the number. Many Zulu speakers have abandoned their own words for numbers and drop English or Afrikaans names into fluent Zulu sentences. Claudia Zaslavsky, who has surveyed African counting and mathematics, describes other examples of languages borrowing number words, from English in the south and from Arabic in the north. What is really striking about all these peoples is how quickly they become numerate and skilled in a full Western system of number words, Arabic numerals, counting, and calculation. In PNG, within a single generation a stone-age culture has produced enough numerate graduates to run a modern society. Australian Aborigines became numerate enough to work as stockmen and operate in a money economy within a few years of contact with white men. This surely suggests that there's a latent capacity waiting to be fully expressed.

Number	Number word	Meaning	Finger gesture
1	nye	'state of being alone'	extend left little finger
2	bili	'raise a separate finger'	extend left little and ring fingers
3	thathu	'to take'	extend three outer fingers
4	ne	'to join'	extend four fingers
5	hlanu	'[all the fingers] united'	extend five fingers
6	isithupa	'take the thumb'	extend right thumb
7	isikhombisa	'point with the forefinger'	extend right thumb and index finger
8	isishiyagalombili	'leave out two fingers'	extend three fingers of right hand
9	isishiyagalunye	'leave out one finger'	extend four fingers of right hand
10	ishumi	'cause to stand'	extend all fingers

Table 2.2 Zulu number words.[46]

NUMBER WORDS: DIFFUSION OF A SINGLE INVENTION OR RESPONSE TO A LOCAL NEED?

The idea of using a sequence of words to stand for numbers is clearly an advance over using a collection of physical objects. They are easier to use, at least when you are familiar with them (I'll discuss how and why children use finger arithmetic in Chapters 3 and 5). Once you have moved from body parts to words, you can name numbers by using the principle of 'additive composition', by which I mean that a number is made up of other numbers, just as a collection contains sub-collections, apart from the collection 1. This means that you can combine number names to make larger and larger numbers with complete precision.

The Origins of European Number Words

It is certainly true that once a system of number words has been invented, it is so useful that it is maintained in the language, wherever it spreads and whatever else about the language changes. Most European languages and many languages of India, Iran, and other places are descended from a language we now call Indo-European (IE). We have no records of this language, and philologists have had great fun trying to reconstruct it from its descendants, especially its early descendants such as Ancient Greek and Sanskrit. When number words from various IE languages are laid out side by side (Table 2.3), it's easy to see their relationship. For comparison, I show two non-IE languages that have had many centuries to assimilate vocabulary from their IE neighbours, but it's quite clear that they have not. The sound changes (called phonetic shifts) that have taken place over four or five millennia have created two classes of IE language: the Kentum languages, in which in the IE form *dekmt*—ten—the initial *d* sound stays more or less the same—*d* or *t*—and the *k* also stays more or less the same; and the other group, the Satem languages, which keep the *d* but soften the *k* into *s* or *sh*. The word for a hundred, IE *kmtom*, keeps the initial *k* sound in Latin and other Kentum languages, while the Satem languages soften the *k* to *s*, as in Sanskrit *shatam*.[47] Table 2.3 also makes it clear that Finnish has very different words for these numbers, though, like IE, these languages use a base-10 number system. It is easy to see that modern speakers of IE languages use number words that descended from IE roots. Figure 2.9 shows the descent of the words for 10 in the two IE groups of languages.

Number	Basic IE	Kentum languages				Satem languages			Non-IE	
		Greek	Latin	Irish	Modern German	Sanskrit	Russian	Finnish	Basque
1	oi-nos, oi-qos	heis	unus	oin	eins	ekab	odin	yksi	bat
2	duuo	dyo	duo	da	zwei	dvi	dva	kaksi	bi
3	trejes	treis	tres	tri	drei	trayah	tri	kolme	hiru
4	quetuor	tettares	quattuor	cethir	vier	chatvarah	chetyre	neljä	lau
5	penque	pente	quinque	coic	fünf	pancha	pjatj	viisi	bost
6	sueks	hex	sex	se	sechs	shash	shestj	kuusi	sei
7	septm̥	hepta	septem	secht	sieben	sapta	semj	seitsemän	cazpi
8	oktou	okto	octo	ocht	acht	ashta	vosmj	kahdeksan	zortzi
9	neun	en-nea	novem	noi	neun	nava	devjatj	yhdeksan	bederatzi
10	dekm̥, dekmt	deka	decem*	deich	zehn	dasha	desatj	kymmenen	amar
100	kmtom	hekaton	centum*	cet	hundert	shatam	sto	sata	eun
1000	sm-gheslom	chilioi	mille	mile	tausend	sahasram	tysjacha	tuhat	milla

* Pronounced with a hard 'c'.

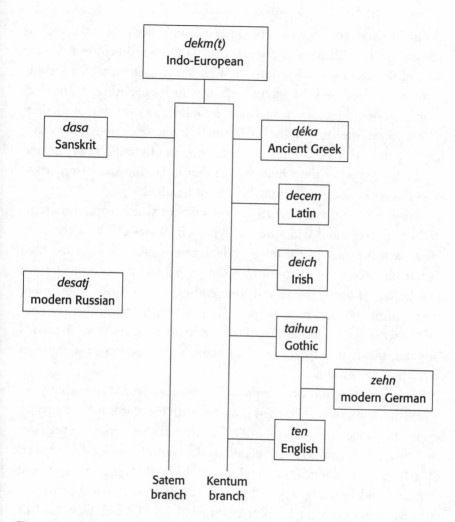

Figure 2.9 The origin of modern European words for 10. In the Satem branch of the Indo-European family, the *k* sound in the IE *dekm(t)* became *s*, while in the Kentum branch, *d* became *t* and later *z* (pronounced *ts*) in modern German. (After Menninger[49])

The IE words for the first ten numbers and for 100 are related to each other, and are possibly derived ultimately from a form *dekmtm*, meaning 'two hands'.[50] The word for 1,000, on the other hand, seems to have several different roots. The Latin *mille* seems to be derived from the Lesbos dialect version of the IE to become *smighsli*, shortened in the ancient Italian languages to *smilli* or *milli*, from which modern Romance languages get their words for thousand. The Sanskrit *sahasram* is also derived from the IE root *sm-gheslom*. If both these derivations are correct then IE possessed a word for a thousand before it divided several thousand years ago into the Kentum languages, which include Latin and Greek, and the Satem languages such as Sanskrit.[51] The Germanic thousand (*tausend*; *thusundi* in Gothic, an ancestor of modern German) is not related to the conjectured IE ancestor, *sm-gheslom*. According to Karl Menninger, the great historian of numbers, it is related to the Gothic word for a hundred, so that in Gothic and its predecessors *thusundi* meant something like 'great hundred'.

This mechanism for creating new number words from old seems to be very basic and widespread. Gypsies in Wales call hundred *baro desh*, which means 'great ten', while gypsies in Russia say *baro shel*, 'great hundred', for a thousand.[52] Our word for million comes from the Italian *milione*, where the *-one* ending means 'great'.[53] Another mechanism may also be at work in IE. It has been argued that the root of the word for hundred, *kmtm*, comes from the genitive of the word for ten, meaning 'of decades' and being a contraction of 'decade of decades', or ten tens.[54]

The construction of a sequence of number words probably took place in several stages. Perhaps it started with the words for body parts, especially fingers, as we saw in PNG. There is some evidence that our words for four and five are related to the root of the word for finger. The Gothic word *fimf* may be related to the Gothic *figgrs*, pronounced 'fingers' and meaning finger. In Slavic languages the word for five is related to the word for fist. For example, in Old Church Slavonic (the ancestor of many modern Slavic languages), five is *petj* and fist is *pesti*. It has been argued that the IE word for five, *penque*, is related to words for hand in many IE languages, along with the suggestion that the word for ten may have originally meant 'two hands'.[55]

Does this mean that proto-Indo-European, a very early stage in the historical development of IE languages, was a base-5 language? Not necessarily. There are suggestions that it could even have been a base-4 language, counting up to four, and then going on 4 + 1, and so on. Menninger[56] and others have noted something odd about the word for eight in IE—it is a dual form (a number inflexion for pairs), perhaps a dual form of a word for four, meaning 'two fours'. They also point out that, even more curiously, in all IE languages the word for nine is very similar to, and certainly related to, the word for new. In Italian, the word for new is *nova*, and for nine *nuove*; in German, *neu* and *neun*, in French, *neuf* for both meanings; in Sanskrit, *nava* and *navas*; and so on. Could this mean that nine was the 'new number' after the pair of fours?

One final fact supports this hypothesis. In many European languages, some of the number words agree grammatically with the collection of things enumerated. In French, only the word for one (*un/une*) agrees in gender. In Latin, there are separate forms of the word for two, according to gender and case: *duo, duae, duo; duorum, duarum; duobus; duos, duas, duo*. For three, there are separate forms for masculine, feminine, and neuter: *tres* and *tria*. There is a similar pattern in Gothic. In both Latin and Greek there is only one form for four. In Ancient Greek, on the other hand, the word for four behaves just like the words for one, two, and three, with separate forms according to gender and case. No language in the IE family has inflected forms for the words for five and above. This makes the first four numbers special in IE. Perhaps its speakers started with words for just the first four numbers, based on fingers and combining the two hands. Menninger even speculates that the IE word for five, *penque*, may originally have meant 'four fingers plus one'.[57]

From Fingers to Words

The important point for the Mathematical Brain hypothesis is this. No one person, or group of people, invented the number words, which everyone then copied. We have seen that separate language families have different sets of words—in IE these are descended from the same roots up to a hundred—but neighbouring, unrelated languages have their own words for the numbers. There is evidence that number words were not all invented at once. IE speakers may have started with words for the four fingers on one hand, and built up vocabulary from these. Words for large numbers—a hundred, a thousand, a million—were invented much later, and indeed we continue to invent names for very large numbers, such as trillion. The traces of body-part counting, especially finger-counting, in the number words of languages suggest very strongly that the use of body-part names for number words preceded and was the basis for the familiar number names in many, perhaps all, languages. This in turn suggests a universal historical progression from body-part counting to number names. If the Mathematical Brain hypothesis is true, then we might well expect brains everywhere to find similar solutions to the problem of expressing numbers. Why the hand should turn out to be so handy is discussed in more detail in Chapter 5.

BASIC BASES

The way we name numbers is not to have one name for each number, which is typical of Type I body-part counting. That would be not just impractical, but impossible, as there are infinitely many numbers. Body-part counters live in a culture where counting rarely needs to go above the counting limit of their system. In modern societies we often need to talk about large numbers, so we construct our number names from a small vocabulary of number words and rules for combining them. The rules reflect the base implicit in the number system. For English and other IE languages, the base is 10.[58] If our ancient Einstein was the sole source of early numbers, we would expect all number sequences to be constructed along the same lines, using the same base and similar mechanisms for constructing numbers larger than the base. On the other hand, if all of us, and our ancestors, possessed a Mathematical Brain capable of coming up with the idea of numbers for ourselves, we would expect all systems to exploit the idea of additive composition, but to find a very wide variety of bases and mechanisms for making large numbers.

The idea of a base may be related to the idea of a 'basic collection' of things—a collection that can be readily referred to by all members of the community. This is why body parts that are always visible, such as fingers, make a 'handy' basic collection, and why the testicles and penis are only used as part of the basic collection by Yupno males. We develop names for members of the basic collection, which may have begun historically as body-part names for many systems. Counting started by associating each object to be counted with a member of the basic collection, and later with the name of the member. Base systems tend to reflect these basic collections of body parts:

five fingers, ten fingers, twenty fingers and toes (visible when we didn't wear shoes).

The base is the number after which names repeat according to rules for their combination. We can speculate that, initially, the base was simply added to non-base numbers, just as *fourteen* adds 4 to the base 10. In body-part systems the base was often called simply 'a man', and body-part names were additively combined with it. More recent base systems give special names to powers and multiples of the base. In English, there are repeated unit names after the name of the multiple of ten which itself repeats: *twenty-one, twenty-two, twenty-three*, and so on. We also have special names for multiples of 10: *ten* (1 × 10), *twenty* (2 × 10), and so on. We have names for 10^2—*hundred*—and 10^3—*thousand*. The South American Indian language Tacana, like some other languages, expresses the powers of its base, *tunka* (10), explicitly, just as we might say 'ten times ten times ten': 1000 is *tunka-tunka-tunka*.[59]

English is not a regular base-10 system. For numbers between 10 and 20 we have special words—*eleven, twelve*, and so on—rather than simple additive combinations, such as 'ten one' or 'ten two'. The names of our decades are not transparent either. Instead of 'two ten' and 'three ten' we have the special words *twenty* and *thirty*. We have no names for powers of 10 between 10^3, *thousand*, and 10^6, *million* (except for the seldom used *myriad* for 10^4). These irregularities make it hard for children to learn the pattern and the meanings of English number names, as we shall see in Chapter 3. It need not be like this. Chinese children have the benefit of number names, also base-10, which are entirely regular: they can count up to ten in the usual way, then proceed ten-one, ten-two, ten-three, up to two-ten, then two-ten-one, two-ten-two, and so on.

English contains residues of other bases that have been used in parallel with base 10, and which historically may have preceded it in Europe. Base 12 was used for money (12 pennies to the shilling), weight of precious metals (12 Troy ounces to the pound), length (12 inches to the foot), and quantity (dozen, gross). The word *twelve* reflects its origins much less transparently than the 'teen' words, which are still clearly in the form 'unit + ten'. The division of day and night, and our clock face, into 12 hours has an ancient Egyptian origin,[60] and is possibly the source of our twelve-counting.

We can also see in English, and in other European languages, the traces of a *vigesimal*—base-20—system. The word *score* means 20, but it also means to keep count generally, and to cut (a mark on a tally). English once used base 20 for money (20 shillings to the pound) and for ages (as in the phrase 'three-score years and ten'). French counts in twenties for 80 and above (*quatre-vingts, quatre-vingt-dix*), and 60–79 form a group of 20 (*soixante, soixante-et-un . . . soixante-dix . . . soixante-dix-neuf*). Modern Irish and Scottish Gaelic counts up in twenties from 20 (in Irish, *fiche* (20), *deich ar fiche* (10 on 20), *da fiche* 20: in (2 × 20), *da fiche's a deich* (2 × 20 on 10) . . .) as does Danish (60 is *tre-synds-tyve* = 3 × 20, 80 is *fur-synds-tyve* = 4 × 20. In the case of French, base-20 counting seems to have been introduced by the Normans in the eleventh century. It included forms from *trois-vingt* (60) through *six-vingt* (120), to *dix-huit-vingt* (360). These spread from northern France to the south with many variants lasting into the seventeenth century.[61] Indo-European is a strictly base-10 system, so the presence of traces of base 20 suggests that IE speakers coming into Europe took over a pre-existing base-20 system. Basque, which is not IE, and may well be the last surviving remnant of pre-IE European languages, is vigesimal.

The base-10 system can be found outside Europe in quite unrelated languages of Africa and Asia, and base 20 was used by the ancient Maya. Their numeration was quite systematic, with separate names for the first four powers (Table 2.4). The Aztec system was the same, so presumably this conceptual technology was shared; it has been handed down to the modern Mixtec of Mexico, who have since borrowed from the Spanish a special word for 100. Both Mayans and Aztecs, but also the Basques, break up the sequence of twenty into groups of five, so strictly they use 5–20 systems of counting. A *sexagesimal* system—base 60—with multiples of 10 was used by the Babylonians, and survives in the way we measure angles and time, and possibly in the way that the structure of some modern European number words changes at 60. Among the earliest written numerals, those of Sumeria showed clearly that the Sumerians had separate words for at least the first two powers of 60, but could and did count beyond that, using multiples of the base, just as we do (Table 2.5).[62]

20^1 (= 20)	20^2 (400)	20^3 (8,000)	20^4 (160,000)
hun	*bak*	*pik*	*calab*

Table 2.4 Mayan number words for the first four powers of 20.

60^0	10	60^1	10×60^1	60^2	10×60^2	60^3
(= 1)	(10)	(60)	(600)	(3,600)	(36,000)	(216,000)
as	*u*	*ges*	*ges-u*	*sar*	*sar-u*	*sar-ges*

Table 2.5 Sumerian number words for the first four powers of 60 and their multiples of 10.

To construct numbers above the base, we have seen three principles used:

Addition of a unit to the base—for example, 7 + 10: *seventeen, dix-sept, shih-ch'i* (Chinese).

Multiplication of the base by a unit—for example, 7×10: *seventy, siebzig, ch'i-shih.*

Creating a new term for powers of the base—for example, 10^2: *hundred, cent, pai.* (This is a 'name-value' system, quite different from the place-value system we use for numerals.)

This might suggest the invention of principles that diffused to speakers of different languages, who then applied them to their own homegrown number words. It may be true that users of these methods learned them from their neighbours, but there are number systems which use other methods based on other principles, and even IE languages may deploy them. One such method is subtraction—sometimes called 'back-counting' or 'overcounting'. We can see it in Latin numerals, which use both addition and subtraction: XI is 10 + 1, but IX is 10 – 1, and XLIX is (50 – 10) + (10 – 1) = 49. In Latin texts we find 19 written as *un-de-viginti* (20 – 1) and 58 as *duo-de-sexaginta*

(60 – 2). Of course, in English we use subtraction routinely in telling time: 'five to six' instead of 'five fifty-five'. Some systems subtract 'half' from the next number up. In modern German, the time *halb neun* does not mean half past nine but 'half to nine' (8.30). In ordinary Danish numbers, *tres* (short for *tre-synds-tyve*, meaning three times twenty) means 60, but *halvtres* means fifty. Similarly, *firs* (*fir-synds-tyve*) is eighty, and *halvfjers* is 70. Here the half refers not to half a decade, but to half the fourth twenty (*fjers = firs*).

There are many examples of subtraction in older forms of modern European languages. Today, we can find subtraction for even small numbers in Finnish (a non-IE language), where 8 is *kahdeksan* (10 – 2) and 9 is *yhdeksan* (10 – 1). For extensive and systematic use of subtraction we turn to the mysterious language of the Ainu of northern Japan and the Sakhalin islands (unrelated to Japanese, Chinese, or Russian), a small group of hunter-gatherers and fishers. (I take this account from Menninger.[63]) This isolated language uses a base-20 system for larger numbers, but is built on the familiar collection of fingers (Table 2.6). The number word for five means 'hand', and that for ten means, elliptically, 'both hands'. In their presumably independent system, they subtract 10 from multiples of 20 rather than add 10 to multiples of 20, as Mayans and other base-20 users have done. The Ainu do not seem to have developed a word for 10^2, or indeed for 20^2; in fact they have no special words for numbers bigger than 20. If they had borrowed their system from neighbours, who had ultimately borrowed theirs from an ancient Einstein in Ur, then we might expect the mechanism for constructing numbers from the 20 base to have been part of the package. This, together with the subtraction method, suggests again a number system that is home-grown.

Most of the systems I have described mix an existing method of base counting with 'upgrades'—new and useful features borrowed from neighbouring systems, or developed independently. The mechanisms of borrowing and development are seen very clearly in PNG counting, where Type II counting developed from Type I; and Types III and IV, with verbal systems, used words to replace body-part names and counting-tokens such as pebbles. (Incidentally, the word *calculus* comes from the Latin word for 'pebble.') Modern languages contain traces of earlier counting methods, and methods borrowed

Number	Word	Meaning
1	shi-ne	'beginning-to be'
2	tu	
3	re	
4	ine	'much'
5	ashik-ne	'hand'
6	i-wan	4 from 10
7	ar-wan	3 from 10
8	tu-pesan	'two steps down'
9	shine-pesan	'one step down'
10	wan	'two-sided' (= both hands)
20	hot-ne	'whole' (man)
40	tu hotne	2×20
60	re hotne	3×20
80	ine hotne	4×20
30	wan e tu hotne	10 from 2×20
50	wan e re hotne	10 from 3×20
70	wan e ine hotne	10 from 4×20
90	wan e ashikne hotne	10 from 5×20
100	ashikne hotne	5×20
110	wan e iwanhotne	10 from 6×20

Table 2.6 Number words in the Ainu language.

from neighbours or tribes they replaced. All this suggests that people have an innate capacity to count—indeed an urge, which may be driven in part by economic or social circumstances—and that they will use whatever comes to hand to do this effectively.

Base Creation

Although languages with specialized number words use bases, which are multiples and powers of one number, there are a wide variety of these bases. The same bases have originated in quite unrelated languages, such as 20 in pre-IE European tongues and the languages of the Maya and the Ainu, which may nevertheless use quite different ways of combining bases and other numbers—some use addition, others subtraction. These features suggest that the idea of a base wasn't invented in one place and diffused to other places, but was the natural and inevitable outcome of people seeking to express the capacities inherent in their Mathematical Brain, especially the ideas of additive composition and collections of collections. Of course, people eagerly snap up useful inventions, so if a neighbour has a good way of doing something it is soon incorporated into the cultural toolbox.

KEEPING ACCOUNTS: THE NEED FOR NUMERALS

The need to make permanent records of numbers has given us a wonderful opportunity to see into the minds of our ancestors, to see how they grasped the concept of numerosity and developed ideas based on it. The concept of numerosity implies principles that could guide the construction of number systems, and in this section I argue that the development of number systems can be explained in terms of these principles. Although these principles have emerged in a distinct order, it is clear that a culture often worked with more than one principle at a time in their construction of numerals.

Stage I: The Tally Principle

We have seen collections of inscribed marks on ice-age bones, and arrays of dots in ochre on the walls of Aurignacian and Magdalenian caves that could be the earliest permanent symbols for numbers. They seem to represent simple numerosities: our ancestors knew how to make a collection of marks to represent the numerosity of a set of objects and, perhaps, people. The idea of making one mark for each member of a collection, making a tally, is thus an ancient idea. It also seems to be clearly related to body-counting, which puts body parts in one-to-one correspondence with the collection of things to be counted.

Tallies have been found all over the world, from ancient Fiji to the Peru of the Incas. It is so pervasive an idea that the word for making the mark, *scoring* in English, and parallel terms in other Germanic languages, means 'counting', and a *tally* can mean the result of counting. The word tally itself is derived from the Latin *talea*, which means 'cut twig' or 'stave'. The Latin word for calculating, *computare*, comes from *putare* which means, literally, 'to cut' (as in amputate, from *amputare*).

Tallying is one of the simplest and clearest manifestations of the concept of numerosity—one mark for each member of the collection to be counted—and for this reason it was used, even by people who could read and write, well into the nineteenth century in monetarily sophisticated countries like England and Switzerland. The use of tallies by the Bank of England was abolished by statute only in 1783, but they continued to be used until at least 1825.[64] According to the historian of money C. R. Josset,

> Some of the tallies represented payments to government departments . . . one of these . . . is eight feet six inches long, and represents the largest amount to which one tally was restricted—£50,000. It owes its existence to the fact that it had never been returned to the Exchequer, as the payment represented a government debt which had never been paid.[65]

Stage II: The Collection Principle (or 'The Poker-Chip Principle')
Although the tallying principle is logical and easily understood because it is based straightforwardly on the concept of numerosity, it is inconvenient when the number gets large. How many I's are there in the following collection?

IIIIIIIIIIIIIIIIIIII

The problem can be made easier by grouping the I's into subcollections:

IIIII IIIII IIIII IIIII

This stage in the development of numerals makes use of the idea that each collection has a numerosity which can be denoted by a single symbol. That is to say, the collection of marks, or of things, can be denoted by one sign. We can think of this as the poker-chip principle (or for older readers, the cash-register principle), where a single chip (or flag) stands for a denomination representing a multiple of the basic unit—chips for 1, 5, 10, 50, 100, 250, 500, (etc.) pounds or dollars. Of course, these chips have their numerical value printed on them, so there is no ambiguity, but they are also distinguished by colour, shape, and size. The process of representing a large number by a single sign is called by Menninger 'encipherment'—creating a cipher to stand for a whole collection.

We have seen how Sumerian accountants used pictographs to represent collections of sheep or of measures of grain (Figure 2.2). The Egyptians of 4,000 years ago also grasped the idea that the numerosity of a collection can be denoted by a single symbol. Like the Sumerian system, theirs was simple and additive. Much of what we know about it comes from the Rhind Papyrus, kept in the British Museum, a roll 33 cm high and 565 cm long. It shows units as collections of vertical lines, with separate symbols for powers of 10, from 10^1 to 10^6 (Figure 2.10).

Once there is a special symbol for a whole collection, then it is a natural next step to give the symbol its own name. This principle is likely to be the origin of name values for bases.

Stage III: The Adding Composition Principle
A third principle has been used for numerals, based directly on the concept of numerosity: that any numerosity, apart from 1, is the sum of other numerosities. We have seen on the Rhind Papyrus that a combination of signs means that the numerical values of these signs should be added together. (It is not inevitable that the conjoining of signs indicates addition: we shall meet examples of multiplication, raising to a power, and of subtraction.) Sumerian accountants clearly used this principle, as we saw above in Section 1.

We have no evidence that prehistoric man had reached Stages 2 and 3 in representing numbers. I have interpreted the marks on bones and walls in terms of the Stage 1 principle. On the other hand,

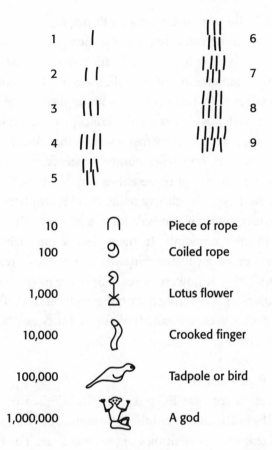

Figure 2.10 Egyptian hieroglyphic symbols for numbers, from the Rhind Papyrus. The Egyptians used a base-10 name-value system, with separate symbols for powers of ten. Numbers are formed by addition only.

there are many obscure symbols for which there is no agreed interpretation, and it is at least conceivable that some stood for large numbers. For example, in Figure 2.3, there are rows of 26 dots next to two 'claviform' symbols. It has generally been assumed, following the great cataloguer and interpreter of prehistoric cave art André Leroi-Gourhan, that the claviform stood for a woman. On the other hand, the claviform symbol could have stood for a large number, perhaps by analogy with the convention in modern body-part counting systems of referring to the limit of counting as 'a man'. So the combination of claviforms and 26 dots meant 'two large numbers + 26'.

Stage IV: The Collection of Collections Principle

The concept of numerosity implies the possibility of a collection of collections. This is what multiplication means: the numerosity of 5×3 is the numerosity of a collection of five collections of three members each. The fact that this is an implication of the concept does not mean that possessors of the concept have grasped it. The idea of joining together the numerosities of collections, in a systematic way, led to an advance on earlier number systems, both conceptually and in the ease and clarity of representing big numbers.

Although the Egyptians clearly understood multiplication—its operation was evident in their symbols for the powers of 10—it was not fully explicit in their numerals. In their hieratic and demotic scripts, simpler and easier to write than hieroglyphics, they created special symbols for multiples of powers of ten. For many of these signs, a version of the multiplier is conjoined with the multiplicand. The signs for 500 and for 5,000 each contain both signs for 5 and for 100 and 1,000 respectively.

Stage V: The Base Principle

It is easy for us to see that Egyptian and Babylonian numerals used bases. We use base 10, and so did the Egyptians. They had special signs for powers of ten, and for multiples of powers of ten. The Babylonians used two bases. The first, and most famous, was 60, which we have inherited in our measures of time and angles. Base 60 was very convenient because it has many factors—2, 3, 4, 5, 6, 10, 12, 15, 20, and 30—which made calculation very easy. Calculating the corresponding fractions—½, ⅓, ¼, and so on—required very little work. Tables for use in schools tended to be for use with problems that weren't so easy, such as calculating the square of numbers, as in Figure 2.1.

Stage VI: The Recursion Principle

Essentially, recursion means applying a rule and then applying it to the result of applying the rule, and so on, as often as you wish. For our numerals, you can take a number, say 657, apply a rule for multiplying it by 10 (the rule for these numerals consists simply of putting a 0 on the right of the number), which gives 6,570; apply the rule to the result to give 65,700, apply the rule to this result, and so on. The

Babylonians could do this in only a very limited way: they had no mechanism for constructing higher and higher numbers in an easily grasped way: 178,975 would come out as something like this—transcribed into familiar numerals:

(1) (10,10,10,10) (1) (10,10,10,10) (10,10,10,10,10) (1)

This was difficult to compose, and difficult to read. The cuneiform numeral for 1 can mean 1, 60 (the base), or any power of 60, just as our 1 can mean 1, 10, or any power of 10. The principal difference between their system and ours is that their 1 is often ambiguous: two numerals next to each other are sometimes meant to be multiplied, sometimes added. This is how the 1's in the above expression should be interpreted:

$$((1^2 = 3,600) \times (40)) + ((1 = 60) \times (40)) + (50 + (1 =))$$

These ambiguities may go some way to explaining why the Babylonian system of numerals didn't stand the test of time.

Since numerosities can be ordered by size, with no upper limit, numerals should be able to express this clearly. Cuneiform can represent only the lower powers of 60, along with multiplication and addition. This does make it possible to express big numbers, but they are very hard to read and even harder (for me at least) to write. In fact, our ordinary numerals are fine for numbers up to about 1 million, but above that they too get hard to read, so about here we start using power notations—it's easier to see that 10^{15} is bigger than 10^{12}, and bigger by a factor of 10^3, than to see that 1,000,000,000,000,000 is 1,000 times bigger than 1,000,000,000,000.

The later Egyptian hieratic script had a more compact system which relied on the poker chip principle, with thirty-six separate denominations of 'chip': for the units and for unit multiples of 10, 100, and 1,000.

The technology of imprinting soft clay tablets with shaped sticks severely limited the set of marks that could easily be used. The Egyptian system exploited the flexibility of writing with a brush on papyrus to increase both the vocabulary of symbols and also the readability of the intended number: far less adding and multiplying in your head was needed. But the Egyptians didn't fully exploit the hieratic system. They created number symbols for each new power of 10—the poker-chip principle—but that is not a systematic approach. There was no general means for representing ever larger numbers in the way that our modern place-value decimal system allows.

Both the Egyptians and the Babylonians could in principle write numbers as large as they wished, but in practice their system was efficient only for small numbers. But both systems were much better than the later Greek and Roman systems, which relied on the poker-chip principle. Greek numbers were represented by the twenty-four letters of the alphabet, plus three obsolete letters *stigma, koppa,* and *sampi,* which they needed because each of the nine units was denoted by a letter, each of the nine decades was denoted by nine more letters, and each of the hundreds was denoted by a letter. Higher numbers were created by arbitrary diacritical marks, such as a comma placed below the units to indicate thousands.

Greek is a model of clarity compared with the more familiar Roman numerals, and it is no accident that Ursula K. Le Guin chose to present the numerals of the Masters in Roman letters, a seriously awkward way of representing large numbers. Roman uses the poker-chip principle, subtraction as well as addition, but no multiplication. Numbers bigger than C (*centum,* 100) and M (*mille,* 1000) are constructed more or less arbitrarily, and there is no recursive mechanism for writing really big numbers. Because Roman numerals are not constructed according to strict rules, over the centuries there has been great variation in how they are written. We use M for 1,000, but the Romans of Cicero's time never did: they used CIƆ, with IƆ for 500. Larger numbers were often made by adding C's, so that 10,000 was CCIƆƆ, and its half was IƆƆ.

Roman numerals are not recursive and don't make for easy calculation.

Stage VII: The Place-Value Principle

A convention of our numerals, and one not strictly derived from the concept of numerosity, is that the value of a digit depends on its position in a string of digits. Thus the 1 in 100 means something different from the 1 in 71. This principle allows us, among other things, to construct numbers as large as we please, though, as we have seen, above about 1 billion these numbers become hard to read. It is generally believed that the place-value principle, along with zero (which I deal with in the next section), were invented by Hindu mathematicians and brought to Europe by Arab traders. This is true, but the interpretation of Babylonian cuneiform numerals does depend on position, as we have seen. For example, the value of the symbol for 1, either as 1 or as (1 ×) 60, depends on its place in the sequence of symbols.

ZERO: FROM NOTHING TO NOTATION

The concept of numerosity can be extended to include the idea of a collection with no members, what mathematicians and logicans call the 'empty set' or 'null set'. Although the idea that we have no bananas is unlikely be a new one, or one that is hard to grasp, the idea that no bananas, no sheep, no children, no prospects are really all the same, in that they have the same numerosity, is a very abstract one. But it does follow quite naturally from the idea that two collections with different things can have the same numerosity. The idea that we should represent this empty set, this nothing, in our system of numerals, was a very difficult one to establish. Even the greatest scientist and mathematician of antiquity, Archimedes (who, as we shall see, constructed a method for numbering the grains of sand in the universe), failed to invent a place-value notation with zero. The great nineteenth-century mathematician Carl Friedrich Gauss speculated regretfully, 'To what heights science would have risen by now if only he had made that discovery!'[66]

If Archimedes failed, how did someone else succeed? If the concept of zero is implied by the concept of numerosity, then we might expect people to try to represent it in their numerical notation when the circumstances were appropriate: it may not have needed an ancient Einstein or an ancient Archimedes to invent it. Was there a single invention site for zero?

Our 'Arabic' numerals have place value and zero, and it is certainly the case that Europeans of the twelfth century learned of these numerals, along with their zero, from Arab traders. But the Arabs invented neither the numerals nor the zero. The Arabs of the eighth century seem to have had no numerals at all, and wrote numbers as words, even in mathematical texts. In AD 773, the Caliph of Baghdad received a copy of the *Brahmasphutasiddhanta* ('Improved Astronomical Textbook of Brahma')—a work written 150 years earlier by the leading Hindu astronomer, Brahmagupta—in which the mathematics was written in the Hindu place-value notation with zero. Muhammad al-Khwārizmī (from whose name our word 'algorithm' comes) wrote his famous 'arithmetic' in 820, explaining the use of these new numerals in calculation. The book was translated into Latin and was widely known in Europe from the twelfth century. (Al-Khwārizmī seems also to have introduced the method of grouping digits by threes from the right, which we still use.[67]) The impact of the Arabic numerals on Europe is illustrated by the various words for 'zero' (Figure 2.11).

The Extraordinary Story of O

Was zero, then, invented by Hindu mathematicians? Our numerals are certainly derived from their Brahmi numerals, which originally represented numbers according to poker-chip conventions, not place values, for units and decades. But the path from these numerals to place values with zero is one of the most extraordinary in the history of science, a path that depends critically on technology, but also on poetry.

The Indus Valley of the sixth century AD had a rich and stormy history. The original inhabitants were driven out by the Aryans who, from late in the second millennium BC, had swept down from the northwest. They brought with them the religion of the Veda written in the Indo-European Sanskrit language, with its base-10 system, and displaced or enslaved the indigenous people and beliefs. The region became a satrapy of the Persian emperor, Darius, and was invaded in 327 BC by Alexander the Great. The Indus Valley remained under Greek influence until Chandragupta drove them out. His grandson, Asoka, established an empire around 250 BC; according to a traditional saying, if greatness is a measure of the number of people revering his memory after his death, then Asoka was greater than Julius Caesar or Charlemagne.

There was a lot of mathematics in the Indus Valley. A mathemati-

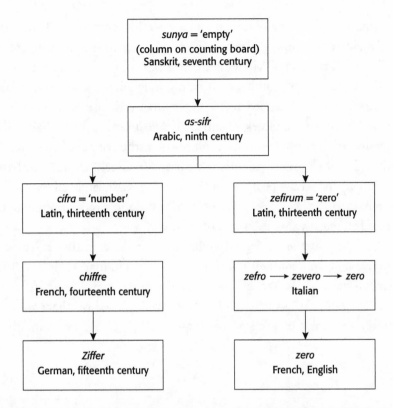

Figure 2.11 The evolution of words for 'zero'. In Sanskrit the zero was called *sunya*, meaning 'empty'. The Arabs, who brought the Indian numerals to Europe, translated this with the word *as-sifr*, literally 'the empty'. It is this word that is the source both for many European words meaning 'numerals' or 'numbers', on the left of the diagram, and for words meaning 'zero', on the right.

cal treatise had been composed at the high point of Vedic literature one thousand years earlier. Gautama Buddha, according to the Sanskrit epic *Lalita Vistara* (written 2,000 years ago), knew the words for numbers up to 10^{53}, and said that there were eight more 'sequences' beyond this. These numbers were probably never used in calculations, but the awareness of their existence may have provided further impetus to develop a notation for representing them.[68] There was contact with Babylon by the overland route, and also by sea traders, and it is certain that Indus mathematicians came to know about Babylonian discoveries; later, the astronomical ideas of Ptolemy reached them from Alexandria, including his notation. By the sixth century AD there was a flourishing school of astronomy, which included Brahmagupta, that made use of the Babylonian place-value system, and also the Ptolemaic convention, in recording the angular positions of heavenly bodies, of using a small circle to indicate zero degrees or minutes.

These ideas—of numbers extending indefinitely, and using a special mark for no degrees (etc.) in angular measurements—were of course known to the Greek scientists of Alexandria, and probably also to many other people who used numbers in the course of their work. Although Babylonian numerals were base 60, Greek, along with Latin and other Indo-European languages in the Eastern Mediterranean, were base 10, as we have seen. Why then did the Greeks not come up with a full place-value decimal notation with zero?

One part of the answer is technological: the counting board. Indian traders and mathematicians were very familiar with counting boards. The boards had columns for the powers of 10—units, tens, hundreds, and thousands—and pebbles were placed on them to indicate the multiples of each power (Figure 2.12). To add two numbers

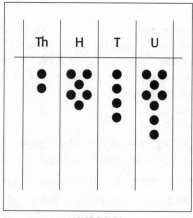

MMDCXLVIII

Figure 2.12 The number 2,648 represented on a counting board, with columns representing thousands, hundreds, tens, and units. Counting boards were common throughout the Mediterranean region for two thousand years. Very few survive; those from the Classical period used columns representing successive multiples of 5 rather than 10. The counting boards were clearly place-valued, but the results of calculations carried out on them then had to be 'transcoded' and written down in the Roman or Greek number system. These systems were name-valued, and the Roman system used subtractions as well as additions.

using the columns of the counting board was very much like our familiar column arithmetic, with carrying. When adding the two collections of pebbles gave a zero in that column, there was a situation logically the same as having a zero place value.

The Greeks and Romans also used counting boards, as can be seen from the fact that many of their words for number processes come from counting boards, as indeed do words in modern European languages (Table 2.7). One problem with Greek counting boards was that they were based on columns of 5's and not 10's, at least that was the case for the earliest identified Greek board, the Salamis Tablet.[69] However, later Greek and Roman boards used columns of ten. Surely, then, zero would have been an easy conceptual step, especially given the Babylonian precedent of a place-holder for zero place value in measuring angles. Perhaps the main barrier to its invention by the Greeks or the Romans, especially the Romans, was their number systems. Once the number was shown on the counting board in Figure

Language	Word	Original meaning	Derived from
Greek	*pempazein*	'to make fives'	Counting on a board with columns of fives
	psephizein	'to move pebbles'	Counting board
Latin	*calculus ponere*	'to place stones'	Counting board
Medieval Latin	*calculare*	'to move pebbles'	Counting board
	computare	'to cut'	Notched tally-stick
French	*jeter*	'to throw'	Counting board
	calculer	(from Latin *caculare*)	
	compter	(from Latin *computare*)	
English	*cast*	'throw'	Counting board
	count	(from Latin *computare*)	

Table 2.7 Number words that come from the use of counting boards.

2.12, it had to be transcribed in way that did not reflect at all the columnar basis of the calculation. Even so, it is perhaps surprising that with all their inventiveness, their interest in mathematics and astronomy, and their extensive trading contacts, more efficient numerals did not emerge from the Greek-speaking world.

The Hindu mathematicians had one secret ingredient that made the step to zero an easy one: poetry. In the popular Sanskrit verse epic *Agni-Purana*, written around AD 300, we find numbers written as words with place value.[70] These were typically not number words, but words that evoked the number. So instead of 1 the poet might write 'the moon' since there is only one of them; similarly, for 2, he might use 'arms', or 'eyes', or 'wings'; for 5 he might use 'arrows', since Kamadeva, the god of love, had five arrows in his quiver. For zero there were many words, including *sunya*, meaning 'empty', but also words meaning 'complete', 'gap', 'whole', and so on. Using a range of words, including number words, a poetic and memorable phrase could be constructed. Successive words represented increasing powers of 10, beginning with the units, followed by the tens, and so on. Where a power of 10 was missing, an appropriate word evoking zero was used in its place. Thus, for example, 1,201 might be written as *sasi-paksa-kha-eka*: 'moon-wings-hole-one'. This is a place-value system with zero. Enciphering the numbers as in poker-chips or by name value was no longer necessary.

The final step was to use special symbols, called Gwalior numerals, which had been derived from the older Brahmi numerals and are clear ancestors of our current numerals, 2 and 3 being almost identical. The earliest known example of place-value notation with zero (a small circle) is a Gwalior inscription from AD 870, which shows the numbers 270 and 187. From here the path to our own numerals is straightforward. The hard work had all been done: it was necessary just to make the numerals a bit clearer, as can be seen from the evolutionary tree in Figure 2.13 (from the historian of mathematics Graham Flegg).

This story shows that our place-value notation did not have a single inventor, or even a single site of invention. The pieces were put together over a period of 2,500 years, from the Babylonian partial system of place-values, with gaps that were sometimes marked, via

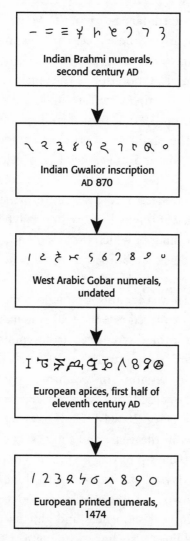

Figure 2.13 The ancestral forms of modern 'Arabic' numerals. They derive ultimately from the Indus Valley Brahmi numerals of the second century AD, which were not fully organized by place value. They also lacked a symbol for zero; this was invented during the fifth century, and the earliest known example is in a Gwalior inscription from AD 870. The forms were brought to the West by Arab traders—hence their name. The first book to describe them in detail was the *Liber abaci* by Leonardo of Pisa (known as Fibonacci), which appeared in 1202. (Adapted from Flegg[71])

the technology of counting boards, the base-10 number words of Sanskrit and its descendants, and the poetry of the Hindu sine tables in the 6th century AD.

The Even More Extraordinary Story of the Maya O

What happens when any of these pieces are missing? Does the Mathematical Brain still have the concept of the empty set that it tries to represent in a numerical notation? The ancient Maya of Central America developed a complex culture and civilization which lasted from about 1000 BC until AD 1500, when they were destroyed by the Spanish conquest. They built great cities and traded extensively with their neighbours. By about 500 BC they had developed a hieroglyphic type of writing, whose decipherment is not yet complete. Many if not most of the texts were destroyed by Spanish priests. One wrote, 'We found a large number of books in these [hieroglyphic] characters and, as they contained nothing in which there were not to be seen superstition and lies of the devil, we burned them all, which they regretted to an amazing degree, and which caused them much affliction.'[72]

Like their modern descendants, and indeed most American Indian languages, the Maya counted in a base-20 system, more specifically in a base-5–20 system, probably derived from counting on fingers and toes. They had words for powers of 20, such as 400 and 8,000, and they had an obsession for counting, particularly counting days, for which they used one step of 18, so that one of their year-counts, the *tun*, gave $20 \times 18 = 360$ days. Of course they knew there were 365 days in the year, and their 'vague year', called *haab*, had 18 periods of 20 days plus one period of 5 days. There was also a sacred year of 260 days that was used for ceremonial purposes. The surviving texts, known as codices, are often devoted to astronomy, chronicling events in year sequences and almanacs, and many of the inscriptions on buildings also have a numerical content. They even had words or phrases for numbers as big as 20 *kinchiltuns*: 18×20^7 or 23,040,000,000 days!

At least as early as 400 BC, the Maya, along with their neighbours, were using a system of numerals with place value, but not with a zero. This was the system of dots for 1 and bars for 5.[73] This may have formed a model for later developments in a way similar to the Hindu mathematicians who used the Babylonian model before them. The Mayans also seem to have had counting boards, and ways of arranging pebbles or cacao beans to make up numbers, perhaps in a manner equivalent to the Hindus. So, the Maya had number words using a base system, they had trade, they had extensive counting practices, including counting boards, they had a writing system. Were they able to represent the empty set systematically, with a zero, when other similarly endowed cultures, such as the ancient Greeks and Egyptians, had manifestly failed? The answer is straightforward: they were. What's more, it is now known that their system preceded the Indian system by at least 250 years, and perhaps as much as 650 years. Their system uses a shell sign for zero, meaning roughly 'completion', and is shown in Figure 2.14.

We have not been able to trace the history of the creation of the Mayan numeral system in the way we did for the creation of the Hindu zero, so we cannot know whether it came about through the accumulation of small, necessary steps, or all at once, as a single

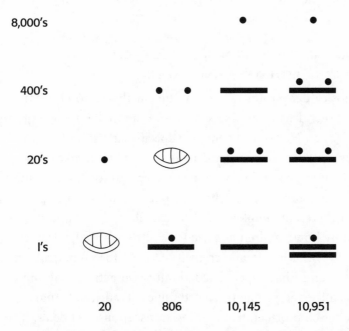

Figure 2.14 Quite independently of the invention of zero in the Indus Valley, and several hundred years earlier, the extraordinary Mayan civilization used a shell sign in a place-value notation to indicate zero. The Maya used two signs, the dot for 1 and the horizontal line for 10. In their vigesimal (base-20) ordinary counting system they used these symbols for multiples of 20^0 (= 1), of 20^1 (= 20), of 20^2 (= 400), and so on. Unlike our numerals, the places are ordered from bottom to top rather than right to left. (Adapted from Sharer[74])

invention. Intriguingly, the Incas, a much later civilization (though one without writing), recorded accounts and almanacs using a system of knots on strings attached to a head-string, called *qipus*. These used place-value notation with a base 10, so that a group of 4 knots nearest the *qipu* would be worth 4×100, while the next group of 4 would be worth 4×10, and a group of 4 farthest from the head-string would be worth 4×1. Knotting systems are still used in Peru, and in fact have been used by many cultures in the Americas and elsewhere, including Japan and Germany. Is it possible that a form of *qipu* existed in the Yucatan peninsula in Mexico, home of the Maya, which provided the idea of zeroes for place values? *Qipus* are interesting from another point of view: the empty place was represented by a gap in the string. This suggests that the idea of representing the empty place may not depend on the insight of a single inventor, or invention site, but rather on how the Mathematical Brain grasps the idea of an empty set.

NUMBERS AND THE BEGINNINGS OF SCIENCE: BABYLONIANS, EGYPTIANS, AND GREEKS

This is not to deny John Locke's argument that a good notation can help you keep ideas of numbers clear and can make the operations on numbers easier. Nor is it to deny that specific circumstances could pro-mote—or retard—people's need to draw out the implications of the concept of numerosity. Every new mathematical tool adds to the stock of cultural resources upon which people can draw to improve their ability to represent numbers and to calculate. In Chapters 3 and 8 I shall show how children acquire (or fail to acquire) cultural tools.

We have seen how trade created the need for numerical accounts in Sumeria, and I have speculated about the practices that could have encouraged ice-age people to record tallies. Trade and ritual gave rise to the poker-chip principle recording transactions and deals. The historian of mathematics Dirk Struik saw this as essential for the administration of the states that emerged in Mesopotamia between ten and five thousand years ago.[75]

Trading, however, does not explain the development of ways of representing and talking about numbers far too large to be involved in deals, nor of systems of numerals that made calculation easy. After all, trading in the Eastern Mediterranean flourished for 11,000 years without place-value numerals. Further developments have been prompted by the needs of science. The Babylonians needed to measure angles, and to make astronomical calculations. No doubt this was made easier in the first place by the base-60 system they had in place for trading quantities of grain or for measuring areas.

In the Rhind Papyrus from ancient Egypt, there are eighty-five problems

> which deal with the strength of bread and of different kinds of beer, with the feeding of animals and the storage of grain, showing the practical origin of this cumbersome arithmetic and primitive algebra. Some problems show a theoretical interest, as in the problem of dividing 100 loaves among 5 men in such a way that the share received shall be in arithmetical progression, and that one seventh of the sum of the largest three shares shall be equal to the sum of the smallest two. We even find a geometrical progression . . . [and] problems of a geometrical nature, dealing mostly with menstruation. The area of the triangle was found as half the product of base and altitude; the area of a circle with diameter d was given as $(d - \frac{d}{9})^2$, which led to a value of π of $256/81 = 3.1605$.[76]

A complete history of the evolution of fractions and decimals would take me too far beyond my current brief, but it is clear that it was scientific speculation and attempts at accurate measurement that led to these developments.

Pythagoras, around 500 BC, took Babylonian ideas about geometry (they knew about 'Pythagoras' theorem' long before he did) and found ways of turning them from rules of thumb into statements that could be proved—theorems, in fact. He and his followers explored the relationship between geometry and arithmetic and were responsible for the classification of numbers into triangular, (see Chapter 9), square, and so on.

The Hindu place-value system, as we have seen, grew out of the use of counting boards, which were probably developed for trading, but the key steps forward—words with a place value, the poetry of tables, and their final expression in numerals—were made by astronomers.

The Maya's system was closely associated with astronomical recordings and with speculations about the nature of time and the universe. They established a system known as the 'long count'. In Maya cosmology, the world went in cycles of destruction and re-creation. They measured their years from the last creation, which they calculated to be 3114 BC in our calendar. The end of the current great cycle, when this world will end, is 21 December 2012,[77] which is, unfairly, just when I will have finished paying off the mortgage. It is clear that the needs of cosmological calculations prompted techniques for counting large numbers, and also counting backwards to an imagined time well before the earliest recorded events in Mayan history.

EVERYBODY COUNTS: THE RISE OF UNIVERSAL NUMERACY

We have found examples of people able to count from the earliest records, even from the prehistoric record. What we do not know is how representative these people were of their communities. Could everybody count? Of course, we have only recently started to collect statistics of mathematical achievement across the whole population, and in some countries even these data are not yet available. So we have to find other ways of discovering what ordinary people knew about mathematics.

It is certainly true that good calculators—by which I mean as good as a well-educated sixteen-year-old nowadays—were exceptional. In the Dark Ages, around the time of Charlemagne, long before Arabic numerals were introduced into Europe, individuals able to calculate well could go far, though they may have had the humblest of origins. The historian Alexander Murray tells of 'a slave from Marseille . . . about AD 570 . . . fully versed in "arithmetical studies" . . . whose skill was rare enough to earn him a high place in the Frankish royal household.'[78]

England around this time was very dark indeed in arithmetical skills. The English couldn't even sort out conflicts between the Roman and Celtic calendars, and the inhabitants of Northumbria, for instance, 'contentedly celebrated two Easters', according to the Venerable Bede in his *Ecclesiastical History* written a hundred years later, in 731.[79]

The *Ecclesiastical History* is justly celebrated as the most influential book of its time, in part because Bede was serious about chronology, and had arithmetical skills enough to get it right. Indeed, Bede's skills were so outstanding that he was called *Beda computator* and *Computator mirabilis*. Murray infers from Bede's exceptionality that England and the rest of the Germanic world of the eighth century were relatively innumerate. Charlemagne himself was very keen on arithmetic, which he learned from an Englishman, Alcuin of York, who had emigrated to Pavia in Italy, and under his influence *computus* (arithmetic) became a major part of the curriculum of episcopal and monastic schools. This suggests that at least the people who attended these schools would have known some arithmetic.

The low level of arithmetical skills has been blamed on Roman numerals, and it is certainly true that calculation was extraordinarily difficult. The historian of mathematics Graham Flegg has made a study of early calculation and describes some of its problems:

> Consider the multiplication of 325 by 47. Using our numerals, the calculation is simple:

$$
\begin{array}{r}
325 \\
47 \\
\hline
2,275 \\
13,000 \\
\hline
15,275
\end{array}
$$

> Now try to multiply CCCXXV by XLVII. In the former system, one had to multiply every single figure contained in 325 with every figure in 47 (altogether 6 simple multiplications), to write the partial results in the right places, and to add them. If one tries to do the same thing with CCCXXV and XLVII, the first problem that arises is that XLVII cannot be decomposed into parts X + L + V + I + I, because the notation XL is subtractive. One can try writing XXXX instead of XL and try computing the product

[of] CCCXXV [and] XXXXVII by a method similar to today's by multiplying every single component C or X or V contained in the first factor by every component X or V or I of the second factor. This method will involve [6 × 8 =] 42 single multiplications, followed by addition of the results.[80]

He calls this, not unreasonably, 'a very cumbersome method'.

Murray argues that to put the blame entirely on the notation is too simplistic:

Roman numerals manifested and partly occasioned the paralysis of early medieval arithmetic. A hypothesis is bound to suggest itself to our modern minds that our ancestors had to wait for Arabic numerals to break the spell ... Our book-learning tends to equate culture with written culture ... To understand mathematical development [in the tenth century] we must block out this element of our education, and realize that it was precisely their freedom from the proprieties of literary culture which led arithmeticians of this period to their breakthrough.[81]

The breakthrough came about because 'the drudgery of numerical calculation was being shifted from the written page to a device: the abacus. Because the abacus turned its back on writing, little record of its early use in Europe remains to the historian nor even to the archaeologist: less than half-a-dozen examples of the medieval European abacus survive.'

One of the key advantages of the abacus was its use of place values; and one of its main practical difficulties lay in converting to and from Roman numerals. (A twelfth-century mathematician, Ocreatus, devised a place-value notation based on these numerals so that 1089 would come out as I.O.VIII.IX, but it didn't catch on.[82]) For many years Arabic numerals were known as 'the script of the abacus'. The great mathematician Leonardo of Pisa—still famous under his nickname of Fibonacci for his eponymous series—wrote in 1202 a massive book called *Liber abaci* about the new arithmetic in the new numerals.

It is reasonable to suppose that traders used the abacus or counting board as part of their everyday work, and that the few educated by the Church had some arithmetic, but we can only speculate about the mathematical competence of the serf in the field or the aristocrat in his castle. Certainly it seems that businessmen were at the forefront of the movement to bring in the new numerals. Many of Fibonacci's examples in *Liber abaci* are drawn from business, and have titles such as 'The man who went to Constantinople to sell three pearls', 'Two men formed a company in Constantinople', and 'Finding the equivalence between bad money and good'.[83] Simplified shortened versions of his book were aimed at the business community and proved popular.

On the other hand, there was resistance to the introduction of these numbers, even from the normally progressive banking community of Italy. The Guild of Florentine Bankers issued a statute in 1299 forbidding their use:

> No member of this guild shall presume to write, or allow to be written by anyone else, in his ledger or account book, or any part thereof where payments and receipts are recorded, any item in what is known as the style or script of the abacus. He shall on the contrary write openly and at length using letters. The consuls of the guild shall be obliged to impose a fine of twenty small Florentine shillings for each occasion and document wherein the offence is commited.[84]

Nevertheless, Italy, and especially the great trading centre of Venice, was leading the change to Arabic numerals. The *Arte dela mercandanta*—or, to give it its full title in translation, 'The Mercantile Art, which is Popularly Known as the Art of the Abacus'—was published in Treviso, near Venice, in 1478, making it the earliest printed book on the subject of arithmetic. The editor of the translation into English, Frank Swetz, writes of that period:

> From the fourteenth century on, merchants from the north travelled to Italy, particularly to Venice, to learn the *Arte dela mercandanta* . . . of the Italians. Sons of German businessmen flocked to Venice to study the *Welsche Praktik*, the foreign practices of

business, commercial arithmetic, and currency exchange. After acquiring these skills, they returned home with such terms as *disagio*, discount; *credito*, credit; *valuta*, value; *netto*, at net price, etc. [not to mention, *agio*, advantage, profit] . . . The flow of German merchants to Venice was so great that a special complex was established to accommodate visiting Germans [called the] *Fondaco dei Tedeschi* [where] the painter Titian served his apprenticeship frescoing its walls.[85]

Menninger reports that 'A citizen of Nuremberg urged his son in Venice to do three things above all: to rise early, to go to church, and to pay attention to his arithmetic teacher.'[86]

Businessmen were learning the new maths, but many others were not. In most books of the thirteenth and fourteenth centuries, numerical information, even dates in works of history and hagiography, was scarce. Peter Abelard, centre of French intellectual life and 'a pioneer in the skills of reason', in his autobiography uses no number above 10 and only one number above 5, and never gives dates at all, except 'a few months later' or 'one day'.[87] There was literary resistance to, and snobbery about, numbers at least until the Renaissance, and which can still be found in British public (i.e. private) schools and the British Civil Service, where mathematicians and scientists rarely achieve the very highest grades.

A particular difficulty of Arabic numerals is the incomplete correspondence between the words and the numerals. As we have seen, European languages are base 10, but irregularly so, and they do not use place values (like Hindu poetry). This means that the translation requires some skill and learning. Why should the term *one hundred* be rendered as '100'? We have to understand that both the words and the numerals mean ten to the power of two. Why should *one hundred and three* be 103 and not, say, '100 3'? The problem of learning to 'transcode'—translate between the verbal code and the numeral— gives children a lot of difficulty, as we shall investigate in Chapter 3. Of course, the difficulty is in some ways more acute for Roman numerals, but at least for each power of ten there was a separate symbol—X, C, M—just as there are separate words—ten, hundred, and thousand. Since people are often reluctant to learn new things, then one source of resistance could have been that the new numerals weren't actually that easy to master.

Little is known about the numerical skills of the business classes, but even less is known about any other class. One indirect piece of evidence comes from the systems of weights and measures that were used in Europe until they were displaced by metrication and decimalization.

In Britain, the Imperial system (Table 2.8) is still in widespread use for weights and measures, though it is increasingly being replaced, with official encouragement, by the metric system. You might ask why people put up with such complicated and unpredictable weights and measures. Why were there not simple systems that went up in standard multiples, as the metric system does, and as the Babylonian system used to? Life was even more complicated than this because there were special units for measuring particular goods. For example, there were special cloth measures called ells—one of which was 'a yard and a handful', 40 in., abolished by statute in 1439, and the 'wine gallon' of 231 cubic inches, abolished in 1824. There was also the problem of standardization. What happened when one of the standards of these measures was lost, as happened to the standard yard and the standard pound in the fire that destroyed the Houses of Parliament in 1834?

In Britain and many of its colonies, money was also measured not as multiples and fractions of a single unit, but in different units—12 pennies in a shilling, and 20 shillings in a pound (not to mention 21 shillings in a guinea, which was, for some reason, the standard unit for buying and selling racehorses and certain other valuables). This system does not reflect (only) British perversity. It was in fact introduced formally in AD 780 by Charlemagne, who called the units in Latin a *libra* (or *talentum*), each of 20 *solidi*, each of 12 *denarii*, and versions of this system were found all over Europe. The French used a *livre* of 20 *sous* (from the word *solidus*) of 12 *deniers*. The Venetians, at the height of their trading might, had two systems organized by 20 and 12, the *lira di piccoli* and the *lira di grossi*, depending on the amount of silver in the units. Each lira was worth 20 *soldi*, and each of these 12 *piccoli* or *grossi*. To make things even more complicated, the famous *ducat* was worth one-tenth of a *lira di grossi*, or 24 *grossi*.

These measures are organized into identifiable, and often small,

Weight	Length	Capacity
16 dr (drams) = 1 oz (ounce)	12 in (inches) = 1 ft (foot)	4 gills = 1 pt (pint)
16 oz = 1 lb (pound)	3 ft = 1 yd (yard)	2 pt = 1 qt (quart)
14 lb = 1 stone	22 yd = 1 chain	4 qt = 1 gallon
2 stones = 1 quarter	10 chains = 1 furlong	2 gallons = 1 peck
4 quarters = 1 cwt (hundredweight) (= 112 lb)	8 furlongs = 1 mile (= 1760 yd = 5280 ft)	4 pecks = 1 bushel
20 cwt = 1 ton (2240 lb)		8 bushels = 1 quarter
		36 bushels = 1 chaldron

Table 2.8 Some Imperial units of measure.

collections of lower-rank units. It is at least a possibility that this organization fitted better our innate concept of numerosity than a system where essentially there is one unit (for a dimension) with multiples and fractions. It may be easier to see in the mind's eye a collection of 4 quarts in a gallon, and a collection of 4 gallons in a peck, than it is to see 100 centilitres in a litre and 100 litres in a . . . a whatever. As a user of the old British money and measures, I still find the idea of a shilling more graspable than 5p, and a pound weight more so than 400 grams. Perhaps by giving distinct names to these collections, their value is easier to bring to mind.

The spread of formal training in mathematics has gone hand in hand with the replacement of old measures by new, which use just one unit for each dimension, such as the metre for length, together with decimal multiples and fractions of it. Formal education allows, even encourages, children—and adults—to manipulate numbers without attending to their numerosity or their meaning. This certainly frees the mind from being constantly aware of the reality of the stuff being measured, which in turn has both good and bad consequences, as we shall see in later chapters.

WHO COUNTS?

The new Arabic notation helped to spread arithmetic skills that we today take for granted. There would still be problems 'transcoding' from number words to numerals, and from numerals to number words, because the two systems operated on different principles, despite their both using a base of 10. Al-Khwārizmī in his 'Algebra' shows the problem of transcoding from numerals to words when the number is large. The number 1,180,703,051,492,863 would have been read as follows, since the Arabs of that time did not have words for millions and above:

> one thousand thousand thousand thousand thousands (five times) and one hundred thousand thousand thousand thousands (four times) and eighty thousand thousand thousand thousands then seven hundred thousand thousand thousands (three times) and three thousand thousand thousands (three times) and fifty-one thousand thousands (twice) and four hundred thousands and ninety-two thousands and a hundred and sixty-three.[88]

Even with our new names for big numbers, it is by no means straightforward to read aloud 1,180,703,051,492,863, as you may easily test for yourself.

Children today have problems transcoding from the teens to numerals. They have to learn to understand why the single words one, two, three ... are represented by single numerals, while the single words eleven, twelve, thirteen, and so on, are represented by two numerals.

Before the introduction of what the editor of the Treviso Arithmetic, Frank Swetz, called the 'new math of the 15th century', people were well able to trade and to use the abacus or the counting board, which required an understanding of the concept of numerosity. These abilities were probably widespread throughout the Classical world of the Eastern Mediterranean, and back through to Babylonian times. We do not know what proportion of the population of Mesopotamia understood the tokens that were used for trading, but it would be reasonable to suppose that they were in very widespread use for nearly 10,000 years for the very reason that they were easily understood by most people.

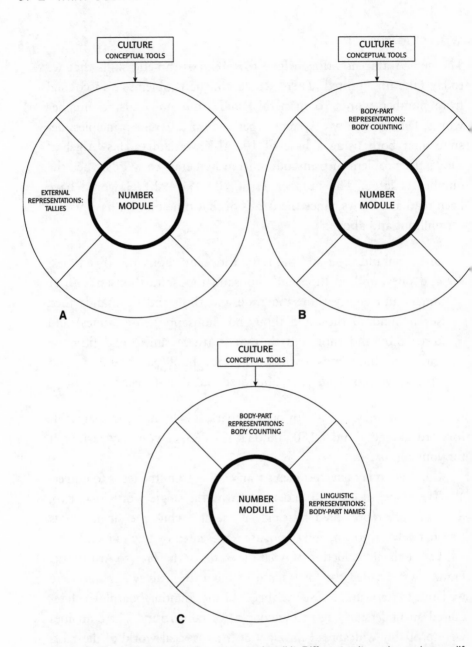

Figure 2.15 Adding tools to the conceptual toolkit. Different cultures have chosen different modes when constructing conceptual tools to extend the power of the Number Module. Ice-age cave painters and the modern Aranda of central Australia (a) used external representations of numerosities, though apparently no body-part counting, while many tribes in Papua New Guinea prefer body-part counting (b). Modern Zulus and early Europeans used both body-part names and body-part counting (c).

The value of a notation, as Locke suggested 300 years ago, is to keep the idea of each number separate in the mind. Before numerals, there were number words. Where the language possesses no specialized words to notate the concepts, people will use parts of the body, such as fingers and toes, but other parts too, to keep track of the ideas; they will also use the names of body parts to stand for the ideas. Many European number words are ultimately derived from these as well, for example 'hand' and 'first', not to mention the word for numbers themselves, digit', which comes from the Latin for finger. But none of this is of any use without an understanding that the things to be counted form a collection that can be put into one-to-one correspondence with another collection whose numerosity is known.

Notations and calculating devices, both conceptual and physical, were ways of extending the capacity of the Number Module in the Mathematical Brain to represent numbers and to calculate with them (Figure 2.15). We don't know whether the human hunter-gatherers of the Upper Palaeolithic used body-part counting, but as far back as 32,000 years ago, when they shared Europe with the Neanderthals, they made marks on bones and on walls that suggest they were keeping tallies. We even saw evidence suggesting that our cousins, the Neanderthals, and even our distant ancestors, *Homo erectus*, may have possessed the concept of numerosity. The Mathematical Brain was part of our common humanity as far back into the historical record as we can trace.

3

BORN TO COUNT

A child, at birth, is a candidate for humanity; it cannot become human in isolation.

FRENCH PSYCHOLOGIST HENRI PIERON, 1959

I argued in Chapter 2 that everyone counts, not because everyone has the opportunity to learn this special skill, but because we are born with special circuits in our brains for categorizing the world in terms of numerosities. Whether a culture has formal arithmetical education or not, whether the lives of its members involve frequent use of numbers or not, indeed, whether its language contains special words for numbers or not, people will be able to carry out basic numerical operations.

This Mathematical Brain hypothesis is a claim about the relationship between nature and nurture in the domain of numerical abilities. I show it graphically in Figure 3.1. Very simply, nature provides an inner core of ability for categorizing small collections of objects in terms of their numerosities, which I have called the Number Module. For more advanced skills, we need nurture: acquiring the conceptual tools provided by the culture in which we live.

There are many precedents for specialized innate abilities. For example, many perceptual capacities are already working in the newborn baby: babies can see colours, distinguish speech sounds from non-speech sounds, and, within a few days or weeks, focus their eyes and see clearly. It is not surprising that newborns can use their five senses, but are they able to categorize the world in a more abstract way? We now know that newborns categorize the world in terms of

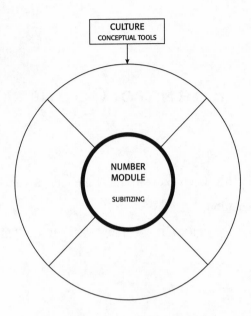

Figure 3.1 The newborn infant can use subitizing (the ability to tell numerosity at a glance, without counting) to discriminate and identify the number of things in a visual array, up to about 4. It has not, of course, had the opportunity to acquire conceptual tools such as counting words or finger patterns.

objects that have a continuous existence in time—if an object disappears, they stare in surprise. They also have expectations about how these objects will behave: one object cannot pass through another, for example. Babies will have had no opportunity to learn about these things: they seem to be built into the brain as part of the genetic code, and they kick into life as soon as the baby leaves the womb. However, being born with a capacity does not mean that it will be immediately evident. For example, we are all born with the capacity to grow pubic hair but it is not present in the newborn, appearing only after about 12 or 13 years of maturation.

The Piagetian Alternative

The influential Swiss psychologist Jean Piaget believed that our reasoning capacities emerged slowly, each new concept building on those previously developed. Numbers, he believed, are intimately connected with the development of the ability to reason logically and abstractly, though the ability for full abstract reasoning, in what Piaget called the stage of 'formal operations', was thought to emerge at about the same time as pubic hair.

> Our hypothesis is that the construction of number goes hand-in-hand with the development of logic, and that a pre-numerical period corresponds to a pre-logical level. Our results do, in fact, show that number is organised, stage after stage, in close connection with gradual elaboration of systems of inclusion (hierarchy of logical classes) and systems of asymmetrical relations (qualitative seriations), the sequence of numbers thus resulting from an operational synthesis of classification and seriation. In our view, logical and arithmetical operations therefore constitute a single system that is psychologically natural, the second resulting from a generalisation and fusion of the first, under two complementary headings of inclusion of classes and seriation of relations, quality being disregarded.[1]

He believed that our idea of numerosity was built on more basic capacities. These included the capacity to reason transitively—that is, the child should be able to reason that if A is bigger than B, and B is bigger than C, then A is bigger than C. Without this capacity, the child could not put the numbers in order of size, which is clearly fundamental. A second capacity the child must develop is the idea that the number of things in a collection is 'conserved', to use his technical term, unless a new object is added to the collection or an object subtracted from it. Merely moving the objects around—for example, spreading them out so they take up more room—does not affect number. Even more basic than either of these two capacities, as Piaget pointed out, is the ability to abstract away from the perceptual properties of the things in the collection. To grasp the numerosity of a collection, one needs to ignore all the particular features of the objects in it: their colour, their shape, their size, even what they are. A collection of three cats has the same numerosity as a collection of three chairs, or indeed of three wishes. The idea of number is abstract, very abstract. And the ideas of 'same number' or 'different numbers' are abstractions from abstractions.

According to Piaget, the emergence of the capacity for numerosity depends on the development of the necessary prior capacities, what Piagetians call 'prerequisites'. It also depends, as do many conceptual and logical abilities, on interacting with the world. The concept of numerosity could emerge as a result of manipulating objects, lining up collections to establish one-to-one correspondence between the members of the two collections, for sharing out sweets or toys.

The Empiricist Alternative
The philosopher Philip Kitcher makes the child's manipulation of objects in the environment the foundation of his approach to mathematics:

> I begin with an elementary phenomenon. A young child is shuffling blocks on the floor. A group of his blocks is segregated and inspected, and then merged with a previously scrutinized group of three blocks. The event displays a small part of the mathematical structure of reality, and may even serve for the apprehension of mathematical structure. Children come to learn the meanings of 'set', 'number', 'addition' and to accept basic truths of arithmetic by engaging in *activities* of collecting and segregating. Rather than interpreting these activities as an avenue to knowledge about abstract objects, we can think of the rudimentary arithmetical truths as true in virtue of the operations themselves.[2]

This approach is a version of 'empiricism', which claims that all ideas, all concepts, are derived from sensory experiences, and abstract ideas are constructed by generalizing from many particular experiences. On this account, children can have no grasp of numerical concepts until they are able to manipulate objects, segregate one group from others, scrutinize, remember the results of the scrutiny (which cannot be a number, since this is what they are setting out to explain), and merge these results with others (whatever this may mean). It is not clear at what age Kitcher believes that children are able to do these things, since he draws on no (empirical) studies of how children actually do acquire arithmetical concepts, but it cannot be earlier than about two or three years of age.

The approaches taken by both Piaget and Kitcher imply that categorizing the world is going to come quite late in the child's development. Piaget thought that the number concept emerged at about the age of four or five. After all, how can an infant—newly arrived in the world, unable to speak, and with the world just a buzzing confusion of colours and noises—use number to categorize what it sees or hears? How could it possibly add or subtract? The obvious, commonsense answer is that the infant cannot.

In this chapter, we shall see that the obvious answer is the wrong answer. The truth is much more surprising. Infants as young as the first week of life do indeed categorize the world in terms of numerosities, and infants of a few weeks, too young to have learned about arithmetic, can add and subtract. We shall see how counting provides the conceptual tools that take the child beyond what can be achieved by using the Number Module alone, beyond the ability to recognize numerosities, to the key idea of a sequence of numerosities ordered by size.

INFANT NUMEROSITIES

A baby just a day old is lying on her side in a hospital bassinet, quiet but alert. About 18 cm from her eyes is a white card with two circular black dots on it. She looks at the card. The card is replaced by another card with two similar black dots, but more widely spaced. The baby stares intently at it. The second card is replaced by the first, and the baby looks at it. All the while an experimenter, out of sight of the baby, is measuring how long she spends looking at each card. As the two cards continue to be presented alternately, the baby begins to lose interest and looks at the cards for shorter and shorter periods. Then a new card is presented, a card with three black dots in a line, and the baby immediately looks longer at this new card, twice as long in fact as at the previous card. Why? Does the baby just prefer looking at more black dots than at fewer? Two new cards are shown to the baby, one at a time. Each card now has three dots in a line, but on one of them the dots are more widely spaced. After a few trials the baby seems to lose interest and barely glances at the cards; then a new card is shown. This time with just two dots. The baby again looks longer at this new card. Is it just something new? To be new for the baby, she has to have a memory of what went before. What is represented in this memory? Is it the fact that there were black dots, or a white card? Is it the pattern of dots? Or could it be the *number* of black dots?[3]

This technique is known as 'habituation–dishabituation', and it makes use of the fact that babies like novelty and will look longer at new things: the same thing over and over again causes them to *habituate*—lose interest—while a new thing causes them to regain interest—*dishabituate*. What makes this technique particularly useful for studying the mind of the baby comes when you ask what counts as new for the baby. That is, what categories can the baby use for classifying her experiences? We know that newborns can make subtle distinctions among sounds. For example, they can categorize sounds into P sounds and B sounds. If they hear a series of P's they habituate, but when they then hear a B sound, they get interested again.[4] We know they can categorize by colour and by shape.[5]

But how do we know to what aspect of novelty the baby is responding in the dot task? It could be any new stimulus. Three American experimenters, Prentice Starkey, Rochel Gelman, and Elizabeth Spelke,[6] carried out a similar type of experiment with slightly older children, 6–8 months, but instead of black dots they used pictures of various objects: an orange, a key, a comb, an egg-beater, and so on. Instead of a card with two dots close together alternating with one with two dots far apart, each card had two objects, but different objects each time. The dishabituating card also had new pictures on it, but there were three pictures this time. Since each card was new for the babies, would they have mentally categorized the habituating cards as showing two things, so that when a card with three things was presented, they would regain interest and look longer? If they did look longer, it could not be because of mere novelty, since each card was new. It turned out that babies did look significantly longer at the card with three pictures on it.

Perhaps babies just like to see more pictures and this is why they looked longer. However, Starkey and his colleagues used the other sequence as well: a habituating series of cards with three pictures on them, followed by a dishabituating card with just two. Again the babies looked longer at the new number. The babies seemed to be sensitive to the number of pictures on the card. They categorized what they saw in a way that is quite abstract: the particular features of each picture—the colour, the objects depicted, their size, their brightness—which change with every card, have to be disregarded.

Stationary pictures of objects have a pattern: one object is a point, two objects will form a line, and three may form a triangle and four a quadrilateral. Perhaps babies are using some form of visual pattern perception rather than numerosity.[7] One fascinating study puts paid to that idea. Two Dutch psychologists, Erik van Loosbroek and Ad Smitsman from the Catholic University of Nijmegen, showed babies of 5 and 13 months not still pictures, but moving pictures. The pictures were of two, three, or four rectangles in shades of grey that moved in random trajectories on a computer monitor. From time to time one rectangle would appear to pass in front of another, occluding part of it. As in the previous studies, after a while the babies looked at the screen for less time, but when the number of rectangles was changed, either by adding one more rectangle or taking one away, they started to look for significantly longer. They cannot have been responding to a change in the pattern, since each of the rectangles was in constant motion, so they must have extracted the numerosity from the moving displays.[8]

We are beginning to find evidence that the infant's sensitivity to numerosity goes beyond collections of objects, still or moving. They are also sensitive to collections of actions. These are very different in kind from objects. Where does one action end and the other begin, and how are actions to be categorized? If I deal from a deck of cards, five cards to five players, is there one action—the deal—or twenty-five actions—each card?

The following remarkable experiment was carried out by Karen Wynn, a brilliant young researcher at the University of Arizona. The baby, this time about six months old, well before he has spoken his first words, is looking at a display stage with a puppet on it. In the habituation phase he sees the puppet make two jumps, with a short pause between the jumps. As with repeated presentation of two pictures, so the looking time gets shorter with each jump. The puppet makes three jumps, and the looking time nearly doubles. Again the reverse was used as a control: three jumps followed by two jumps.[9]

I have focused on numerosities of visible collections, but numerosities are supposed to be abstractions, distinct from perceptual
properties. Are babies sensitive to the number of sounds, say the beats
of a drum? Prentice Starkey's team used a virtuoso version of the
habituation technique. They habituated babies to pictures of two dots
or three dots, then showed them a black disk that emitted either two
or three drumbeats. If the babies had been habituated to two dots
they would stare longer at the black disk when it emitted two beats; if
habituated to three dots, they would stare longer when it emitted
three beats. For the babies to behave like this, they would have to
have formed a mental representation that puts the *number* of dots
and the number of beats into the same category, a category that is
independent of whether the things were seen or heard.

It seems as though anything that a baby can think of as separate
entities it can enumerate. Its behaviour can be guided by the number
of things that it experiences independently of what those things are. It
is born with the ability to form a representation of the numerosity of
a collection of things, and because its behaviour changes when the
number changes, it can also tell whether a new collection has the
same numerosity as a previous collection. This in turn implies that it
can store in its memory and retrieve, at least in the short term, the
numerosity of the previous collection.

Is there an upper limit to the baby's concept of numerosity? Can it
enumerate 4 or 10 or 100? The maximum seems to be 3, though in
some tasks the baby can distinguish 'more than 3' from 3, and it has
been claimed that in certain circumstances babies can distinguish 5
from 4. However, we cannot be sure that this limitation lies in the
baby's idea of numerosity rather than in its ability to perceive and to
remember what has been perceived. Our understanding that numerosities have no limit seems to depend on our sense that it is always
possible to keep adding one. Thus any limitation on the infant's part
may have more to do with its ability to carry out successive additions,
and the chain of reasoning needed to get from that to the idea that
numbers have no upper limit.

The most likely limitation is the ability to take in the numerosity
of a visual array of objects at a glance, and without counting. Even in
adults, the limit is about 4. This seems to be a specialized process in

visual perception,[10] which is usually given the name *subitizing*. Stanislas Dehaene, a psychologist, and Jean-Pierre Changeux, a neuroscientist, working in Paris, have created a computer model of this process which very simply and effectively extracts the number of objects from a visual display, disregarding their size, shape, or location. The representation that is extracted can then be trained to make comparisons. It is tempting to think that something like this has been built into the visual processing system of the infant's brain.[11]

INFANT ARITHMETIC

Possessing a concept of numerosity implies more than just being able to decide whether two collections do or do not have the same numerosity. It implies an ability to detect a change in numerosity when new members are added to the collection, or old members taken away. Are babies born with the ability to do this? How can we tell? We certainly cannot ask them: not only can babies not speak, they cannot understand speech either. This lack may not prevent babies from having *arithmetical expectations* based on their concept of numerosity. The problem is to discover whether they do.

Imagine now that you see me put one doll into a box you know to be empty, and then I add another. You will *expect* to find two dolls in the box. This expectation will be based on your knowledge of arithmetic, among other things (such as the fact that objects do not just appear or disappear). If I show you that there is just one doll in the box, your expectations will be violated and you might stare longer into the box, wondering what could have happened to the other doll.[12] Similarly, if you see me put two dolls into a previously empty box and then remove one, you will expect there to be one doll left. Again, this will be an arithmetical expectation. If you now find two dolls in the box this expectation will be violated, and you may again show some surprise. The question now can be framed as follows: will a baby have the same expectations as you? Will it expect adding one doll to another doll to produce two dolls and show surprise if it does not? Will the baby expect taking one doll away from two dolls to leave exactly one doll, and show surprise if it does not?

This is what Karen Wynn set out to test in her Infant Cognition Laboratory at the University of Arizona.[13] She made use of the fact that babies look longer at events that violate their expectations; to discover whether babies had arithmetical expectations turned out to be really very simple. Babies of 4 to 5 months were seated facing a small stage. In the addition experiment, they would see one Mickey Mouse doll on the stage; then a screen would come up concealing the doll. A hand would then appear holding a second doll, which would be placed behind the screen. The screen would come down revealing either two dolls, which is what the babies would expect if they had addition expectations, or one doll, which is what they would not expect. Did they look longer at the single doll? Indeed they did. Perhaps, the sceptical reader is already asking, one doll was for some reason more interesting for the babies to look at, and that's why they looked at it longer.

Wynn had two ways of countering this potential criticism. First, she pre-tested the babies by measuring their looking times at one doll and at two dolls. No difference. Second, she carried out a subtraction experiment. This time the babies looked at a stage with two dolls on it. The screen came up, but now a hand went behind the screen and could be seen to remove a doll. The screen came down to reveal one doll, which is in line with a subtraction expectation, or two dolls, which is not. Would the babies now look longer at two dolls? Indeed they did, suggesting that they expected that two dolls, take away one doll, would leave just one doll.

Now we have a nice control for which display the babies might have preferred without any arithmetical expectations at all. A display of one doll was expected in the subtraction experiment but not in the addition experiment; so, if the babies did have arithmetical expectations, they should look longer at the same display after seeing the subtraction occur. This is just what happened. Similarly, a display of two dolls would be expected in the addition experiment but not the subtraction, and again the babies looked longer at the same display when it followed an arithmetical process that makes it unexpected.

This result has been replicated by Tony Simon at the Georgia Institute of Technology and his co-workers Susan Hespos and Philippe Rochat at Emory University.[14] They introduced a new twist to the experiment. Will babies (this time from 3 to 5 months) actually give more weight to arithmetical expectations than to other kinds of expectations about objects? In their experiment, the babies saw two kinds of doll—Elmo and Ernie, from the TV show 'Sesame Street', which are different in shape and colour. This allowed the experimenters to violate expectations about the identity of the object—Elmo surreptitiously changing into Ernie—as well as arithmetical expectations. They used 'possible' and 'impossible' trials in the addition experiment in which the baby saw one object, then the screen came up and they saw a hand put a second object behind the screen (Table 3.1).

The remarkable finding was that the babies responded very strongly when the outcome was arithmetically impossible, but did not seem to care at all when Elmos changed into Ernies. It is beyond all question that babies of this age are well able to discriminate shapes and colours and they do have expectations about objects appearing or disappearing without obvious reason, and about at least some of their physical properties. This seems to me good evidence not only that babies are born with the capacity to form arithmetical expectations of this simple sort, but that it is actually more important to them than some other, more obvious types of expectation.

Babies, as we have seen, have a sense of numerosity and can carry out a process of adding or subtracting one from small numerosities to develop accurate arithmetical expectations. We do not know whether babies' arithmetical expectations are really general, as ours are. For

Possible outcomes	Impossible outcomes
Elmo + Elmo = 2 Elmos	Elmo + Elmo = Elmo (impossible arithmetic)
Ernie + Ernie = 2 Ernies	Elmo + Elmo = Elmo + Ernie (impossible identity)
Elmo + Ernie = Elmo and Ernie	Elmo + Elmo = Ernie (impossible arithmetic and identity)

Table 3.1 Outcomes of trials with Elmo and Ernie.

example, do they have a general expectation that whenever you take an object from a collection you are left with one fewer? Do they even have expectations that apply to all collections of a given numerosity, that whenever you take 1 away from a collection of 2 you will be left with 1? They probably have this latter expectation, but we cannot be sure. We cannot even be sure that they have in mind the numerosities that they can distinguish in these experiments, in the sense that they can think about them in the absence of a collection with that numerosity, or whether indeed they can think about them at all.

We believe that if you take one thing away from a collection, then the collection will be smaller, it will have fewer members. It is by no means clear that babies understand this just because they notice a *difference* from their expectations when you take one doll away from two dolls. Similarly, we believe that adding one increases the numerosity of a collection, and again all we know about babies is that they notice the difference from their expectations.

Where babies have arithmetical expectations, we as adults also have arithmetical *beliefs* which we can formulate explicitly if we have to. Now, babies may also have beliefs about adding and subtracting, but it is very difficult for us to find out because the best evidence—explicit formulation in words—depends on speech. Nevertheless, babies' behaviour does appear to be constrained by the truths of arithmetic, even if they do not actually believe that if two objects are presented and just one of them is removed, then exactly one of them will be left. In this sense, they do seem to possess a kind of innate arithmetic.[15]

The reason why learning to count is so important is that it helps the baby build on these innate capacities so that it understands that numerosities have a size sequence, so that it can bring to mind individual numerosities, and so that it can have entirely explicit beliefs about the relationship between numbers and the effects of operations on numerosities.

LEARNING TO COUNT—SOME SIMPLE WAYS

Counting is basic. It makes the first bridge from the infant's innate capacity for numerosity to the more advanced mathematical achievements of the culture into which it was born. The least mathematical of cultures enable their members to do much more than the infant can. The members can keep track of quite large numerosities by counting with special number words or body-part names; they can do arithmetic beyond adding or subtracting one from small numerosities which they will need for trading or for ritual exchanges.

As any adult knows, counting is one of the easiest things to do. So why, if children are born to count, does it take so long for them to learn to do it? They start around two years old, and may be more than six years old before they have a good grasp of how to count and how to use counting.

Counting, it turns out, is not as simple as it first seems. Let us reflect for a moment on what practical skills we need to have mastered to count a collection of five toy dinosaurs. First, we need to know the number words from 'one' to 'five' (or, more generally, we need to know five counting words that we always keep in the same order). Second, we need to link each of these words with one and only one object: no word must be used more than once and all objects must be counted. That is, we must put each object in *one-to-one correspondence* with the counting words. Third, we must be in a position to announce the number of toy dinosaurs by using the last counting word used: 'One, two, three, four, five. Five toy dinosaurs.'[16]

Learning the sequence of counting words is the first way in which children connect their innate concept of numerosity with the cultural practices of the society into which they are born. As we saw in Chapter 2, not all societies use specialized words for counting. Many use the names of body parts. But all use the words in a fixed, unalterable sequence. You could count with the word sequence 'one, seven, five' so that each time 3 objects were counted, 'five' was announced. In this case the word 'five' would just mean 3. Similarly, you could count 'thumb, wrist, shoulder' every time so that the word 'shoulder' meant 3. What you cannot do is change the order, for then 'five' or 'shoulder' would have different meanings each time they were used and no one could understand how many had been counted.

Even learning the sequence of number words is not that straightforward. Children of two or three years often think of the first few number words as just one big word—'onetwothreefourfive'—and it takes them some time to learn that this big word is really five small words.[17] Of course, if there's just one big word, they cannot put the sequence into one-to-one correspondence with objects to be counted. It also takes a while for children to get the word sequence correct:

> A child of 3½ trying to count eight objects: 'One, two, three, four, eight, ten eleben. No, try dat again. One, two, three, four, five, ten, eleben. No, try dat again. One! two! three-ee-four, five, ten, eleben. No. .... [finally] ... One, two, four, five, six seven, eleven! Whew!'[18]

But knowing that there is a fixed sequence of separate words is not sufficient for knowing that these words are used for counting, that they have a role in finding the numerosity of a collection. As I pointed out at length in Chapter 1, number words have many meanings, not just a numerosity meaning. The child therefore has to separate counting uses from other uses which may be much more frequent around the house or school: telling the time, measuring, putting things in order, classroom numbers, TV channel numbers, house numbers, and so on. This suggests (though there is no direct evidence) that the acquisition of the word sequence and its use in counting will depend heavily on how it is taught and on the contexts in which it is learned.[19]

One-to-one correspondence appears at about two years of age quite independently of learning the sequence of counting words. At two, children happily give one sweet to each person, put one cup with each saucer, and can name each person in a room or a picture—or point to them—once and only once: 'Daddy, Mummy, Amy, Auntie Carole, me!'[20] If you show a 'puppet who is not very good at counting' counting the same object twice or missing an object altogether, children of three-and-a-half are very good at spotting these violations of one-to-one correspondence.[21] And almost all children point to each object when they count, even when they can use the number words correctly, so there is one-to-one correspondence between objects, points, and words.[22]

Children of three-and-a-half are also proficient at giving the last word in the count as the number of objects counted. Rochel Gelman, a psychologist at the University of California at Los Angeles (UCLA), whose work on children's number abilities has been the most influential since Piaget, calls this the cardinal word principle.[23] She, and others, have pointed out that merely doing this doesn't mean that children really know that the last number spoken is the numerosity of the set. They could just be imitating an adult routine. We can ask children of this age to count a collection of toy dinosaurs, and they can reply, correctly, 'One, two, three, four.' If we then ask them, 'How many toy dinosaurs are there?' they may well go back and count them again. This may be because they don't understand that the process of counting will give them the numerosity of things counted. On the other hand, given that they've just counted how many, they may think that the adult has detected an error and is asking them to do it again.

Some children of this age, though they may count in some circumstances, do not always see the point of it. If you ask them to give you three toy dinosaurs, they may just grab a handful and give them to you without counting. Karen Wynn[24] calls them 'grabbers'. Although they do use the last word of a count to say how many, grabbers often have not yet grasped the role of number words in counting—sometimes they think that the number word is just a label that attaches to an object. Here is what Adam, a grabber, did in one of Wynn's tasks:

EXPERIMENTER (E): So how many are there?

ADAM (A) (Counting three objects): One, two, five!

E (Pointing towards the three items): So there's five here?

A: No, that's *five* (pointing to the item he'd tagged 'five').

. . .

E: What if you counted this way, one, two, five? (Experimenter counts the objects in a different order than Adam has been doing.)

A: No, *this* is five (pointing to the one he has consistently tagged 'five').

Other children, whom Wynn calls 'counters', usually a few months older, will count, either aloud or silently, passing you the toys one by one. They also reliably give you the last word of the count in answer to 'How many?' These children are initially able to count only small numerosities, and probably build up their competence systematically from 1 to 2, from 2 to 3, from 3 to 4, and so on. In a give-a-number task, they will start by being able reliably to give 1, then to give 2, but perhaps not 3, then 3 but perhaps not 4. So by three-and-a-half most children have a grasp of small numerosities, and know that counting is a way to find the numerosity of a collection.

Children also need to understand that it doesn't matter in which order they count the objects in a collection, or indeed what those objects are. Gelman calls these the 'order-irrelevance principle' and the 'abstractness principle'.[25] It is, however, true that even when they normally obey these principles, they are still better at counting solid objects than actions or sounds, especially objects they can actually move about,[26] and also do better when the objects are lined up in a row and they start at one end rather than in the middle. It's generally believed that these differences in performance are due not to a weakness in the basic ideas, but to other problems in carrying out the task, including the effects of practice. For the same reason they are better at counting with small numbers than large. They have much less practice with large numbers: who would teach their child 'one hundred and seventy-three' before they teach 'three'?

Gelman's three 'how-to-count principles'—cardinal word, order-irrelevance, and abstractness—along with a fourth principle for one-to-one correspondence guide the acquisition of verbal counting skills. It is clear that a grasp of the principles follows from understanding the concept of numerosity. Collections are not intrinsically ordered. Understanding this means that you understand the order-irrelevancy principle. There is also no constraint on the kinds of things that can be members of a collection, provided they can be individuated. Understanding this implies holding the principle of abstractness. Of course, children, and adults, may possess the concept of numerosity without fully understanding and without having derived all the principles that validly follow from it.

The how-to-count principles for putting counting words to members of a collection are complex, since counting means being able to link each member of a collection, once and only once, to a fixed sequence of words. In this way, the further you count in the sequence the larger the numerosity you have counted. If you count from the word 'one' to the word 'five' in the usual English sequence, then the members counted at the word 'four' are a sub-collection of the final collection of five objects; similarly, the members counted at 'three' are a sub-collection of the collections of four and five.

Specifically, the cardinal word principle—the last number named in a count is the numerosity of the collection counted—also follows from the concept of numerosity, since you are establishing a correlation between members of a collection whose numerosity you do know, the number words up to five, say, and members of the collection of things to be counted, whose numerosity you do not know. It may follow in a practical way as well. Recall that infants can recognize the numerosities of objects up to about 3. In children and adults this ability to take in the numerosity of a visual array of objects at a glance, and without counting, is known as *subitizing*.

Karen Fuson, from Northwestern University in Illinois, who carries out her research in some of the toughest schools and homes in Chicago's notorious South Side, suggests that children may notice that when they count a collection 'one, two, three', they get the same number as when they subitize the collection. This helps them to see that counting up to N is a way of establishing that a collection has N objects in it.[27]

Repeating the count, and getting the same number as was obtained from subitizing, will reinforce the idea that every number name represents a unique numerosity. Again, this is something obvious to us adults, but it may not be obvious to children, especially as in practice children will sometimes count the same collection and get different results. They will count (or miscount) 'one, two, three dinosaurs', and may count again 'one, two, four dinosaurs', and then again 'one two three four dinosaurs'. They may wonder whether different number words can name the same numerosity, the numerosity of the collection of dinosaurs. Perhaps they will ask themselves: 'Does counting always give me the numerosity I get from subitizing?' (though they are unlikely to frame the question in exactly those words).

One of the child's real problems at around this age, about four years old, is, in my view, the conflict that can occur between the numerosities they achieve by counting and the numerosities provided by their innate ability to subitize small collections of objects. Suppose that subitizing yields four objects but counting comes up with five; which are they to believe? Will they suspend judgement and recount? At the moment, little is known about the causes and consequences of this conflict.

The child will have still other ways of estimating the numerosity of a collection. In general, they will have noticed that more things take up more room than fewer things, so the size of the array will be a useful clue. Packing density will also be a clue to numerosity. Piaget was among the first to see that a full grasp of the concept of numerosity meant being able to abstract away from—or ignore—these superficial clues, so that you do not think, for example, that there are more things just because they are more spread out (or more closely packed together). He saw the development of the child's thinking in general as a move away from the particular to the general and abstract (indeed he thought that really abstract formal reasoning doesn't emerge until puberty—which may not correspond to the intuitions of parents with teenage children[28]).

Children also use one-to-one correspondence to establish which of two sets has more things in it. Even children as young as four can give two people the same number of sweets by using a 'one for Bill, one for Mary' strategy. In one experiment, the experimenter counted out Bill's share, and then asked the children who had successfully shared out the sweets how many sweets Mary had, but less than half of them spontaneously made the inference that Mary had the same number as Bill. Most tried to count out Mary's share. So the match between *these* two ways of determining numerosity—one-to-one correspondence and counting—is by no means clear to children at this stage.[29]

The conflict between the innate systems and counting becomes most surprising when children actually change their mind about the numerical relationship between the collections. Piaget observed that moving objects around, without adding or subtracting an object, will make children as old as five or six think that the numerosity has changed. He would lay out two lines of coins, one above the other, so that each coin in one line was clearly paired with a coin in the other. The children under these conditions had no trouble saying whether or not the two lines had the same number of coins. Then, in full view of the children, Piaget spread out the coins in one line so that the line was longer than the other line. It was clear that he had added none and taken none away. He asked the children which line had more coins, and they said the longer line.

The conflict between the different sources of evidence—different 'cues'—for the numerosities can be seen very clearly in the way children between four and six try to establish whether two sets have the same number. What seems to happen is that during this period, they come to suppress perceptual cues such as the spacing of objects, and to depend exclusively on genuine numerosity information, such as correspondence and counting. They cease to be fooled by changing the spacing of objects. In Piagetian terms, number is 'conserved' under perceptual transformations. There are three stages in the child's progress to conservation.

Piagetian Stages in Achieving 'Conservation of Number'[30]
(The basic situation: six little bottles, about one inch high, the kind used in dolls' games, are put on the table, and the child is shown a set of glasses on a tray.) Look at these little bottles. What shall we need if we want to drink? *Glasses.* Well, there they are. Take off the tray just enough glasses, the same number as there are bottles, one for each bottle. (*Child's responses in italics.*)

Stage I: No correspondence or equivalence. Here the child seems to rely solely on perceptual cues like spacing, and doesn't count or use one-to-one correspondence.

Car (5 years 2 months) arranged them so that each bottle had its glass. (He had taken all the glasses, so he removed some and left 5. He tried to make these correspond to the 6 bottles by spacing them out so as to make a row the same length.) Is there the same number of glasses and bottles? *Yes.* Exactly? *Yes.* (The bottles were then moved closer together so that the two rows were no longer the same length.) Are they the same? *No.* Why? *There aren't many bottles.* Are there more glasses or more bottles? *More glasses* (pushing them a little closer together). Is that the same number of glasses and bottles now? *Yes.* Why did you do that? *Because that makes them less.*

Stage II: Children can do one-to-one correspondence, but still rely more on perceptual cues. In Piaget's terms, they haven't yet achieved 'conservation of number' under perceptual transformations.

Mog (4; 4) estimated that he needed 9 glasses for the 6 bottles, then made one-one correspondence and removed the 3 that were left over, and said spontaneously: *No, it wasn't the right number.* And are they the same now? *Yes.* (The glasses were put closer together and the bottles spread out a little.) Is there the same number of glasses and bottles? *No.* Where are there more? *There are more bottles.*

Children can be quite explicit about the evidence they are relying on to make a judgement. Counting can override perceptual cues at this stage.

Gal (5; 1) made 6 glasses correspond to 6 bottles. The glasses were then grouped together. Is there the same number of glasses and bottles? *No, it's bigger there* (the bottles) *and smaller here* (the glasses). (The bottles were then grouped together and the glasses spread out.) *Now there are more glasses.* Why? *Because the bottles are close together and the glasses are all spread out.* Count the glasses. *1, 2, . . . 6.* Count the bottles. *1, 2, . . . 6.* They're the same then? *Yes.* What made you say they weren't the same? *It was because the bottles are very small.*

Stage III: Children have achieved conservation of number. They now rely on one-to-one correspondence or counting and are not deceived by changing the preceptual cues.

Lau (6; 2) made 6 glasses correspond to 6 bottles. The glasses were then grouped together. Are they still the same? *Yes, it's the same number of glasses. You've only put them close together, but it's still the same number.* And now, are there more bottles (grouped) or glasses (spaced out)? *They're still the same. You've only put the bottles close together.*

Piaget believed that counting, and learning number words to do it, was not important, and certainly not necessary, for constructing the concept of numerosity, which he thought was built up from logical concepts and reasoning, around the ages of four to six, until possession of the concept was demonstrated by conservation of number under transformations. Following Piaget, the French virtually outlawed teaching counting in nursery schools: clearly there would be no point if the child has first to develop the Piagetian prerequisites of transitive inference, class inclusion, and so on.[31]

COUNTING LARGER NUMBERS:
WHY IT'S EASIER IN CHINESE

The conceptual tools provided by the culture are not all the same, even for something as basic as counting. In Chapter 2 we saw that there were lots of different counting systems, some using body-part names; some with bases of 20 or 60; others, like Ainu, which used overcounting and subtraction; others, like ours, that used only addition; some with big numbers always first, like our numeral system; others with the smaller number first, as in German *ein-und-zwanzig* ('one-and-twenty'). The child will have different problems to solve in trying to master these local counting systems. Do some of them make life harder for the child, or are they all really much the same? Unfortunately, research in this area is just beginning, but there is one feature of counting systems that we now know makes life harder: irregularity.

The innate structure of our representations of numerosity is not in base-10 form. It may work only for numbers less than 10: the evidence from infants has shown abilities only up to about 4. Even if nature has endowed us with a way of constructing mental representations of numbers as large as we choose, there is no reason to suppose that it will be in base 10. However, English-speaking children need to learn the local cultural practice of counting in tens. In fact, they have to learn two quite different principles of counting in tens. The first learned is the verbal system, which is not a place-value system but an enciphered or 'name-value' system. We have special names for (some but not all of) the powers of ten: 'ten', 'hundred', 'thousand', 'million'. We say 'two hundred and twelve', not 'two one two' (which is how the poet-astronomers of the fifth-century Indus Valley civilization did it, as we saw in Chapter 2). We also have to learn the numeral system, which is indeed place-value. And we have to learn how to 'transcode', to use the technical term, from one to the other. The most basic thing that children have to learn is that larger numbers are composed of smaller numbers, that both systems use 'additive composition'. That is, they have to learn that *twelve* and *12* both mean ten plus two.

Now, different languages can make the additive composition of the number-word system clear or obscure. In English, we count from

1 to 9, with each number represented by a single word. *Ten* is a word, so are *eleven*, *twelve*, and so on up to *twenty*. In Chinese, each number up to 10 is also represented by a single word, but thereafter things are regular (Table 3.2). For Chinese children there is no trouble with the teens, as they do not have to learn special words for them. But how is the English-speaking child to know that *eleven* is really ten plus one, or *twelve* ten plus two? They sound like single words, and are written as single words. Some children pick up on the fact that there is a new, teen, series after ten. This can lead to mistakes such as over-regularizing from the later teens to the earlier. Some children briefly count *ten, eleventeen, twelveteen*. The first decade is irregular not only in being single words—other decades are two words—and not only in having the first two words not sounding at all like teens; but those that have the word teen in them have teen in the wrong place—after the unit number ('thirteen' is a 3, 10), rather than before for all other decades in English ('twenty-three' is 20, 3).

Our children have to learn that *-ty* is the bit of the word that stands for 10, and that *twen-*, *thir-*, and *fif-* (none of which are words in English) mean two, three, and five (or twice, thrice, and five times). Chinese children, on the other hand, need to learn no new words or new bits of words for the decades: the number of tens is explicit—*two ten, three ten*, and so on. When it comes to representing units, the unit number always comes straight after the ten, unlike in French, where decades plus one are different from decades plus a higher number—*vingt-et-un*, but *vingt-deux*. Does this simplicity really give Chinese children an advantage in learning their numbers? Do they learn the principle of additive composition more easily?

Chinese-speaking Taiwanese children of 4, 5, and 6 years old turn out to be spectacularly better at counting than their US counterparts. The US children were far worse when they got to the teens, while the Taiwanese children scarcely made any mistakes.[32] What is more, Taiwanese children understand how tens and units are added together in the base-10 system that is common to Chinese and English; in fact they seem to understand how to add numbers together to make a target number far better than US children do. This was shown recently by a study by Peter Bryant with six-year-olds. He used a simulated shop where things cost 6p or 11p, and children

1	*yi*	20	*er shi*
2	*er*	21	*er shi yi*
3	*san*	22	*er shi er*
4	*si*	23	*er shi san*
5	*wu*	24	*er shi si*
6	*liu*	25	*er shi wu*
7	*qi*	26	*er shi liu*
8	*ba*	27	*er shi qi*
9	*jiu*	28	*er shi ba*
10	*shi*	29	*er shi jiu*
11	*shi yi*	30	*san shi*
12	*shi er*		
13	*shi san*	100	*yi bai*
14	*shi si*		
15	*shi wu*	200	*er bai*
16	*shi liu*		
17	*shi qi*	231	*er bai san shi yi*
18	*shi ba*		
19	*shi jiu*		

Table 3.2 Chinese number words.

had 1p, 5p, and 10p coins (or their Chinese equivalents). Both groups were equally good at counting out the 1 units, but the Chinese children were much better at paying with 10 + 1 rather than eleven 1's, which is what one would expect if the transparency of the Chinese verbal system makes additive composition so much easier to understand. What is more, they seemed to understand the principle better, since they transferred this to paying 5 + 1 for the 6-unit purchase.[33]

Even when children understand that their language uses a base-10 representation, there is still the conflict between the way the base is encoded in the name-value system of the words and in the place-value system of the numerals. Children learn that *ten* is encoded as 10, *twenty* as 20, *one hundred* as 100, *two hundred* as 200. They will also have learned about additive composition. So *one hundred* plus *one* can be formed simply by sticking the two parts together (with an *and* in between) as *one hundred and one*; *one hundred* plus *forty-seven* is *one hundred and forty-seven*. It is perhaps not surprising that in the early stages of learning to write numerals, English children write 'one hundred and one' as 1001, or 'one hundred and twenty-nine' as '10029'.[34] An explanation for this was proposed by Richard Power and Maria dal Martello, from the University of Padua in Italy, who had studied the writing errors of Italian children aged six and seven.[35] They tested the children's ability to write numbers to dictation. The children did fine with two-digit numbers, like 27, and with multiples of powers of 10, such as 100 or 200, but many were still making mistakes writing three-digit numbers like *due cento venti sette* and *tre cento cinque*. Instead of writing 227 and 305, they wrote '20027' and '3005', just like the English children. They were writing the name values 200 and 300, and using additive composition to stick on the other part of the number. But why didn't they write *venti sette* as 207? In a previous study with one of the founding fathers of artificial intelligence, Christopher Longuet-Higgins, Power had figured out the few general rules that relate number words to numerals in a very wide range of languages. In fact, they wrote a computer program that would work out the relationship for any language, no matter which base system it used, given just a few examples. Two of these rules seemed to have a direct application here. One they called 'concatenation'. For two-digit numbers, the child need only take the 'major term', the multiple of the tens (2), and the 'minor term', the multiple of the units (7), and concatenate them to get the correct way of writing 27. However, for three-digit numbers this doesn't work. Children need to extract another rule from the examples they hear and see, which Power and dal Martello called 'overwriting from the right'. For *two hundred and seven* the rightmost 0 must be overwritten by the 7; for *two hundred and twenty seven* the two rightmost 0's must be overwritten by the 27. This is a more complicated rule than concatenation, and since children learn three-digit numbers after they have learned two-digit numbers, it will be acquired later. So there will be a stage when they have the easier concatenation rule but are still working on the overwriting rule.

In learning about numbers larger than those readily grasped by the innate Number Module, the child has to confront the conflict between two conflicting representational principles: name value in words and place value in numerals. This makes learning difficult, especially, as we have seen, where the name-value system is irregular, as it is in English and other European languages.

In Figure 3.2 I summarize how children add to their conceptual toolkit, by using body parts such as fingers, number words, and numerals. One of the problems they face is how to coordinate these different systems.

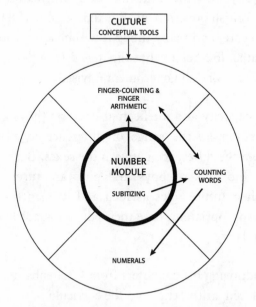

Figure 3.2 The child at about four years uses subitizing to support learning what the number words mean and how many fingers are held up. Numerals are learned primarily in connection with the number words.

ARE THERE SEX DIFFERENCES
IN NUMBER ABILITIES?

Is there something about the female brain that makes it, on average, worse at mathematics than the male brain? This is an important question for our enquiry because if numerical capacity is sex-linked then this is positive evidence for its being coded in the genes. The development of primary sexual characteristics is of course sex-linked and coded in the genes; so is average brain size: human females everywhere have brains 20% smaller than males—1,200 cm^3 versus 1,500 cm^3.

However, it has been very difficult to show that differences in brain size have any cognitive consequences at all. There is no difference in average IQ. In academic achievement, boys have in the past outperformed girls by the age of eighteen. However, girls in England now outperform boys in all subjects at all ages. There is one exception to this general rule: mathematics. Girls are still doing worse at mathematics than boys (but read on).

This has been an official worry since Dr Cockcroft and his Committee of Inquiry into the Teaching of Mathematics produced his report for the British government. But that was in 1982. Before then, few seemed to care, and many thought it almost improper for girls to be good at maths. In a relatively enlightened *Handbook for Teachers*, issued in 1937, the British government advised:

> In mental capacity and intellectual interests [boys and girls] have much in common, the range of difference in either sex being greater than the difference between the sexes. But in early adolescence the thoughts of boys and girls are turning so strongly towards their future roles as men and women that it would be entirely inappropriate to base their education solely on their intellectual similarity.[36]

A father, withdrawing his daughters from Cheltenham Ladies' College when it introduced 'arithmetic' into the curriculum, wrote to Dorothea Beale, the headmistress, 'My dear lady, if my daughters were going to be bankers, it would be very well to teach arithmetic as you do, but really there is no need.' From the middle of the nineteenth century, when female education became an issue, until the Cockcroft report, the curriculum was designed to reflect its usefulness to boys and girls in their adult lives. Differences in mathematical performance were generally attributed to lack of interest on the part of girls, who would be mainly concerned with their future roles as wives and mothers. In 1923, the Board of Education attributed 'girls' inferiority' in mathematics partly to 'an impression among parents, which has influence on the timetable, that mathematics is unsuitable for girls'. Maths was frequently sacrificed to needlework. The Board even suggested that girls' poor performance could be due 'partly to unskilful teaching of an old-fashioned kind'.[37] This is scarcely surprising since very few females wishing to teach maths had had the opportunity to go to university, and fewer still to follow a graduate course in mathematics.

In many countries before the Second World War, including Britain and in many ways the more educationally progressive Austria and Germany, women were strongly discouraged or even prevented from doing mathematics at university. Margaret Wertheim, in her fascinating history of female exclusion from the 'priesthood' of mathematical physics, notes that in the oldest of all mathematical priesthoods, Pythagoras' community in Croton (southern Italy), women were full members, *mathematikoi*. There were even women teachers of mathematics, including Theano, Pythagoras' wife. This was not to last. In the ancient world there was a fundamental division between the male realm and the female realm, the Sky Father and the Earth Mother. For the later Pythagoreans this became a division between the realm of the psyche, which was male, and the realm of the body, which was female. Numbers were in the realm of the psyche, and so naturally a male pursuit, and women came to be excluded from its study. With very few exceptions, women were excluded from mathematics until very recently indeed.

Emmy Noether was one of the team that David Hilbert, perhaps the greatest mathematician of his time, assembled in Göttingen to help Einstein find the right mathematics for the relativistic theory of gravity. She made fundamental contributions to algebra, and to the search for a unified theory of general relativity and quantum mechanics. Yet her life illustrates what obstacles even the most talented of mathematicians had to overcome if they were women.

Despite being the daughter of a professor of mathematics, she was denied entry to university, and spent three years at teacher training college. She then was allowed to attend classes in mathematics at Erlangen, her father's university, but only as an 'auditor'. It was not until five years later that she was allowed formally to enrol. Her doctoral thesis was described as 'an awe-inspiring piece of work' by Hermann Weyl, one of the most celebrated mathematicians of his day. However, as Wertheim puts it, 'It was one thing for a woman to be educated in Germany; it was another matter for her to be employed'.[38] For the whole of her working life in Europe she never received a proper salary, even when she was finally offered an official position at Göttingen.

In the first half of this century, most girls in Europe and the USA harbouring the hope of going on to university were attending single-sex schools where they were taught by female teachers. With these obstacles to getting a degree in mathematics, there were very few properly qualified teachers of mathematics. There is no doubt that this put girls at a disadvantage. Today, when presumably girls and boys have more or less equivalent teaching, have the girls caught up?

In a provocative review, David Geary, a psychologist from the University of Missouri, assembled evidence from a wide range of industrialized countries to show that boys, on average, still outperform girls in mathematical problem-solving.[39] Among US teenagers, there are more boys than girls in the upper reaches of the SAT-M (Scholastic Aptitude Test—Mathematics), a requirement for university admission. The difference between boys and girls gets larger higher up the range.

Geary attributes the male advantage to their superior visuo-spatial skills, needed in the competition for mates when man was a hunter and woman a gatherer. These visuo-spatial skills, tempered in habitat navigation, will be evident in geometry, but also in solving non-geometrical problems formulated in words. One problem with this theory is that even in the USA at 17 years the *average* difference between boys and girls is still only 1%. The most recent cross-national comparisons using the same tests in all countries, the Third International Maths and Science Survey (TIMSS),[40] reinforces the overall picture that in most countries, including the USA, boys do not outperform girls at all (Table 3.3). However, there are still a few countries in which boys significantly outperform girls, most dramatically in

Age nine to ten			Age fourteen		
Country	Mean (points)	Difference in favour of boys	Country	Mean (points)	Difference in favour of boys
Singapore	625	−10	Singapore	601	0
Scotland	520	0	Hungary	502	1
USA	544	2	Canada	494	2
Canada	533	3	Germany	485	2
Hungary	549	5	Scotland	464	3
England	513	5	USA	476	5
Norway	502	5	Sweden	478	5
Japan	693	8*	France	493	8
Netherlands	577	15*	Japan	571	11*
			Switzerland	506	14*
			England	476	17*

*Statistically significant difference.

Table 3.3 International comparisons of sex differences at two ages in points.[41]

England. Interestingly, the gap between boys and girls gets bigger with age, indicative of the critical influence of educational practices. What is certainly clear from the TIMSS data is that the differences between countries, between educational practices, has a vastly greater effect on performance than the difference between the sexes.

TIMSS provides a snapshot of the situation three years ago, but in the most recent public examination figures in England, January 1997 at the time of writing, at the age of sixteen girls are outperforming boys in every subject, including mathematics. In some educational authorities girls are, overall, outperforming boys by nearly 50%.[42] So the urgent question is no longer why girls are performing less well than boys, but why teenage boys are doing so badly! No one has yet suggested that boys are inherently less intelligent than girls, nor that they might be better fitted to manual work than to brain work.

Geary refers to numerosity recognition and ordering, counting, and simple arithmetic as 'biologically primary abilities'.[43] These are precisely the abilities that seem to be functioning in infants, and, as we shall see in the next section, in our primate ancestors. Now, if there is to be a biological difference between males and females, here is where we should find it, since more advanced numerical skills will be deeply affected by educational opportunities. However, Geary admits he was unable to discover any evidence at all for sex differences in these biologically primary abilities.

The fact that there are no sex differences in these basic abilities, and probably no biologically based sex differences in higher abilities, does not mean that the basic abilities are not coded in our genes. It tells us only that they may not be sex-linked properties of the genome. So we shall have to look elsewhere for the genes.

BACK TO THE BEGINNING:
OUR ANIMAL ANCESTORS

An innate capacity for numbers coded in our genome implies that we have inherited that coding from our parents, and they from their parents. How far back in our evolutionary history can we trace it? We have seen that the earliest *Homo sapiens* appeared to possess the capacity, and possibly our Neanderthal cousins too. We have no direct evidence that our common ancestor, *Homo erectus*, could count, since the surviving artefacts offer no clues. It is, however, possible to test descendants of our more distant ancestors, the chimpanzees, who split off from the human lineage about 6 million years ago.[44] If we can find evidence that chimpanzees categorize the world in terms of numerosities, then this opens up the possibility that the genetic endowment goes back to at least the ancestor of both humans and chimps. Of course, other animals may have this number sense too, in which case it originates much further back in the evolution of life.

But there is one crucial caveat to this line of reasoning. To show that an ability has been inherited from an ancestral animal, the mere fact that we can both do the same thing is not enough. Bees and birds can both fly, but the flying apparatus of birds is completely unrelated genetically to that of bees. For more abstract abilities it is necessary to show that doing the same thing is the result of the activity of genetically related brain structures. In chimps' brains, which are very like ours though smaller, I would be happy only if equivalent brain structures are implicated. Of course, if chimps cannot use numerosities then the whole issue will not arise, and we may assume that these abilities originated no earlier than the first hominids, perhaps even just with *Homo sapiens*.

So how can we find out whether animals possess a concept of numerosity, given that animals do not count aloud? There are two basic methods. First, we can see if it is possible to train an animal to respond to numerosity, and just the numerosity. Second, we can see whether an animal's behaviour is governed by numerosity without training. For example, we may be able to use the same methods used to study equally speechless infants. Naturally, for a capacity to have survived millions of years of evolution, it is likely to have been of use to individual animals in improving their reproductive success, or at least to have been closely linked to some other capacity that has improved their reproductive success.

Since animals cannot use number words (apart from Alex, an African Grey parrot (see p. 138), we should avoid the word 'count', which is closely associated with the use of number names. Let us talk instead of 'enumerating'. The great German student of animal behaviour, Otto Koehler, called genuine examples of animal enumeration 'thinking unnamed numbers', where the animal uses 'inner marks' to keep track of numerosities.

Trained to Enumerate

Let me start with an example of an animal who, despite appearances, did not count: the horse Clever Hans. Clever Hans, who flourished at the turn of the century, was able to produce answers to arithmetical problems by tapping his foreleg. Some of these arithmetical problems would be too difficult for many US high-school graduates[45]: he was, for example, able to add fractions such as ⅖ and ½, and gave the answer by tapping out the numerator, 9, and the denominator, 10, separately. He could find factors, and tapped out correctly, 1, 2, 4, 7, 14, and 28 when asked to find the factors of 28. He could give square roots and cube roots. His owner, Van Osten, a mathematics teacher and horse trainer, was entirely convinced that these talents were genuine, and allowed a panel of experts, which included a psychologist, an animal trainer, a circus manager, and the director of the Berlin zoo, to carry out extensive tests. They were puzzled and could see no evidence that the trainer was cueing Clever Hans. The chairman of the panel, the psychologist Carl Stumpf, wrote, 'I could not believe that a horse could perceive movements which escaped the sharp eyes of a circus manager . . . One would hardly expect this feat on the part of an animal who was so deficient in keenness of vision.' Stumpf was, in keeping with the post-Darwinian zeitgeist of 1904, willing to believe in the essential similarity between the human and the animal mind. He noted that even 'educators were disposed to be convinced because of the clever systematic method of instruction [but] which had not, until then, been applied to the education of a horse'.

Of course, the horse had been extensively trained, and rewarded whenever he produced the correct answer. But his arithmetical skills were not due to training. One man, Oskar Pfungst, was not stumped by this. He discovered the explanation by careful experimentation with Hans and other horses. Hans was cued to stop tapping his foot by the movements of the questioner's head, eyebrows, or dilation of his nostrils. Van Osten, quite inadvertently, began to produce these cues near the answer, which Hans, who was indeed a clever horse, picked up, and was then rewarded for doing so. Hank Davis, a leading expert on animal counting from the University of Guelph in Ontario, noted that

> Pfungst determined that it was not even necessary that such cues be sent by Van Osten. Hans was 'clever' enough to learn the signaling systems of other interrogators. As long as the questioner knew the correct answer, Hans was also likely to succeed . . . The inadvertent delivery of cues resulted from the normal buildup of tension in the questioner as Hans approached the correct answer. Perhaps most telling was the fact that Pfungst, himself, could not stop Hans even after he knew the nature of the signaling system and had attempted to suppress it.[46]

Scientists today take extraordinary precautions to avoid a repeat of the Clever Hans phenomenon. For example, any experimenters in view of the animal must not know what the correct response should be, so they could not cue the animal correctly even if they wanted to.

It might seem to us that the obvious creatures to test would be our nearest relatives, the ones with brains most like our own—chimpanzees. Chimpanzees we now know are highly intelligent, social animals, who in the wild make and use tools and even, to some extent, create a culture. They can be trained to communicate very effectively with humans, and with each other, using the sign language of the deaf.[47] There is a good chance, therefore, that chimps might show some ability to enumerate. However, studies of chimp enumeration have been held back because Behaviourism, the dominant philosophy in most US animal labs until recently, worked on the assumption that animals lacked any kind of cognitive concept, including number concepts, and indeed many Behaviourists believed that concepts were superfluous to the explanation of *human* behaviour. What was critical to the Behaviourist was the establishment of simple links between a stimulus and a response, and it really didn't matter what 'organism' was used, provided they could register the stimulus and physically produce the response. Why, then, use chimps, which are rare, expensive, large, strong, and dangerous, when they could use rats, which are small, cheap, and safe?

There is another tradition, going back to Darwin, which doesn't shrink from attributing concepts to animals. One of Darwin's students, George Romanes, was the first to try to train a chimp to use numbers. He reported in 1898 how he taught a chimpanzee to give the right number of straws on a verbal command, up to five.[48] Interestingly, two chimps trained by a strict Behaviourist took half a million trials to match numerals 1 to 7 to numbers of objects, and naturally no numerical concepts were invoked to explain this performance.[49]

It is only recently that chimpanzee enumeration has come under scientific scrutiny. The Japanese researcher Tetsuro Matsuzawa trained a chimpanzee called Ai to select Arabic numerals that corresponded to the number of items in a display, such as pencils, gloves, and spoons, up to six.[50] Even more impressive numerical abilities have been elicited by scientists at the Yerkes Primate Research Center in Georgia.

Sarah Boysen[51] trained Sheba, a three-year-old female chimpanzee, to use Arabic numerals up to 4 in a range of standard number tasks that a three-year-old child might find difficult. The training was long and complicated, and proceeded in four stages, each with several steps.

Stage I: Sheba Is Trained to Use One-to-One Correspondence
In this stage Sheba has to learn to match a small collection of marks on a card with one of three collections of gumdrops in circular 'wells'. When she is correct she is rewarded with gumdrops, a tasty treat.

Step 1. Sheba learns to point to the location of a gumdrop, indicated on a card in front of her, in one of the three wells (Figure 3.3a).

Step 2. Sheba learns to pick out the number of gumdrops corresponding to the cards, but with one distractor (2 v. 1, Figure 3.3b). Here she is discriminating between two numerosities.

Step 3. Sheba learns to pick out the number of gumdrops corresponding to the card, with two distractors (1 v. 3 v. 2, Figure 3.3c). Now she is discriminating among three numerosities.

Mastery of this task enables her to go on to learn how to use numerals instead of collections of gumdrops. But again she is rewarded when she picks the correct number.

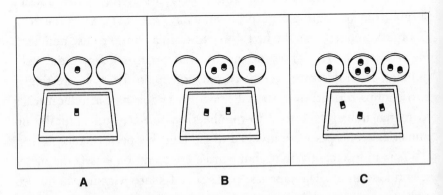

A   B   C

Figure 3.3 Sheba the chimp learns to match numerosities. She is rewarded for matching the numerosity of the marks on the rectangular card with gumdrops placed in circular wells. This is the first stage in training her to understand Arabic numerals. (From Boysen[52])

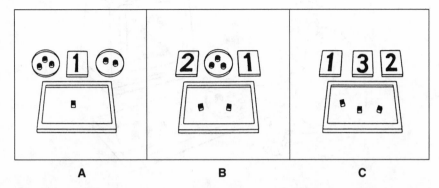

Figure 3.4. Sheba learns Arabic numerals. She is rewarded for picking the numeral that corresponds to the numerosity on the card. She starts with one numeral, then goes on to two, and finally has to pick one of three numerals corresponding to the numerosity. (From Boysen[53])

Stage II: Sheba Learns Arabic Numerals

Step 1. Sheba learns to pick the numeral from three wells (Figure 3.4a); she already knows that one gumdrop on the card does not correspond to the gumdrops in the two wells. In this way she begins to learn the meaning of '1', '2', and '3'.

Step 2. Sheba learns to pick one numeral from a choice of two numerals, reinforcing the training of Step 1 (Figure 3.4b).

Step 3. Sheba learns to pick the correct numeral from a choice of three (Figure 3.4c).

Stage III: Sheba's Understanding of 1, 2, and 3
Is Tested in a New Task

Sheba is shown a numeral on a computer screen and has to point to the well with that number of objects (Figure 3.5). She is rewarded with gumdrops when she is correct.

Stage IV: Transfer of This Knowledge to Simple Addition

Finally, Sheba showed that all this training could result in two remarkable achievements—adding objects and indicating the sum in numerals; and adding numbers denoted by numerals.

Figure 3.5 Sheba learns the numerical value of the numerals. In this stage of the learning she must pick the well with the numerosity corresponding to the numeral on the computer screen. (From Boysen[54])

Step 1. Oranges were hidden at two of three locations in Sheba's work area: a tree stump, a food bin, and a plastic dishpan (Figure 3.6). Sheba found the oranges and then pointed to one of the numerals to indicate the sum of the two.

Extraordinarily, she did this on the very first trial of the session, without any training at all, and maintained this performance for two weeks.

Here, Sheba may be showing us that she can add together the numbers of oranges she found in two of the three hiding places. Alternatively, she may have been counting them as she found them, perhaps as three- or four-year-old children add by counting on. When they are adding 3 and 2 they may go, 'one, two, three' for the first number, and then 'four, five' to add the second.

Step 2. Arabic numerals, rather than oranges, were hidden at two of the locations, and she had to add together the numbers she found. She learned this task very quickly.

Sheba thus learned to use abstract representations—Arabic numerals—for small numbers. Human children can use their emerging knowledge of numbers in a range of tasks. David Geary, as we have

Figure 3.6 Sheba shows that she can add. In the first version of the task, oranges are hidden in three locations in Sheba's work area. She has to find the oranges and then pick the numeral corresponding to the sum. Having already learned the meaning of the numerals, she was successful on her very first trial. Having mastered this task, the numerals were substituted for oranges at these locations (as shown here), and again Sheba was successful at selecting the numeral in the tray corresponding to the sum. (From Boysen[55])

seen, postulated three 'biologically primary abilities'—discriminating numerosities, counting, and simple arithmetic. To these, I would add ordering numbers by size, or at least being able to select the larger of two numbers. So important and basic is this ability, that I devote the whole of Chapter 6 to it. Can Sheba use her knowledge of numbers in these four skills?

Sheba was able to learn to pick the larger of two numbers—the basis for ordering by size. She learned pairs that differed by 1, such 1 v. 2, 2 v. 3, 3 v. 4, and in each trial she was rewarded when she picked the larger number. When she was proficient at this, she was presented with a pair of numbers that she hadn't seen as a pair before, such as 2 v. 4, which she was able to manage well.

Another very basic human skill, as we have seen, is counting. The child learns to map each member of a collection of objects to a sequence of words. Since chimps do not know spoken words, and cannot learn them, I have been careful not to talk about 'counting', but about 'enumeration'. But can chimps do something that is equivalent? Can they put objects in one-to-one correspondence with mental tags of some sort? We cannot show that any of Sheba's achievements depended on being able to count in this sense. One experiment by colleagues at the Yerkes Primate Research Center in Georgia shows that counting is possible. Yerkes was famous in the 1980s for teaching chimpanzees to communicate in a symbolic language. The most famous of these chimpanzees was Lana, trained by Duane Rumbaugh and his colleagues. Rumbaugh and David Washburn set out to see if Lana, by now a seventeen-year-old, could count.[56]

They now wanted to use a method which would force Lana to use mental tags, and which therefore had to exclude the possibility of her using other cues, such as the spatial arrangement of the collection to be counted. They devised a method that depended on making the right number of objects disappear from a computer screen. To do this, Lana had to remember how many objects she had made disappear. She was already skilled at using a joystick to control the position of a cursor on a computer screen, but she needed to understand the new task. In the training phase, she was shown a numeral, 1, 2, or 3, had to select boxes until she had reached that number, and then demonstrate her understanding by moving the joystick back to the numeral.

In a typical early trial, Lana saw the numeral 3, and at the bottom of the screen a line of rectangular boxes. As Lana removed two boxes by moving the cursor into them, the numerals 1 and 2 appeared in their place and two 'feedback boxes' that turned blue. This was designed to give Lana assurance that she was proceeding correctly. To complete this trial successfully, Lana had to remove a third box and return the cursor to the target numeral, 3. When she was successful she got a reward, but if she returned the cursor too early (after 2, for example) or too late, then the computer would emit a raucous tone.

Once Lana had mastered the training, she went on to the experiment proper. Now the boxes were arranged differently for each trial, and there was no feedback, either from the feedback boxes or in the form of numerals appearing in place of the selection boxes. Lana showed that she could manage all the numerals from 1 to 4 very efficiently. Something very like human counting must have been involved, because she had to keep a *mental* tally of the *number* of boxes she had removed from the screen. There were no external cues she could have relied on in the final test sessions.

Sheba's ability to add small numbers was matched by Sherman and Austin, two language-trained chimpanzees in Rumbaugh and Washburn's lab.[57] Not only could they add two numbers together, they could accurately compare the size of the sum with the result of a second addition. The way they did this was simple and elegant, and actually required very little training. Sherman and Austin would see two trays, and quickly learned to choose the tray with more chocolates on it (Figure 3.7). Not surprising, you may think, but there was a catch. In each tray were two wells with pieces of chocolate in them. To decide which tray had the most chocolates, Sherman and Austin had to add the contents of the two wells, and then select the larger of the two sums. This is a task then that demands the use of three primary abilities: recognizing the numerosities (of the wells and the sums), adding, and ordering.

Of course, these two chimps may not have been adding so much as applying a 'counting all' strategy to the two wells. Nevertheless, if children added the pieces of chocolate together this way, we would be quite happy to say that they were adding, but using a particular technique to do it.

Higher Maths in 'Lower' Animals

Can we find any of these biologically primary skills in ancestors of both chimpanzees and humans, or indeed in any other animals? The seminal demonstration comes not from mammals but from birds. It has long been thought that birds can count the number of eggs in a nest. Whether they can or not, Otto Koehler showed in a series of classic experiments between the late 1930s and the 1950s that birds can use numerosities to guide behaviour, and perhaps even use mental tags to count. Koehler put forward a new and important hypothesis which, like much of his work, has been largely ignored, one suspects because

Figure 3.7 Austin has learned to select the tray with more pieces of chocolate on it. Since each tray has two wells with pieces of chocolate in them, he must add the numbers together and select the larger sum. (From Rumbaugh & Washburn[58])

he published almost exclusively in German, and around the time of the Second World War.[59] What he proposed was that humans would never have started counting without two pre-linguistic abilities: the ability to compare two numerosities presented simultaneously, and the ability to remember numbers of objects *presented sucessively in time*. Both these abilities, he showed, we share with birds.

In one experiment, a raven called Jakob was rewarded when he tried to open a box with the same number of spots on its lid as there were on a large 'key' card (Figure 3.8). The arrangement of spots was always different on the lid and the key card. The wrong lid always differed by just one spot. Jakob solved the task by finding the lids with same numbers as key cards, and learned eventually to distinguish 2, 3, 4, 5, and 6 spots.

Figure 3.8 A raven matches numerosities. The great German ethologist Otto Koehler trained his raven Jakob to pick one of two small boxes that had the same number of blobs on its lid as there were on a big card. Notice that the pattern on the correct lid is quite different from the pattern on the card: This is one of a classic series of experiments with birds that demonstrated their numerical ability. (after Thorpe[60])

Koehler next showed that animals could 'act upon' a number. So jackdaws were trained to open the lids of a row of boxes until they had taken from them a given number of pieces of food, say 5, and then stop. To do this, they, like Lana, had to keep track of the pieces of food they had taken. They had to create what Koehler called 'inner marks', mental tags, similar to (though of course not the same as) our silent counting using number words. Jackdaws did this very successfully.

This was demonstrated in an experiment with a jackdaw, given the task of raising lids on a row of boxes until he had taken 5 pieces of food. One trial in the many that made up the experiment was remarkable. The pieces were distributed in the first five boxes 1, 2, 1, 0, 1. The jackdaw opened only the first three lids, and so had taken only 4 pieces of food. Koehler, a meticulous experimenter, was just about to record 'one too few, incorrect solution', when the jackdaw came back to the row of boxes. The great British pioneer in bird behaviour, W. H. Thorpe, described what happened next.

The bird went through a most remarkable performance: it bowed its head once before the first box it had emptied, made two bows in front of the second box, and one before the third, then went farther along the line, opened the fourth lid (no bait) and the fifth and took out the last (fifth) bait. Having done this, it left the rest of the line of boxes and went home with an air of finality. This 'intention' bowing, repeated the same number of times before each open box as on the first occasion when it found baits in them, seems to prove that the bird remembered its previous actions.[61]

Koehler, who was always extremely cautious in putting forward interpretations of animal behaviour, thought that the bird must have created 5 inner marks, unnamed numbers, which it used to compare its own actions with those required by the task.

To what extent are these inner marks like our numbers? Koehler thought that they were 'equal marks', rather like our using one nod of the head for one, two nods for two, and so on. Each nod is to equal the others, and they are the *mental equivalent of tallies*. He called the creation of a collection of these inner marks 'thinking unnamed numbers'. Our numbers are unequal in this sense. 'Three' is qualitatively different from 'two', and in a fixed order in relation to it. Koehler did not rule out the possibility that animals may have mental marks like ours, but they were not necessary to explain his experimental results.

One particularly striking example of bird counting comes from Alex, an African Grey parrot trained by Irene Pepperberg at the University of Arizona. When Alex is asked how many objects there are on a tray, or even how many red objects there are, he will actually say the number. Of course, this has taken many, many years of training, but it is impressive because he has learned not just to associate the right number name (more correctly, the right vocal response) with the numerosity of the array, but also because he is able to apply the name to a collection of objects he has not been trained with. This is important because it shows that Alex's representation of numerosity is not tied to a particular collection of objects, but is more abstract than that.[62]

Since Koehler's time, many researchers have found evidence both for the ability to compare and select from simultaneously presented numbers, and for 'acting upon' a number, in a wide range of species. Rats, for example, can learn to count shocks, or learn the number of doors to ignore before entering the arm of a maze which contains food.

Birds and rats have small brains, even taking into account their much smaller bodies. The animals with the largest brains for their body size are, of course, humans. But the next-largest brains are not in our closes relatives, the chimpanzees, but in dolphins. There has been almost no research on dolphin numerical abilities, and none at all on the kinds of ability they may share with chimpanzees, rats, and birds.[63]

The Evolution of the Number Module

Laboratory experiments show that animals have a latent capacity to do simple numerical tasks. As well as in the recently evolved apes, it is found in birds, which evolved after the dinosaurs. For this capacity to be preserved for millions of years, it must surely have offered some advantage to those species that possessed it. But what could this be? The life of the individual animal—the *phenotype*—depends on feeding and safety from predation. Securing these helps all members of a species similarly endowed—the *genotype*—to survive and reproduce better and, other things being equal, to reproduce more offspring than species members without the endowment. In this way, the valuable capacity to carry out these simple numerical tasks will remain in the gene pool. However, the genotypic capacity may persist even though it offers the phenotype no advantage.[64]

Squirrels will have more nuts for winter if they consistently choose branches with three nuts rather than two, and in general foraging will be more effective if the animal can decide which patch has the most food. It is certainly true that animals make more trips to patches where there is more food. If there are two patches, A and B, so that A has twice as much food as B, then animals tend to go twice as often to A as to B, and make the ratio of trips match the ratio of food. Why they do not spend all their time at the patch with the most food, which would seem to be the optimal strategy, is a problem we cannot go into here. The main point for us is this: animals can estimate and compare two quantities. Many researchers have suggested that this is precisely what constitutes the adaptive advantage of number capacity.[65] But squirrels may not be counting nuts; they may be relying on a concept of quantity that is not numerousness—the amount of nut-stuff on the two branches. This is how we estimate the volumes of milk or granulated sugar, for example. Foraging success critically depends on making quantitative estimates without using numbers. Even invertebrates do this. Worker bees, for example, when they have found an abundant source of pollen or nectar, return to the hive and 'dance' a message to the other bees indicating the direction and the distance of the food source. When the quantity of food decreases below a certain threshold, the bees may still visit the patch but will not dance on their return. They thus make estimates of relative quantity.[66]

Evolutionary explanations of behaviour can easily become Just-So stories, whose acceptability depends too often on the imagination of the teller and the gullibility of the audience. What is needed are documented examples of behaviours in the wild that cannot depend on quantity estimates, but must depend on numerosities. These examples are almost impossible to discover, since numerosity in nature almost always varies with quantity. This may of course be why a sense of numerosity is adaptive.

As we have seen, birds can be trained to make use of a number sense which, in exceptional individuals, can go up to 7. Do they use this in the wild? Bird-nesting children have always wondered whether birds can count the number of eggs or chicks in the nest. There would seem to be a good reason for being able to do so. In normal circumstances, egg-laying continues until incubation behaviour is triggered. Too many eggs could mean that the parents will be unable to feed all their chicks, which may be detrimental to *all* the chicks in the nest; too few would reduce the chance of the genes surviving. If eggs are taken during laying, birds will usually lay extra eggs; and if eggs are added, they will stop laying, perhaps even reabsorbing eggs that have formed inside their body. Even after the birth of the chicks, the female may cannibalize some offspring if she cannot feed all of them.[67] But does this mean that birds count their eggs and their chicks? Does it mean they have a sense of their absolute numerosity, of 'fiveness', say? Does the female think to herself, in effect, 'I can only support five chicks, so I'd better eat the sixth?' Birds probably do have a real sense of numerosity, but one can imagine other ways of reaching the same decision. They could be using some perceptual cue, such as the visible ratio of eggs to nest, or of chicks to nest, as judged simply in terms of the proportion of light (eggs, chicks) to dark (nest).[68] This behaviour is certainly consistent with its being controlled by a Number Module, but it is also consistent with its being controlled by a mechanism sensitive to relative quantity more generally.

There is another activity in which birds seem to count, and that is

in singing. Songbirds such as the chaffinch, lark, or canary are genetically programmed to sing their own species-special song, but it has
been known since at least the eighteenth century that the birds also
learn. Canary-fanciers prize 'schoolmaster canaries', particularly good
singers from whom other canaries learn. In fact, there are local
'dialects' of birdsongs.[69] A dialect can be the exact number of repetitions of a note—seven in this forest, but eight in the distant meadow.
This means that the offspring learn the number of repetitions of the
note from the parent, and countersinging adult neighbours copy this
number of repetitions. The German ethologist Uta Seibt argues that
this is really a very abstract concept of number: the perceived number
of notes is transformed into the performed number of notes.[70]

One extraordinary recent demonstration shows that rhesus monkeys can use numerosities in the wild. In a monkey colony on the
island of Cayo Santiago in Puerto Rico, Marc Hauser and his colleagues from Harvard University carried out the same Mickey Mouse
experiments as Karen Wynn had with infants. Since the monkeys
were wild, and could not be confined to their mothers' laps, like
Wynn's babies, the experimenters had to wait until a monkey took an
interest in their apparatus, which was a field version of Wynn's
Mickey Mouse experiment using pieces of aubergine instead of dolls.
Just like the infants, the monkeys showed surprise when 1 piece + 1
piece did not yield 2 pieces of aubergine; and when 2 pieces – 1 piece
did not yield 1 piece.[71] This shows that they are able to use numerosity representations to estimate food supply, but it still does not show
that they will do so when not prompted by an experiment.

The best examples so far of number use in the wild do not come
from foraging. In the Serengeti National Park in Tanzania, a lioness is
returning at dusk to her pride. Eighteen females, one adult male, and
seven cubs are waiting over a kilometre away. She hears a roar, one
she does not recognize. It must be an intruder into her territory. Her
cubs are safely with her sisters, and she is all alone. She hears the roar
again, it's the same lion. Should she try to drive off the intruder? It
would be an even match—her against one intruder—and it could turn
into a real fight. With lions, that could be fatal. Dusk turns to the
inky black of night, and she returns silently to the pride.

The following week, again at dusk, she hears roaring 500 metres away. She hears one unfamiliar voice, then a chorus of roars, one overlapping the next, and none of them the familiar voices: three intruders. This time she is with four of her sisters from the pride. Three of them, five of us. Their ears prick. The roaring is coming from a stand of trees over to their left. They wait, they peer into the night and at each other. One of them, the leader, approaches the roaring cautiously at first, as the others join her, more quickly until they are charging headlong into the trees.

By the time they reach the trees, the roaring has stopped and there is no sign of the intruding lions. This is not surprising. The roaring was actually coming from a loudspeaker set up by Karen McComb and her colleagues at the University of Sussex.[72] She was testing a theory about the way lions make a numerical assessment of the threat from intruders and the strength of the defence forces. The theory predicts that lions (like many other animals, fighting among which would be costly) will contest resources only when they are very likely to win; otherwise they will withdraw. The one exception is when a lioness is with her cub: then she will always attack an intruder. The lions' decision to attack depends on the number of intruders—in this experiment one or three—and how many adult defenders there are. The lioness leader identifies roaring as coming from individuals who are not members of the pride; she will also represent the defenders as known individuals. The best explanation of her decision is that she enumerates the number of distinguishable roarers and the number of her sisters, and the compares the two numbers. Only when the number of defenders is greater than the number of intruders will she launch an attack. This is remarkable because the number of intruders comes from the sound they make (they are not visible), while the number of defenders comes from another sense or other senses, vision probably, and is stored in the lioness's memory. Thus she has to abstract the numerosity of the two collections—intruders and defenders—away from the sense in which they were experienced and then compare these abstracted numerosities.

Chimpanzees are social animals like lions, but unlike lions they use tools. West African chimpanzees use stones to crack nuts, with a large stone as an anvil and a smaller stone as a hammer, while East African chimpanzees do not do this.[73] This has led to suggestions that chimpanzees have cultures that are passed from generation to generation by social learning, just as human cultures are. Indeed, when an individual who knows how to crack a nut with a stone is introduced into a culture which doesn't do this, members pretty soon learn how to do it, particularly the younger adults. The key question for us is this: can the use of numerical skills be part of a chimpanzee culture? Can a wild chimpanzee community learn to use their latent numerical ability in a way that is particular to them?

The story of Brutus, an alpha male, is an extraordinary and unique example of just this. He was observed by Swiss zoologist Christophe Boesch in the forests of the Taï National Park in Côte d'Ivoire. Brutus was the leader of a community of eighty chimpanzees. Like other communities, parties of around ten would go off in search of food, often travelling in one direction for hours in silence. These travelling parties would keep in touch by pant-hooting and by drumming on trees with buttresses, which are very resonant and can be heard for thousands of metres through the forest. Boesch noticed that sometimes after he had heard drumming, all the parties in the community would change direction. Many months of patiently following the community made Boesch realize that it was only when Brutus was drumming that the community changed direction. Analysis of the drumming and the reactions to it led Boesch, a famously careful researcher, to the astonishing conclusion that Brutus was signalling to his community in a 'symbolic drumming code' based on the *number* of drumbeats. Brutus conveyed three completely specific messages:

1. Drumming *once* at two different trees indicated the direction he was proposing, which was the direction followed by Brutus when moving between the two drummed trees.

2. Drumming *twice* at the same tree meant rest for an hour. The community activity stopped for an average of 60 minutes. In twelve observed instances, the rest was never less than 55 minutes and never more than 65 minutes. Once Boesch observed Brutus drumming four times on the same tree, and the party rested for 2 hours!

3. Drumming *once* at one tree and *twice* on another tree meant change direction to the one proposed, and then rest for an hour.[74]

For this form of communication to work, Brutus and other members must be able to use their numerical capacity to distinguish 1, 1 from 2 from 1, 2. It is only found in this one community in the Taï Forest: it was part of their culture and no one else's. I say 'was' because Brutus has now stopped using the code. Poaching, the greatest threat to chimpanzee survival, has killed or kidnapped so many prime males that the number of travel parties has since declined dramatically.

These examples suggest that animals can and do use numerosity skills in the wild. This seems to help them to resist predation and communicate while foraging. According to Hank Davis, an expert in the numerical abilities of rats, 'I believe that *absolute numerosity* is a distinctly human invention. No nonhuman animal needs this form of numerical competence in order to lead a successful, totally normal life.'[75] What animals use, he says, is just *relative numerosity*. They do not need to understand that each time they see a collection of 3 things, it has the same numerosity, only that in the course of comparing it with other collections, they can tell which has more, that is, it has more than 2 and less than 4 things. We have seen lions compare the numbers of intruders and defenders. In these circumstances, knowing the absolute number of defenders, or of attackers, may not be necessary. Brutus's chimpanzee companions may have relied on 2 being more than 1, and 2, 2 being more than 2, or 1, 2. However, the basis of the comparison could still be the ability to extract from the surroundings the absolute number of things in a collection and remember this for comparison with the numerosity of other collections. The lioness counts three intruders, remembers this (as did Koehler's jackdaw), and compares it with the number of defenders, including herself, before making a decision to attack or withdraw. The chimpanzees may similarly have remembered that two beats on the same tree means 'rest', while two beats on different trees means 'change direction'. At the moment we do not know which is the best account of the numerical capacities of our ancestors.

ARE THERE GENES FOR BUILDING THE NUMBER MODULE?

For us to have inherited a capacity for numerosity, this capacity must be encoded in the genome—the genetic instructions that control the building of our body. The human genome consists of 46 chromosomes, arranged in pairs, which we inherit from our mother and father. These chromosomes contain, we now believe, about 100,000 genes, about half of which go into building the brain.

How can we find out which genes are for numbers? In principle, it is very easy. We find people who are bad at numbers and work out where their genome is defective. Of course, there are many reasons for being bad at numbers—inadequate teaching for a start. So the first job is to find a group of people who are bad at numbers for reasons that are independent of environmental causes. The next job is identifying the part of each person's genome to see which ones are defective (and hoping that all members of the group show the same genetic defect). This means checking an enormous number of locations along each chromosome. We do now have some ideas about which regions on which chromosome are unlikely to be involved, but it still makes looking for a needle in a haystack seem easy.

There is another problem. No one has yet been able to identify genes responsible for any single cognitive function. No one has found the genes for language, for example. David Skuse and his colleagues at the Institute of Child Health in London have come nearer than anyone else to finding genes for a cognitive function, what they call 'social cognition'. This seems to consist of a range of social skills that might all depend on seeing another person's point of view.[76]

Skuse studied a population of females with Turner's syndrome. This is a chromosomal disorder in which one member of a pair of X chromosomes (45; 46) is missing or damaged. Normally, each member of the pair will be 'imprinted' according to whether it comes from the mother, called Xm, or from the father, Xp. In boys, who will have an X and a Y, the X will come from the mother. So in girls with Turner's syndrome, those with just the Xm will be much more like boys, and these are the ones with poor social cognition.

The other striking feature about Turner's syndrome compared with control subjects matched for age is that they are worse at mathematics but not at reading or spelling. On the whole they seem to be about two years behind. It is not clear from the one detailed study that exists, by Joanne Rovet and her colleagues at the Hospital for Sick Children in Toronto,[77] where or why these children are worse.

Do they fail to acquire more advanced skills? Do they lack some 'biologically basic abilities'? It remains to be discovered.

In collaboration with David Skuse and his team, I have started to carry out tests on females with Turner's syndrome. If there is a set of genes that build the brain circuits for the Number Module, then we may be able to track them down over the next three or four years. If there are not . . .

Laboratory experiments demonstrate that many species of mammals and birds can be trained to carry out simple tasks that depend on numerosity. With ingenuity, experimenters have been able to ensure that the animals are responding to the numerosity of a display rather than to the quantity of stuff in the display. The capacity to use numerosity information may offer its possessors an adaptive advantage, though it is very difficult to separate out the advantage of being able to use quantity information from being able to use numerosity information. Two examples from mammals in the wild support a specifically numerical interpretation—a lioness repelling intruders and a chimp leader directing his troop. These animals no doubt use quantitative information in other circumstances as well.

Are these animals using the predecessor of our Number Module? The answer is, we do not know. To establish this claim it is not enough to show that we and they both respond to the same numerosity properties of our environments. We also have to show that we have inherited their bodily mechanisms for doing it—not just eyes and ears, which we have indeed inherited from our simian ancestors, but brain circuits too. Unfortunately, as I write, we have absolutely no evidence as to which brain areas chimps, lions, or birds use to carry out numerical tasks. It is possible that they use different brain areas from one another, and from us. The evidence for a deep evolutionary source for the Number Module is tempting, compatible but incomplete.

Nevertheless, it now abundantly clear that infants are born with a capacity to recognize distinct numerosities up to about 4, and to respond to changes in numerosity. They also possess arithmetical expectations: if you take 1 doll away from 2, they expect to find 1 doll remaining; and if you add 1 doll to 1 doll, they expect to see

2 dolls as a result. These laboratory findings suggest that infants can compare numerosities and select the larger of two small numbers. These three abilities—to recognize numerosities, to detect changes in numerosity caused by adding or taking away from a collection, and to order numbers by size—are the biologically basic numerical capacities, the ones that are embedded in our innate Number Module.

4

NUMBERS IN THE BRAIN

Signora Gaddi[1] is sitting at her desk in the office of the family hotel in Friuli, northern Italy, where for many years she has kept the accounts. She is a small, neat woman of fifty-nine years, well organized and clearly very competent, with thirteen years of education behind her. She speaks clearly and fluently about her family and the problems of running a hotel. My colleague Lisa Cipolotti places five small wooden blocks in front of her, and asks her to count them. *Uno, due, tre, quattro. La mia matematica finisce qui.* 'One, two, three, four. My mathematics finishes here.'

Lisa takes away the blocks and shows Signora Gaddi a card with three dots on it, and asks her to say how many there are. She looks carefully at each dot in turn, mentally counting them, and says *Tre.* Lisa asks her to do it without counting, but she cannot. She then shows her a card with two dots on it. Again Signora Gaddi counts in her head: one, two. She clearly cannot do what the rest of us can do— see at a glance, without counting, how many dots there are, at least up to four. This process, called subitizing, can be carried out by small children, probably even by infants and by many species of animals, as we saw in Chapter 3. But Signora Gaddi cannot subitize.

Lisa tests other basic abilities. First, how accurately and quickly can she judge which of two numbers, two single-digit numbers, is the bigger? She is shown a card with the numerals 2 and 3, and she correctly picks the 3. She is shown 2 and 4 and she correctly picks the 4. Then she is shown 5 and 10, which is a bigger absolute difference than in either of the two other trials, but she confesses she is completely at a loss, and guesses that 5 is the larger. Perhaps, we think, there is something amiss with her ability to read and understand the numerals. So we try the same test with dots instead of numerals. We get exactly the same results. For up to four dots she was accurate if very slow; for four or more she was completely confused, and resorted to guessing. Then we ask her to compare one number that is 4 or less with one that is larger than 4. Now she is really quite good, scoring 70% with numerals and almost 100% with dots. So she has a sense that there are numbers beyond the reach of her counting, which have to be bigger than the numbers she can count. She knows it isn't numbers that finish at 4, just *her* numbers that finish at 4.

Counting objects, as children have taught us, is not as simple a task as it seems to us adults. We need to coordinate the sequence of words with tagging each of the objects as counted or to be counted. There are lots of ways in which this can go wrong. A possible problem could be in remembering the sequence of number words. To test this, we asked her just to recite the number names, starting at 'one'. But again, she could not get above 'four'.

Even number facts, which seem to require just memory, were extraordinarily difficult for her. To retrieve the number of wheels of a car, she summoned up the image of a car, and counted aloud the wheels she could see in her mind's eye. To answer Lisa's question about the number of arms on a crucifix, she asked Lisa to hold out her arms and then counted them. If numbers up to 4 were hard, those above 4 were impossible. She could not recall the number of days in the week, her house number, her age, or her shoe size.

Fifteen months earlier, Signora Gaddi had suffered a stroke that damaged the left parietal lobe of her brain. This is the classic site for a condition called *acalculia*—an inability to use numbers—but we had never seen a patient, or even heard of a patient, so severely affected by a stroke that they could not even subitize two dots. Since her stroke, her life had been one of frustration and embarrassment. She was unable to do things that previously had been second nature to her. She could not give the right money in shops; she had no idea how much she was spending or how much change she was getting. When she got to the check-out, all she could do was to open her purse and ask the assistant to take the right amount of money. She could not use the phone. There was no way to call her friends. In case of emergencies, the phone was specially adapted so that by pressing one button it rang pre-set numbers in sequence until one answered. She was unable to tell the time, or catch the right bus. She could not convey ordinary facts if they involved numbers. Despite her best efforts, her performance did not improve in the year and half we were testing her.

THE INDEPENDENCE OF THE NUMBER AREAS

We immediately realized that this could be an important case. The brain is organized into different specialist regions, each doing its own job. One of the best ways of finding out which bit of the human brain does which job is to find patients whose brain cannot do a particular job, and try to link the disability to the location of the brain damage.

In a stroke, the person affected suffers an interruption to the blood supply to the brain. A blood vessel bursts or becomes blocked, cutting off the supply of oxygen to the neurons—nerve cells—in the affected region. Sometimes the cells seem to recover, and sometimes the brain finds other ways to carry out the functions of the damaged neurons. In other cases, patients are left with difficulties that can profoundly change the whole course of their lives. In Signora Gaddi's case, her language was quite severely affected by her stroke, but later recovered fully; her numerical abilities did not recover. What makes the victims of stroke so interesting and important to science is that the damage is confined to just the area fed by the affected blood vessel. This often means that just one function of the brain is disturbed, so we can see how the brain divides up the work it has to do, and how a disturbance in one function will have knock-on effects on other functions. Stroke patients are often happy to cooperate in neuropsychological studies, even when the main purpose is scientific rather than rehabilitative. One reason is that stroke victims like to feel that some general good may come from their own personal tragedy. Another reason is that the scientific tests provide very sensitive and accurate measures of exactly what is wrong, and exactly what still works well, and if the tests are repeated at regular intervals they can tell the patient objectively how well different functions are recovering or not. For this method to work for Signora Gaddi, we needed to be sure that her problem really was numerical, and not the result of some other cognitive deficit.

We were encouraged by the old findings of Salomon Henschen, a neurologist who worked in the Karolinska Institute in Stockholm until the late 1920s, and introduced the term 'acalculia'. He had collected data on 260 neurological patients with some disturbance to their numerical abilities, out of a total collection of over 1,300 cases. On the basis of this extraordinary database, he concluded that there 'exists in the brain an independent system subserving arithmetical processes and that it is independent, or nearly so, of the systems for speech and music.[2] However, at the time when we were testing Signora Gaddi, it was by no means generally accepted that core numerical abilities were an independent system. Many, following Jean Piaget, saw the number concept as emerging from more primitive logical concepts without, as it were, a life of its own, at least not in the development of the child.[3] Perhaps by the time the child becomes a fully competent adult, the number concept could have freed itself from its logical past. Others, following Noam Chomsky, believed that number was just a special aspect of language.[4] There was also a whole school of thought which claimed that the core mental representation of numbers, the representation of their size, was not numerosity but analogue. It was as if each number were represented in the brain by a rod of a particular length (plus or minus some margin of error).[5] Neurologists too had tried to explain acalculia in terms of more general abilities. One review, published in the same year as our report on Signora Gaddi, argued that there was no one site in the brain for acalculia, since acalculic symptoms could appear following damage to many different brain areas. Yet other neurologists tried to argue that our number abilities are based on general intelligence and reasoning, or on our spatial abilities, or on linguistic abilities, or on some combination of the three, in various proportions; and that different types of symptom arise from damage to the areas of the brain supporting reasoning (frontal lobes), spatial awareness (parietal lobes), memory for general knowledge (left temporal lobe), or linguistic ability (left temporal lobe).[6]

The Language of Numbers Is Not Language

It was critical to establish that Signora Gaddi's problem with numbers could not be explained in other ways. We had already seen that her spoken language was unimpaired,[7] but perhaps the brain damage had affected non-modular capacities—those we deploy in a wide range of processes and tasks—such as the ability to reason, the ability to deal with any kind of quantity, or just memory for any kind of fact, not just numerical facts. We developed a whole new battery of tests to check each of these functions. She passed all with flying colours. Not a hint of a problem. She scored 100% on our reasoning tests. She could solve unerringly problems such as, 'Giorgio is taller than Carlo, Pietro is shorter than Carlo: who is taller, Pietro or Giorgio?' She could still remember all kinds of geographical and historical facts she had learned at school, provided they didn't involve numbers. She had no problems with remembering her friends and family, or her past history. So there was clearly nothing wrong with her memory. With respect to quantities, she knew which was heavier, a kilo or a gram, a kilo or a tonnellata;[8] which was longer, a metre, a centimetre, or a kilometre. She had no trouble ordering pictures of objects according to their size in real life. It was clear from these tests that language, memory, and reasoning were not sufficient in themselves for good number performance. Something crucial was clearly missing. But was the number circuit really independent of these other systems?

To be confident that there was an independent number region in the brain, we needed cases the converse of Signora Gaddi. Could there be people with good numerical abilities but minimal language, severely defective memory, and very poor reasoning? To begin with, perhaps, someone whose language was disastrous, but who could still calculate. Even Henschen had never seen such a patient; they were bound to be rare. Language processes take up a large chunk of the left hemisphere of the brain, so anything that damaged the language circuits could well affect neighbouring regions, including the inferior left parietal region, which we suspected were critical. These cases would be very different from stroke victims like Signora Gaddi. They would be the result of a disease which causes widespread damage, and moreover which leaves a kind of island of spared brain. These diseases are associated with the dementias. The best known is Alzheimer's disease, which spreads slowly, or quickly, through the brain. These are truly tragic conditions that ultimately affect most brain functions. Unlike strokes, there is no recovery.[9]

Even today, only one or two such cases have been discovered in which widespread damage has spared numerical processing. Martin Rossor, Elizabeth Warrington, and Lisa Cipolotti from London's National Hospital for Neurology and Neurosurgery have recently reported a patient, a Mr Bell, suffering an awful degenerative disease of the brain called Pick's disease, whose effects are similar to those of Alzheimer's.[10] Mr Bell's language had almost completely disappeared. He was left being able to utter just a few stereotyped phrases, such as 'I don't know' and, curiously, 'Millionaire bub'. His understanding of speech or of written language was almost nonexistent. Nevertheless he was still pretty good at calculation, and could accurately add and subtract, and though he seemed to have lost some multiplication facts he still showed a good understanding of what it was and how to do it, as you can see from Figure 4.1. He could also select the larger of two- and three-digit numbers, showing that he still understood about numbers as being ordered by size, and the way the Arabic numeral system worked.

The nineteenth-century neurologists Paul Broca and Carl Wernicke discovered that language processes are for most people in the left hemisphere, in particular in part of the left temporal lobe (now know as Wernicke's area) and also in part of the left frontal lobe (Broca's area), and in the brain circuits connecting these two regions. Mr Bell's disease attacked the left temporal lobe, and possibly the left frontal lobe, so it is not surprising that his language was affected. It seems to have spared the left parietal lobe, the region we were beginning to home in on as the main site of the core number abilities—of the Number Module itself.

We had now taken the first steps on the long road to understanding how numerical abilities were organized in the brain. We knew from Signora Gaddi and Mr Bell that numerical abilities were separate from

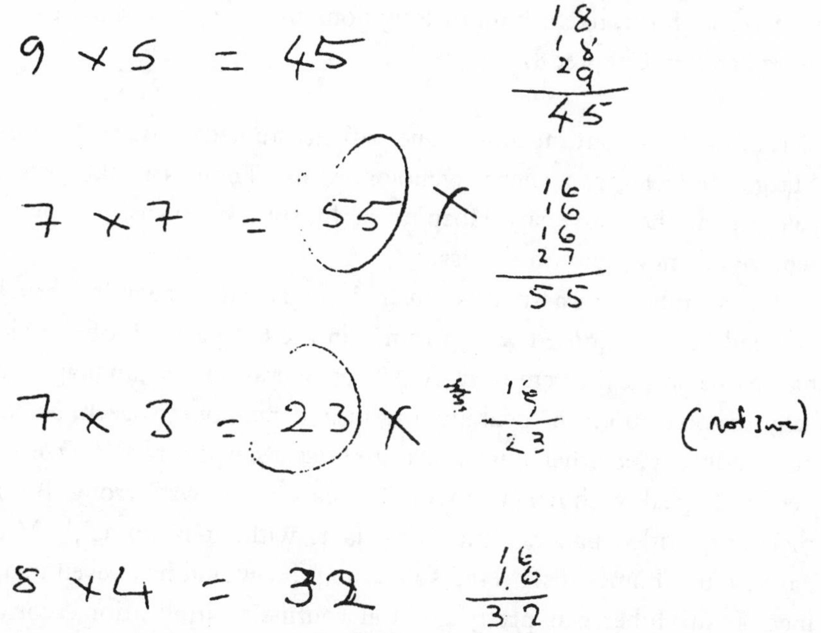

$9 \times 5 = 45$

$7 \times 7 = 55$

$7 \times 3 = 23$

$8 \times 4 = 32$

Figure 4.1 Even though brain disease had almost completely destroyed his language ability, Mr Bell was still good at arithmetic. These are examples of his written multiplication when he could not recall the answer directly and work it out. His strategy of repeated addition demonstrates that he still understood the principles, and that his good performance isn't simply down to rote memory. (From Rossor *et al.*[11])

language abilities, first, because you can be very bad at one while remaining good at the other, and second, because the brain areas involved seemed to be different. Now these were only two cases, a dangerously small base on which to erect a grand theoretical pyramid.

Also, we were going against the grain of common sense and some expert opinion which robustly maintained that language and numbers are intimately connected, and this is not an implausible position. After all, much of what we know as adults about numbers we learned as children by means of language: counting, multiplication tables, and so on. Of course, Mr Bell does not prove that we do not store some number facts in verbal form, only that there is another form that we *can* use which does not depend on language. Which form is more important? Certainly, common sense and educational opinion suggest that the knowledge of the multiplication tables we use in calculating really is in verbal form, like a kind of long nonsense poem (I discuss this in more detail in Chapter 8).

Verbal facts without meaning. One patient, studied by our colleagues Margarete Delazer, a neuropsychologist, and Thomas Benke, a neurologist, at the University Hospital at Innsbruck, Austria, throws a remarkable new light on this issue.

Frau Huber ran a small farm in a pretty valley near Innsbruck. She had been diagnosed with a tumor in the left parietal lobe, which had to be surgically removed. After her operation her language was fully restored, both in speaking and in understanding speech, as was her reading. Her other intellectual abilities seemed intact.[12] To meet her or to speak with her, you would think nothing was wrong. But in their aptly titled paper, 'Arithmetic facts without meaning',[13] Margarete and Thomas discovered something few would have even imagined. Frau Huber was pretty good at routine multiplication, scoring 59/64 on problems from 2×2 to 9×9. While this is not wonderful, it is not bad for someone who left school at thirteen and had undergone a major operation on her brain. No surprises here. There were surprises when she was asked to do simple addition and subtraction. Now her performance was distastrous. She failed to score at all on a standard clinical test. When she was asked to make a number out of poker chips, she got very few correct, and some of her mistakes showed that she had a very shaky understanding of written numbers. In this task, Frau Huber was given poker chips marked with the values 1, 2, 5, 10, 20, 100. She was asked to make up the numbers presented on cards. What she did is shown in Table 4.1. This shows a lack of understanding of the numerical system, at least, and probably of the way numbers combine to give other numbers, what is called 'additive composition'.

When she couldn't remember the answer, she didn't spontaneously try to use her fingers, as a child might and many of our other patients do. Even when Margarete asked Frau Huber to use her fingers, she just looked at them helplessly, and denied that they would be any use in adding up. She just didn't seem to understand numbers or arithmetic any more. Margarete and Thomas checked this by inventing a new test. She was given a sum with its answer and then asked

Number on card	Chips selected	Frau Huber's comment
12	5 5 5 2 2 2 2 2 2	
103	100 100 100 1	'Three times a hundred plus one'.
52	50 50	'I need two fifties'.
38	10 10 10 5 1 1	

Table 4.1 Frau Huber counting with poker chips.[14]

about a new problem that was related to it by a familiar law of arithmetic. So she would be told that 13 + 9 was 22, something she could no longer work out for herself, and then asked to solve 9 + 13. She did very badly on this. Even on multiplication, where she could recite tables efficiently, she failed all the trials. When she was told that 12×4 was 48 (in Austria, they only learn their tables up to 10), she could not say what 4×12 was.

Frau Huber's brain damage had spared her verbally coded, rote-learned number knowledge, but the understanding of the numbers and of arithmetic had been lost. Without understanding, these verbal facts are of very little use. This also has theoretical implications. In their theoretical model of numerical representations, Dehaene and Cohen[15] claim that number facts are stored verbally. This is certainly supported by the case of Frau Huber. Tables, like most of arithmetic, are taught using words, so it is not surprising that some of the verbal coding—just like Lewis Carroll's poem 'Jabberwocky'—sticks in the mind (well, in *my* mind).

But the case of Frau Huber also shows that facts stored in verbal form do not connect up with other parts of arithmetic. For her, these facts are divorced from their meanings as numerosities. This is why it makes no sense for her to use her fingers to try to calculate answers when she cannot recall the words. Contrast her performance on multiplication with that of Mr Bell, who performed at a similar level in terms of overall scores. When he failed to remember an answer he used a numerosity-based strategy to work it out. He wasn't always right, but his attempts showed he understood that multiplication is equivalent to multiple additions. Frau Huber does not seem to understand that at all.

Number Memory Is Not Just Memory

Neuroscientists and psychologists distinguish three separate memory systems, each with its own location in the brain. First, there is long-term autobiographical or 'episodic' memory, for events we have experienced in our life, tagged for when and where these events happened. These are the memories lost in amnesia. Second, we have long-term 'semantic' memory for general knowledge, including what we learn in school. Items in semantic memory are not tagged for where or when we learned them. Semantic memory is the repository for facts like the capital of Botswana or the meaning of 'verisimilitude', and also the verbal form of multiplication tables. In cases of classic retrograde amnesia, patients may have forgotten where they went to school or that they are married, but can still recall the capitals of European states, the meanings of words, and tables. Third is 'short-term memory'. For psychologists, this is the capacity, measured by 'span', for keeping a list of unrelated items, for example a list of digits, in the right order until needed. Without rehearsal the items are lost within a few seconds. The normal span is about seven digits or six words. Whether the items are presented visually or auditorily, and whether they are letters, words, or numerals, there is good evidence they are stored in verbal form. Looking up a telephone number and keeping it in mind to dial is the textbook use for short-term memory.

Now the question for us is this: which of these memory systems do we use to store our knowledge of numbers and arithmetic? One could make a plausible case for all three. There is that indelible memory of a sunlit classroom. You were waiting for the bell to ring so that you could run into the playground, when Miss Brown asked you for the answer to 8×7. Flustered, you ventured 'fifty-four, Miss'. Humiliatingly, your worst enemy Lucy confidently piped, 'that's wrong, Miss, it's fifty-six'. Maybe we do have a few of these memories. But what about those table facts when you weren't the humiliated—or the humiliator? One way of finding out is to study the numerical abilities of severely amnesic patients. Have they lost their arithmetical facts as well?

Long-term autobiographical memory. Margarete, Thomas, and I studied a group of amnesic patients,[16] all of whom suffered both retrograde and anterograde problems. That is, they were very bad at recalling what happened before their illness began (retrograde), but also very bad at remembering things that had happened to them since (anterograde). They would usually be unable to remember whether they had been to the clinic before, though they all had, frequently. These patients were tested with standard arithmetical tests, and also with some special tests of our own devising. On tests of simple arithmetic most were just as accurate and just as fast as our control subjects with normal memories. This suggests that for number facts, autobiographical memory is not really very important.

My collaborators had the ingenious and original idea to use 'priming' with these patients. Priming is a technique I had been using for quite other purposes with normal subjects. If you see the same multiplication problem twice, you are able to answer it faster the second time. The first occurrence of 7×9, which we call the 'prime', activates the fact $7 \times 9 = 63$ in memory. This activation dies away only slowly, so when you encounter 7×9 for the second time, which we call the 'target', that fact is still more active than it was first time, which makes it quicker to retrieve. Eventually, after some minutes or hours, the activation is back to its previous level. We also used a slightly more sophisticated version, where the subject sees 7×9 but later has to solve its complement, 9×7. In the experiment subjects just had to answer a long string of problems presented one at a time on a computer screen. They were not told that they would sometimes see the same problem more than once. The amnesic patients have no conscious recollection of the problems they have just seen.

A typical sequence of trials went like this:

$\ldots 7 \times 9$ (prime), 3×3, 4×1, 6×8, 1×5,
7×9 (target), 2×2, $8 \times 7 \ldots$

Subjects were asked to say the answer as quickly as possible. There was an additional task. After each target, subjects were asked if they had seen the problem before in the task. The control subjects were right on 91% of occasions, but the amnesics were right only for 31% (and they could have been guessing). Normal subjects produced answers to targets faster than answers to primes, and so did the amnesic subjects.

This shows that arithmetical facts can be well preserved in the long-term semantic memory of amnesics: they are not 'amnesic for arithmetic'. What is more, arithmetical problems elicit the same responses in the amnesic brain as in the normal brain—the activation seems to decay in the same way—except that the amnesics don't remember having recently seen the problem. It fails to register in their autobiographical memory. We can therefore rule out autobiographical memory as the locus for stored numerical knowledge.

Long-term semantic memory. What about semantic memory, where our general knowledge is stored? Signora Gaddi had well-preserved semantic memory. There are also the converse cases, where general knowledge can be severely affected but arithmetic is well preserved. These cases are rare because impairments to semantic memory are usually the result of progressive diseases of the brain, like Alzheimer's, which cause widespread damage and in the end affect most brain areas. Recently, a French neurologist and a team of Belgian neuropsychologists have described a really extraordinary case: Monsieur Van, whose semantic memory was severely compromised, but whose calculation remained almost at prodigy level.[17] I describe Monsieur Van in more detail below (see p. 163).

Short-term memory. When we do a mental arithmetic problem which involves more than two digits, carrying or borrowing, most of us have the sensation of saying the intermediate results in our heads. This helps us keep track, or seems to. Try adding 87 and 56. Did you hear something like 'carry 1' in your head after adding 7 and 6? If you did, this was your short-term memory working. This is the verbal code in which you store information for brief periods. Is it necessary for mental arithmetic, or is it a kind of epiphenomenon, something that pops up in consciousness while the real work, the real calculating, is being carried out elsewhere?

We know from studies of normal children and normal adults that short-term memory span—how many digits you can repeat back immediately after a single presentation—correlates highly with scores on arithmetic tests.[18] Short-term memory professionals, and there are hundreds round the world who make a decent living out of studying our ability to recall lists of unrelated items, stress its importance. Charles Hulme and Susie Mackenzie, in their book *Working Memory and Severe Learning Difficulties* (short-term memory is often called 'working memory') write that 'Such temporary storage is obviously necessary for a wide variety of tasks . . . such as mental arithmetic.'[19] However, as we all know, correlation is not cause. We cannot say whether short-term memory helps arithmetic, or arithmetic skills help short-term memory. The other problem is that span correlates with all sorts of cognitive abilities, and could therefore be used to diagnose mental ability generally. Oliver Wendell Holmes called it 'a very simple mental dynamometer which may yet find its place in education.'[20] Looked at the other way round, lots of other abilities may also be contributing to span performance.

There is one way to find out what role short-term memory plays in arithmetic: test someone whose short-term memory is very poor and see what effect this has on their calculation skills.

One day I was attending a case conference at the National Hospital for Neurology and Neurosurgery in Queen Square, London, the oldest neurology hospital in the world. This is a meeting where a patient is tested before an 'audience' of neurologists and psychologists who together apply their expertise in an attempt to make sense of the symptoms, formulate a diagnosis, and recommend a treatment. The patient was Mr Morris, a brisk, well-dressed, confident man in his fifties. We heard that he had been a pharmacist and still owned a chain of chemist shops. He had suffered a stroke to his left hemisphere that had left him with halting speech and a mild form of Broca's aphasia (a condition in which speaking is affected more than understanding speech). He was being presented by Professor Elizabeth Warrington, head of the neuropsychology department and one of the founders of modern neuropsychology.

Elizabeth showed that Mr Morris had difficulty uttering grammatical sentences, and was also suffering a rather rare kind of dyslexia that was a result of his stroke. She then asked to Mr Morris to repeat back a list of numbers. She started with one number, then went on to two numbers. No problem. He could clearly hear the numbers properly and he could say them. But when she got to three numbers, e.g. 6, 2, 9, he started to make mistakes. He would miss out one of the numbers, or get them in the wrong order. The best he could manage reliably was two digits. Most people can manage at least six numbers, so this was really defective short-term memory. Here was an ideal opportunity to explore the contribution of short-term memory to arithmetic. So, what was his mental arithmetic like?

Elizabeth tested him with examples from her own Graded Difficulty Arithmetic test, a mental arithmetic test known to neuropsychologists around the world by its initials, GDA. It starts easy and gets harder. The first question is 'fifteen add thirteen', the fifth is 'one hundred and twenty-three add twenty-nine', and the twelfth 'Two hundred and forty-four add one hundred and twenty-nine'. If you complete this question or if you fail three questions in a row, you continue with subtractions, starting with 'nineteen take away seven' and ending with 'two hundred and forty-six take away one hundred and seventy-nine'. Note that all these questions exceed Mr Morris's span of two digits.

Mr Morris astonished us. He seemed to have no trouble at all with most of the questions. Even questions such as $128 + 149$ and $119 - 35$, which he would find impossible to repeat because they were 3 or 4 items greater than his span, he answered correctly. As Elizabeth fired questions at him, I was trying to answer the questions in my head, but he got his answer out quicker than I could most of the time. When I checked with my colleagues afterwards, they confessed to exactly the same reaction. Now, these impressions at a case conference are not enough. Elizabeth, Lisa Cipolotti, and I followed up by systematically testing Mr Morris's short-term memory and his calculation, both 'mental' and written. The results confirmed our impressions. Even when we tested his short-term memory in a way that didn't require him to use his impaired speech, by pointing to the numbers, he still showed a span of about two items. His performance on the GDA put him in the 63rd percentile—that is, he was better than 63% of the population. We concluded that 'short-term memory measured by span, has a very marginal role in arithmetic'. Of course, Mr Morris had to remember the problem in order to work out the answer, but we think that rather than using the general-purpose, verbally coded short-term memory, arithmetic uses a special-purpose memory. In Mr Morris's case, this memory was still a working memory.[21]

Reasoning and Arithmetical Reasoning

It's natural to think of the ability to reason logically as being important in mathematics. Piaget stressed the fundamental importance of logical reasoning in developing ideas of number. However, the fact that infants can recognize and mentally manipulate numerosities without being able to reason logically (see Chapter 3) suggests that reasoning about numbers might depend not on general reasoning abilities but on something more specialized.

To establish that number reasoning is separate from general reasoning ability, we need to show that, despite good general reasoning, even simple arithmetic can be severely impaired; and also that, despite poor general reasoning, arithmetical skills can still be good. The case of Signora Gaddi illustrates the first part: her reasoning, including reasoning on Piagetian tasks as measured by our tests, was flawless; but her numerical abilities were disastrous. Now, was there a patient unable to reason, but who nevertheless could carry out arithmetical tasks accurately and fluently? No one like that had ever been reported, until a team from the Catholic University of Louvain, one of the leading neuropsychological research centres, discovered Monsieur Van.

Monsieur Van is an eighty-six-year-old manual worker whose schooling finished after primary level. He said that his teachers were surprised at how good he was at arithmetic when he first went to school. When he was admitted to the clinic he was in the early stages of an unfortunate dementing condition, probably Alzheimer's disease. As a consequence he was confused about where he was and his long-term autobiographical memory was poor, in this respect rather like the amnesics I described earlier. His most remarkable deficit lay in his inability to reason. For example, he was given 27 playing cards from 1 to 7 in each of the suits, and was asked to find the missing card. In the words of the investigators, 'He proved totally unable to organise the search.'

Extraordinarily, he was also quite unable to carry out the tasks Piaget had labelled a prerequisite for having the idea of numerosity, and which a child of four can manage. For example, he twice failed a simple number conservation task, where a row of ten wooden cubes was lined up in one-to-one correspondence with a row of ten wooden disks. He agreed that there were the same number of cubes as disks. When three of the disks were removed he correctly said that there were fewer disks than cubes, indeed that there were three fewer disks. Then the two rows of ten cubes and ten disks were set out again. This time the experimenter spread out the cubes, but without adding or subtracting any cubes or disks. Monsieur Van now said that there were more cubes than disks. On a second trial, the disks were squeezed together, and again he said that there were more cubes than disks. Surely he would understand, as even a child of four understands, that to change the numerosity of a collection a member must be taken away or a new member added. Monsieur Van was unable to do it. You will recall that our very severe acalculic, Signora Gaddi, succeeded at it. Now, if this kind of reasoning ability underpins our skill at using numbers, then Monsieur Van should be very bad indeed. Was he?

Quite the opposite. He had no trouble estimating the number of dots in a display, and he performed well on a number comparison task. He was as good as normals half his age on standard tests of arithmetic, but what made his performance exceptional was the way he tackled difficult calculations. For example, he was able to tell which of a set of three-digit and four-digit numbers, such as 839, 841, 4096, and 4099, were squares and which were not. In another task, he had to pick the square root for a four-digit number: he would see 3844, for example, and be asked to choose 42, 61, 62, or 68. It is not easy. He was quick to solve these problems, but was not completely error-free. This contrasts strikingly with his general reasoning skills, where he performed very poorly indeed, as we saw.

So, now we have both halves of the double dissociation: good general reasoning but very poor arithmetic (Signora Gaddi) and strikingly impaired reasoning but excellent arithmetic (Monsieur Van). This supports the idea that the brain organizes arithmetical processing in circuits that are separate from the circuits used for general logical reasoning.

Common sense and some expert opinion suggest that our numerical abilities are closely bound up with our linguistic abilities, with our ability to memorize, to hold information in a short-term working memory, and with our ability to reason. What these patients show is the exact opposite. In the brain, these abilities are separable. For each ability we can find people who are good at it, but bad at numbers, and other people who are bad it but good at numbers. In the technical vocabulary of neuropsychology, these are called *double dissociations*, and they are a key method for establishing the independence, the separability, of mental processes. A *single dissociation*—good at X and bad at Y—isn't enough. This may show only that Y is just a more difficult version of X, and it is generally true that the easiest skills survive best in cases of injury. My own knee injury, for example (about which I am happy to talk at great length at the slightest opportunity), has affected my running but not my walking. Walking is easier, and it would be remarkable indeed to find someone who could run but not walk. Analogously, it is possible that brain damage can make easy things hard and hard things impossible. If we had found only patients who were good at language but bad at numbers (or bad at both), we could deduce no more than that number tasks are harder than language tasks. With the other dissociation—bad at language but good at numbers—this difficulty explanation is ruled out.

These patients show the following:

Independence of number and language—Signora Gaddi was good at language, but very bad at numbers; Mr Bell was very bad at all language tasks, but still good at arithmetic.

Independence of number and memory—Amnesics still perform normally on number tasks, while many of the alcalculic patients I have described, including Signora Gaddi, are not at all amnesic.

Signora Gaddi can still be very good at remembering everyday facts, like capitals, word meanings, and so on, but cannot remember any facts at all that involve numbers above 4.

Mr Morris's short-term memory was so bad that he could not repeat back more than two numbers, but he was able to carry out mental calculations on two three-digit numbers accurately.

Independence of number and reasoning—Monsieur Van's reasoning abilities were on many tasks worse than that of a four-year-old, yet his calculation was excellent. Signora Gaddi, on the other hand, performed flawlessly on reasoning tasks at which Monsieur Van failed, yet her number skills were disastrous.

These dissociations are summarized in Figure 4.2.

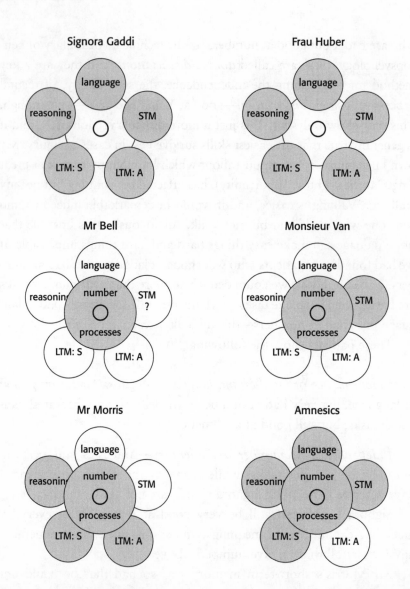

Figure 4.2 The independence of the number circuits. These diagrams summarize the dissociations shown by the patients I have described. Five non-numerical abilities may be contrasted with numerical processes: language, short-term memory (STM), long-term semantic memory (LTM: S), long-term autobiographical memory (LTM: A), and reasoning. A shaded disk indicates an ability that is still functioning at normal or near-normal levels; an unshaded disk indicates that it no longer functions. The diagrams show that it is possible to be in possession of all these abilities and still have lost basic number processes, and also that it is possible to be good at arithmetic while having lost some or all of them.

Let me add a note of caution. These double dissociations are found in the performance of adult patients, and suggest that number abilities are independent of these other abilities and probably depend on brain circuits separate from those used for numerical tasks. It may nevertheless be the case that all these abilities are necessary for acquiring the conceptual tools provided by culture. For example, although skilled adults may not need tables in their verbal form, it may be that language-coding acts as a ladder: you need it to climb up to the level where you can represent the facts in terms of numerosities, but once there you can kick the ladder away with no ill effects (unless you need to come down again when you forget the mental representation in numerosities). There may also be reasoning and memory ladders for some arithmetical processes (I discuss this issue in more detail in Chapters 7 and 8).

INSIDE THE MATHEMATICAL BRAIN

The exercise books used by children in France have tables on the back, not just multiplication tables, but also addition, subtraction, and division tables. Children are expected to learn them all. The information is thus divided up by operation, and within operation by number. Is this how information is organized in the mathematical parts of the brain? Even if, as I have argued, there are circuits in the brain specialized for numbers, this does not mean that within that region our number facts are neatly sorted as they are on French exercise books. The world of numbers is very tidy, very orderly, but in the brain does the representation of number facts and numerical operations, the conceptual tools we acquire from our culture, reflect that orderliness, or does it reflect the disorderliness of how we learn these facts?

Our way of finding out is to look at how the system breaks down after brain damage. Imagine that the back cover of the French exercise book is perforated between the tables. If I were to pull even crudely on the two sides, it would separate the multiplication and addition tables from the subtraction and division; or if I pulled top and bottom, the addition and subtraction would be separated from multiplication and division. Other forces would separate the tables in different ways, but would almost always segregate the information by table because the perforations between the tables are the lines of least resistance. But is this a valid model of real human brain organization? Is it really possible for people to lose neat parcels of knowledge in this way: multiplication without losing addition, or addition without losing multiplication? Or, indeed, are arithmetical facts really separate from everything else we know about numbers? Do we really keep the fact that 7 + 5 = 12 separate from a procedure for adding numbers together?

Facts and Procedures

The first major clue to the way the brain organizes arithmetic came in 1979, when Dr Constable, a consultant physician, strode into Elizabeth Warrington's office at the National Hospital and demanded to be tested, twice a day. He had suffered a stroke which affected his speech, temporarily, and his vision, but left his consultant's personality untouched.[22]

When he was asked to solve 5 + 7, he replied, '13 roughly'. When he was tested formally he turned out to be normal on all cognitive tests except arithmetic. He complained that before his stroke addition and subtraction were 'automatic', but now they were slow and difficult. Given enough time, he thought he would be able to solve such problems by counting forward for addition or backward for subtraction. He even managed to solve the most difficult problem on a standard test: 'A man earns £60 per week. If 15% is withheld for taxes, how much does he receive each week?' He verbalized his solution process as follows: 'So we do it 10% first, is £6, half of that is £3, equals £9; £60 minus nine is £51'.

It was clear that he understood all the arithmetic operations, and the sequence of operations for carrying them out. He never made silly errors, like saying that the sum of two addends was smaller than either of them, which many patients do. Warrington writes, 'He claimed he often knew the approximate solution but not the exact solution and indeed before attempting a calculation he would often say "approximately ... N"'. So what was wrong? Why did he score so badly on timed tests?

If you look at Figure 4.3, you will see that the graphs of his addition and multiplication response times show two interesting things. Dr Constable was, as I have said, slow, but he wasn't always slow. Sometimes he was as fast as the controls (five consultant physicians at the National Hospital). Occasionally, he seems to have been able to

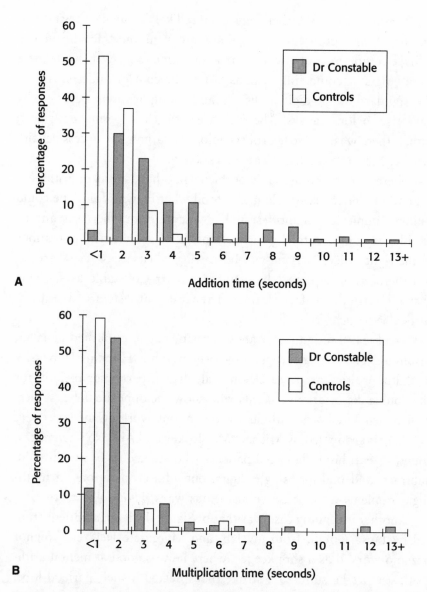

Figure 4.3. Mr Constable's addition times (a) and multiplication times (b). He was generally much slower than control subjects at solving single-digit addition and multiplication problems. Most of the time he seemed unable to access his memory for these previously familiar facts, having to work them out anew. (Adapted from Warrington[23])

remember the answer to these very simple problems, most other times not, and it is then that he had to resort to counting backwards or forwards, or to other strategies. When the answer was relatively large,

8 + 9 rather than 2 + 3, then he was more likely to make a mistake. It was not, Warrington discovered, that there were some facts he seemed to have forgotten, and always took a long time to answer, while there were others he could still recall as fast as the control subjects. Any of the standard single-digit additions and multiplications occasionally gave rise to long delays. The facts were thus not permanently lost; rather, there was, to use neuropsychologists' jargon, an 'access deficit'. Getting access to the facts was the problem.

There were no comparable problems in other aspects of arithmetical and numerical skills. He understood what he was doing; he could estimate numerical quantities; he had a sense of number size; and he could carry out accurately, for the most part, arithmetical operations in the right order, carrying and borrowing when necessary. Warrington therefore interpreted the results from Dr Constable as showing that the retrieval of facts formed a separate subsystem of the arithmetical system.[24]

The breakthrough paper about Dr Constable, published in 1982, inspired a group of neuropsychologists at Johns Hopkins University in Baltimore to start research on acalculia, in particular to look for the double dissociation: patients who show the opposite deficit—facts well remembered but arithmetical operations working incorrectly, if at all. This group, led by Michael McCloskey and Alfonso Caramazza, found several brain-damaged patients who seemed to be able to add, subtract, and multiply single digits, but whose operations in multidigit problems were defective in various ways (Figure 4.4).[26]

Another intriguing case was that of Signor Tiziano, a patient studied by Luisa Girelli, from my lab, and Margarete Delazer.[27] Signor Tiziano worked as a shopkeeper, where he was good at mental arithmetic, before he suffered a stroke that affected his left parietal lobe. As a consequence he was left with what Luisa and Margarete call a 'subtraction bug'—a flaw in his mental subtraction program. Figure 4.5 shows what he did. Can you work out what he was systematically doing wrong? Signor Tiziano always subtracted the larger from the smaller, whether he should have done or not. This is rather like the mistakes children make: 'three take away four is impossible, so it must be four take away three'. There was one exception. When he was subtracting a two-digit number from a three-digit number, he

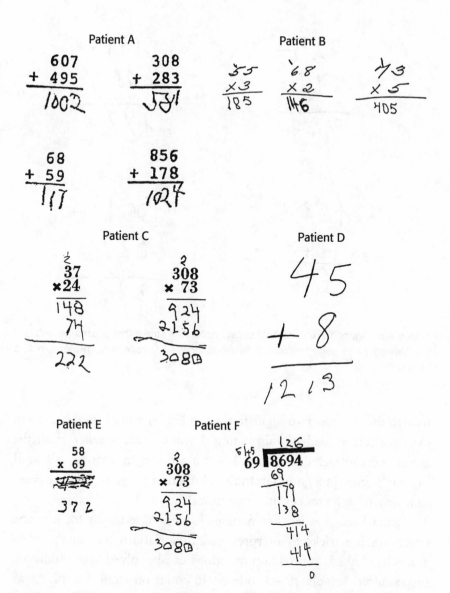

Figure 4.4 Six patients with deficiencies in their arithmetical procedures. Patient A has lost his carrying procedure. Patient B has a bug in his carrying procedure. Patient C fails to shift the intermediate product in the second row. Patient D is confused, combining components of both addition and multiplication procedures (8 + 5 and 8 + 4). Patient E is confused, but seems to be able to recall that $9 \times 8 = 72$. Patient F fails to carry out the long multiplication procedure correctly, but can still do long division. (From Caramazza and McCloskey[25])

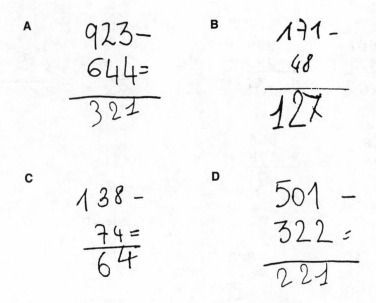

Figure 4.5 Signor Tiziano, a shopkeeper, suffered a stroke that caused his subtraction procedure to become faulty in a revealingly systematic way. (From Girelli & Delazer[28])

treated the leftmost two digits in the top line as a single number. So in example (c), instead of subtracting 3 from 7, the smaller from the larger, he subtracted 7 from 13, getting the right answer. It's as if there is a 'bug' in Signor Tiziano's subtraction program, so that every time he runs it he makes the same mistake.

Remarkably, patients sometimes lose, or lose access to, just one operation. It is tricky to interpret these dissociations because the operations are linked. Subtraction questions can be solved using addition: for example, to solve 9 – 3, one could count on from 3 until 9 was reached. Division depends on knowledge of multiplication, and both long multiplication and long division procedures depend on knowledge of multiplication facts. But you can see from Figure 4.4 that Patient F seems to have the facts at his fingertips but still has bugs in his long multiplication, though not his long division, procedure.

For most of us, subtraction depends on carrying out operations which include the retrieval of previously learned facts, often facts of addition rather than specific facts of subtraction. Most patients we test are worse on subtraction than on comparable additions. However, two or three cases have been reported recently in which the patient is actually better at subtraction than addition.

Madame Bonnard, a patient studied by Xavier Seron's team in Louvain, Belgium,[29] was very bad at single-digit arithmetic, making errors in over 30% of additions, and, even worse, in over 50% of multiplications. However, she made only 10% of subtraction errors. This suggests that representations of addition (and multiplication) in the brain are segregated from subtraction; we do not yet know how. So here was a case of preserved subtraction procedures when a lot of factual knowledge seemed to be lost.

Taking all these patients together, we find a double dissociation. Patients like Dr Constable and Madame Bonnard are poor at retrieving facts, but still good at carrying out arithmetical procedures. On the other hand, Signor Tiziano and the patients reported by Alfonso Caramazza and Mike McCloskey have well-preserved facts but make mistakes, usually quite systematically, in applying simple arithmetic procedures. It seems, therefore, as though arithmetical facts and arithmetical procedures occupy different circuits in the brain.

Addition and Multiplication Tables

On the cover of French exercise books addition and multiplication facts are separate. But is this really how the brain organizes these facts? In school, addition is taught before multiplication, but most of the time we are carrying out real-life multiplications, in combination with addition and subtraction. This raises an intriguing general question: does the brain like to organize information in terms of what we might call its experiential history—items being linked together according to whether they were experienced together—or are items filed neatly by subject matter, addition here, multiplication there? The case of Signor Bellini turned out to be very revealing.

Signor Bellini was an accountant before he suffered a stroke that left him with damage in the left hemisphere. He was treated by neurologist Gianfranco Denes and his team at the University Hospital in Padua, Italy. After three years he still had problems in speaking and in moving his right arm. On standard tests of arithmetic he scored within the normal range. Clinically he was not acalculic at all, but, as you will see, his is one of the most extraordinary stories, only one part of which I shall tell here.

First, some historical background. Franco, as Gianfranco is always known, had for many years been working with Dr Carlo Semenza, a brilliant psychiatrist, psychoanalyst, neuropsychologist, and professor of psychology. They had published a series of important papers on the effects of brain damage on memory and on language. I had got to know them both at an annual neuropsychology workshop they started in 1980 in the beautiful medieval town of Bressanone in the Italian Dolomites. The best neuropsychologists in Europe, and elsewhere, came regularly to discuss their latest research, attracted not just by the scientific proceedings: Carlo and Franco had rightly judged that good food, a congenial atmosphere, and the chance to ski in some of the loveliest mountain scenery in the world would be a winning combination. And so it proved. This annual meeting has probably done more to advance neuropsychology in Europe than any other single action. Many senior scientists leave the meeting having set up some new research, and many junior scientists leave having found a lab that would welcome them for extra training. Carlo, who worked in the Psychology Department at the University of Padua, suggested that we exchange students under a European Community scheme known as ERASMUS, which we did. Through this, we began joint research on disorders of language, usually involving the students we were exchanging. One year, riding a ski lift above Val Gardena, Carlo and I hit on the idea of joint research on acalculia, which we felt was important and, in those days, neglected. A couple of years earlier, Elizabeth Warrington had presented the case of Dr Constable to the workshop, and the idea had been slowly germinating in the back of our minds (though probably in the front of our brains). Together with Franco and Elizabeth, Carlo and I drew up a proposal, which we sent to the European Community for funding. Fortunately they agreed, with only small cuts to our estimated budget. Even more fortunately, we managed to persuade two outstanding students, Lisa Cipolotti and Margarete Delazer, to work with us on the project. Lisa came from Padua to work in Elizabeth's department, and Margarete left Innsbruck to work in Franco's.

So, when Signor Bellini walked into the neuropsychology lab in Padua, Margarete, Franco, and Carlo had an idea what to expect. They noticed that although he scored 20/20 on a written multiplication test, he seemed to be doing it slowly and oddly. When he was re-tested on single-digit multiplication, with visual presentation, and asked to respond promptly without working out the answer, he scored only 3/20. He scored well, and answered quickly, on addition or subtraction, so difficulties in hearing, understanding, or speaking couldn't explain the difference.

On repeated testing, he was always slow on the same multiplication questions. He could manage his ten-times table easily—but of course there's a trick to that. He didn't have to dig the answer out of memory. Questions from the two-times table were also answered swiftly. Again, these could be solved by adding rather than retrieving memorized table facts. Most of the rest, he had to work out. And if he had already worked out the answer to, say, 8×7, in one test, he would still work it out anew on all subsequent tests. This made him different from Dr Constable. Whereas Dr Constable had an access deficit, some-times being able to find the answer in memory, sometimes not, Signor Bellini seemed genuinely to have lost his multiplication facts. How he worked out the answers I'll deal with in Section 3.[30]

Signor Bellini, understandably, also had to work out even very simple division questions, even on the complements of multiplication questions he had already done. So, even if he had worked out 7×6, he still had to work out $42 \div 6$; whereas if he could retrieve 8×2 from memory, then he swiftly produced the answer to $16 \div 2$.

Division
This is evidence, perhaps not surprising, that multiplication is the basis for solving division. But multiplication is not enough. A patient studied by Lisa Cipolotti and Angelo Costello had largely intact multiplication, but still couldn't do division. The patient, a civil engineer, following damage to the left parietal region, could still multiply 2×2, but could-n't solve $4 \div 2$, or even $2 \times ? = 4$. In fact, when he was tested on the multiplications he got right, he was almost always unable to solve the corresponding divisions. Again, it may not be surprising that there are extra operations involved in division, but it is surprising that brain

damage can affect just those operations, suggesting that circuits in the left parietal lobe have become specialized for division procedures.[31]

Signor Bellini's inability to retrieve from memory multiplication facts he had surely known before his stroke suggests that they were stored in circuits separate in the brain from those for addition. But this is a single dissociation, and it remains possible that multiplication is simply harder than addition—just as running is harder than walking— unless we can find the other half of the dissociation: good multiplication fact retrieval but poor addition. There is such a case: Frau Huber. She was, you will recall, far better at pulling out multiplication facts than anything else in arithmetic. It is beginning to look as if we have a case for saying that our brain does like to keep multiplication and addition in separate circuits. For division, we have yet found only a single dissociation with multiplication, and we cannot know what other cases might turn up. However, for most people, carrying out division does depend on a knowledge of multiplication. A simple division is usually solved by turning it into a multiplication problem with an unknown. For example, I solve $63 \div 7$ by trying to find the number which, multiplied by 7, gives 63—in other words, $7 \times ? = 63$. Now, if I am typical (and we have done some research on this which suggests that I am[32]), then the other half of this dissociation will not be found. You can't be good at simple division without being good at multiplication.

UNDERSTANDING NUMBERS

Although Signor Bellini had lost his multiplication tables, he nevertheless was able to solve all the multiplication problems that were put to him. How did he manage it? Of course, to solve 3×6 he could have done $6 + 6 + 6$, but there are more efficient ways of solving multiplication problems, if you know the laws of arithmetic. What Signor Bellini did, making the best possible use of what he knew, is shown in Table 4.2. Although brain damage had severely affected Signor Bellini's memory for his multiplication tables, these strategies show him to be in full command of the laws of arithmetic as they apply to multiplication. These include:

Multiplier	Strategy
2	$N + N$
3	$(N \times 2) + N$
4	$(N \times 2) + (N \times 2)$ $(10N \div 2) - N$
5	$10N \div 2$
6	$10N \div 2 + N$
7	$10N - (2N + N)$ $(10N \div 2) + 2N$
8	$10N - 2N$ $10N \div 2 + (2N + N)$
9	$10N - N$

Table 4.2 Signor Bellini's strategies for muliplying N by numbers from 2 to 9.[33]

Commutativity

$$A \times B = B \times A$$

He always treated complementary problems the same.

Associativity

$$(A \times (B \times C) = (A \times B) \times C) \quad \text{or} \quad A \times (B \div C) = (A \div C) \times B$$

For example, the strategy for 5 uses it explicitly, but with an interesting complication. He takes a problem such as 8×5 and turns it into $10 \times 8 \div 2$, which is equivalent to $10 \div 2 \times 8$. That is, he sees the equivalence of $(10 \times N) \div 2$ and $(10 \div 2) \times N$.

Distributivity

$$(A \times (B - C) = (A \times B) - (A \times C)), \quad (A \times (B + C) = (A \times B) + (A \times C))$$

Strategy	Example
$A \div B = X$	$49 \div 7 = X$
Guess value of X in $B \times X = A$	Guesses 5
	$7 \times 5 = 35$ (solved with strategies)
If not:	
$A - (B \times X) = C$	$49 - 35 = 14$
$C \div B = D$	$14 \div 7 = 2$
$X + D = $ result	$5 + 2 = 7$

Table 4.3 Signor Bellini's strategy for division.[34]

There is an example in the strategy for 8, which he applies to 7×8: $7 \times (10 - 2) = (7 \times 10) - (7 \times 2) = 56$.

He has also retained command of division, for example the laws of cancellation, where $(A \times C) \div (B \times C)$ can be reduced to $A \div B$. So, for example, $28 \div 4$ was solved by first reducing it to $14 \div 2$. And he was able to put laws together to form a quite complicated series of moves to solve what most of us would find a very simple problem: $49 \div 7$, as shown in Table 4.3. This is someone who understands arithmetic well, but has just lost his multiplication facts. Dr Constable, you will recall, also understood arithmetic well, but found it difficult, sometimes impossible, to find the answers in memory.

Unruly Rules

Michael McCloskey and his team at Johns Hopkins University stressed the importance of separating such table facts from arithmetical rules. One of their patients, referred to as 'P.S.', was rather poor at multiplication, making errors in about 20% of single-digit problems, but seemed to have entirely lost her grasp on problems with 0 in them. She almost always said N, in $N \times 0$ or $0 \times N$, for example, $0 \times 6 = 6$. For some reason, halfway through testing, she started to get all these 0 problems right, while still showing the same level of difficulty with other multiplication facts. Other patients have trouble with these rule questions, but then so do normal people. In testing *control* subjects, McCloskey found that they were making a lot of errors.[35] All this suggests that our knowledge of rules like this are stored separately from tables of facts.

READING, WRITING, AND ARITHMETIC

When we learn about numbers at school, and elsewhere, there is more to it than just calculation. We have to learn the numerals, and in the right order. We have to learn how to pronounce each numeral and to be able to write down the numerals we want, or write them to the teacher's dictation. Being able to translate, or, more technically, *transcode*, among the different forms of numbers—spoken, heard, seen, written—is an important skill.

Transcoding is not as easy as it seems. Witness the difficulty children have learning the numerals even when they already know the number words. There are three reasons. First, the basic principle of coding the numbers is different: words are name-valued while numerals are place-valued, as we saw in Chapter 2. We indicate 'one hundred' in words by having a special word to name that value, while we represent it in numerals by placing the 1 to the left of two zeros. Second, and consequently, the syntax of the number words and the numerals is quite different. Third, the sequence of English number names is irregular, with special names for the teens and the decades, while the numeral system is entirely regular (as discussed in Chapter 3).

The input to both the arithmetic system and the transcoding system can be spoken number words, written number words, or numerals. Similarly, the output can be spoken number words, written number words, or numerals. How are these systems linked with the reading and writing of words? Are there separate routes through the brain for *five* and for *fine*, and even a separate route for *5*?

The first clue came in 1892, when Jules Dejerine, a great French neurologist, published the first case of a reading disorder following brain damage. His patient was unable to read words, though he could still write words, but he was able to read and write numerals. Many similar cases have been reported since then. One explanation sometimes proposed has nothing to do with letters and numerals taking different routes through the brain, but with the fact that there are just 10 numerals, but 26 letters and lots of words. The combinatorial problem of reading words is just so much greater than that of reading numerals, even multi-digit numerals. Evidence for separate routing would be strong if we could find a double dissociation—a patient who could read words but not numerals. Signora Gaddi, who could not count above 4, was completely unable to read words or letters. She could not even recognize letters in a task that required her only to pick letters out of an array of similar-sized nonsense shapes. On the other hand, she was still able to read and understand the numerals 1, 2, 3, and 4.

Recently, Lisa Cipolotti discovered two patients, one English and one Italian, who were much better at reading words, including the number words, than the corresponding numerals. The Italian patient was a banker in the early stages of Alzheimer's disease. Dottore Foppa was almost perfect on all Lisa's tests of reading words, including very long words and number words. However, he had great difficulty reading aloud numerals of two digits or longer: he could read *cinquante quattro*, but not *54*. However, he did seem to understand the numerals he couldn't read aloud. For example, Lisa gave him sets of four long numbers to order by size: (e.g. 15,680; 17,630; 1,568; 156,800), and he managed flawlessly. There seemed to be a problem in getting from the numerals to the spoken number words.[36]

In another case Mr Lamb, a retired printer, suffered bleeding in his left parietal lobe and as a result was very poor at reading even single digits. He found two-digit numbers almost impossible. On the other hand, he could read number words without difficulty.[37]

Both these cases had good visual abilities, as their word reading shows, so that their problem with numerals, considered together with other cases in which patients were able to read numerals even though suffering severe dyslexia for words and letters, is evidence that there is a separate input route for numerals.

An even more spectacular dissociation between numbers and words was found in a highly literate woman who underwent surgery on her left frontal lobe. After surgery she complained of reading and writing difficulties. A series of detailed tests by Steven Anderson and his colleagues at the University of Iowa[38] revealed that she was well able to read and write numbers but completely unable to read and write words (Figure 4.6). Even on single letters she could name only half of them. Her visual capacities were intact, since she could read numbers perfectly and carry out other visual tests satisfactorily. And her ability to control her hands was also well preserved, since she was able to write numbers and also draw competently. So, soon after the visual stimulus arrives in the brain, the routes for numbers and words must diverge, and remain separate until just before the final common path leading to the hands.

Our method of double dissociation has revealed again that numerical abilities separate themselves from other, apparently similar, skills. Writing words and writing numerals, reading words and reading numbers, all involve distinct brain circuits, despite having common input pathways from the eyes and common output pathways to the hands.

Within the number transcoding pathways themselves, things can go wrong, as they can in a single transcoding sub-pathway, as Lisa Cipolotti's group discovered with one of her patients, Mr Drummond, who suffered a stroke that affected his left parietal lobe. One type of transcoding was entirely unimpaired: he could read numerals, even six-digit numerals, fluently and flawlessly. But when it came to writing numerals to dictation he made errors when the number had four digits or more. For example, when Lisa tested him on the first day, he wrote, '3000,200' for 'three thousand two hundred'. Even familiar numbers, such as 'one thousand, nine hundred and forty-five', were written as '1000,945'. These are reminiscent of children's errors when they are trying to convert from the name value of words to the place value of numerals, and we interpreted them as the loss of one rule. This is the rule of 'overwriting from the right',[40] for combining the major term, in this case, 'one thousand', with the minor term, 'nine hundred and forty-five' (which in turn has its major term, 'nine hundred', and minor term, 'forty-five'). The major term is 1000, and the minor, 945; to combine them, overwrite the three rightmost zeros with the three numerals of the minor term. If you simply use the developmentally earlier 'concatenation rule', which sticks the major and minor terms together, you get Mr Drummond's error. We are not sure why he always applied overwriting to the hundreds, but we do know that children manage to overwrite in the hundreds when they are still concatenating in the thousands.

On the second day, Mr Drummond began to notice that he

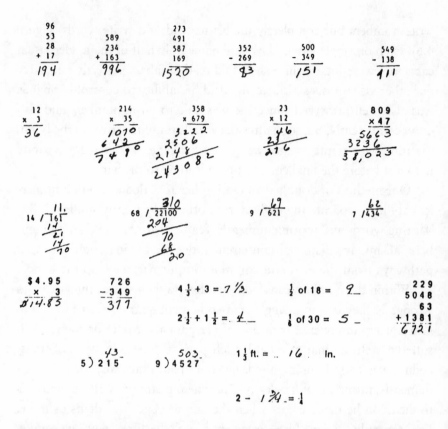

Figure 4.6 The patient who can write numbers but not letters. Donna's visual capacities were intact, since she could read numbers perfectly and carry out other visual tests satisfactorily. And her ability to control her hands was also well-preserved, since she was able to write numbers, and also to draw competently. So, somewhere soon after the visual stimulus arrived in her brain, the routes for numbers and words

was not writing down what Lisa had dictated, since his reading was entirely intact. He'd look at the number and remark, in a puzzled voice, 'That's not what you said.' By the end of the second day he was getting all the dictations correct, and was flawless on day three.

I now turn to the question of how transcoding is organized in the brain in relation to other number skills, and also in relation to verbal skills, including reading. Again, our best evidence comes from careful studies of people with brain damage to find out which subskills are always linked together and which can dissociate. To see whether transcoding and calculation are separate processing streams in the brain, we need to find someone who can calculate but not transcode.

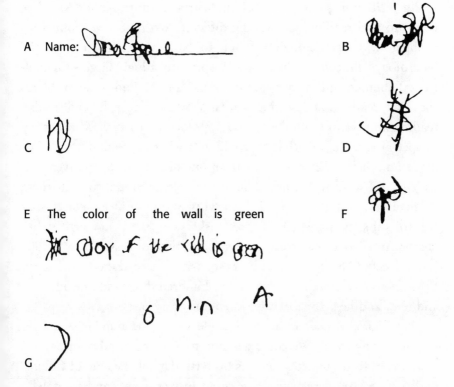

A Name:

B

C

D

E The color of the wall is green

F

G

diverged, and remained separate until just before the final common path leading to the hands. As can be seen, her written arithmetic is neat, confident, and accurate (opposite page). But writing tasks involving letters are a different matter (this page): (a) name; (b) name with eyes closed; (c) letters A and B; (d) letters A and B written left-handed; (e) copying; (f) 'dog' written to dictation; (g) name written with eyes closed and examiner moving the paper. (From Anderson et al.[39])

Not surprisingly perhaps, there are many patients, including, for example, Dr Constable and Signor Tiziano, who despite calculation difficulties could read and write numerals with no problems, and could count and say number words faultlessly. This may mean simply that reading and writing numbers is easier than calculating, and less vulnerable to brain damage. So perhaps this is a pointless search. After all, to calculate we need to understand either the words or the numerals in which the question is posed, and at the same time be able to produce accurately the answer either in spoken number words or in written numerals. If you can do all that, surely you must be able to read the numerals aloud, or write them to dictation.[41]

In 1990, a fifty-seven-year-old industrial chemist, Signor Amadeo, began to find reading and writing difficult. Within a few months his problem was bad enough for him to be referred for tests at the Neurology Clinic in the University Hospital in Padua. His general intellectual abilities and memory were normal, but he had some problems speaking, reading, and writing words. Most strikingly, he had trouble reading and writing numbers. Lisa Cipolotti and I devised a battery of special tests to see what he could and what he couldn't do.[42] We made up a list of 220 test items from one digit (e.g., 6) to seven digits (e.g., 1,469,756). We asked him to read them aloud, to write them to dictation, and also to read them when written out as words. Our control subjects managed all three tasks with just a few errors, but Signor Amadeo was correct only half the time or less. For example, he read '5,000' as 'fifteen hundred thousand'; he read the words *seven thousand one hundred and ten* as 'five hundred thousand one hundred and ten'; and he wrote 'two hundred and forty one' as *2,045*.

But Signor Amadeo had no trouble seeing the numbers, and no trouble saying them. We could ask him to give the number of days in the year, or to recite dates, such as his birth date or the date of Columbus's voyage to America, which he could answer readily and accurately. More remarkably, he was still good at arithmetic, whether spoken (mental) arithmetic or written arithmetic. Even when we gave him sums and subtractions of up to six digits, he was correct 98% of the time.

We then tested him on just those numbers on which he had made transcoding errors—that is, misreading them or writing them incorrectly to dictation. Signor Amadeo was almost perfect when asked to say or to write numbers that were generated internally from a calculation, even when he had previously failed to read them aloud or write them to dictation. Here are a couple of examples. When asked to write to dictation *settanta mila* (seventy thousand), he wrote '17,000'; yet he correctly wrote the answer to the problem '56,748 + 13,252 =', which is 70,000. He read '4,070' as *quattrocentomila settanta* ('four hundred thousand and seventy'); he wrote *quattromila settanta* ('four thousand and seventy') as 1,070. Yet, for the calculation '2,561 + 1,509', he wrote the answer correctly as 4,070.

Overall, he was saying or writing about half the numbers correctly, when he was transcoding, and around 90% when they were produced after a calculation. So it wasn't just that he had lost the ability to write or say certain numbers: he could get them out if they were the result of the calculation. He made errors just in transcoding. It seemed to us highly implausible that writing '70,000' to dictation was *harder* than finding it as the sum of 56,748 and 13,252. Indeed, most patients—and most of us—will be more likely to make more mistakes on the latter. This makes another double dissociation.

We concluded from this case, and others with the opposite and very common condition that they could transcode but not calculate accurately, that there must be two routes from input to output. One is used for calculation, and was still functioning well for Signor Amadeo; a second route is for transcoding—reading numbers aloud and writing them to dictation—and for Signor Amadeo this second route is somewhat damaged. If we have two routes, then we need a way of making sure that we use the right one. So, for example, in an arithmetic test, when we see '$7 \times 9 =$' it is not appropriate simply to say 'seven times nine equals'. This means that when we select one route we have to be able to prevent the other one from operating.

MISSING THE MEANING[43]

Signor Strozzi was a market trader in northern Italy when a stroke damaged his left hemisphere, severely affecting his speech.[44] My colleague Margarete Delazer assessed him as having difficulties both in speech production and in understanding what other people said. His general intellectual ability on a non-verbal test, however, quickly recovered. He could read and write single digits, and count out loud up to 10. Margarete noticed that when he was asked to pick the larger of two numbers, or two arrays of dots, he was abnormally slow. Even more strikingly, he was as bad on simple calculations as anyone Margarete had tested. He found it impossible to add 2 and 2, whether you showed him the numerals or read the problem to him. He couldn't subtract or multiply, either. There was one further thing he could do: If you presented the addition in dots, not numerals, he could work out the answer. This he did by counting all the dots in the problem (Figure

4.7). Signor Strozzi turned out to suffer one of the most specific and profound deficits we had ever seen in a patient, a deficit that targeted the core meaning of number expressions, their numerosities.

Margarete and I had had many discussions about number meanings. In Chapter 1, I discussed the way in which numerical expressions can have quite different meanings: there are numerosities (five eggs), but there are also numbers for ordering (fifth house) and for labelling (Channel 5). Children learning about numbers have to keep these meanings separate and clear, even though their environment mixes them up. We were influenced by the work of Karen Fuson in Chicago on the way in which these meanings are learned, and the role of counting in both learning the separate meanings and, later, integrating the meanings into an ordered sequence of numerosities.[46]

The critical test was number comparison: having to pick the larger of two numbers. If you have no idea of the sizes of numbers—of their numerosities—you will be unable to do this task in the normal way. However, Margarete had already seen that Signor Strozzi could do this accurately, though slowly. There is an absolutely solid result, perhaps the most reliable effect in cognitive psychology, though, strangely, it was not discovered until 1967.[47] It is this: the time it takes to identify which is the larger of two numbers (or the smaller) depends on their difference. It takes longer to pick 9 from the pair 9, 8 than from the pair 9, 1. There's even a mathematical law that relates the difference to the time.

There are few abilities more basic to numeracy than being able to decide which is the larger of two numbers. Whole numbers are completely ordered by numerosity. Any abnormality in how Signor Strozzi compared numbers would indicate a very serious problem indeed, since it implies that something could be amiss with his grasp of the core concept of numerosity itself. As I argued in Chapter 1, numerosity is the foundation of arithmetic. Addition of A and B means finding the numerosity of the *union* of the two collections with numerosities A and B. Children understand this: if a collection of sweets with numerosity A is added to a separate collection with numerosity B, then you put the two collections together and count the result, the union, to give you the sum of A and B. If arithmetical facts are normally represented and organized by numerosities; if, for exam-

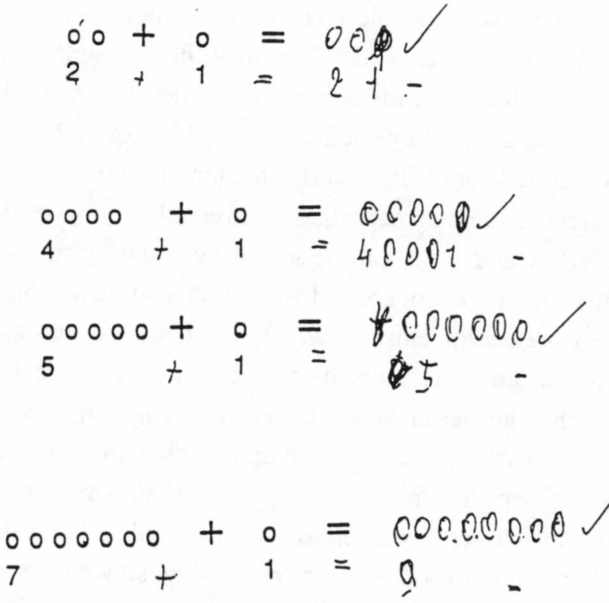

$$oo + o = ooo \checkmark$$
$$2 + 1 = 2 \; ... \; -$$

$$oooo + o = ooooo \checkmark$$
$$4 + 1 = 4 \; ooo1 \; -$$

$$ooooo + o = ooooooo \checkmark$$
$$5 + 1 = 05 \; -$$

$$oooooo + o = ooooooo \checkmark$$
$$7 + 1 = 9 \; -$$

Figure 4.7 Signor Strozzi, a market trader, suffered a stroke which severely affected his ability to do simple calculations, although he was still able to count. He used counting to carry out almost all the numerical tasks we presented to him. When faced with problems expressed both in numerals and in the form of strings of O's, he was able to add only by using a counting procedure and applying it to the O's. (From Delazer & Butterworth[45])

ple, multiplication or addition facts are ordered by the size of one of their operands, as indeed they are when they are taught to us, then what would become of these representations if the idea of numerosity itself has been affected by brain damage?

Margarete created a test to see how long Signor Strozzi took to compare two single-digit numbers. He would see two numerals on a computer monitor; his task was to press the right button if the larger was on the right and the left button if it was on the left. And he was to do it as quickly as possible. Remarkably, when the difference, the 'split', as we call it, was larger, it took him *longer* to make the judgement. This is absolutely contrary to the normal result. Why was this? Suppose that, instead of comparing the numerosities of the two numbers directly, he tried counting from one to the other. Then it would take him longer to get from 1 to 9 than from 8 to 9. Of course, he wouldn't know which one to start with, so he would pick one at random perhaps, or choose the leftmost one, to start with.[48] We knew he was able to count. The decision as to which was the larger would then be made like this: if I start with A and get to B by counting, then B is larger; if I don't (if, say, I get to 10 before I get to B), then A is the larger number.

Margarete made a remarkable discovery that supported this interpretation. $A + 1$ and $1 + A$ can be solved by counting the next number after A, but only if you understand what numerosities are. Signor Strozzi couldn't do these problems. However, whenever he was asked 'What number comes after A?', which is numerically but not conceptually equivalent, then he was always able to give the right answer. After a few weeks, his comparison times speeded up and the pattern became increasingly normal: smaller splits taking longer than larger splits. Fifteen weeks after his stroke, his comparison times looked normal, if a shade slow. As his comparison times were recovering, so were his arithmetical skills, not to normal levels admittedly, but he was scoring about 75% on single-digit problems. We could attribute his arithmetical improvement to the restoration of his sense of numerosity; however, we have only a correlation, and we cannot infer causes from correlations alone. The case of Signor Strozzi shows that the logical differences in number meanings outlined in Chapter 1 are reflected in brain organization.

Taken together, the ways in which brain damage either impairs or spares the different abilities in the patients provide the outline of how the Mathematical Brain is related to other cognitive and perceptual functions in the brain, and also the way the components of the Mathematical Brain are organized. Neuropsychologists call the diagram of relationship of these processes their 'functional architecture' (Figure 4.8).

LEFT BRAIN, RIGHT BRAIN

The next problem is to locate the functional architecture in the actual architecture of the brain. How are the number circuits arranged in the brain? Are they all in the same hemisphere? Is there a single brain region dedicated exclusively to numerical processes—is the Mathematical Brain a well-defined neural structure? To begin to answer these questions, we

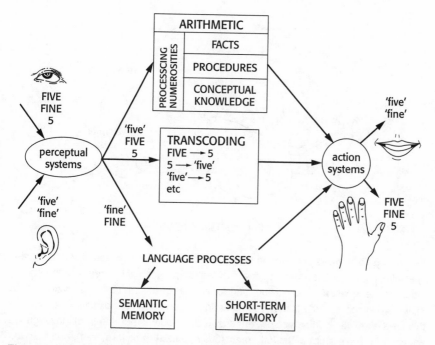

Figure 4.8 The 'functional architecture' of arithmetic. People experience numbers in many ways—as spoken words, as printed numerals, and so on. This means that the brain has two jobs. First, it has to separate numbers from other inputs, such as words that don't refer to numbers, and second, it has to treat numbers in a way appropriate to the current task. Our studies of patients show that there are separate routes through the brain from input to output for the task of 'transcoding' (reading and writing numbers) and for arithmetic. However, both routes converge on the same systems for saying and writing numbers.

have to understand the overall structure of the brain. Figure 4.9 shows how the main perceptual and action circuits are arranged.

The brain is organized into many specialist areas which have quite definite tasks. In perception there are specialists for detecting edges of objects, colour, location in space, and so on. There are also specialists for controlling action. One curious feature of brain organization is that the specialists for the right side of the body are in the left hemisphere of the brain, and for the left side of the body in the right hemisphere. That is, the main perceptual and action circuits cross over: the left hand is controlled by the right hemisphere, sounds going into the left ear are analyzed primarily in the right auditory cortex, and the left visual field (what you see to the left of your centre line) is analyzed in the right

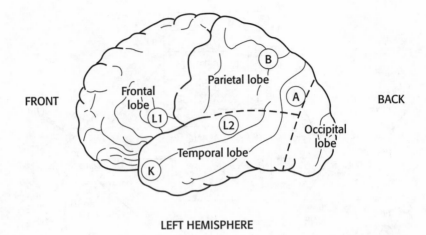

LEFT HEMISPHERE

Figure 4.9 The areas of the brain in which numbers are processed. The brain areas specialized for processing numbers are in the left parietal lobe. Area A in the inferior lobule is the location for subitizing, and forms part of the circuit for analyzing where things are in space. Area B may control hand shape and finger position (I explain why this area is critical in Chapter 5). Areas A and B are both separated from the language areas L1 (Broca's area) in the left frontal lobe and L2 (Wernicke's area), and from the principal repository of general knowledge (K), both of which are in the left temporal lobe. (Areas which serve number processing but other functions as well, such as the visual, auditory, and motor areas, are not shown.)

hemisphere. The two hemispheres are linked by the *corpus callosum*, a massive tract of more than 200 million long neural fibres that carry information from one hemisphere to the other.

Number processes share the main perceptual and action systems with other processes. But one brain area emerges as a key area for numbers: the left parietal lobe. It is the area that is almost always demonstrably damaged in cases of acalculia. Patients with other cognitive abilities shot to pieces, but with preserved numerical skills, seem to have the left parietal lobe intact. This doesn't mean that no other brain areas are specialized for some number abilities. Does the right hemisphere play any part in number tasks? We all know, or at least many people believe, that the left hemisphere is sequential, logical, and analytic, while the right hemisphere is parallel, global, and artistic. Perhaps the left brain does all the work while the right brain appreciates the beauty of numbers. How can we find out what the right side of the brain does? There are four ways.

What are the effects of right-hemisphere damage? First, we can study patients with lesions in the right hemisphere to see what effects this might have on numerical skills. The problem here is that we are not sure which part of the right hemisphere we should be looking at, and lesions in irrelevant areas will have no effect. There are two ways round this. We could survey a whole group of patients with right-hemisphere lesions and compare them with a group of patients with left-hemisphere lesions. For simple arithmetic, as measured by Jackson and Warrington's Graded Difficulty Arithmetic test, lesions in the left hemisphere caused severe acalculia in 16% of patients (patients who scored worse than 99% of control subjects), while lesions in the right hemisphere resulted in no such severe problems.[49] On the other hand, there is evidence that one of the most basic numerical abilities, the ability to subitize, may be represented in both the left and right hemispheres since damage to the right parietal lobe will, in some cases, lead to an impairment in this ability.[50]

Nothing left. A second approach is to find people who have had the whole of their left hemispheres removed, so that whatever they can still do must be the responsibility of the right hemisphere. One such patient was a Vietnam veteran studied by Jordan Grafman and his colleagues.[51] Normal arithmetic seemed to have been abolished almost completely, though the patient could still identify the numerosity of a collection of objects, recognize numerals, and compare number magnitudes. Incidentally, almost all language ability, a left-hemisphere function, had been lost.

Split brains. Third, we could look at 'split-brain' patients in order to examine what happens to the specialist processes in each hemisphere. If a visual stimulus, for example a numeral, is presented to the left visual field it will be processed in the right hemisphere. If it is presented in the centre of the visual field, which is where you are now reading, then it will go into both hemispheres. Similarly, if you touch an object with your left hand, this information will be processed by your right hemisphere. In most of us, the brain areas that control speech are in the left hemisphere. This means that when you name a numeral presented to the right hemisphere, the information has to be passed across the corpus callosum into the left hemisphere so that it can make contact with language systems.

In practice, finding out which side of the brain does what turns out to be very difficult. Normal human brains, as you may expect, transfer the information through the corpus callosum, when necessary, to the specialist that normally does the job in hand. The most we can observe is that material presented to the wrong side of the brain is processed slightly more slowly because extra time is needed, often just a few milliseconds, to transfer it from the wrong side to the hemisphere containing the appropriate specialist. When the corpus callosum has suffered damage or has been deliberately cut by the surgeon, then the two hemispheres operate more or less independently, so we can see what each does. This is why these patients have been so important in the development of neuropsychology, and why Roger Sperry, the pioneer investigator of split brains, received the Nobel Prize for Physiology or Medicine in 1981.

Most of the brains split by the neurosurgeon had been suffering from severe intractable epilepsy. This is why the operation is carried out: to stop the epileptic seizures spreading from their focus into the other hemisphere and making their effects so much more intense. Non-surgical lesions occur when a blood vessel bursts. This usually destroys just part of the corpus callosum, thereby interrupting the transfer of just particular types of information—those processed by brain areas immediately adjacent to the damaged fibres.

This is what happened to a patient referred to Paris's famous neurological hospital, La Salpêtrière (where Jean-Martin Charcot taught Sigmund Freud about advanced neurology, and hysteria). The posterior part was destroyed, which prevented communication between the visual areas. In a brilliant series of experiments, comparing the presentation of stimuli to one side of the brain or the other, Laurent Cohen and Stanislas Dehaene showed that the patient could recognize numerals in both hemispheres. We have known since the work of Jules Dejerine in the late nineteenth century that the right hemisphere could recognize and read numerals even when reading words was impossible.

The patient could even compare the magnitude of single-digit numbers in both hemispheres, though with a 13% error rate, and she was slower than when the numerals were presented to the right hemisphere. She was very bad at naming numerals presented to the right hemisphere, but errors showed an interesting and important pattern. When she was wrong, the number name she produced was similar in magnitude to the target (more similar than one would expect by chance). If she saw '5', she might say *quatre* or *six*. What she could not do was arithmetic of any sort. Cohen and Dehaene conclude that she was unable to transfer the identity of the numerals across the corpus callosum to the left hemisphere for naming, whereas she could transfer approximate size information. The reason for this is that the anterior fibres of the corpus callosum, the fibres that connect the two parietal lobes, were still intact; according to their theory, the parietal lobe in each hemisphere is able to process analogue magnitudes—sizes. Since the information is only approximate, she will make mistakes, but these won't be outlandish mistakes. She will never say *neuf* when her right hemisphere reads '2'. Although her right hemisphere was able to manage these very simple numerical tasks, though less efficiently than the left hemisphere, calculation was virtually impossible. She made errors on half the occasions she was asked to add 1 to a single digit. Even when the task did not require a spoken response—and hence the involvement of the left hemisphere— but a pointing response or just indicating whether a sum was right or wrong, she was still very bad. This supports the idea that calculation is exclusively the job of the left hemisphere.[52]

Is numerosity represented in both hemispheres? According to Cohen and Dehaene, when we compare numbers we use an analogue representation of their size, in much the same way we might compare the water levels in two glasses. They claim that this representation is used by both hemispheres, and is what can still be transferred across the anterior fibres in their patient's corpus callosum. Even if the right hemisphere uses analogue magnitudes, which is why responses originating from it tend to be approximate, the left hemisphere could still be using numerosity representations, which is why responses originating there are almost always exactly right. Of course, the left hemisphere might be able to represent analogue magnitudes as well, but the crucial point is that only the left hemisphere can represent numerosity.

Imaging the brain in action. Fourth, it is now possible to image human brain activity while it is occurring, using one of several new methods that do not require the skull to be opened up (though there is that method as well). They all depend on the fact that when brain areas become active, the blood flow to them is increased, and with it comes an increase in the metabolism of glucose and in electrical activity.

Measuring electrical activity is the easiest, and the longest established, technique—known as electroencephalography (EEG). Electrodes are attached to the scalp and they respond almost instantaneously to changes in electrical activity in the brain. The problem is to discover which part of the brain is generating the electricity: the electrodes are not on the brain itself, of course, so electrical currents are refracted through the fluid surrounding the brain, and through bone, skin, and hair. The more electrodes there are, the better is the fix on the underlying generator.

Measuring blood flow and glucose metabolism is more difficult. An increase in metabolism means an increased consumption of oxygen. Now, if you are breathing a radioactive isotope of oxygen, $^{15}O_2$, which emits positrons, a machine can detect the by-products of this emission: gamma-rays emitted when the positron collides with an electron and both are annihilated. Clever use of detectors and computers has meant that the source of the positrons in the brain can be calculated. This method is called positron emission tomography (PET). To get a good picture of what is going on, the brain really has to be doing the same thing for a considerable period of time—half a minute at least, even with the newest machines and the fanciest statistical techniques. Most of the brain tends to be active all of the time, so it is a problem to pin down the part of that activity, as measured by PET, that is due to mathematical work and not to daydreaming, worrying about the mortgage, or even doing other things relevant to the task in hand, such as reading the numbers or speaking the response. The way daydreaming is eliminated is by averaging over many trials of, say, mental multiplication, and over several brains, with the assumption that the different daydreams or worries will somehow balance out, and the most consistent activity will be from the mental multiplication task.

But within that task, how can we tell which brain states are due to numerical processes—say, multiplication—and which are due to visual processing of the stimulus, and which are due to generating a spoken response? The standard method is this. Find a task that requires everything that the multiplication task requires, except for the multiplication itself. One possibility would be to have a task in which the subject reads aloud the digit. In both tasks there is visual processing of the stimulus and a spoken response. One can even arrange the two tasks so that exactly the same stimuli are used in them, or exactly the same responses. For example, in the multiplication task you see 6 × 3 and say 'eighteen'; in the control task, you see 6 × 3 but simply read aloud 'six times three'. Then you measure all the brain activation for the multiplication task and all the brain activity for the reading, and subtract the second from the first, point by point in the brain, leaving just the extra activity for the multiplication task. With any luck, this will be located where you expect it: namely in the parietal lobe.

Unfortunately, this exact investigation has yet to be done. Studies of numerical processes using functional brain imaging are still in their infancy, but they hold out the hope of being able to localize the circuits with much more accuracy than is possible from lesion studies, and, combined with EEG, we should be able to determine very precisely both when and where these processes are occurring.

THE LEFT PARIETAL LOBE

We have seen a whole series of patients whose numerical abilities were affected when just one brain area was damaged: the parietal lobe in the left hemisphere. We have also seen patients whose brains have suffered damage, often quite widespread, that have affected other cognitive processes, but have spared the numerical ones.

The parietal lobe is actually quite a big area of the brain, stretching from the central sulcus all the way back to the occipital lobes. Not all of this area is devoted to numbers. The current best guess is that a relatively small part, the inferior lobule, is the core of our numerical abilities. It is difficult to be precise for two reasons. First, our best evidence at the moment comes from patients, and unfortunately the things that cause the brain damage—strokes and diseases—don't target just this part of the brain. In every patient the damage will affect other regions, possibly unconnected with numbers, but we cannot tell which part of the lesion is which. Second, everyone's brain is different in size, in shape, and in the pattern of folding. Although the major landmarks are easy to locate, a small area might be much harder to identify in different brains. In one brain it could be tucked into the side of a sulcus (groove), while in another it may be nearer the top of the gyrus (the bump).

The best hope of pinning down the crucial part of the left parietal lobe is through imaging the brain in action while it is doing very well-defined and well-understood numerical tasks. But imaging methods are still in their early stages of development, and we don't yet know quite what we are seeing through the scanning cameras. We are in a position similar to Galileo using the first telescopes. This made possible unprecedented advances in astronomy. He knew that light from the sky was causing the images he could see, but he had no theory of optics. There was thus a big logical jump from the spots of light on the eyepiece to the moons of Jupiter. Crucially, when we image the brain in action, we need to identify just those bits of the activity that are devoted to numbers. Since the brain is always busy doing lots of tasks, from monitoring the environment to controlling breathing to wondering about dinner, we still need to find good ways of sorting out the activity we are interested in.

Nevertheless, it is now clear that our Mathematical Brain is located in the left parietal lobe. Why it should be there is the subject of the next chapter.

HAND, SPACE, AND BRAIN

For *Fingers*, by ordinance of nature, and the unrepeatable statute of the great Arithmetician, were appointed to serve for casting counters, as quicke and native digits, alwaies ready at *Hand* to assist us in our computations.

JOHN BULWER, *CHIROLOGIA*, 1644

In this chapter I want to ask, and try to answer, a rather strange question: why is the number area in the left parietal lobe of our brains? This is a strange question because we don't usually ask why—it just is where it is. However, it can be a sensible question. We know why the primary visual cortex is in the occipital lobe at the back of the brain: it is because this is where the nerves from the eye project. We can trace the nerves from the retina in the eye via just a few synapses, joins between nerves, to this region of cortex. There is thus a simple anatomical answer.[1]

But this seems a rather distant analogy. The primary visual cortex is connected to a special organ, the eye, which has evolved for detecting visual features of the world. On the other hand, the essence of number, as I have argued, is its abstractness. The visual properties of things to be counted do not matter much, even to the infant (as we saw in Chapter 3), and we can count things that have no visual properties at all, such as drumbeats or virtues. There can be no number-detecting organ analogous to the eye, so no brain region hard-wired to it for analyzing its output.

A closer analogy is our ability to use language. Until very recently in evolutionary time, the only channel for language has been between mouth and ear. Speaking involves controlling about a hundred muscles, most of them in the head, but also the muscles of the larynx in the throat and the respiratory muscles in the chest and abdomen. In the course of normal speech we make about 14 different sounds per second, which implies some 1,400 instructions to the muscles. Speech is thus a highly complex motor skill. Similarly, decoding the speech we hear requires us to identify 14 different sounds per second, or about 2 words a second, and identifying which, of the 75,000 words we know, each of them is. This requires fast, and very sophisticated, auditory processing.[2] But the elements of language are also abstract—the words and the sentences, the mental lexicon and the mental grammar that underlie them, the meanings and the connotations. Where in the brain are these abstract elements organized? The answer turns out to be instructive. The first main area was discovered in 1861 by French neurologist Paul Broca, and it is now known as Broca's area. It turns out to be an extension of what is called the motor cortex—a strip of the frontal lobe critically involved in the control of movements. What's more, it lies very close to those parts of the motor cortex that control the lips and the tongue. When Broca's area is damaged, causing Broca's aphasia, typical symptoms are problems with speaking, though understanding speech may be preserved.[3]

The other main area was discovered by a young German neurologist called Carl Wernicke in 1874, and this is adjacent to the auditory cortex in the temporal lobe. Needless to say, the area is called Wernicke's area, and the symptoms of damage to it are called Wernicke's aphasia. Unlike Broca's aphasia, speech remains fluent; the principal difficulty is in *understanding* speech. It is as if the relatively abstract language functions have colonized brain areas adjacent to the main motor and sensory areas that serve it. There is one potentially complicating factor. Both Broca's and Wernicke's areas are lateralized, which means that they are in just one hemisphere, usually the left hemisphere, which is the one connected to the right hand—for most of us the dominant hand. For most left-handers, perhaps 70% are also left-lateralized for language, compared to over 95% for right-handers.[4] You will recall from Chapter 4 that, like language abilities, numerical abilities are lateralized in the left hemisphere.

At a broad-brush level, then, there is a precedent for looking for the brain circuits for relatively abstract abilities. There are also two intriguing facts which suggest that 'why' may not be a silly question after all.

First, damage to the human parietal lobe can result not only in difficulties with numbers, but also in problems with orientation in space, with control of actions, and with representations of our own bodies. This bundle of difficulties goes together under the name of 'Gerstmann's Syndrome'. Josef Gerstmann was the first, in 1924, to notice that these disorders are often found together. There has been a long debate over whether these difficulties are bundled together because the regions that do the job happen to be close together in the brain, irrigated by the same artery, so that damage in that region is likely to affect all the jobs. Gerstmann himself thought that they were related functionally, because our representations of numbers are intimately bound up with our representations of space and body, especially our fingers. A few of us, perhaps about 14%, think of numbers in spatial terms.[5] Try for a moment to picture in your mind's eye the sequence of numbers from 1 onwards. Does it form a line? If so, in which direction does it go? For most people who do see a line, it is from left to right, though some report right to left, and for others the line goes straight up.

The second fact is that all of us, at some time or another in our lives, count on our fingers. There seems to be a very close connection between fingers, counting, and number. Could it be that the representation of numerosities that we form in our brain has something to do with the representations we form of our fingers? This is the idea I want to explore in this chapter: does the connection between fingers, space, and numbers explain why numbers are in the parietal lobe?

FINGER-COUNTING AND EARLY ARITHMETIC

The historian of numbers Tobias Dantzig wrote, 'Whenever a counting technique, worthy of the name, exists at all, finger-counting has been found either to precede it or accompany it.'[6] The etymology of our number names is rooted in the words for fingers and hands—the words for 'five' and 'fingers' share the same Indo-European root; in Slavic languages the word for 'five' is very similar to the word for 'fist'; and in many, quite unrelated languages, the word for 'five' is the word for 'hand'. In English the word 'digit' also means a finger or toe. It seems clear from this that counting on fingers preceded counting with special words.

We saw in Chapter 2 that some cultures count on their toes, and on other parts of the body too, including the testicles and penis. These cultures use body parts—and their names—as a standard collection that can be used to determine the numerosities of other collections. This method uses the principle of numerosity because it matches the numerosity of the body parts to the numerosity of the collection to be counted. Naturally, the most commonly used body parts are fingers. There are obvious reasons for this. First, they are handy. They are usually not covered by clothing; they are readily visible to the counter and any audience; they are movable and manipulable (literally). Most important, it is easy to put them into clear one-to-one correspondences with the collection of things to be counted, whether they are physical objects or abstract entities (think how you announce a collection of points you wish to make in an argument).

Actually, body-part counting, such as that used by the Yupno (Figure 2.8), is more advanced than the principle of numerosity. First, the body parts are always used in the same order: counting always starts with the left little finger, 6 is always the right little finger, and so on, until 33, the penis. This means that each body part (or its name) can denote a number without the need to count out each of its predecessors. This method implies a strict ordered succession of numbers in terms of their size: each successive body part denotes a bigger number than its predecessor. This may seem obvious, but it's a big conceptual step forward. Holding up three fingers on the left hand and four on the right hand in itself implies no order: they are just two numerosities; as we saw in Chapter 3, children and animals may be able to distinguish numerosities without being able to order them by magnitude.

Finger Dialects

You might have imagined that there is only one way to use your fingers in counting using just the principle of numerosity—namely, the way you happen to have learned how to do it. You would be wrong. Here's a test: hold up fingers to represent 3. If you held up your index, middle, and ring fingers, you are from Northern Europe or one of its colonial outposts (USA, Australia, etc.). If you held up your thumb, index, and middle fingers, then you are from the Mediterranean. France, by the way, is divided north–south by finger-counting. As a consequence, holding up a thumb does not mean '1' to a Northern European, nor does holding up an index finger mean '1' to a Mediterranean.

Finger dialects can therefore be as much a clue to a person's origins as their spoken dialect was to Professor Henry Higgins in Shaw's play *Pygmalion*. The cosmologist John Barrow gives an example:

> During the Second World War, in India, a young Indian girl found herself having to introduce one of her oriental friends to an Englishman who appeared at her home. The problem was that her girlfriend was Japanese and would have been immediately arrested were this to become known. So, she sought to disguise her nationality by telling her English visitor that her friend was Chinese. He was somewhat suspicious and then surprised them both by asking the oriental girl to do something very odd: 'Count with your fingers! Count to five!' he demanded. The Indian girl was shocked. Was this man out of his mind, she wondered, or was this another manifestation of the English sense of humour? Yet the oriental girl seemed unperturbed, and raised her hand to count out on her fingers, one, two, three, four, five. The man let out a cry of triumph, 'You see she is not Chinese; she is Japanese. Didn't you see how she did it? She began with her hand open and bent her fingers in one by one. Did you ever see a Chinese do such a thing? Never! The Chinese count like the English. Beginning with the first closed, opening the fingers out one by one!'

Barrow doesn't report what became of the Japanese girl once her nationality had been exposed.[7]

Being suspicious myself, not of nationalities but of what I read in books, I tried this experiment on my Japanese colleague, Naoki Shibahara. I asked him to show me five on his fingers. He raised his fingers, just as I would do. Was he secretly Chinese pretending to be Japanese? Had Barrow got it all wrong? No. Showing numbers is not the same as counting out. When I asked him to count one, two, three, four, five, he duly started with an open hand and bent his fingers successively. If you watch English people counting by touching their fingers, they don't always start with 'one' on the index finger, 'two' on the middle, as they would if they were displaying a number. They might count from their little finger, or from their thumb.

No one nowadays is formally taught to finger-count in the locally approved way. But like many informal gestural systems, there are 'dialects'. For example, rotating an index finger against the temple, where I come from, means 'mad', while in Italy it means 'thinking', showing that some aspects of these systems are learned from other members of the society.

Bede's Finger Bending

Once the principle of numerosity has been succeeded by the name principle, then numbers larger than the numerosity of fingers, or of other body parts, can be devised. Because it's so useful, finger-counting methods—actually, one finger-counting method—has been an important part of our heritage from classical antiquity. Juvenal wrote:

> Happy is he who so many times over the years has cheated death
> And now reckons his age on the right hand.[8]

His readers would all have known that one hundred was counted on the right hand. The practice continued long after Juvenal's Rome was no more, as we shall see in a moment.

The greatest historian of the Middle Ages,[9] the Venerable Bede, wrote a very influential book, *De computo vel loquela digitorum* ('On Calculating and Speaking with the Fingers'), at the beginning of the eighth century. The finger-counting system depicted therein seems to represent the Roman system of at least 700 years earlier, perhaps with extensions. We have no Roman manuscripts of the period, but two coins in the British Museum have VII and VIII on one face with the finger signs on the reverse, and these are identical to those described by Bede. The system was universal throughout Europe.[10] As you can see from Figure 5.1, this system goes beyond the principle of numerosity. Bede went on to show how you can represent 1,000,000, which is rather more than the numerosity of the fingers of two hands. The system involved positions of individual fingers, bending the fingers at the first joint (articulus) for the units up to 5, and at the knuckle for units above 5. There is a lot of finger-bending—*flexus digitorum*.

Bede explained how it was possible to go beyond 9,000:

If you wish to say ten thousand, place the back of your left hand against your chest with the fingers extended, and point to the neck ... [for 90,000] place the left hand over the small of the back, the thumb pointing toward the groin (ands thus forward). Then for one hundred thousand up to nine hundred thousand do the same on the right side of the body in the same order. For ten times one hundred thousand (which is one million), place both hands together with the fingers interlaced.[12]

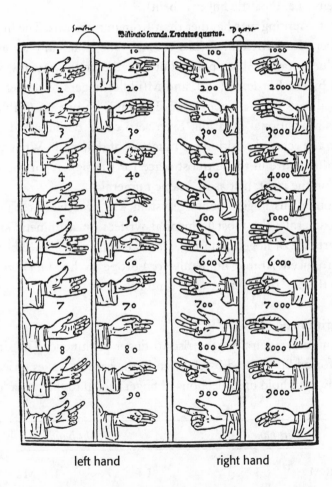

left hand   right hand

Figure 5.1 Bede's finger counting, as depicted in the *Summa de arithmetica* of the Italian mathematician Luca Pacioli (see Chapter 2). The book was published in 1494, nearly 800 years after Bede described the system, demonstrating the enduring value of finger-counting to arithmetic. (As reproduced in Menninger[11])

This system continued to be depicted in books, presumably because it was still in widespread use, well into the eighteenth century.

Although Europeans now count by extending their digits, rather than bending them, bending is probably as widespread as extending, even for small numbers. We have seen that this is still the Japanese method, and many indigenous American tribes, such as Dene-Dinje, use this method, starting with the open hand and bending the little finger for 'one', the ring finger for 'two', and so on until there is a complete fist. Their words for numbers exactly reflect this: 1 is 'the end is bent' (i.e. the little finger is bent).[13]

Finger-counting was handier than Roman numerals. The historian of numbers Karl Menninger has argued that it actually anticipated place-value notation.[14] He points out that the units were always represented by the L(ittle), R(ing), and M(iddle) fingers of the left hand; the tens always by the I(ndex) and T(humb), and so on (Table 5.1). This was a positional notation. Even zero could be indicated, by the fingers in the relaxed position for numbers of that rank. What's more, although units are in the leftmost place for the signer, for the viewer they are on the right, just as in Arabic numerals!

Although this finger-counting system was eventually replaced by Arabic numerals, the most influential writers on arithmetic stressed the importance of finger-counting, from Leonardo of Pisa (Fibonacci), who introduced Arabic numerals to Europe in his *Liber abaci* in 1202, to the end of the eighteenth century.

Finger Arithmetic

Finger-counting naturally gave rise to finger arithmetic. The simplest method for addition, used by children in the earliest stages of learning arithmetic, is to hold up collections of fingers equal to the two addends,

Left hand		Right hand	
L R M	I T	I T	L R M
Units	Tens	Hundreds	Thousands

Table 5.1 Positional notation in finger-counting.

for example 3 fingers on the left hand and 4 fingers on the right, and then count all of the fingers raised. Much more sophisticated methods, based on the system Bede described, were very widely used.

Using fingers for more advanced calculation is now almost unknown among adults in numerate cultures, yet, as Dantzig notes, 'Only a few hundred years ago finger counting was such a widespread custom in Western Europe that no manual of arithmetic was complete unless it gave full instructions in the method.'[15] In his *Liber abaci*, which introduced arithmetical methods based on Arabic place notation, Leonardo of Pisa nevertheless abjures his readers that 'multiplication with the fingers must be practiced constantly, so that the mind like the hands becomes more adept at adding and multiplying'.[16] The greatest ingenuity was displayed in devising rules for adding and multiplying numbers on one's fingers. The art of using fingers in counting and arithmetic was one of the chief accomplishments of an educated man, ranking with reading and writing words.

Here's one way of multiplying on the fingers, as described by Dantzig:

> To this day [about 1930], the peasant of central France (Auvergne) uses a curious method for multiplying numbers above 5. If he wishes to multiply 9×8 he bends down 4 fingers on his left hand (4 being the excess of 9 over 5), and 3 fingers on his right hand ($8 - 5 = 3$). Then the number of bent-down fingers gives him the tens of the result ($4 + 3 = 7$), while the product of the unbent fingers gives him the units ($1 \times 2 = 2$).[17]

This method was once very widespread, and is probably very ancient.

Use It or Lose It

To use finger-counting required precise accurate control of finger movements and handshapes, and of the positions of the fingers and hands in space. Even for the Yupno, the left little finger meant 1, and the right little finger meant 5. In Bede's system the difference between units and hundred was encoded by left and right. To be skilled meant exercising the parts of the brain specifically responsible for handshapes, finger positions, and orientation in space, particularly the personal space defined by one's own body coordinates. We are now coming to realize that, with use, the brain areas become larger, and the brain cells within them become more densely interconnected.[18] And conversely, when a brain area isn't used, just like other unused parts and organs of the body become atrophied, it shrinks and cells within it die more quickly. Using finger-counting on a regular basis would therefore increase the size, structure, and efficiency of the brain areas that control it in the parietal lobes, especially in the left parietal lobe.

LEARNING WITH FINGERS

Even in cultures which possess perfectly good number words and perfectly good numerals, people still use fingers to count and to do simple arithmetic. Children do it in all cultures, apparently without any explicit instruction, indeed often where formal instruction discourages or even forbids the use of fingers. As adults, we frequently touch the objects we are counting to ensure that each object has been counted once and once only. Even Sarah Boysen's chimpanzees (Chapter 3) have been observed to touch the objects that they have to enumerate.

Children who have yet to acquire more than two counting words can still use their fingers to represent numerosities. A nice example of this comes from a study of Julien, son of the French psychologist Rémi Brissiaud. Being a product of a French nursery school, where our familiar numerals and number words were forbidden, Julien's only exposure to counting was at home. Here's what happened when Brissiaud tried to teach Julien to count to three. The boy was 2 years 11 months old and knew only the words for one and two.

FATHER: See, there is one, two, three: there are three tokens. Go ahead, do what I did.

JULIEN (pointing to each token successively): One, one, one.

Julien shows here that he can point to each token once and only once, and he can put each token into one-to-one correspondence with a counting word; it just happens that the word is 'one'. However, he can use his fingers to count beyond one, or even 'two', his other counting word, as you can see in the next dialogue.

> FATHER (displaying a set of two tokens): Show me with your fingers how many tokens there are.

> (Julien raises the thumb and the index finger of the right hand.)

> FATHER: Good! Now what do you call that in tokens?
> JULIEN: Two.
> FATHER (displaying a set of three tokens): Show me with your fingers how many tokens there are.

> (Julien looks at the set of tokens and then at his fingers. He holds up his thumb, his index finger, and the middle finger of his right hand while holding down the ring finger and little finger with his left hand.)

> FATHER: Yes! What do you call that in tokens?

> (Julien makes no response.)

Julien went on to increase the numbers he could reliably show on his fingers, but did not learn to recite the corresponding words for nearly two more years. He even did simple addition and subtraction in his head by imagining the appropriate hand shapes. Here is how we know that this is what happened:

> FATHER: Do you remember how many mistakes [in a picture] there are?
> JULIEN (holding up six fingers): Six.
> FATHER: How many have you found?
> JULIEN (counting on the picture with his index finger): Four.
> FATHER: So how many more do you have to find?
> JULIEN (immediately holding up his two thumbs): Two.[19]

Now, normally Julien made '2' with two fingers, or sometimes a finger and thumb. To make '4', he would fold down his thumb, leaving four fingers outstretched. To make '6', he would use five fingers and a thumb. If he had worked this out without imagining his hand shapes, he would have shown two fingers. But if he had imagined a hand plus a thumb, and then taken away four fingers, he would have been left with two thumbs![20]

Julien was at a stage sometimes called 'pattern-making', using a pattern of fingers to represent a numerosity. The fingers are put in one-to-one correspondence with the object to be counted, obeying what I called the principle of numerosity. In this example, the objects were very abstract—mistakes in a picture. If the same pattern is used over and over again for the same number—say, all four fingers but not the thumb for 4, and all fingers on the left hand for 5—then each numerosity becomes associated with the same hand shape and the same visual pattern.

Children use their finger-counting skills for a range of tasks, including, we recently discovered, deciding which of two numbers is the larger. At four or five years old, they use finger-counting more often than verbal counting. Erica (aged four-and-a-half), deciding between 4 and 9, exclaimed 'It's definitely the 9! You need two hands for 9, it's the one close to 10, but you only need one hand for 4.'[21]

What happens next is that children start to match each number word in the counting sequence to each finger. For example, they might start with the left index finger and count 'one', middle finger 'two', ring finger 'three', little finger 'four', thumb 'five'. This immediately leads children to think about numbers in two ways, which might well be new to them. First, it makes clear that the numbers are ordered by size. You get to four before you get to five, and more fingers are raised for five than for four.

The Finger-Name Principle

Second, you will reach the same finger each time you count the same number—for example, the left thumb each time you get to five—provided you always use the same hand shape to represent a given numerosity. This could result in thinking that the counting name of that finger is the number of fingers displayed. We saw in the last section how giving each pattern of finger positions a number allowed Bede and his classical sources to represent numbers up to 1,000,000, way beyond the number that could be represented by one-to-one correspondence between fingers and numerosities. But now there are two, potentially conflicting systems that the children have to manage—their original numerosity representation and the new name-value system.

To see how these conflicts arise and become resolved, let us start with how children represent numbers. The important thing to realize, and many educationalists do not realize this, is that each child invents this system for themselves: they do not learn from family or teachers. For numbers up to five they use the fingers and thumb of one hand. Since children develop this system individually, there will be idiosyncrasies. Some use the right hand, others the left; we do not know whether this choice has anything to do with handedness. Some start by representing 1 on the forefinger, others on the little finger, still others on the thumb. It is likely that in the beginning children are by no means consistent in the pattern they use to represent these small numerosities.

Much more consistent is children's use of 5 + *something* for numbers bigger than 5. Seven-year-olds, who in Sweden have just started school, do not, for example, represent 7 by 4 fingers on one hand plus 3 fingers on the other, or 8 by 4 + 4, but always by 5 on one hand and 2 on the other: 5—the whole hand—is very salient for children.[22] This means that with practice a number, say 4, can be represented in two quite different ways: a numerosity (as four fingers), or by the finger named 'four' by the child counting aloud (the forefinger if the child habitually starts at the little finger). Lisa, a seven-year-old studied in school by Dagmar Neuman in Gothenburg, allowed the two ways to lead her into saying that 4 + 5 = 5. First she represented 4 on four fingers, using the numerosity principle, but then added the five by raising her thumb using the finger-name principle. The total therefore was the whole hand—the numerosity representation of 5![23]

Thus, even when children have some number words, they may still use their fingers, not only for addition but also for other computational purposes. Neuman shows how seven-year-olds use fingers to solve problems with an unknown, such as 3 + ? = 7. They start by putting up seven fingers. Some will know the pattern already, others will count out fingers until they have seven. Then they will look to see how they can find a pattern of three in the seven fingers (Figure 5.2). Using fingers helps children understand that the numbers—and their representations in words and fingers—are ordered by size. When you count 3, for example, you have already counted 1 and 2, so these are collections included in the collection of 3. I am not saying that children

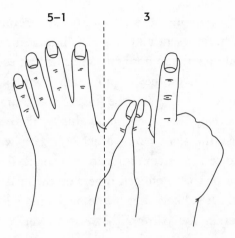

Figure 5.2 Three plus what equals seven? Children work it out on their fingers, first making the seven in the normal way with the whole of the left hand plus a finger and thumb from the right hand. They can see that taking out the rightmost three of these seven digits leaves the whole left hand minus its thumb—that is, with four. (Adapted from Neuman[24])

did not already understand this idea, but it fixes it more firmly in the mind, and it also fixes the ordering of the number words.

Using fingers to teach yourself arithmetic, which is what children do, turns out to be complex. Several different abilities need to be very precisely coordinated. Think for a moment about adding 4 and 3. What do children have to be able to do in the simplest case, using the principle of numerosity? They have to:

- know the numerosity of 'three' and 'four'.
- represent 3 and 4 as collections, using their fingers. Either they will have to count out four fingers and then three fingers; or they may already know a familiar pattern for each, e.g. raising the four fingers for 4, or raising the index, middle, and ring fingers for 3.
- understand that 'adding' means finding the numerosity of the union of the two collections.
- find a way to do this. If they do this by counting all the fingers raised, then additionally, they have to:
  — know the number-word sequence up to at least 7;

- know that counting all the members of the union will give them the sum;
- be able to count each finger once and only once;
- know that the last number counted is the sum.

This is the earliest stage of finger arithmetic. Karen Fuson, the psychologist and educationalist from Chicago, has documented the development from this stage to more sophisticated methods (Figure 5.3).

Children's use of fingers becomes more efficient and more abstract. From counting all the fingers, they progress to 'counting on' from one of the addends displayed as a pattern on the fingers, and then to counting on from the larger of the two addends. Then it dawns on them that if they are counting on, the first addend needs only to be spoken—it doesn't need to be displayed. This becomes particularly useful when counting over 10. By this stage, the fingers are used primarily to keep track of the counting on: they can see how many they have counted by the pattern of fingers raised. These more advanced methods require accurate control of all the abilities listed above, plus an understanding that the sequence of number (names) represents an ordered succession of numerosities. So starting with the word 'four' brings to mind the collection with the numerosity 4, and counting on the second addend is enumerating the rest of the union of 4 and 3.

Strangely, perhaps, even when adults have learned calculation procedures at school, many will continue to use their fingers. One reason, I suspect, is confidence. If they are able to use tried and tested methods, especially ones where any mistake will be readily apparent on the fingers, then they will be reassured that they have found the solution. I personally don't do this for calculation, but I confess I still do it for solving time problems, such as how many days I'll need to rent a car for. If it is Wednesday to Monday inclusive, it has to be six. I know that, but I still count out the days on my fingers. I need to be absolutely sure, given car rental charges in Europe!

Laying Down the Traces
Children don't need to be taught to use their fingers to do arithmetic. They seem to discover this method on their own, though no doubt hav-

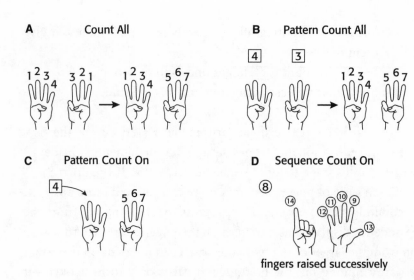

A   Count All   **B**   Pattern Count All

C   Pattern Count On   **D**   Sequence Count On

fingers raised successively

Figure 5.3 The development of finger arithmetic. (a) Counting all. The child counts out the addends 4 and 3 on the fingers of each hand, and then counts the raised fingers. (b) Pattern count all. The child recognizes the finger patterns made by the numbers and doesn't need to count out the addends on fingers; even so, all the raised fingers are counted. (c) Pattern count on. The child realizes that it is not necessary to raise fingers for both addends. The first addend, 4, is announced, and the second addend is counted on verbally, raising the fingers until the pattern for 3 is recognized. (d) Sequence count on. The method used in (c) can be applied to 8 + 6: 8 is announced, followed by counting on, raising the fingers until the pattern for 6 is recognized. (Adapted from Fuson & Kwon[25])

ing models in front of them—teachers, parents, or other children—may be a spur and a guide. This is speculation, however, since no one has yet done the research to test this. An enterprising researcher might look at finger-counting by blind children, to whom models for hand shapes would have to be deliberately presented by touch. Neither do we know whether it's the feel of the hand shape or the look of it that is critical in calculation. We know that sighted children do look at their hand shapes when counting or calculating, and use patterns to keep track of counting on. Could blind counters use just the feel—feedback from the position of the muscles and the joints—of their own hand shapes to keep track? We just don't know. (It's not enough just to ask blind people. Adults may have forgotten whether they used fingers in learning arithmetic; and children may not be very good at introspecting about the feel of fingers and the role this plays.)

What we do know is that calculating with fingers is very natural, and that children do it even when discouraged by teachers. This could mean that somehow in the child's brain the representation of numbers is very closely linked to representations of hand shapes. Using finger calculation would reinforce these links.

WHICH WAY DOES THE MENTAL NUMBER-LINE GO?

At the beginning of this chapter I asked whether you saw a line of numbers in your mind's eye. According to Xavier Seron and his team of neuropsychologists in Louvain, Belgium, about 14% of us do. More than a hundred years ago, Sir Francis Galton, one of the first experimental psychologists, found that people reported seeing number lines with strange shapes, like those shown in Figure 5.4. Galton called these 'number forms'. They arise in some people's minds automatically and spontaneously. But why? Is our very conception of numbers so intimately bound with our conception of space that we think of numbers as being organized in space? Like the vast majority of people, I don't have a number form. What is it that distinguishes those who do have one from those who don't? It isn't mathematical ability. Some mathematicians have them, some don't; some people who are poor at maths have them.

One thing all number forms have in common is that numerals are represented, not words. Most, as we see in Figure 5.4, mark the decade boundaries and treat the first 10 numbers as special. However, this is not universal, since one number form reported starts with 12 in a circle, followed by the teens before looping off into the decades. These observations suggest that there is an important learned component to number lines: they use the local way of writing the numbers, and the local base system to organize the shape of the line. Some subjects report being able to 'zoom in' on the number they wish to focus on, but all report that this number seems somehow clearer or brighter than the other numbers. Most of the reports collected by Seron's team had the numbers going from left to right, with one going right to left. Numbers also tended to go upwards; only one subject reported his line going downwards.

In 1949 a patient was admitted to the Radcliffe Infirmary in Oxford, where he was examined by a neurologist by the name of Spalding, and one of the pioneers of neuropsychology in Britain,

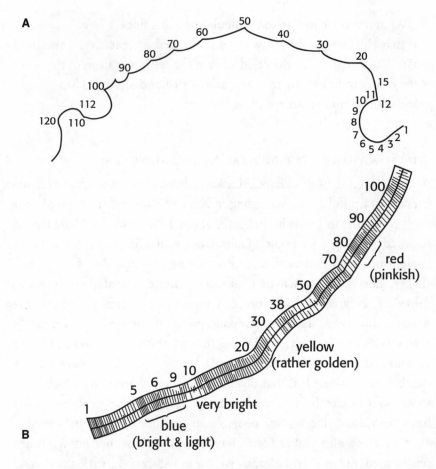

Figure 5.4 Two of Galton's 'number forms': (a) with a clock-like beginning, (b) with changes in brightness and colour. (From Galton[26])

Oliver Zangwill.[27] The patient had been injured five years earlier during the war by a piece of metal entering his brain in the left parietal lobe, and ending up in the right frontal lobe. He had largely recovered from this, but he now found it very difficult to find his way around, even in very familiar places such as his home town and the hospital. He got left and right confused, and his visual memory was poor. His calculation was extremely bad, with both written and oral presentation (Table 5.2). Spalding and Zangwill wrote in their report:

> He spontaneously said that he 'used to have a plan of numbers, but had lost it', or, more accurately, it was no longer distinct. He

Problem	Patient's answer	Correct answer
Oral presentation		
2s 6d + 5d =	2s 11d	2s 11d
3s 6d – 11d =	2s 2d	2s 7d
3s 1d + 11d =	4s 0d	4s 0d
3s 4d + 1s 3d =	5s 8d	4s 7d
Written presentation		
3s 0d + 1s 3d =	5s 1d	4s 3d
1s 2d – 4d =	10d	10d
2s 6d – 1s 8d =	×	10d
3 × 6 =	18	18
7 × 7 =	×	49

Table 5.2 Calculations by Spalding and Zangwill's patient, involving sums of money in pre-decimal currency: shillings (s) and pence (d).[28]

drew this plan of numbers as far as 12, and the remainder was drawn under his instructions. A few days later he drew the complete plan himself. He was very hesitant and uncertain, but the two plans are similar, and from them and his comments on them the plan . . . was constructed . . . He stated that this form was seen against a vague background which he thought might have been his old school playground. The bottom of it was on ground level a few yards from him and the form sloped away from him at an angle of about 40° to the horizontal. He saw all parts of the form simultaneously but the particular number he was seeking stood out with special distinctness . . . The form had been with him as long as he could remember, and had remained unchanged until his injury.[29]

This number form, shown in Figure 5.5, is typical of the types described by Galton and by Seron, which their users claimed helped them with their calculations. This patient attributed his difficulties with numbers to

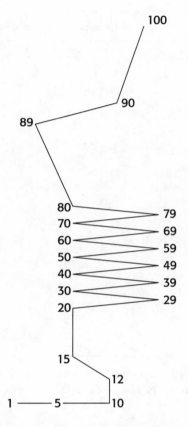

Figure 5.5 A number form that no longer functions. The patient whose number form this was attributed his loss of calculating ability following brain damage to the fact that he could no longer use it. (From Spalding & Zangwill[30])

the fact he could no longer use this number form. It may be, then, that for those who are aware of them, number forms are a way of representing the numbers which actually has some utility.

This spatial aspect of numbers fits in with a view of the mental and neural representation of numbers, powerfully advocated by Rochel Gelman and C. R. Gallistel, whose book *The Child's Understanding of Numbers*[31] has been immensely influential. In this book and later work, number magnitudes are represented as segments of a single mental number line. If we imagine this line as starting at 0 (or at 1), and being marked off at intervals of 2, 3, and so on, it can be seen that segment length will depend on number size. Calculations can be carried out using this kind of representation. For example, 4 and 3 could be added by combining the lengths of the two addends, and re-laying it on the number line, so that one end is on the 0 and the other will be roughly on the 7. The problem is that only one of Seron's subjects reported doing anything even remotely like this when adding. Of course, the whole process could be unconscious.[32]

The French neuroscientist Stanislas Dehaene has recently used an ingenious experimental technique to show that even people who are not conscious of having a number line do seem to arrange their mental numbers from left to right.[33]

Dehaene and his colleagues asked subjects to decide whether a number was odd or even. Half the subjects had to press one button with their left hand if the number was odd, and another with their right hand if it was even. The other half had to do it the other way around. The results were extraordinary. When the number was small, the subjects were faster with their *left* hand, but when it was large they were faster with their *right* hand. Dehaene called this effect the spatial-numerical association of response codes—or the SNARC effect (echoing Lewis Carroll's poem *The Hunting of the Snark*). He argued that since the larger number will be more to the right of personal space it would be easier and quicker to associate it with a right-handed response. Intriguingly, Iranian students, who read from right to left, did not show this effect as a group, though individually, those who had lived longest in the West (in Paris) were more likely to show it. This suggests that the orientation of the mental number line depends in some mysterious way on the direction of reading.

As Seron and his team discovered, only a minority of people are aware of a number form or number line, and it seems to be formed in childhood.[34] It remains a vivid and automatic accompaniment to numerical tasks in those who have it. Exactly how it is used in calculation is still obscure, and whether everyone who has one uses it is also unclear. What about people who are unaware of such a number line? Is theirs simply an unconscious version of it that shows up in effects like the SNARC? We do not know. Why do some number lines go to the right, some to the left, and some up and yet others down? Again, we don't know.

What is clear is that our representation of space, and of left and right, is intimately bound up with our representations of numbers.

The intriguing thing is that the area of the brain primarily responsible for our sense of space is also in the parietal lobe. Patients with parietal lobe lesions often suffer a serious and mysterious problem with space: they 'neglect' the half of space that lies on the side opposite to the brain damage. It's not that they cannot see what's on the neglected side, as careful experimentation can demonstrate, it's rather that they pay no attention to it. This problem can be so extreme that if they hear a voice coming from the neglected side of space, say the left, they won't turn to the left to see where the voice is coming from; instead they keep turning to their right until the source of the voice comes into view in the right side of space.

Dr Gerstmann's Mysterious Syndrome

In Chapter 4, I introduced three patients whose brain damage left them with very severe acalculia: Signora Gaddi, the hotelier, was totally unable to deal with numbers above 4; for Frau Huber, the farmer's wife, numbers had lost their meaning even though she could still recite her tables; and Signor Strozzi depended entirely on being able to recite the sequence of number words to carry out any number task, even comparing the size of two numbers. These three patients all had lesions to their left parietal lobes,[35] but there was something else they shared. They each had the four cardinal symptoms of a condition known as Gerstmann's syndrome.

Dr Josef Gerstmann, a shrewd clinician, reported in 1924 his tests of a fifty-two-year-old woman who, he noticed, was unable to name her own fingers, or point to them individually on request. This applied to other people's fingers too. He called this deficit 'finger agnosia'—a lack of knowledge about fingers. Further testing revealed that she couldn't tell easily which was her right hand or her left, nor Dr Gerstmann's right and left hands. Her calculation was unusually poor, and she had great difficulty in spontaneous writing (though she was able to copy words, showing that her vision and muscular control were still working), a condition called 'agraphia' (loss of writing ability).[36] Gerstmann collected two more patients, re-examined the reports of patients studied by other researchers, and concluded that these four symptoms go together to form a syndrome:

1. finger agnosia
2. acalculia
3. left–right disorientation
4. agraphia

His idea was that the key symptom was finger agnosia. We all possess a 'body schema'—a mental representation of our own bodies—including representations of our hands and fingers. This representation can be damaged, leaving a problem naming and pointing to body parts. Patients can't point to their elbow or to their knee on request. Most often, they confuse left and right parts of their body. This can happen even though they can feel and see their body without difficulty, and can move parts of their body normally. (For those who enjoy collecting technical vocabulary, this condition is called 'autopagnosia'.) Patients with Gerstmann's syndrome may be able to name and point to all parts of their body quite satisfactorily, until they reach their hands—then they have serious problems. Finger agnosia is therefore a highly specific case of this disturbance of body schema confined to representations of fingers. Gerstmann pointed out that even in cases of finger agnosia, patients may still be able to name and point to the thumb, and to the ring finger if it has a ring on it; that is, if there are extra clues to which finger is which.

Gerstmann believed that the loss of finger sense in combination with the left–right confusion caused the acalculia. This has been a source of fierce debate. Many have pointed out that every combination of the four symptoms has been observed, so they don't necessarily hang together. It even seems possible to have finger agnosia without acalculia; and it is certainly possible to have an acalculia without finger agnosia.[37]

In 1962 two British pioneers of neuropsychology, Marcel Kinsbourne (who happened to be my psychology tutor at the time) and Elizabeth Warrington (from whom I later learned much of what neuropsychology I know—see Chapter 4), published reports on nine patients with the complete set of four symptoms.[38] In one test some of the patients could not tell without looking whether the experimenters were touching one finger or two. 'The fingers have lost their individuality . . . The fingers are as if fused together in a solid lump.' Significantly, all these patients were severely acalculic, just like our patients Signora Gaddi, Frau Huber, and Signor Strozzi. Something very basic in their numerical abilities seems to be missing.

The British neurologist Macdonald Critchley suggested that 'Calculation entails motility . . . "Acting calculation" . . . This is illustrated by the child's use of counters—and also by the very etymology of the term calculation, implying the manipulation of little pebbles. An ideokinetic apractic factor in dyscalculia would not therefore be a matter of surprise.'[39] In translation, this means that calculation involves moving things about, so not having a clear idea of where things are and where things have to go could well cause calculation problems. However, this hand-waving just highlights the real problem for Gerstmann and his supporters: they haven't explained in detail *how* loss of the finger sense will lead to acalculia in skilled adults who, like our patients, no longer count on their fingers.

Born with Gerstmann's Syndrome

These patients were presumably normal before suffering brain damage. However, if fingers are important in the development of numerical abilities, what would happen to children born with finger agnosia? I would predict that they should have great difficulty representing even the most basic numerosities.

In another piece of pioneering research, in 1963, Marcel Kinsbourne and Elizabeth Warrington described their investigation of seven children referred to Great Ormond Street's world-famous Hospital for Sick Children. Their speech had developed normally, and they were all within the normal range for intelligence, with two testing very high on a standard IQ test. All these children were selected as having finger agnosia, Gerstmann's key symptom. What of their number skills? All but one were at least two years behind the average for their age, and they all had problems with simple addition and subtraction. 'Even the simplest additions were beyond the scope' of three of the children.[40] Four or five of these children probably suffered some damage to their brains during birth or from early diseases. However, two did not, and had perhaps inherited a condition that affected the normal growth of their parietal lobes, which in turn affected the conception of space and of motor control, especially in tasks like drawing and writing, that required both good perception of spatial relationships and fine control of movement through space.

Marcel and Elizabeth started with finger agnosia and found numerical disabilities. More recently, the US psychologist Byron Rourke has started with children who have specific arithmetical problems and found that many of them do indeed suffer from Gerstmann's tetrad of symptoms.[41] An Israeli team from Jerusalem has described in detail an eleven-year-old boy, intelligent and with fluent language, who not only is very poor at simple arithmetic but finds counting on his fingers problematic, and fails even Piaget's number conservation task.[42] (A row of objects is spread out or pushed closer together. A four-year-old will say that there are more objects when they are spread out, and fewer objects when they are pushed closer together.)

These findings lend support to the idea of an intimate connection between representations of fingers and representations of numerosities in the parietal lobe. More than that, they suggest that where the finger representation fails to develop normally, it can have knock-on effects on the development of number skills.

FINGERS IN THE BRAIN

At least five distinct brain areas are involved in representing the fingers. The details of the first two were discovered in the 1950s by Dr Wilder Penfield, a neurosurgeon working in Montreal, using a then novel technique reminiscent of Dr Frankenstein.[43] Penfield was pioneering surgical treatment for intractable epilepsy. The idea was to remove 'the epileptic focus'—the misfiring brain tissue that caused the fit. The surgeon's problem is to cut it out while avoiding cutting out tissue that could leave the patient with devastating side-effects. This is particularly apparent with the part of the brain called the primary motor cortex. Surgery here could cause muscle weakness or loss of control of movements. To reduce the risk of these side-effects, Penfield had to map which bits of the motor strip did what. This can be done only with a conscious patient.

In the operating theatre, a powerful local anaesthetic would be administered so that the skull could be opened, exposing the surface of the brain, while the patient remained conscious. Penfield then stimulated the brain with an electrode, and noted the reactions. For the motor cortex, stimulation would cause an involuntary twitching of the part of the body linked to the stimulated brain cells. Proceeding systematically along this part of the cortex, Penfield was able to map one brain region that controlled the movement of body parts. Moving back across the central fissure, there is a parallel brain region called the primary somatosensory cortex. When you feel a sensation in part of your body, this is the destination to which the nerves send a message. To map it, one really does need the active cooperation of the patient. When the cortex is stimulated, the patient must report where he feels an itch, a pain, or a tingle. Proceeding systematically again, Penfield was able to determine which sections of the somatosensory cortex are linked to which body parts. The results of this investigation were truly extraordinary. It turns out that the brain maps body parts in a very systematic way. In general, adjacent parts of the body are adjacent in the brain, but not to scale. The parts that are specially sensitive, or where control of movement is most complex, require more neurons and hence a bigger portion of the brain. In Figure 5.6 you can see in the 'homunculus' map that the thumb gets more brain space than the other fingers. This is because it is more sensitive and is involved in more complex actions than the other fingers.

The motor cortex sends messages down the nerves in the spinal cord to the hands and fingers, and receives messages from nerves in the fingers and hand that ascend the spinal cord to the somatosensory cortex. But movement control is fantastically complex, and four other main areas are also involved. There is the cerebellum, a kind of mini-brain that specializes in coordinating action; and there are subcortical circuits, deep inside the brain. But of special interest to us are two further cortical areas, recently identified as forming a circuit with the motor cortex.

Rizzolatti's Mirror Cells

One of the most exciting developments recently has been the discovery of 'mirror cells' by the neuroscientist Giacomo Rizzolatti and his colleagues at the University of Parma in Italy.[45] These are cells in the region of the brain known as the pre-motor cortex. This is where messages go before proceeding to the primary motor cortex. The nerve cells

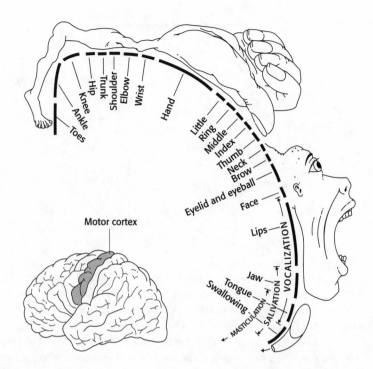

Figure 5.6 A cross-section of the left hemisphere, and the motor homunculus. A strip of cortex just in front of the central sulcus is devoted to working out how to move the muscles so as to carry out our intended actions. Many more cortical neurons are devoted to moving body parts over which we have precise, fine control, such as the fingers, than to those parts over which only broad control is needed, and indeed is mechanically possible, such as the trunk or hip. (From Penfield & Rasmussen[44])

there are responsible for the planning of movements, while the primary motor cortex is responsible more for their execution. One way of thinking about its role is as a kind of lexicon of movement plans, containing the basic vocabulary of movements.

What Rizzolatti found when testing monkeys was that these nerve cells become active when the brain is planning a very specific hand movement. One cell becomes active just when the brain is planning a precision grip with the index finger and thumb, as one might use in picking up a raisin. Other cells become active when further specific hand movements are planned. Rizzolatti called them mirror cells because they were found to become active when an animal was observing the same action. Thus the cell for precision grip responded at the sight of it as well as to execution of the action.

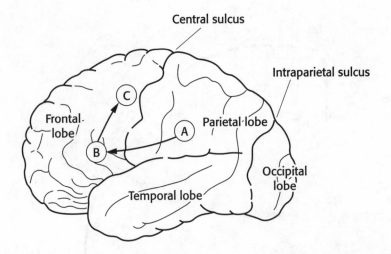

Figure 5.7 The 'mirror cell' circuit for controlling hand shape. It is now known that there are three main cortical areas that control hand shape and finger movements. Area A, in a deep sulcus in the parietal lobe, is where intended actions are thought to be planned. This area is connected to area B, called the 'premotor cortex', which contains the mirror cells that control specific hand shapes. They are so called because they are involved not only in planning one's own hand shape but also in recognizing other people's hand shapes. Once the hand shape has been selected, instructions are sent to the motor cortex, which programmes the sequence of muscle movements needed to make the hand shape. (Adapted from Jeannerod et al.[46])

Deep in the sulci (grooves) of the parietal lobes (of monkeys) there are neurons that participate in the planning of hand and finger movements in relation to an object—for example, planning the appropriate precision grip in relation to the size of a raisin and its location in space (Figure 5.7). These parietal neurons are thought to project into the mirror neurons. We can see how this arrangement implements levels of planning a hand shape. At the first level, in the parietal lobe, you decide on the shape you wish to make—for example, raising the first three fingers. This command is passed along connective nerve cells from the parietal lobe to the mirror cells in the pre-motor area, where the program for the appropriate hand shape is selected. To make this hand shape, some fingers will need to be raised and others lowered; exactly which will depend on the current hand shape. These decisions will be made in the motor cortex. (This is not the end of the story: there are several other brain circuits below the level of the cortex that are involved in the detailed planning of muscle movements, coordinating movements with current body posture, and sending commands to the muscles of the hand and arm.)

Braille Readers' Fingers
Each finger has a distinct group of cells representing it in the brain. Blind readers of the tactile alphabet invented by Louis Braille use their fingers, often just one index finger to read. After some years of reading like this, what happens to the brain? We now know, following a series of brilliant experiments by Alvaro Pascual-Leone and his colleagues, that the reading finger—and just the reading finger—is represented by far more brain cells than non-reading fingers (whose representation is similar to that of the fingers of sighted people). The extra meaning that can be derived from the feel of the little Braille bumps on the page seems to have extended the size and presumably the kind of representation the reading has. The critical areas with the expanded representation include the left parietal lobe (for right-handed readers).[47] This shows that what you do shapes the way your body is represented in your brain. The expanded representation of the reading finger reflects the new use to which the finger has been put.

FINGERS AND COUNTING IN THE BRAIN

We have seen that finger use plays a critical role in the development of counting and arithmetical skills. For several years children will be daily, perhaps even hourly, raising and lowering their fingers and simultaneously looking at finger configurations, thinking about numbers and saying number words, and doing calculations. Finger movements and finger positions are constantly associated with numerical meanings. It would not be surprising, therefore, if some of these meanings stuck to their fingers, or to the representations of these fingers in the parietal lobe, just as letter and word meanings stick to the representations of the Braille reader's reading finger.

If this is correct, then several puzzles are solved. First, it explains why the representation of numbers is in the parietal lobes: it's where fingers and hand shapes are represented. Second, it goes some way to explaining why the four symptoms of Gerstmann's syndrome go together so often: damage to the left parietal lobe could affect the representation of fingers and the nearby representation of basic number concepts. This was not Josef Gerstmann's own explanation: he thought that damaging finger representations would in itself damage number representations. However—and this is the third puzzle—why does the presence of finger agnosia in childhood (in developmental Gertsmann's syndrome) so often lead to dyscalculia? My hypothesis is that, without the ability to attach number representations to the neural representations of fingers and hands in their normal locations, the numbers themselves will never have a normal representation in the brain.

The Number Module, which I claim human infants are born with, and which we share with non-human species, is known to function only for numerosities up to about 4, 5 at the very most. That is, our brain is genetically programmed with the capacity to represent numerosities up to 4. There is as yet little evidence as to where in the brain this module is located. The best bet is the inferior (lower) parietal lobe of the left hemisphere certainly, and the right hemisphere probably.[48] This brain area is at the junction of the occipital lobe at the back of the brain, the site of the main visual processing systems, with the temporal lobe, the site of most language processing and semantic memory.

The question, then, is how do we get beyond 4? Historically, a key development has been the universal use of fingers, even where there are no specialized words for numbers. Finger control, as we have seen, has a primary site in the parietal lobe and, if monkey brains are like human brains in this respect, deep in the intraparietal sulcus. (A sulcus is a fold in the cortex.) I suggested in Chapter 3 that children use their ability to recognize small numerosities—subitizing—as a way of checking the results of counting aloud, using the counting words. We have seen that finger patterns are important in children's simple arithmetic. My hypothesis, therefore, is that as the child grows and develops, the subitizing circuits in the inferior parietal link up with the finger circuits in the intraparietal sulcus. The fingers therefore gain an extended representation by this link: they come to represent the numerosities.

6

BIGGER AND SMALLER

'Which is bigger: 2 or 9?' This is not a trick question—you just have to choose the right number. But it is a very easy question. Almost everyone who is familiar with the numerals will get the answer, and get it very quickly. Even acalculic patients who cannot add or subtract can usually manage to do this task. I could present the same problem in words—'Which is bigger: two or nine?'—or with dots— 'Which is bigger: • • or • • • • • • • • •?' The results would be essentially the same: a very easy problem. Why should the way we solve such a trivial problem be important or even interesting?

There are two things any Number Module worth the name must be able to do. First, it must be able to categorize the world in terms of numerosities, at least small numerosities. We have seen that human infants and many other animal species are able to do this. Second, it must be able to order these numerosities by size, since this is absolutely fundamental to the idea of numerosity. If I am right, then our genes should contain a program for building circuits in the brain to represent number size, enabling us to judge which of two numbers is bigger.

There is another way of comparing numerosities. We can use conceptual tools we have learned from our culture. For example, we could use counting to tell whether 9 is bigger than 3. We could start at 1 and count up until we hit the first number—in this case, 3. We can then infer that 3 is smaller than 9, and hence that 9 is larger than 3.

A cognitive module, according to the philosopher Jerry Fodor,[1] must operate quickly, automatically, and in a 'domain-specific' way—that is, it must operate only on a certain type of input. To be a module in Fodor's sense, the Number Module must therefore operate quickly and automatically just on numerosities—the most basic sense of numbers.

Fodor, as I noted in Chapter 1, further stipulates that a module must be 'hard-wired'. That is, it must consist of definite neural circuits, and these circuits must be innate. Unlike Steven Pinker (author of *The Language Instinct*[2]), with whom he shares many beliefs, Fodor wasn't in the least interested in constructing an evolutionary story for why the mind is equipped with a battery of modules for analyzing the environment of the brain containing those modules. But it is possible to tell such a story. It often happens that being able to categorize a situation quickly and accurately in terms of its key features could aid the survival of the phenotype (individual): for example, being able to categorize the dark shape overhead as a predatory bird, or to recognize prey from an unusual angle. If the phenotype survives then it will have a better chance of reproducing. I argued in Chapter 3 that the ability to estimate the number of attackers is why Karen McComb's Serengeti lionesses flee when outnumbered but attack when not. Similarly, a creature equipped to estimate the number of nuts on a branch, or the number of prey, will do better in the competition for survival than its brothers and sisters not so equipped.

We have already seen in Chapter 3 that human infants are sensitive to the number of things in a visual array. Infants seemed to be the same as adults in their ability to identify almost instantaneously up to about four visual objects. But the ability to discriminate between numerosity A and numerosity B is not the same thing as having a sense of which is the bigger, and this is what the lionesses appear to do, and it is how numerical abilities could make for more efficient foraging.

For animals with a lot of neocortex, that is, those with flexible responses to environmental conditions—those which learn—it could be advantageous to relegate some processes to modular status. Because modules act automatically as well as quickly, the animal will not need to use central processing resources in trying to categorize the situation. The module will have served up the answer: it's a predator. The only decision central processes will then have to make is flight or fight. In general, it may be advantageous to relegate routine, if vital, categorization decisions to a module.

Is the ability to order numerosities by size a function that is carried out by the Number Module? First, we need to discuss the 'signature' of the way the brain represents number size. This is important because there are several ways in which we could decide which of two numbers is larger without considering number size at all. For example, we could base the decision on which number comes later in the sequence of counting words, in just the same way as we would judge which of two letters comes later in the alphabet, or which of two months comes later in the year.

THE SIGNATURE OF NUMBER SIZE

Look at Figure 6.1. In which case is it easier to pick the larger, Problem 1 or Problem 2? Introspectively both seem equally easy, indeed trivially so. This is one of the problems with introspection as a method of investigating mental processes, and it is why psychologists do experiments rather than simply asking people to introspect on what they are doing. Experimentally, it turns out that Problem 1 is reliably easier than Problem 2 in the sense that it's answered faster and with fewer errors. This is because the difference between the two numbers in terms of their sizes is greater in (1) than in (2). The numbers 2 and 9 are more dissimilar. This difference between the problems doesn't depend on using numerals. The same result can be achieved using the words *two, eight, nine*, or the arrays of dots • •, • • • • • • • •, • • • • • • • • •. The effect of the 'distance' between the numbers is one of the most robust and reliable in the whole of experimental psychology. We can make a simple plot of the time taken to make the decision, called the comparison time, against this difference.

Problem 1   Problem 2

    2   9   8   9

Figure 6.1 The distance effect (1). In which case is it easier to pick the larger number?

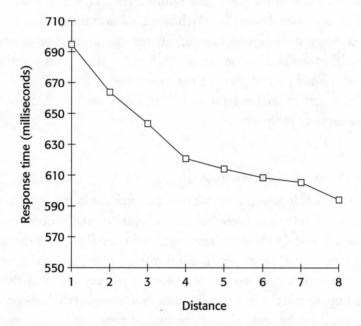

Subject sees	3	6	9	8	2	7
Distance		3		1		5

Figure 6.2 The distance effect (2). It takes longer for subjects to select the larger of two numbers when they are numerically similar. Similarity is measured here as the 'distance' between the two numbers (some examples are given above the graph). (Data from Butterworth et al.[3])

In Figure 6.2, the comparison times are the response times for the subject to name the larger of two numerals presented on a computer screen. The times are plotted against the distance between the smaller and the larger number: e.g. the difference between 3 and 6 is 3, and that between 9 and 8 is 1.[4] Difference turns out to be a good predictor of comparison time, as it does for many size-like dimensions, including weight, length, loudness, and brightness. This was formulated as a law in the nineteenth century by Ernst Weber (see Chapter 1). If you look at the scale on the left of the graph, you will notice two remarkable features. First, the times are very short: around half a second to identify the numerals and their sizes, decide which is the larger, retrieve the name of that number, and utter it. Second, the difference between the fastest times and the slowest times is about a tenth of a second. It is thus scarcely surprising that intuition does not distinguish between the ease of solving the two problems above.

It's worth comparing this result with other conceivable outcomes: the comparison times could have depended on the visual similarity of the numerals (6 looks more like 8 than like 1), or on similarity in sound ('four' sounds more like 'five' than like 'seven'); or it could have turned out that no systematic factors determine comparison time. There is another possibility: comparison times could have got *longer* as the difference between the two numbers got bigger. The line in Figure 6.2 would then go up instead of down from left to right. In the whole of psychology, we find that the more similar things are the harder it is to discriminate between them in making any kind of judgement (see Chapter 1). This is simply the application of Weber's law to other dimensions. To find the exact opposite would be an extraordinary result. Think of it in terms of brightness, for example: it is as though, if asked which of two lamps is brighter, you would find it easier when the two lamps are both bright (or both dim) than when one is bright and the other dim.

I mention this possibility since we have recently made the remarkable discovery that this pattern of comparison times—quicker when the numbers are close together than far apart—is diagnostic of an impairment to the Number Module (see Section 4 below). In any case, the take-home message is that the measure of the time it takes the brain to make a comparison depends on the numerical size of the difference.

The distance effect has been found in young children;[5] and even in monkeys. The monkey effect is measured differently. In a study by David Washburn and Duane Rumbaugh of the Yerkes Regional Primate Research Center at Emory University in Georgia, two rhesus monkeys called Abel and Baker were trained to pick the larger of two numerals from 0 to 9, using a computer joystick.[6] In the first phase, they were shown pairs with 0 and one other numeral, say 4. If 0 was selected they would get no food pellets, whereas if 4 was picked they would receive four pellets. They were thus rewarded only for selecting non-zero numerals. In the next phase, they saw two non-zero numerals, for example 4 and 2. In this case they would get four pellets if they selected 4, and two if they selected 2, so both choices would be rewarded, but the larger numeral would yield a bigger reward.

Now, although Abel and Baker were seven-year-olds, experienced in the ways of lab experiments, they had not been trained on numerals before. After a few hundred trials both monkeys were selecting the larger numeral most of the time. However, they did less well when the numerical difference between the numerals was small, and best when it was large—the distance effect. We know that Abel and Baker were genuinely using number size, and not some other principle, because of some ingenious controls built into the experiments.

For example, they would first be trained on the pairs 8, 6 and 7, 6. How would they solve the new pair 8, 7? They would have learned that 8 is better than 6 and 7 is better than 6, so they could order both 8 and 7 with respect to 6, but not with respect to each other. Just remembering the *ordinal* relationships between the numerals would not be sufficient. Nevertheless, Abel was selecting the larger of these new pairs from their very first presentation. How did he do it? One possibility is that he simply remembered the *number* of pellets associated with each numeral, and selected the numeral associated with the larger number—he was using number size. (He could have been remembering that 8 is two pellets more than 6, while 7 is only one pellet more, but this is a kind of indirect number size relationship.)

There is also evidence that at the end of some 1,100 trials both Abel and Baker had fixed in their brains the relative sizes of all the numerals from 0 to 9. In a further experiment Abel and Baker saw several numerals together, sometimes as many as five, and would be rewarded best if they selected the largest. Although they were not so good at this as at the pairs task—it is after all much more difficult, even for humans—Abel managed to pick the largest of five numerals 68% of the time, and Baker 57% of the time. We can speculate that the relative ordering of the numerals is based on the *absolute* numerical size of the collections of pellets used to reward the selections. That is, Abel and Baker remembered that '7' was associated with a collection of seven pellets, while '6' was associated with a collection that was, perhaps, exactly one less than the collection associated with '7'.

Recently, Elizabeth Brannon and Herbert Terrace at Columbia University trained two rhesus monkeys named Rosencrantz and Macduff to identify which of two cards had the largest number of elements (dots, rectangles, silhouetted figures, and so on), and this they were able to do for cards with eight and nine elements. However, one striking feature of this study was that the monkeys had not been trained on arrays with eight and nine elements, but on arrays with one to four elements. Brannon and Terrace concluded that rhesus monkeys spontaneously represent the numerosity of novel visual stimuli, and can use this representation to select the largest numerosity. What is more, they appear to understand how to extend to a larger pair the abstract rule for selecting the larger of two numerosities, having learned it on smaller pairs.[7]

These results suggest that the brains of our very distant ancestors—the common ancestor of the rhesus monkey and humans—were capable of selecting an action on the basis of numerical size. They could choose bigger from smaller.

STROOP

Let us start with another task, in fact, with two tasks (Figure 6.3). In the first task you have to choose the *numerically* larger number, just as you did in the task above. In the second, you have to select the *physically* larger numeral. In Problem 3 the numerical comparison and the physical comparison lead to the same answer, 9. In Problem 4, the numerical comparison and the physical comparison lead to competing answers: 9 and 2 respectively.

This is a numerical version of a task J. R. Stroop invented in the early 1930s.[8] In his original study, subjects were asked to name the colour of the ink in a series of stimuli. Some of those stimuli were words: in particular, some of the words were names of colours, as

Problem 3   Problem 4

Figure 6.3 The distance effect (3). In which case *now* is it easier to pick the larger number?

Stimulus	Ink colour	Correct response
▼▼▼	green	'Green'
TABLE	green	'Green'
GREEN	green	'Green'
GREEN	red	'Red'

Table 6.1 Stimuli eliciting the 'Stroop effect'.

shown in Table 6.1. Here, the stimuli ▼▼▼ and TABLE are neutral with respect to colour, whereas GREEN in green ink is congruent with respect to colour. Stroop and all his successors—and there have been many—found that the word GREEN printed in red ink slowed the saying of the response 'Red'. Even though the task is just to name the ink colour, subjects couldn't help reading the word and understanding it, and this interfered with naming the ink colour. There was conflict and competition between the two responses, 'Red', which is correct, and 'Green', which is not. This slowing is now universally known as the 'Stroop effect'.

This is a very robust effect. Try it on your friends and family—I guarantee you'll reproduce it. Make up rectangles of paper or cards with one each of the following on them: a shape, say a square, for each of the three colours red, green, and blue, three neutral words in each of the colours, and finally each of the colours in conflicting colour words. Explain to your subjects that the task is to name the colour of the ink as quickly as they can. Then show them the rectangles of paper one at a time in this order: shapes, neutral words, conflicting words. Although you will not be timing them, the slowness and the errors when it comes to the conflicting words should be immediately apparent. Scientists are intrigued by the Stroop effect because it shows that there are some things you just cannot help doing, even though they interfere with the task in hand. In this case, you cannot help reading *and understanding* the colour words. No amount of practice completely prevents the interference.[9]

The numerical version of the task shows exactly the same kind of effect. People reliably answer Problem 4 more slowly than they do Problem 3.[10] Of course, this shows only that the physical size of the stimuli interferes with a judgement about the numerical size. But if you do the task the other way round, ask for a judgement of the physical size, then the numerical size interferes with it. Again, Problem 4 is answered more slowly than Problem 3.[11] This shows that the numerical sizes of both numerals are automatically activated *and compared*, and, what is more, the comparison is made quickly enough to interfere with the comparison of physical size. This is one symptom of a quick and automatic numerical process.

In a remarkable recent experiment, Stanislas Dehaene and his colleagues in Paris have shown that the meaning of a numeral is accessed unconsciously—that is, even when you are not conscious of seeing it. Their experiment depends on the effect called 'pattern masking'. When a visual stimulus is presented for a very short time, four hundredths of a second, and is immediately followed by a 'mask'—a pattern that appears in exactly the same area of the visual field—viewers are unaware of the visual stimulus and will say that they saw nothing at all before the mask appeared. In this experiment, subjects were shown a numeral or a number word before the mask, and another numeral or number word after the mask. They were fully aware of this second number, and their task was to press one button with their right hand if it was larger than 5, and another button with their left hand if it was smaller. There were two measures of whether the subjects responded in any way to the masked numeral, the one they didn't know they had seen. First, did it make any difference to their response to the second numeral they saw: did it 'prime' the response? It turns out that it did. If both numerals were larger than 5, then responses to the second were quicker than when the masked numeral was smaller. Similarly, if both were smaller then the response was quicker than if the first was larger and the second smaller. For the second measure of response, scalp electrodes recorded brain activity. When the masked number was larger than 5, there was an increase in brain activity in the left hemisphere which controls the right hand, and when it was smaller than 5 there was increased activity in the right hemisphere, just as there was when the subject was responding to the second number. The subjects' brains were not only registering the masked number, but they were responding to its numerosity without being conscious that they'd even seen it![12]

LEARNING AND STROOP

For the physical version of the numerical Stroop task to show an effect, the subject needs to be able to associate the numeral with its meaning—its numerical size. This association, of course, takes the child some time to learn, perhaps about a year for the single digits and two to three years for multi-digit numbers. But the more the child attends to the numerals and thinks about their meanings, the stronger the association becomes. On the whole, a strong association between *A* and *B* in the brain implies that *A* will activate *B* quickly. For a weak association, the activation will be slow.

I and some colleagues recently studied both types of Stroop task with subjects from four years old to adulthood.[13] We assumed that they would very quickly notice physical size differences, even from the earliest age. Thus when we asked them to make *numerical* comparisons, the *physical* size would interfere. However, at the age of four, we reasoned, there would be a strong enough association between the numerals and their meanings for the numerical size to be activated quickly enough to interfere with the physical judgement.

As you can see from Figure 6.4, in the numerical task, when the subjects were asked to name the numerically larger number, conflicting physical size always interfered, even from the earliest age. This indicates, unsurprisingly, that children automatically processed the comparative physical sizes of the numerals even though these were not relevant to the task at hand. However, in the physical task the youngest children showed no interference from the numerical sizes of the numerals. This indicated that the association between the numerals and their meanings is not strong enough for the meanings to be activated fast enough to interfere with the very fast physical size comparison.

In Chapter 5, we saw that one four-year-old, who took part in this experiment, used her fingers to decide which of the two numbers was larger. At four or five years, children use finger-counting more often than verbal counting, and so associations involve an intermediate step via the fingers, which makes the link between numerals and

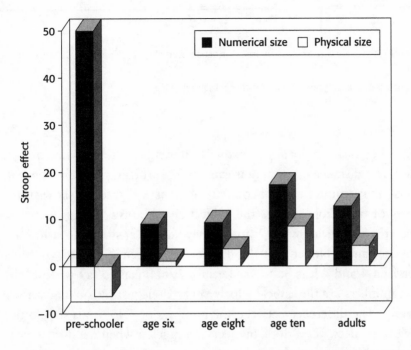

Figure 6.4 The Stroop effect. Two Stroop tasks show how access to number meanings changes with age (J. R. Stroop was the inventor of tasks where two dimensions of the stimulus are put into conflict). In the numerical task, subjects have to judge which of two numerals is numerically larger, while in the physical task they have to judge which of two numerals is physically larger. The Stroop effect comes about when the two dimensions are incongruent—that is, where the numerically larger numeral is the physically smaller one. When this happens, response times are slowed. The bar chart shows the size of this effect, calculated by subtracting the congruent response times (where the numerically larger numeral is the physically larger one) from the incongruent, dividing by the congruent response times, and multiplying by 100. The graph shows that, for all ages, the numerical judgement is slowed when the dimensions are incongruent, but for the physical judgement, incongruency slows only the older subjects. (Data from Girelli *et al.*[14])

number sizes indirect and slower. As Figure 6.4 shows, by the time the children have reached eight or nine years of age these associations are strong enough to produce interference.[15]

We can find the distance effect—the signature of use of a representation of number size—in a rather different task that pits numerical size against physical size. This task may seem even more trivial than number comparison, or even physical size comparison. This 'number

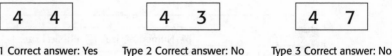

Figure 6.5 Three types of number-matching task.

matching' task simply asks whether two numbers are the same or not. Finding a distance effect here is even more surprising than finding it in a task that requires explicit comparison of size. Figure 6.5 shows three types of trial. For Type 1, the subject should answer 'Yes' (they are both the same); in Types 2 and 3 they should answer 'No' (they are not the same). Notice that the difference between 4 and 3 is 1, while between 4 and 7 it is 3. Now, the subject only has to say whether the two numbers are the same—which can be done just by looking at their shapes. The difference between the numbers on 'No' trials should not have any effect, yet it does. Subjects are quicker when the difference is larger—the distance effect again. They are automatically activating the number sizes and comparing them, even though it is quite irrelevant to the task. Activating this aspect of the meaning of the numerals seems obligatory: one cannot help but do it. The distance effect is found in children as young as six[16] (it hasn't yet been tried with younger children). So, even after just two or three years of systematically learning the numerals, the size meaning comes to mind unbidden.

In Chapter 3, we saw that children of four were still failing Piaget's number conservation task. In this task the child sees two rows of objects, say, a row of six red buttons and a row of six green buttons. To begin with, they are arranged so that each red button is lined up with a green button. The experimenter asks the child whether there are more red or more green buttons, and the child reliably answers that there are the same number. The experimenter then spreads out the row of red buttons, clearly not adding any or taking any away. When asked again, the child typically will say that there are now more red buttons. That is, their judgement is influenced by the perceptual cue of the area covered by the buttons. This is despite the fact that they will have a good grasp of the role of one-to-one correspondence, and know that adding or taking away an object from a collection will increase or decrease its numerosity. In general, they won't be fooled by transformations that don't actually affect number, but in some cases the perceptual cues seem to outweigh the numerical. And there's no need for adults to feel smug. With collections beyond the subitizing range—the numerosities that can be taken in at a glance without counting—above five, say, the perceptual cues of area covered and density are important in making numerical estimates. In fact, the way the objects are arranged affects the speed and accuracy of estimation.[17] One question that arises, therefore, is this. At the age of four, is the lack of interference in the physical task—the number size plays no part—also due to children's natural focus on perceptual cues that steers them in the wrong direction in Piaget's task?

The Stroop task shows that it is just as hard not to process the numerical size of the numerals as it is not to process their physical size, or indeed their colour. The brain is set up to extract this information from the world, whether we need it or not. Perhaps, you are wondering, there's something a bit fishy about the Stroop manipulation, where I have deliberately put into conflict two dimensions which both happen, in English, to be describable by the words 'bigger' and 'smaller'. I have tried to allay your scepticism by showing that exactly the same thing happens with a quite different task, the number matching task. Here subjects just have to say whether the numerals are the same or not. It turns out to be easier and quicker to say 'No' when the numerals are numerically distant. Numerical size is again swiftly and automatically activated—even though it is again quite irrelevant to the task in hand.

DYSCALCULIA—BLINDNESS TO NUMEROSITIES

We normally think of arithmetic as operations on numerosities (though we may not formulate it to ourselves in exactly this way). The addition of A and B is a process of finding the numerosity of the union of the two distinct collections denoted by A and B. Put another way, when we add 5 to 3, we are finding the numerosity of the collection formed by putting a collection of 5 together with a collection of 3. (This is why it doesn't matter in which order the numbers are taken:

the answer is the same.) Children and some adults, as we saw in Chapter 5, do arithmetic by using collections of fingers—and other body parts. For many children, making the numerosity meaning explicit is an important bridge to understanding and to fluent calculational skills.

Back in the early 1950s, the British neurologist Macdonald Critchley, writing of severe acalculia, recognized the importance of the numerosity meaning of the numerals, and proposed that the patient 'may lose the meaning of numbers although possibly still be able to identify and to name the various numerical symbols'. Without this meaning, he went on, the patient 'may not be capable of deciding whether 7 is greater than 6, for example. Even such fundamental conceptions may be wanting as the idea of bigger or smaller.' Critchley associated this deficit of number meaning with failures of simple addition and subtraction, even of the part–whole relationship between numbers (3 is a part of 7). This fundamental deficit, 'however, is rare'.[18] Unfortunately, he reported no patients in whom he had tested number comparison and found it wanting.

Signor Strozzi

Recall from Chapter 4 our patient Signor Strozzi. He was indeed very severely acalculic, despite having spent his working life as a market trader. When we first tested him and asked him to add pairs of single-digit numbers greater than 1, he got none correct! He was very poor even when one number of each pair was 1! My colleague, Margarete Delazer, and I concluded from a long series of experiments that Signor Strozzi had lost the numerosity meaning of the numbers. As suggested as a possibility by Critchley, he still retained the ability to name numbers, and could indeed recite the number names up to 'twenty'. If he could carry out one of our tasks using the sequence of number names, he was fine. This enabled him to add two collections of dots by counting them out. And, although he could not add 1 to number A in his head, he could easily give us the next number after A!

What about his number comparison times? If Critchley's intuition were right, and if I am right about numerosity meanings, then these should be grossly abnormal because he would not be able to use mental representations of numerosities to carry out the comparison: he would have to do it in some other way. When we tested him, not only was he very slow, taking more than twice as long as normal subjects, but as the difference between the two numbers increased so the comparison times became *longer*—the exact opposite of the normal pattern. We do not know for sure why this was, but it is consistent with the idea that he made the comparison by some kind of counting process that utilized the sequence of number names, which he could still recite. For example, if he used a strategy of counting from the numeral on the left to the one on the right, then he would have to count more and longer from 3 to 7 than from 3 to 4. When he reached the right numeral he would know that it was bigger than the left number. Of course, if the larger number was on the right, he would never reach the left number by counting. He would then need some kind of stop rule. For example, if the pair was 4 and 3, and he started with 4, he might stop when he reached double figures, 10, and then deduce that the 4 had to be bigger than the other number.

Both Signor Strozzi's calculation and his sense of numerosity are severely impaired. Does this mean that one causes the other? To find out, we tested him at intervals over a year. As his numerosity sense recovered, and the pattern of his number comparison times became more normal, so his calculation recovered. Ten months after the stroke that caused his impairments, his comparison times were more or less normal in speed and pattern (he was now taking longer for pairs with the smallest difference); and his calculation, though not yet normal, was very much better.[19] But correlation is not cause, and even correlation over time can never be completely convincing. In this instance, general brain recovery could have affected both numerosity and calculation, and other capacities as well.

Although this case was very suggestive, we needed a quite different kind of case, and one that we have never read about in the literature. We needed to see what would happen to someone born without the ability to represent number sizes normally. Would this person have difficulty calculating and doing other very simple tasks that depend on representations of number size, including number comparison?

Charles—Born Blind to Numerosities?
It just happened that some months before we saw Signor Strozzi, I had been testing a very bright young man, called Charles, who had A levels and a university degree in Psychology. He was then working as

a psychological counsellor. Charles came to see me because he had always had problems with mathematics. These were exceptionally severe. He still solved single-digit sums and multiplication on his fingers, and usually took ten times as long as normal adults to solve very simple problems. Subtraction, division, and multi-digit problems were almost always impossible. Numbers seemed not to have the same meaning for him as they do for most of us. Not only did his difficulties prevent him from passing the usual school exams, but his life, both in and out of school, was plagued by daily embarrassments. Shopping was a dreadful experience. He didn't really understand the prices of goods, he was unable to work out whether he had enough money to pay for his purchases, and he couldn't check his change. Naturally, he did his best to cope with practical problems, and to conceal them from others. It was like being an adult unable to read in a world where reading was taken entirely for granted.

Charles willingly subjected himself to our battery of tests. He was hoping to understand why, despite his other academic and personal achievements, he found so difficult what all his friends and family found so easy. The psychology books he had read didn't describe anyone with his condition. Of course, many children and many adults are bad at arithmetic (for reasons I discuss in Chapter 7), just as many are bad at music or history or French. Some will end up two or three years behind their peers' average level of attainment. Many harbour fears about numbers (Chapter 8). But Charles wasn't just delayed and anxious about numbers. He turned out to be much more like a dyslexic who, despite every effort, is constitutionally, genetically, unable to read normally; or like someone born colour-blind. Numbers seemed to lack meaning for Charles. He scored very poorly on all our usual tests, but this didn't help us to get to the root of his problem. Having excluded factors such as defects in reasoning and short-term memory we decided to look at the most basic of his numerical abilities: could Charles tell bigger from smaller?

There was clearly something very deeply wrong with his whole conception of number, but we had no idea what it could be. He seemed to be using cultural tools, in particular counting with words and fingers instead of using his Number Module. We therefore decided to test for the most basic aspects of numerosity. Did he show normal patterns of number comparison? Was he 'Strooped'—that is, were numerosities automatically activated when he saw a numeral?

Figure 6.6 shows a summary of the number comparison results. We used the usual numbers, all combinations of 1 to 9. Charles just had to name the larger number. One extraordinary thing was that his comparison times were more than *four times slower* than our normal control subjects (and I had to use different scales in Figure 6.6 to present the results). The other thing is that the pattern is in the opposite direction: he took longer as the difference between the two numbers increased. In other words, this is an example of an inverse distance effect. And we know why in this case. Although he couldn't explain very clearly what he was doing—as I have said before, introspection is often a poor guide to these processes—we could see him using his fingers to do number comparisons! To work out which was bigger, 3 or 7, he counted from one to the other. We speculated that Signor Strozzi used a stop rule when he started counting from the larger number, and we are pretty

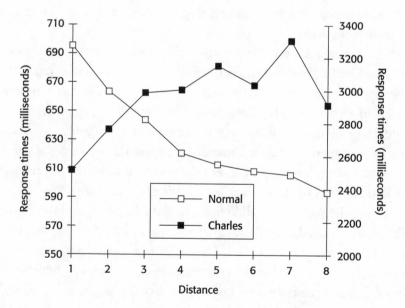

Figure 6.6 Charles's comparison results. Charles (the right-hand scale) is not only very much slower than normal (the left-hand scale) in comparing two numerals, he also shows a reverse distance effect. He uses a counting strategy to compare the numbers. (Data from Girelli *et al.*[20])

sure this is what Charles did. After all, he's not stupid (and his reasoning is not affected by recent brain damage, as Signor Strozzi's might have been). He knows that both numbers are less than 10 because they are both single digits. So if he had started counting from the 7 and hit 10 before he hit 3, then 7 must be the bigger of the two.

We tried number comparison using a Stroop manipulation. Normal subjects are much slower to select the bigger number in pairs like

$$\textbf{2} \qquad \textbf{9}$$

than they are to select the bigger number in pairs like

$$\textbf{2} \qquad \textbf{9}$$

as I discussed above. Sometimes they are quickest of all if the physical size and the numerical size go in the same direction, as in the pair

$$\text{2} \qquad \textbf{9}$$

Charles was not like normal subjects. He was very slow, but also he was slowest when both the numbers were the same physical size. This is a very strange result, indicating that Charles was doing this task in a very strange way.

These were such unexpected and striking results that, with the help of Luisa Girelli, we did the experiments again. Same results. Luisa also tried the physical version of Stroop, where you simply have to judge which of two numerals is the physically the bigger. Remember that children of nine show a distance effect on this task, being quicker to select the numerals when the numerical difference between the pair is large than when it is small. Charles showed no distance effect, suggesting that he was not automatically activating number size.

Just to be sure that, unlike other adults, he really didn't activate the number size, Luisa decided to try the number matching task I described earlier (Figure 6.5). If Charles automatically activated number size, then he should show a distance effect on the 'No' judgements. This task was even easier. He just had to decide whether two numerals were the same or not. If he was activating number size, then he should be quicker to say 'No' on Type 3 problems than on Type 2 problems, since he would see more quickly that 4 and 7 are different than for 4 and 3. Again, he failed to show the normal distance effect; in fact he again showed an inverse distance effect, being quicker on Type 2 problems than on Type 3. But he was very, very slow: taking 5 seconds where normal subjects would take about half a second! So again, his performance on this very simple task was very strange.

Given that his ability to tell bigger from smaller numbers is so abnormal, we wondered whether he even could subitize. Experiments on newborn babies show that this innate ability to recognize the numerosity of up to four objects in a visual array is ready to go as soon as the child enters the world. I argued in Chapter 3 that this ability underpins the later development of counting and more advanced concepts of numerosity. It turned out that even this was impossible. Even for two dots, Charles had to count.

Of course, Charles is not literally blind to numerosities. But when he sees numbers, he doesn't see what we see. They make little sense to him. He has to go through elaborate, time-consuming, difficult, and error-prone processes to figure out what they mean. Without a functioning Number Module, the numerical size of the numerals doesn't seem to be activated. His failure to do the simplest number tasks in the normal way turns out to be diagnostic of a very deep-seated problem.

Numerical Size Does Matter

I have tried in this chapter to show how the most basic of numerical abilities, the representation of numerical size, operates in the brain using the simplest of tasks, those involving judgements of bigger and smaller, and of absolute numerosity. These tasks tell us about normal brain functions, and whether processes operating on numerosities really form a cognitive module, in Fodor's sense. More surprisingly, very simple tests asking subjects to make judgements of 'bigger' and 'smaller' can be used to diagnose profound abnormalities in numerical skills.

7

GOOD AND BAD AT NUMBERS

My nature is subdued
To what it works in, like the dyers hand.

WILLIAM SHAKESPEARE, *SONNETS*, 110

Why are some people good at numbers and others bad? In the movie *Good Will Hunting*, our hero, played by Matt Damon, is a young man working as a janitor at MIT, the most prestigious scientific university in the world. As Will mops, the maths professor sets his class an end-of-term test. They have the whole vacation to find the solution, and whoever can solve it will prove himself or herself to be the most outstanding mathematician in a class of students already outstanding by virtue simply of being good enough to get to MIT. After the lecture theatre has cleared, Will Hunting leaves his mop to write the solution on the blackboard. Next day, the professor, astonished, asks the solver to step forward, but of course none does. Eventually he discovers that it was Will, who turns out to be a mathematical prodigy comparable to Ramanujan, the greatest prodigy of them all. However, instead of studying to become a professional mathematician, Will prefers to go out drinking and getting into scrapes with his friends from the neighbourhood. The professor, despite being a Fields Medallist (like a Nobel prize for mathematics, but awarded only every four years instead of Nobel's every year), is in awe. 'I am nothing compared to this young man,' he confesses.

So where does the talent come from? Will tries to explain to his girlfriend. He compares himself to Mozart: 'He looked at a piano . . . he could just play. I could always just play. That's the best I can explain it.'

There are two opposed ideas about mathematical abilities. Nature: it is some kind of biological gift, like the gift for music, perhaps. And nurture: it is all due to hard work and educational opportunities. There is also, of course, the 'sweet pickle view': mathematical ability contains both nature ingredients and nurture ingredients, in variable proportions. As with all human abilities, there are really two distinct questions. First, why am I a bit better at sums than Eric and a bit worse than Diana? That is, what explains the variation in skills among 90% of the population? The second issue concerns the extreme cases. What is it that makes some people real-life counterparts of Will Hunting, and why are other people absolute duffers?

A Biological Gift for Numbers?

A few years ago the papers carried the story of the (re)discovery of Einstein's brain. His left parietal lobe had cells more densely packed than normal. As we saw in Chapter 4, this is the area of the brain crucially involved in numerical processes. Is being born with these extra cells in the key brain area what made him a great mathematician? The theory of the biological gift goes something like this: our genes (and perhaps our early nutrition) will determine the number of parietal-lobe neurons we are born with; those with more will be better at numbers than those with fewer. This sounds plausible, but it cannot be proved simply by correlating the number of parietal neurons with numerical ability. Being good at numbers could be the *cause* of more neurons rather than the consequence—that is, the brain could assign more parietal neurons to number tasks, or hold on to more parietal neurons (since neurons start dying from the day we are born), precisely because that part of the brain is constantly 'exercised'.

The important thing to remember is that what gets us beyond simple numerosity is acquiring what I call 'cultural resources': the words for numbers, the notations we use for recording and manipulating numbers, the myriad methods and inventions our predecessors have bequeathed to the great subject of mathematics, and so on. One of the things that makes *Good Will Hunting* so implausible is that Will does not seem to have spent much time acquiring these resources. Imagine, if you can, asking Archimedes, the greatest mathematician of antiquity, to solve the equation that follows:

$$2a^2 + 3ab - 4b^2 = 0$$

He would have less chance than an averagely educated fourteen-year-old, simply because he would not know what the strange symbols 0, 2, 3, and 4 mean because they weren't invented till seven centuries after his murder; nor '+' and '–', German inventions of the fifteenth century; not to mention '=', which was invented by the Englishman Robert Recorde in the sixteenth century. He would also have had a problem with the idea that equations can have negative roots. As to calculus, no chance at all. Of course, Archimedes could have learned readily enough, but he would still have had to spend time just mastering the notation and getting up to date on ideas that were not around in his time. How, then, could Will even understand the problems that the MIT professor was setting his class? However gifted, he would have to have spent less time in his cups, and more time in his books.

Here's a tale that mathematicians tell to one another:

> A lawyer, an artist and a mathematician are arguing over whether it is better to have a wife or a mistress. The lawyer argues for a wife, stressing the advantages of legality and security. The artist argues for a mistress, emphasising the joys of freedom. The mathematician says, 'You should have both, then when each of them thinks you are with the other, you can get on with some mathematics.'[1]

The Dyer's Hand

Mathematicians like nothing better than doing maths, and they spend as much time as possible doing it. Even idiot savants, who are calculators rather than real mathematicians, spend an extraordinary amount of their time playing around with numbers and working out problems. They need to, because there is so much to learn. Will Hunting seems to do none of that, and has none of that characteristic passion.

I will argue that differences in mathematical ability, provided the basic Number Module has developed normally in our Mathematical Brains, are due solely to acquiring the conceptual tools provided by our culture. Nature, courtesy of our genes, provides the piece of specialist equipment, the Number Module. All else is training. To become good at numbers, you must become steeped in them. This is the 'dyer's hand theory'.

Surely, you will be thinking, there was some essential and innate difference between the children in your class at school who seemed to find maths really easy and those who always found it a struggle. I am not denying that there may be. In particular, I would not deny that there may have been differences in their capacity for concentrated work or in what things they found interesting. My claim is that there was no difference in their innate capacity specifically for maths.

NORMAL AND ABNORMAL VARIATION

All maths examination results show a big spread from the best to the worst. There are all sorts of reasons why children do badly in exams. Some are sick during their exams; anxiety causes others to underperform drastically; some have dreadful home lives; others have dreadful school experiences. As I shall discuss, in any population of children, over 3% will suffer from dyscalculia, a severe innate inability to deal with numbers normally.

There is a standard test used by the Third International Mathematics and Science Survey (TIMSS) which has been used for comparisons of thirteen- and fourteen-year-old schoolchildren in 25 countries (see box). We can therefore compare differences between individuals within a country and between countries. In England, if the top and bottom 5% of fourteen-year-olds are excluded,[2] the difference between the worst and the best is about 300 points on the TIMSS scale. How much of this can be attributed to natural differences in talent and how much to acquiring cultural resources? One clue comes from comparing the worst country on the list with the best. The average score for children in Singapore (the best country) is about 225 points higher than the average score for children in the worst performing country—the Islamic Republic of Iran.[3] What this amounts to is that the average score for the Iranian children is equivalent to the scores of the worst 5% of children tested in Singapore.

The difference in average performance between Singapore and Iran is surely due to culture. Not just teaching, of course, but attitudes to secular learning, the state of the schools, nutrition, peace or war, and so on. The difference between the best students in Singapore and the best in Iran is even larger, suggesting that the Iranian system fails its ablest students even more than it fails its average students. And the longer the child is

QUESTIONS FROM TIMSS

Here are some examples of questions set to thirteen- and fourteen-year-olds. At the end of each problem, I give the percentage of thirteen-year-olds tested who got the right answer, and also the percentage in the highest-scoring country.

1. Fractions and number sense

A. Luke exercises by running 5 km each day. The course he runs is $\frac{1}{4}$ km long. How many times through the course does he run each day?

Answer: _____

(International average 42%, Best country 72%)

B. Teresa wants to record five songs on tape. The length of time each song plays is shown in the table.

Song	Amount of time
1	2 minutes, 41 seconds
2	3 minutes, 10 seconds
3	2 minutes, 51 seconds
4	3 minutes
5	3 minutes, 32 seconds

ESTIMATE to the nearest minute the total time taken for all five songs to play, and explain how this estimate was made.

Estimate: _____

Explain: _____

(International average 31%, Best country 74%)

2. Algebra

If m represents a positive number, which of these is equivalent to $m + m + m + m$?

A. $m + 4$

B. $4m$

C. m^4

D. $4(m + 1)$

(International average 47%, Best country 77%)

exposed to the Iranian and Singapore systems, the bigger the gap between them. At nine years, the earliest testing age in the TIMSS study, the difference is 180 points. Had there been a test for newborns, the difference would have been zero!

In Chapter 3 I described how performance differs between two groups defined not by nationality but by gender. I argued that these are best explained by the cultural contexts of the two groups. One important difference between them turned on how difficult it once was for women to get degrees in mathematics. This meant that girls in girls' schools were much more likely than their male counterparts to be taught by someone without a degree in maths. They had access to less maths expertise, and their learning would suffer as a consequence. As the proportion of qualified female teachers of maths increased, and coincidentally, as the proportion of girls going to mixed schools increased, where the maths teacher might well be a (qualified) man, so the difference between boys and girls decreased. According to recent figures, girls have now caught up with boys, and are beginning to outstrip them.[4] Of course, this would not mean that girls have suddenly acquired more innate talent for maths than boys, only that the girls' (sub)culture in England in 1998 encourages them to work harder at all their school subjects, including mathematics.

If group differences can be attributed to cultural differences in comparing groups, then why not to the individuals that make up the groups?

Of course, the kinds of tests used by TIMSS will be very culture-dependent. Is there a way of measuring normal variation in underlying basic numerical abilities, in the abilities that we might be born with? These abilities are reflected in tests that require no learning beyond the meaning of the number names: tests of number comparison and of visual numerical estimation (subitizing). These tests, I have argued in Chapters 3 and 6, can be used to assess the capacity of the Number Module.

Normal Variation in Arithmetical Tasks

Timing responses is a good way to test abilities on simple arithmetic tasks. Clearly there is an important difference between someone who has to solve 8 + 7, or indeed 8 × 7, by finger-counting and someone who can give the answer almost immediately. Even if fingers are not used, some kind of internal counting may be, and this again would lead to a slower response than would be expected from someone with fluent skills. In a literate and numerate society, the most obvious variation in numerical skill is correlated simply with age, and timing how long it takes to solve the same problems is a good way of tracking this. What we find is that as they get older, children get very much faster at basic arithmetical tasks such as single-digit addition and multiplication. In our study of Italian schoolchildren, the average time taken to produce the answer to a single-digit multiplication decreased from 6 seconds at age eight to less than 3 seconds at age ten.[5]

The explanation for these age trends is an important clue to variations in individual skills. The child of four or five adds by counting, as I described in Chapter 3, often using fingers or tokens. Most children go through three stages of adding by counting.

Stage I: Counting all. For 3 + 5 they can count out 1, 2, 3, and then 4, 5, 6, 7, 8, keeping track of the second addend, sometimes with their fingers; often they recognize the pattern of all the fingers on one hand as five fingers. At an early stage, in my (English) culture, they may count out both 3 and 5 on separate hands, and then count all the fingers raised.

Stage II: Counting on from first. Here they start with the first number presented, 3, and then count on another five, often using their fingers to keep track.

Stage III: Counting on from larger. Here they select the larger of the two numbers, and count on from it. That is, they will first say 'five' and then count out the next three numbers.

Moving through the stages speeds up solution times because there is less to do at each successive stage. In Stage 1, each number has to be counted out separately and then together. In Stage 2, only the second number has to be counted out. And in Stage 3, only the smaller number is counted out, which of course takes less time than counting the larger, which will happen frequently in Stage 2.

This speeding up is due to acquiring, either through learning or by working it out for oneself, more efficient procedures. Counting on from larger may follow from the realization that addition is commutative—or at least that it doesn't matter which number is taken first.[6]

There is one further factor. We saw in Chapter 6 that as they get older children get faster in comparing the magnitude of two numbers. This is largely as a result of being able to access the meaning of the numerals more quickly. Both improved strategies and faster access to numeral meanings are a direct consequence of steeping the Mathematical Brain in numbers. The more numbers are practised and played with, the more they are thought about, and the more fluent the skills become.

The next stage in the ordinary child's mastery of addition comes as addition facts become stored in the memory. These facts may be taught by parents or teachers, or may be arrived at by counting procedures, or both. Now, instead of working out each sum, the child will be able to retrieve from memory the answers to some of them. Over the next few years the proportion of sums solved by retrieval from memory will increase, and retrieving answers, even for five-year olds, takes half the time needed for counting on fingers.[7]

The difference between quick and slow adult subjects is over half a second per addition problem. That might not sound a lot, but it is an increase of nearly 100%, from 0.63 to 1.2 seconds among our university subjects.[8] Solutions simply retrieved are produced 20 to 50% more quickly than those that need some working out. Well-educated subjects retrieve from 33 to 100% of answers to single-digit additions, and the proportion of retrievals is closely related to their overall mathematical skills.[9] Thus good maths skills go together with having memorized the most facts. This certainly reinforces the role of practice and learning. It doesn't exclude the possibility that the best subjects are also the ones who started off as biologically the most gifted, though it offers no evidence in support.

Applying an Understanding of the Basic Laws of Arithmetic

There is of course more to numbers than remembering simple facts. There is understanding. Even treating $9 + 7$ and $7 + 9$ as the same problem implies understanding the *commutativity* of addition. This is a property of the addition operation that follows directly from understanding that 9 and 7 denote numerosities, and that addition is the process of finding the numerosity of the union of two separate collections, with numerosities 9 and 7. Children take a collection of nine dolls, say, combine it with another collection of seven dolls, and count this new, bigger collection. It becomes clear that it doesn't matter at all whether you take the collection of nine and add to the collection of seven, or start with the seven and add the nine to it.

Similar understandings of the commutativity of multiplication follow from the more basic idea that the union of three collections of five is the same as the union of five collections of three. Understanding commutativity makes it unnecessary to remember both that $9 + 7 = 16$ and that $7 + 9 = 16$, and to remember both $9 \times 7 = 63$ and $7 \times 9 = 63$. Of course, this will be so obvious to readers as to be tedious. So I invite you to try the false-compensation problems shown in the box, which also require very basic arithmetical laws for their solution.

The key to the problems in the box is very simple. It involves two principles which most people should understand. However, our research shows that ordinary, non-mathematical university students get only about a third of these problems right. These students almost never realized that, logically and arithmetically, the problems are all equivalent. Many students studying for a mathematics degree *did* realize that they were equivalent. This doesn't mean that the maths students got all the questions right; in fact, they still failed on 40% of the problems overall, even when they seemed to understand correctly the underlying principles. These principles are:

Any number greater than 1 is the sum of two (positive whole) numbers, e.g. $9 = 6 + 3$.
Multiplication is *distributive* over addition:
$(a + b) \times n = (a \times n) + (b \times n)$, e.g. $9 \times 7 = (6 \times 7) + (3 \times 7)$.

Let's see how these principles apply to Problem 1.

1. The car park in Fulham Street has 690 places per row and 64 places per column. The car park in Berkeley Street has 680 places per row and 74 places per column.

Fulham Street Places:
$690 \times 64 = (680 + 10) \times 64 = (680 \times 64) + (\mathbf{10 \times 64})$
Berkeley Street Places:
$680 \times 74 = 680 \times (64 + 10) = (680 \times 64) + (\mathbf{10 \times 680})$

Now it's easy to see that there are far more places in Berkeley Street. There's no need to calculate the products 690×64 and 680×74.

FALSE-COMPENSATION PROBLEMS[10]

These problems come from an experiment we carried out on university students, including maths students. All you have to do is select the answer you think is correct, without carrying out the calculation.

1. The car park in Fulham Street has 690 places per row and 64 places per column. The car park in Berkeley Street has 680 places per row and 74 places per column.

  a. The car park in Fulham Street has more places than the car park in Berkeley Street.
  b. The car park in Berkeley Street has more places than the car park in Fulham Street.
  c. The two car parks have the same number of places.
  d. Without calculation one cannot tell which park has more places.

2. Caroline and Frances have to fill glasses with orange juice for a birthday party. Caroline fills 230 glasses of 38 cl each. Frances fills 220 of 48 cl each.

  a. Caroline pours more orange juice.
  b. Frances pours more orange juice.
  c. They pour the same quantity of orange juice.
  d. Without calculation one cannot tell who pours more orange juice.

3. Peter earns £380 per month for 170 months, while David earns £370 per month for 180 months.

  a. Overall, Peter earns more money than David.
  b. Overall, David earns more money than Peter.
  c. Overall, David and Peter earn the same amount of money.
  d. Without calculation one cannot tell who earns more.

4. I. 568 x 257   II. 567 x 258

  a. I is larger than II.
  b. II is larger than I.
  c. I = II.
  d. Without calculation one cannot tell which is larger.

For reasons that are not yet clear, our non-mathematical students found the problems framed in terms of money much easier than those frames in terms of rows and columns. Their most common error was to think that the two products were the same—what we have called 'false compensation'. On the other hand, the students with more maths training were not only better at getting the right answers, but also less affected by the form in which the questions were set. That is, they were operating at a more abstract level. Although this helps, we are still trying to find out why maths students, most of whom could explain how the problems worked, nevertheless didn't apply this understanding to all the problems. There was even one student who actually produced the correct formula, and explanation with examples, but still didn't get all the answers right.

WHAT DOES IT TAKE TO BE A PRODIGY?

In our study of 'false compensation' in multiplication, the fact that maths students do better than other students may not reflect their training so much as the abilities they had before they opted to do advanced maths at school. In fact, having good natural abilities for maths may be exactly the reason for choosing maths in the first place. So is it possible to separate some kind of native talent from training? Surely, the greatest prodigies started with a few more of the relevant brain cells than you or I. Or do we all really start equal? The grandfather of the theory of natural ability, Sir Francis Galton, wrote this in 1869 in his book *Hereditary Genius*:

> By natural ability, I mean those qualities of intellect and disposition, which urge and qualify a man to perform acts that lead to reputation. I do not mean *capacity* without *zeal*, nor zeal without capacity, nor even a combination of both of them, without an adequate power of doing a great deal of *very laborious work*.[11] [my italics]

Galton was clear that natural ability didn't just mean capacity (e.g. number of parietal lobe cells), but also 'disposition', what we might now term 'drive'—those traits that enable or encourage you to work hard. The biological gift theory is usually thought of as a theory of capacity only. In this picture, Mozart wasn't just a special musical talent, he was also a hard worker. Whether this is true of music or not, is it true of numerical abilities?

Zeal: The Romantic Tragedy of Ramanujan

Let me start with the mathematician with whom Will Hunting was compared—Ramanujan, one of the greatest of mathematicians and also a calculating prodigy. His story, however, is more extraordinary and more romantic than even Hollywood could devise, and sadder than it would allow. Like Will, he grew up poor; and like Will, as a young man, he supported himself with menial work. There was a professor figure: G.H. Hardy, Professor of Mathematics at Cambridge, winner of many prizes and the most distinguished mathematician in Britain. Like the MIT prof, he was awed by Ramanujan's prowess. He wrote, 'I still say to myself when I am depressed, and find myself forced to listen to pompous and tiresome people, "Well, I have done one thing *you* could never have done, and that is to have collaborated with . . . Ramanujan on something like equal terms."'[12] And not out of modesty. He boasted, or confessed, that he had for a time, been 'the fifth best mathematician in the world', but it was clear to him that Ramanujan rated above him.[13] He was in the Bradman class of mathematicians.[14]

But that's where the similarity with Will Hunting ends. Srinavasa Ramanujan was born in 1887 in a small town in the south of India, not a great intellectual centre like Boston, but also on the wrong side of the tracks. His family were desperately poor, but high-caste, Brahmins. On 16 January 1913 he sent a letter to Hardy:

Dear Sir,
I beg to introduce myself to you as a clerk in the Accounts Department of the Port Trust Office at Madras on a salary of only £20 per annum. I am now about 23 years of age. I have had no University education but I have undergone the ordinary school course.[15]

He enclosed with the letter some of his ideas about numbers, written on nine pages of cheap paper. As bait to catch Hardy's attention, he included a way of finding the value of a particular function that

Hardy had recently written had not yet been determined. His letter concluded,

> I would request you to go through the enclosed papers. Being poor, if you are convinced that there is anything of value I would like to have my theorems published.

Hardy was not the first famous mathematician Ramanujan had written to, but he was the first to reply. As C. P. Snow writes in his foreword to *A Mathematician's Apology*, Hardy's autobiographical memoir, 'Famous mathematicians ... are unusually exposed to cranks. [Hardy] was accustomed to receiving manuscripts from strangers, proving the prophetic wisdom of the Great Pyramid, the revelations of the Elders of Zion, or the cryptograms that Bacon had inserted in the plays of the so-called Shakespeare.[16] Hardy discussed the matter with his long-time collaborator, J. E . Littlewood, the same evening. 'Before midnight they knew, and knew for certain, the writer of these manuscripts was a man of genius. That was as much as they could judge, that night. It was only later that Hardy decided that Ramanujan was, in terms of *natural* mathematical genius, in the class of Gauss or Euler.' He offered to help in any way he could and immediately set to work to get this poor Indian clerk to Cambridge, contacting the India Office and Gilbert Walker, head of the Indian Meteorological Department in Simla, who was persuaded to visit Ramanujan in Madras. Hardy was convinced that Ramanujan had already made original contributions to number theory, but could do much more in Cambridge, where he would have access to all the latest books, some of the best mathematical minds in the world, and freedom from money worries. Hardy was right.

If anyone could be thought of as having a biological gift for numbers, of being a mathematical Mozart, it was this poor Indian clerk. What was the basis of Ramanujan's genius? We cannot know whether he had more parietal-lobe neurons than Hardy, or more even than normal people. What we do know is that, from the earliest age for which there is evidence, Ramanujan was passionately interested in numbers and mathematics and absorbed every book he could lay his hands on. Being desperately poor, there were not many of these. One of the books he was given just before he left school was G. S. Carr's *A Synopsis of Elementary Results in Pure and Applied Mathematics.*

> The book was a compilation of five thousand or so equations, written out one after the other—theorems, formulas, geometric diagrams, and other mathematical facts, marching down the page . . . great chunks of mathematics as it was known in the late nineteenth century . . . The book was a distillation of coaching notes.[17]

In a brilliant analysis, Robert Kanigel, Ramanujan's biographer, makes the point that this was exactly the right book for him. Unlike other maths textbooks it contained almost no proofs. The student was not required to follow the author's logic from premises to theorems. Rather, it gave a series of statements of the theorem with only the briefest indications of the reasons behind them. But it did have what Kanigel calls 'flow': you feel as though you are going somewhere.

For example, the first statement in the book is

$$a^2 + b^2 = (a - b)(a + b)$$

The second statement is a natural extension of the first:

$$a^3 + b^3 = (a - b)(a^2 + ab + b^2)$$

but again with no proof. Of course, it would be possible to write out many more powers of a and b, but instead Carr gives the generalization:

$$a^n - b^n = (a - b)(a^{n-1} + a^{n-2}b \ldots b^{n-1})$$

Kanigel writes, 'It is hard to imagine a book *more* apt to influence a mathematically precocious teenager, at least one like Ramanujan. For in baldly stating its results it almost dared you to jump in and prove them for yourself. To Ramanujan, each theorem was its own little research project.'[18] One of his Indian biographers describes him 'ranging with delight' through the new world this book opened up for him.[19]

He went on a scholarship to the local Government College, but his energies were all focused on maths, even during lectures on other subjects. He began keeping notebooks of his proofs for the theorems in Carr's book, and other mathematical ideas he had. Almost all his ideas, even at that tender age, were about pure mathematics, not the trivial mathematics of 'real life'—problems about how many ditches can be dug by however many men in however many hours. Inevitably he failed exams other than maths, and his scholarship was taken away from him. Without it he couldn't continue. The fees were 32 rupees a term, as much as his father made in a month and a half to support the growing family.

However, some fellow Brahmins with interests in mathematics helped out financially for a while, and he was able to spend all his time doing mathematics. A friend who came to see him recalls 'him lying on a mat, his shirt torn, his long hair carelessly bound up with a piece of thin string, working feverishly, notebooks and loose sheets of plain white paper piled up around him'.[20] By 1911 he had even managed to get a paper published in the *Journal of the Indian Mathematical Society*, and immediately started working on others. The first step onto the world stage of mathematics had been taken.

With a young wife to support, he needed a job. His friends found him a post at the Port Trust Office at Madras. Although the job was not demanding, it gave him less time for mathematics. His wife 'would later recall how before going to work in the morning he worked on mathematics; and how when he came home he worked on mathematics. Sometimes, he'd stay up till six the next morning, then sleep for two or three hours before heading off to work.'[21] This obsessive commitment and self-sacrifice is not unusual in prodigies. Hardy, himself an outstanding mathematician at an early age, wrote in *A Mathematician's Apology* that 'If a man has any genuine talent, he should be ready to make almost any sacrifice in order to cultivate it to the full.'[22] Hardy got Ramanujan to Cambridge in 1914, and, at the remarkably young age of thirty, he was elected a Fellow of the Royal Society. They did great work together, and the mathematical world is still mining Ramanujan's *Notebooks* for new ideas to explore.

The story that started as a romance ends as a tragedy. Ramanujan indeed made the ultimate sacrifice for his mathematical passion. Living in damp, cold Cambridge, away from his wife, his family, his religion, his customary foods, he contracted illnesses that led to a suicide attempt in 1918, and to tuberculosis. Snow, in whom Hardy confided during his final years, writes that Hardy used to visit Ramanujan as he lay dying in hospital at Putney. It was on one of those visits that there happened the 'incident of the taxi-cab number'. Hardy entered the room in which Ramanujan was lying, and said, probably without preamble, '"I thought the number of my taxi-cab was 1729. It seemed to me a rather dull number." To which Ramanujan replied: "No, Hardy! No, Hardy! It is a very interesting number. It is the smallest number expressible as the sum of two cubes in two different ways."'[23] [$1729 = 10^3 + 9^3 = 1^3 + 12^3$]

He died in the arms of his wife back in India in 1920, at the age of thirty-three, with perhaps his greatest work ahead of him.

Deliberate Practice and 'Mental Yoga'

Ramanujan's passion led him to greedily acquire as much of the cultural resources as he could, including a vast range and variety of number facts—the factors of 1729 being just the most famous example. This is entirely typical of calculating prodigies, even those who were not serious mathematicians. In a fascinating review of the whole field of expertise, the US–German team of Anders Ericsson, Ralf Krampe, and Clemens Tesch-Römer have found a ten-year rule: 'The highest levels of performance and achievement appear to require at least around 10 years of *intense* prior preparation [my italics].' This is true of swimming, musical composition, chess, and mathematics.[24] They argue that the key is deliberate practice, which is usually solitary. It is indeed laborious, and to be effective it needs intense concentration. Their conclusion is a simple one: more deliberate practice leads to better performance. There is no other significant factor.

Ericsson and his colleagues had studied violin students at the prestigious Music Academy of West Berlin. They compared the hours of practice of the best students, those rated by their teachers the most likely to play professionally at the highest level, with the hours of practice of good students, but ones judged likely to have a career as teachers of music. The former group practised *alone* over 24 hours a week, the prospective teachers only 9 hours on average. By the age of twenty, those destined to teach had accumulated an estimated 4,000 hours of solitary practice, while the top students had accumulated an estimated 10,000 hours. They also discovered that top professionals keep practising alone for 24 hours a week. They found too that the very best violinists of the twentieth century started younger on average than other excellent violinists. Starting younger of course gives you more time to practise. Exactly the same has been found for chess. Judit Polgar, who became a chess grandmaster at the age of fifteen, as had Bobby Fischer, learned chess at the age of four from her father and was taught at home by her parents *precisely* to demonstrate the effects of early training.

There have been no similar systematic studies for the acquisition of numerical and mathematical skills, but there is abundant evidence that the best calculators, from idiot savants to professional performers, spend a great deal of time learning facts and techniques. In a study of perhaps the greatest twentieth-century calculating prodigy, Alexander Aitken, the psychologist Ian Hunter writes about the tremendous 'intellectual effort' put in at an early age: 'There was clearly that cumulative, hierarchically organised progression which so pervasively characterises the acquisition of any comprehensive skill.'[25] Aitken himself wrote that between the ages of thirteen and seventeen, when he left school, he 'underwent what can only be described as a mental Yoga. I tried harder and harder things until, in the end, I was so good at arithmetic that the master didn't allow me to do arithmetic.'[26]

Wim Klein, who held the word record for extracting roots—he can extract the 13th root (the number multiplied by itself 13 times) of a 100-digit number in under 2 minutes—uses a method that requires taking logarithms of the leftmost group of numbers. For this, he laboriously learned the logs of the integers up to 150.[27]

Prodigies work very hard to learn the tricks of their trade, and the more imaginative and better educated invent procedures to make solutions easier on the memory or quicker to carry out. One 'trick' for solving squares was what got Aitken started. Before he was thirteen, he wasn't interested in arithmetic or mathematics at all. But his teacher

chanced to say that you can use this factorization to square a number: $a^2 + b^2 = (a + b)(a - b)$ [+b]^2. Suppose you had 47—that was his example—he said you could take b as 3. So $(a + b)$ is 50 and $(a - b)$ is 44, which you can multiply together to give 2200.

Then the square of b is 9, and so, boys, he said, 47 squared is 2209. Well, from that moment, that was the light, and I never went back.[28]

Martin Gardner, in his elegant analysis of calculators' tricks of the trade, reports how the adult Aitken used this formula to find the square of 777.[29] Again he added a smaller number, 23, to turn 777 into a number with zeros. Of course, Aitken had also memorized all the squares up to 100, so finding the square of 23 was as easy for him as finding the square of 4 would be for us. So,

$$777^2 = [(777 + 23) \times (777 - 23)] + 23^2$$
$$= (800 \times 754) + 529$$
$$= 603,200 + 529$$
$$= 603,729$$

Easy when you know how.

Aitken's powers of calculation were truly extraordinary. A mathematician who accompanied Aitken to an exhibition of desk calculators, wrote in a letter, 'The salesman-type demonstrator said something like "We'll now multiply 23,586 by 71,283." Aitken said right off 'And get . . .' (whatever it was). The salesman was too intent on selling even to notice, but his manager, who was watching, did. When he saw Aitken was right, he nearly threw a fit (and so did I).'[30]

There was a famous case of mentally retarded autistic twins who demonstrated a phenomenal capacity for identifying prime numbers. This is a really hard task since there are no simple rules for finding or testing primes. Many facts and the ability to hold many intermediate results in memory are essential. The twins seemed to spend all their waking hours contemplating numbers, sharing numbers with each other and, presumably, calculating factors and primes. Oliver Sacks, one of the people who studied them in the 1960s, wrote, 'The twins live exclusively in a thought-world of numbers. They have no interest in the stars shining, or the hearts of men. And yet numbers for them, I believe, are not "just" numbers . . . [they] are holy, fraught with significance.'[31] This is certainly zeal, and the cause of much work.

Capacity. One possibility, already considered over a hundred years ago by Galton, is that inherited capacity sets an upper bound to achievement. This makes sense. Genes are a principal factor in determining body size. Size is clearly critical for eminence in shot-putting and gymnastics. You will never be an Olympic champion shot-putter without being big; at the same time, you will never be a champion gymnast if you are big enough to be a shot-putter. Is there an optimum size for mathematicians? Put another way, does brain size matter?

At its crudest, no. Women's brains are 10% smaller than men's, but their IQ (one measure of general capacity) is on average the same. In any case, general capacity seems to bear little relation to eminence (nowadays measured as job success), even in a domain like chess.[32] The calculating prodigy Shankutala Devi was tested by the American psychometrician Arthur Jensen, a keen supporter of the genetic determination of intelligence, including IQ differences among races. He found that she was not much better than average on standard IQ tests, and was actually slower than average on some tests of the speed of mental processing. As the French neuroscientist Stanislas Dehaene notes, 'Devi's calculation feats were obviously not due to a global speed-up of her internal clock: Only her arithmetic processor ran with lightning speed.'[33] This was because she had built into her arithmetic processor a prodigious number of facts, procedures, and tricks of the trade.

As Devi shows, prodigious calculation does not require great intelligence, although some calculating prodigies were indeed people of extraordinary ability who achieved great eminence—for example Carl Friedrich Gauss, Leonard Euler, and André-Marie Ampère. But there are also the idiot savants, who score around 60 on IQ tests, and whose grasp of mathematics, even of aspects of arithmetic on which they are not prodigious, is very weak. One remarkable calculator studied by psychologists Beate Hermelin and Neil O'Connor in London not only tested with an IQ of 67 on one scale, but was severely autistic and totally without language, spoken or gestural. Nevertheless, he was able to recognize prime numbers up to five digits long in under 3 seconds, and generate them in under 10 seconds, which is four or five times faster than a control subject with a maths degree. He was also able to factorize large numbers faster and more accurately than the control.

Hermelin and O'Connor attribute the sometimes extraordinary skills of autistic idiot savants to their tendency to 'become preoccupied with repetitive actions or ideas . . . [often in] specific domains such as calculation, music or drawing'.[34] The additional factor that makes some autistic people savants cannot be intelligence, or even general speed of mental processing, since they perform poorly outside their domain of expertise. Obsession, however, does seem to be a necessary ingredient.

Nor does it require a generally exceptional memory. Steven Smith, in his brilliant account of prodigies, quotes a contemporary account of the nineteenth-century prodigy Henri Mondeux: 'He, who knows so much, has never learned anything. Facts, dates, places, pass before his brain as before a mirror without leaving a trace.'[35] On numbers, of course, his memory, like that of other prodigies, was prodigious. Aitken, when he heard the year 1961, immediately thought of it as 37×53, *and* as $44^2 + 5^2$ *and* as $40^2 + 19^2$. He was also able to recite π to the first 100 decimal places.[36]

Many prodigies begin to show their extraordinary abilities at a very young age indeed, in the case of Gauss and Ampère at three. But Smith finds that these are usually the ones who hear numbers in their head as they calculate, what he calls the 'auditory type'. Visual calculators, those who 'see numbers in their head' often start much later, in their teens or even their twenties. This suggests to me, that the form taken by prodigious ability is determined not by biological gifts but by which cultural resources are available when laborious work begins. Children of three are likely to experience numbers mainly as spoken words, while older children and adults are likely already to be fluent with visual numerals. If calculating prodigies were all cut from the same biological cloth, one might have expected that the way this manifested itself would be similar.

Perhaps the most striking demonstration that anybody can be a prodigy was provided by the French psychologist Alfred Binet. At the turn of the century he compared two prodigies, who made their living demonstrating their calculating prowess, with three university students and with four cashiers at the Paris department store Bon Marché. The prodigies were much faster than the students, but on most tests they were *slower* than the cashiers! Table 7.1 gives the calculation times for two problems carried out by the two professionals,

Inaudi and Diamandi, and by the best cashier.[37] Now it's true that in those days a cashier was recognized as highly skilled. It was certainly different from working a modern supermarket check-out. It required many different calculations, including multiplying mentally a wide range of quantities—such as lengths of fabric, weights of foods, numbers of needles—by a wide range of unit prices. The cashiers who took part in Binet's tests had on average fourteen years' experience, and were very good at their job. Although cashiers did not need special qualifications beyond ordinary schooling, I don't doubt that self-selection played a part: those who couldn't do it or didn't enjoy doing it moved on to other positions within the store. Nevertheless, here we can see a fairly random bunch of ordinary Parisians outperforming celebrated professional prodigies. This undermines the case for exceptional 'natural ability' and reinforces the case for 'very laborious work'.

Parental Contribution

Sir Francis Galton noticed that eminent individuals were likely to have close relatives who were also eminent, though not always in the same domain. At first sight, this looks like an argument for the inheritance of some extra capacity. Some parents will bequeath a fat bank account—will others bequeath additional brain cells? Galton thought so. Monozygotic twins (identical twins from the same sperm and egg, and hence with the same genes) are known to be more alike in mathematical abilities than dizygotic twins (from different eggs).[38] Many people have concluded from this that mathematical ability is inherited.

	638×823	$7,286 \times 5,397$
Inaudi	6.4 seconds	21 seconds
Diamandi	56 seconds	2 minutes 7 seconds
Best cashier	4 seconds	13 seconds

Table 7.1 Alfred Binet, inventor of the IQ test, measured the calculating speeds of professional theatrical calculating prodigies and of experienced cashiers at the Bon Marché department store in Paris. The best cashiers were at least as good as the best prodigies; on these two tasks the best of them all outperformed the prodigies Inaudi and Diamandi.

However, there are several reasons to be cautious about drawing this conclusion. First, the vast majority of monozygotic twins share the same placenta, and hence have a more similar intrauterine environments than dizygotic twins, who do not share a placenta. Second, identical twins tend to be treated more similarly than non-identical twins, a tendency that is reinforced by dressing them alike.[39] If one twin is thought of as a potentially good mathematician, then the other will be too. However, there is one very nice piece of evidence against such a simple genetic picture: a case of idiot savant identical twins (who therefore have the same genes) where one brother began calendrical calculations at the age of six, but the other only took it up some years later, and never achieved quite the same level of performance.[40]

Of course, there are many other reasons why eminent individuals might have eminent parents: doors can be opened, ropes will be known. An eminent family member is living demonstration of what is within reach. And the best tutors, the best equipment, and the best education can be bought. But there is another link: the encouragement parents give their children. Convincing evidence comes from musical expertise. Children with the most supportive parents achieve the highest levels of performance, especially if the support strengthens as the expertise increases. The parent follows rather than leads the child. The critical factor is the degree of involvement: encouraging practice and helping the child to organize his or her own patterns of practice.[41]

The other striking finding is that it is not necessarily the parents with the greatest musical ability who produce the most musically gifted children, which is what we would expect if the difference lay in the inheritance of extra ability. In fact, if a parent is a good musician, this could be detrimental to the child's own musical development. When my children were able to play recognizably even 'Twinkle, Twinkle', I was impressed and showed it, because here they were at seven years old doing something that I could not. Having a mother who can play a bit and can read music probably helps even more than my indiscriminate encouragement, since she is better able to ensure that their *deliberate* practice is well structured and doesn't contain too many mistakes. One can think of many examples of children with famously encouraging parents who have become eminent in an activity in which the parents themselves did not: to take just the first examples that come to mind,

Venus and Serena Williams in tennis, Tiger Woods in golf, and the Polgar sisters in chess. And Ramanujan. Behind an eminent child there is probably a dedicated parent. This doesn't mean that being a pushy parent guarantees eminent offspring, but being supportive certainly helps.

DEVELOPMENTAL DYSCALCULIA — BORN NOT TO COUNT

If practice, with parental help, is the key to being good, what is the key to being bad? There are many reasons for being bad at arithmetic, just as there are for being bad at any school subject. But school maths is like a house of cards: the cards in the bottom layer must be firmly and accurately constructed if they are to support the next layer up. Each stage depends on the last. If a lower level is shaky, the house will eventually fall down. Similarly, if a pupil, for whatever reason, misses out at Stage N, then it will be hard to build Stage $N + 1$ securely, and if N and $N + 1$ are shaky, then Stage $N + 2$ will be even more fragile. The gap between the concepts currently being taught in class and the pupil's understanding will get wider and wider. In many other subjects this is not the case. If you miss out on the geography of Australia it won't compromise your learning the geography of Ireland. Of course, this is an oversimplification. Geography is now taught in a progressive way, so that concepts introduced as they apply to one country are re-applied to another country later in the curriculum; likewise some aspects of mathematics are relatively independent, for example (Euclidean) geometry and arithmetic. Nevertheless, maths is particularly sensitive to problems at school.

Is maths failure like failing to learn to read? After decades when poor reading was put down to laziness, stupidity, or behavioural problems, we now know that about 4% of children fail to learn to read normally because they suffer from a constitutional disability, dyslexia.[42] Some dyslexics may learn to read quite well by using special compensatory strategies, and indeed may become quite skilled, but they will never read normally. Let me give one example from our own studies. Rosalind was a bright 22-year-old, with three A levels and a good degree. She was quite unable to read aloud letter strings she had never seen before, even very simple ones such as HOO and BANT; but she scored in the normal range for someone of her age and education on a standard reading test.

On more advanced reading tests she proved able to read aloud correctly rare words with uncommon or irregular spelling patterns, such as PHLEGM, IDYLL, and PUERPERAL. And she could define them. Her disability meant that every time she came across a new word she had to ask someone else to tell her the pronunciation, which she then had to memorize. She couldn't rely, as normal readers do, on 'phonics'—that is, on assembling the pronunciations of the individual letters. So although she was reading at statistically normal levels, the *way* she was reading was abnormal.[43] Many dyslexics never manage to read or to spell as efficiently as Rosalind, and suffer lifelong disadvantage as a consequence.

Is there an analogy for numerical abilities? Are there 'developmental dyscalculics', the arithmetical equivalents of Rosalind, who, despite hard work, intelligence, and educational opportunities, will never be able to deal with numbers in the way most of us do? One clue comes from an epidemiological study of over a thousand English children, in which 36 of them (1 in 28) with otherwise normal abilities had 'specific learning difficulties' in arithmetic.[44] Similar results have been obtained in the USA and in Israel. This proportion of 1 in 28 is extraordinarily high: more than one per class in an average school. This is about the same incidence as dyslexia. Other estimates put the true proportion as high as 1 in 17.

The idea that people could be bad just at arithmetic is not a new one. It probably dates back to the golden age of phrenology, when each aptitude and trait was located in a 'bump' on the cranium. People, including Queen Victoria, would visit phrenologists to 'have their bumps felt'. There was meant to be a separate bump for numbers, located behind the eye.[45] The first evidence for a separate specifically numerical ability came at the end of the nineteenth century from the work of a Glasgow eye surgeon, a Dr Hinshelwood. He noticed that there were children who had learned to read numbers but not words, and there were boys who 'excel in their studies in other departments, but are the greatest *"duffers" in arithmetic'*.[46]

'Duffers in Arithmetic'

The Mathematical Brain hypothesis implies that there might indeed be children who, through genetic abnormality or for other reasons, are born with an abnormal brain development which selectively affects their Number Module. We are just beginning to diagnose children as suffering from development dyscalculia. A foremost American expert, David Geary, has found that developmental dyscalculia often involves 'immature problem-solving strategies', for example adding 5 + 4 by counting rather than retrieving the fact from memory.[47] One patient of ours, Julie, though now a well-educated adult, still calculates on her fingers. Geary implies that developmental dyscalculia is really a matter of *delayed* development, rather than *abnormal* development. But we shall see that some people with developmental dyscalculia are not just delayed, but think about numbers quite differently from normal people.

A few years ago we were approached by a Canadian student, whom we will call Julie. She told us that from her primary-school days she had been classified as 'learning disabled' in mathematics. By this time, we had ceased to be surprised that intelligent and well-educated people could be duffers at arithmetic. What did surprise us was the extent to which she relied on her fingers to do even the simplest calculation.

Although she had successfully completed one degree and had been accepted on a postgraduate course, she was very worried that she was still struggling on simple calculation, and embarrassed in case people saw her counting-on 3 from 5 when adding the two numbers together. She solved subtraction by counting up from the subtrahend (the number subtracted), again using her fingers to keep track. So, given the problem 9 – 4, she started with the 4 and counted up 'five, six, seven, eight, nine' (keeping track of how many numbers she had counted on her fingers), 'five!' One task she failed at was counting by threes. She couldn't do this at all, except by counting all the numbers and emphasizing every third— 'One, two *three*, four, five, *six*, seven, eight, *nine*, ten, . . .'.

Our tests revealed that she had retained very few arithmetical facts in her memory, and was very slow indeed on problems that take most of us less than a second, because she was counting, often aloud, and raising and lowering her fingers. Nevertheless, with years of practice she had managed to become proficient enough with her fingers and a few facts to be accurate 90% or more of the time on single-digit problems. Relying, as she did, on counting and fingers, anything more complex than single-digit problems posed an insuperable practical and conceptual hurdle. She had no sense of the meaning of fractions. She thought that ⅙ was smaller than ⅛ 'because 6 is smaller than 8'. Three-fifths of 500 was impossible for her. Anything algebraic was a total mystery—she believed that a/a had to be a since 'the result of an operation with letters cannot be a number.' For $c \times c$, she understood $2c$. The areas of geometrical figures were another mystery.[48]

Julie's dependence on counting and fingers seems to stem from a weak concept of numerosity. It's as if she can't rely on numerosities to organize her memories, and has to use counting instead.

Charles: No Numerosities

In Chapter 6 I described the case of Charles, the most remarkable case of dyscalculia I have studied. I first met him in 1993, when he was acting as a psychological counsellor to a PhD student, but when he entered my office it was not as a counsellor but as someone seeking counselling. The student had mentioned my work on mathematical disabilities, and Charles was wondering if I could help.

He was thirty-one years old. At the age of fourteen he had been diagnosed as a high-IQ dyslexic, severe enough to obtain a disability certificate, but his calculation problems somehow escaped notice. A year or two later, after another batch of standard tests, the educational psychologist wrote: 'Charles also experiences difficulty in the handling and calculation of money with any degree of confidence.' He told me that school had always been a struggle because of dyslexia, and also because in arithmetic he had been permanently stuck at the bottom of his class. Nevertheless, he managed to achieve three good A levels and a degree in psychology, though it all took him much longer than usual. Since psychology degrees involve quite a lot maths, especially statistics, I asked him how he managed those parts of the course. He said that he always did well in statistics exams, but these, he pointed out, do not involve him in any calculation. The calculations are done on a computer. His grasp of the logic of statistical tests may have been a little shaky, but then it is for the majority of students, and not a few research psychologists. You can do well enough in stats exams if you can remember which tests to apply in which situations, just as those who have no real grasp of the principles of cooking can manage reasonably well with a copy of Elizabeth David's *Provincial French Cooking* at their side.

Many people think they are bad at maths, and they are, but they're not dyscalculic. Usually they've been badly taught, or had unfortunate experiences that reduced zeal to near zero. As a result they fell further and further behind their classmates, got more and more anxious about it, and lost confidence in their ability. There are ways of helping these people back to normality and restored confidence, as discussed in the next chapter, but I had no idea whether Charles was in this unfortunately very common category. I gave him a few informal tests, and was immediately struck by two things: he was very slow even at the simplest additions and subtractions, and he always used his fingers for calculation.

In both these respects he was like Julie. Like her, he relied almost entirely on counting to carry out arithmetical tasks in his head or on paper. And also like her, he would use his fingers for calculation. To multiply 5 by 3, he would count up to 5 on his left hand, and raise one finger on his right; count from 6 to 10 on his left hand, and raise a second finger on his right hand; and finally count from 11 to 15 on his left hand and raise a third finger. After each left-hand count he would check his right hand to see how many fives he had counted. He was almost always correct when both numbers were below 5, but he found it hard to keep track when one of them was above 5, complaining that he needed another hand.

At this point I decided that it was time to consult Lisa Cipolotti, with whom I had been investigating neurological patients with acquired acalculia and who probably knew as much as anyone about testing individuals with number difficulties. Together we ran Charles through some of the batteries of tests that we had used with the patients. He performed well on tests of reasoning, of general intelligence, and even of reading, which shows that hard work can compensate for dyslexia to the extent that one can learn to read efficiently. This is not, however, the same as reading normally. He could read and write numbers fairly accurately up to about three digits, but then he started to make lots of mistakes. This was unusual, but perhaps not a sign of some profound disturbance. But his calculation was still almost at the bottom of the scale for competence, not just 'lacking confidence'. Even though he worked hard at his maths he was never able to compensate to the same extent as he did in his reading.

Can he subitize? Where Charles's problem was more profound than Julie's was revealed in the very simplest number tasks: number comparison. In Chapter 6 I mentioned Charles's abnormal performance in deciding which of two numbers was the larger. Not only was he abnormally slow, he took longer to decide that 9 was larger than 1 than to decide that 9 was larger than 8. This is exactly the opposite of the normal pattern, where the greater the difference between numbers, the easier and quicker is the decision. This was our first real clue that Charles's deficit was quite unlike anything we'd come across before.

The second clue was, if anything, even more extraordinary. Charles was simply unable to subitize: that is, to recognize the number of dots in an array without counting. The way subitizing is assessed is by looking at the time it takes to name the number of dots in an array. Normally, it takes about the same time to name one, two, three, and four dots; after that the curve rises steadily at about 0.05 second per dot, which suggests some kind of internal counting; the exact time increment depends on the pattern of the dots and the individual. Charles was counting at over 0.4 second per dot, nearly ten times normal. This is about the speed at which he would count out loud, and he was counting at this rate from two dots onwards. So he was always counting and never subitizing. In Chapter 3, I presented evidence that newborn babies can subitize (at least, normal ones can) and that this ability underlies the development of ideas of numerosity.

My colleague George Mandler produced the definitive study of adult subitizing in 1982.[49] Mandler showed that it takes no longer to name the number of dots when there are four dots than when there is just one dot. For more than four dots the time taken increases systematically with each additional dot. He concluded that for more than four dots we engage in some kind of fast silent counting. Interestingly, he found that if the dots are arranged in what he called a 'canonical' pattern, such as is seen on dice or on playing cards, then counting time is quicker because the viewer can make use of the regularity if not the familiarity of the array. Even for three and four dots there is a slight difference between a random pattern and a canonical pattern. Three dots, unless they are in a straight line, will always form a triangle, and four dots will always form a quadrilateral, and our visual pattern-recognition system can take advantage of that fact. The 'subitizing range' is from one dot to the upper limit of the number that can be accurately estimated without counting—that is, before the line on Mandler's graph begins to go up. For most of us, the limit is four.

A key component of the Number Module is thus the ability to subitize. How does it function in Charles's brain? We carried out the Mandler tests on Charles and on control subjects, using both random and canonical arrays of dots. The results are shown in Figure 7.1. It is clear that Charles cannot subitize. The time it takes him to name two dots is greater than one, three is greater than two, and four is greater than three. In fact, he takes about half a second (500 milliseconds) per dot. Not only does he count, where the rest of us subitize, he counts very slowly—slowly enough to be using the counting words. For more than four dots our control subjects were counting at less than 150 milliseconds per dot: too fast for them to be saying the numbers out loud, or even in their heads.

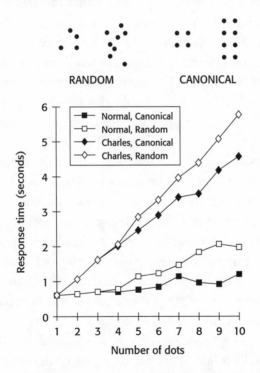

Figure 7.1 Charles's dot enumeration. In this task, subjects have to say the number of dots in the array as quickly as they can. Normal subjects can see the number of dots at a glance in the 'subitizing range' of 1 to 4 dots. For larger numbers of dots an unconscious counting process is used, which takes about 0.2 second per dot, depending on whether the dots are arranged in a familiar 'canonical' pattern or at random. Not only is Charles much slower than the normal subjects, taking about 0.5 second per dot, but he starts counting at two dots.

Does Charles have a mathematical brain? In subitizing, as in comparison, Charles is relying on the sequence of counting words to do a numerosity task that we would do in a quite different way. He was unable to do something that comes quite naturally to human infants, and indeed to the young of some other species. It seems as though the machinery for subitizing, present in the normal brain, is not working in Charles's brain, or is even not there at all. So, what's the matter with Charles's brain? He has no history of neurological illness, and is clearly intelligent and well educated. Why, then, is he unable to carry out the very simplest numerical tasks normally? It cannot be put down to a general cognitive impairment, since that would have prevented him from achieving what he has done in school and at university. Nor can it be blamed on his mathematics education, either formal and informal, since subitizing requires no education, apart from a knowledge of the number names and their meanings. He has a good general vocabulary, so it cannot be accounted for by a failure to words in general. As I said, I think the root of his problem has been a failure to represent the meanings of number words. But why should this be—what has prevented him from acquiring mental representations of the numerosities even of very small numbers?

As with colour-blindness and dyslexia, part of the brain has failed to develop normally. There are two possibilities. First, at some point in his development, probably before he went to school, he suffered damage to his brain that affected the part critical to processing numerosities. Second, if our genes contain instructions to build a special part of the brain to represent numerosities, as I claim, then my guess (and at the moment it is no more than a guess) is that Charles's genes did not contain the right instructions, so the necessary part of the brain was never configured. The Number Module in our Mathematical Brain is very specialized and very hard-wired. If it is damaged early on or if it fails to get built, no other part of the brain can satisfactorily take over its job. Charles manages his arithmetical tasks as best he can by working around the deficit, using other ways of representing numbers: notably the sequence of counting words and finger representations of numerosities.

Without a sense of numerosity, he was unable to tell which of two numbers was bigger in the way the rest of us do. He had to resort to a strategy of counting from one to the other. Our tests showed that he took longer to say that 9 was bigger than 8 than to say that 9 was bigger than 1—the complete opposite of the normal pattern, which is that the more similar in size two numbers are the longer it takes to say which is the larger. (Julie, on the other hand, was fairly quick on this test and showed the normal pattern of being faster when the difference between the two numbers was greater.) Charles managed to store almost no arithmetical facts. When we first tested him he took 8 seconds to add 8 and 6, 12 seconds to subtract 2 from 6, and he failed on 7 + 5 and 9 + 4. This puts him in the bottom 1% of the population. In later tests he was better, but abnormally slow because he was calculating with his fingers.

Prosthetics—pocket calculators and computers—helped him tremendously, since he was able to learn the correct procedures by heart, and this could mask even his weak conceptual grasp. One incident illustrates this nicely. On a multiplication test he would say $N \times 0$ was N (which is not a completely unknown error even among undergraduate students at universities with highly selective intakes). He also said that $N \times 1$ problems had N as the answer. Of course, his pocket calculator would always get the right answer to both types of problem. I pointed out to Charles that in the course of the test he had said both that 6×0 was 6 and that 6×1 was 6. How did he explain that? All he could offer was that both 'sounded right' to him.

Without the normal basis for numerosity, as revealed in the subitizing and comparison tests, Charles never seemed to develop the normal adult understanding of the basic concepts of arithmetic. I believe that these concepts provide the organizing principle for our memory for arithmetical facts. The popular idea that we must (or ought to) depend on sing-song recitation of tables for efficient arithmetic is, in my view, quite wrong. In Chapter 4 I described the case of Frau Huber, who was able to recite her multiplication tables but couldn't add or subtract, and never even tried to use her fingers. The words in these tables seemed quite cut off from their meanings. Without the meanings—the numerosities—the ability to repeat the words is little help in arithmetic. Something must have gone wrong with the development of the number circuits, the Number Module, in Charles's brain. These provide the inner core of our number understanding. The conceptual tools we learn at school or discover for ourselves are built onto this core.

Cathy with the Strange Number Line

I saw my very first case of developmental dyscalculia back in the early 1980s before I'd even heard of it, and long before I had any idea of how to test for it. It came about like this. My partner, Diana Laurillard, was at the University of Surrey researching the use of new technologies in university teaching, particularly as applied to mathematics, her subject. One day a psychology student came to see her about her own maths incompetence. For as long as she could remember, any kind of arithmetic had been a disaster area for her. Cathy had no problems with the rest of her course. She was getting good marks, could think logically enough to program computers (which had been her job before coming to university to read psychology), and was doing well at statistics, which needed logic and computer skills rather than calculational skills.

But on even the simplest addition with a sum greater than 10 she was awful. Not only did she get the wrong answer, she had no confidence at all in her answers. For 8 + 6 she would say, '15, I think. I'm not sure.' She didn't count on her fingers to solve problems. In those days, I hadn't discovered that timed tests of subitizing and comparison were diagnostic of deep deficits of basic number concepts. Our tests consisted of finding out which sorts of sum she could do and which she couldn't, then asking her to describe what went on in her head when she was trying to get the answer. We were very puzzled. We didn't know that there could be learning difficulties confined to numbers, so why couldn't this smart young woman do what even a child of six could do?

In one of our test sessions, Diana, who, unlike me, sees a number line in her head when she's calculating, asked Cathy to draw out *her* number line. What she drew is shown in Figure 7.2. Cathy had been using this scheme since primary school, and she'd never noticed anything wrong with it. Her mental picture was based on it. So when she thought about 5, she thought of it as at the middle of the 1–10 line, and 3 as at the middle of the 1–5 line. But what was at the middle of the 5–10 line? Was it 7 or was it 8? Decades were represented twice, once at the beginning of a line and once at the end. This scheme would not have survived a simple counting test: 'One, two, three, four, five, five, six,

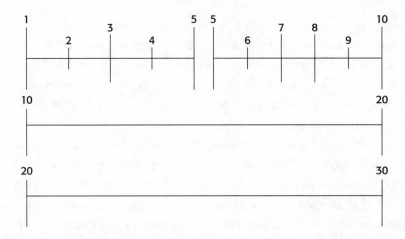

Figure 7.2 Cathy, a highly intelligent, well educated dyscalculic in her late twenties, drew for us her number line. She had been thinking about numbers in this way since she was a young child, but this was the first time she had committed the scheme to paper.

seven, eight, nine, ten, ten, eleven.' She seemed to have failed to connect numerosity with counting, or either of them with calculating. She seemed to have memories, often vague and uncertain, for some numerical relationships. So how could Cathy have used a number scheme so profoundly wrong for so long? We never found out, but Diana did give her the correct scheme to practice with before she disappeared from our lives and our research. We have never met anyone like her since.

A Gene for Numbers?

Why are otherwise intelligent children so bad at numbers? To say that they suffer from 'developmental dyscalculia' is just to give a name to the condition. There's no evidence that it runs in families, in the way dyslexia does, though there has been very little research.

One important clue was discovered by Marcel Kinsbourne and Elizabeth Warrington. They found that Gerstmann's syndrome can occur in children. Sufferers from this syndrome have defective mental representations of the fingers—they cannot tell which finger is being touched, without looking, are confused about left and right, and have difficulty writing and drawing. As I suggested in Chapter 5, using fingers for counting is intimately linked with the development of normal concepts of numerosity, and the fact that the representations of numerosity in the brain are right next to the representations of fingers. If the brain representations of fingers are defective in the child, could this lead to abnormalities in the basic concept of numerosity? Kinsbourne and Warrington found that the children with Gerstmann's syndrome were certainly much poorer at simple arithmetic than matched control subjects were, and some even had difficulty in counting.[50]

Byron Rourke, a US psychologist specializing in developmental disorders, looked at the issue from the opposite perspective. Starting with children whose academic abilities are poor only in arithmetic, he found that many of them also have the other symptoms of Gerstmann's syndrome.[51] Children with Gerstmann's syndrome often have a history of difficult births or diseases of infancy which may have damaged the sensitive developing brain, but some do not.[52] If brain injury is not responsible for all cases of developmental dyscalculia, then what is? Could it be in the genes? If, as the Mathematical Brain hypothesis claims, our genes code for building a specialized Number Module in the brain, then something could go wrong with this process. Of course, finding dyscalculics with no obvious cause of brain injury doesn't mean that the cause is genetic. One would need to be able to establish a genetic abnormality quite independently of the dyscalculia.

One group with poor numerical skills are those born with Fragile X syndrome, an abnormality of a sex-determining chromosome. The abnormality is now known to be located on the long arm of the X chromosome, though it is still not known why. These children often develop Gerstmann's syndrome, with severe dyscalculia. Another group are females with Turner's syndrome. To oversimplify, these girls are missing one of the two X chromosomes that makes them girls rather than boys, who have one X and one Y chromosome. This condition seems to have no effect on language skills, memory, or general intelligence, but arithmetical abilities are about two years behind the average for their age.[53]

It still needs to be established whether it is this genetic abnormality in the chromosomes that has affected these girls' capacity to carry out the simplest number tasks—subitizing and comparison—or whether their poor performance has some other cause. But connecting genes with behaviour, even if we could do it, is only part of the story. This is why all those newspaper stories about a gene for IQ or for mothering instinct are silly. The missing link is the brain. We still need to establish that the genetic abnormality has affected the development of the key brain circuits. (No one has the slightest idea what these are for IQ or for mothering.) But we do have good evidence that the parietal lobes, especially the left parietal lobe, are where most number work is carried out (see Chapter 4).

The answer to the puzzle has to connect genes, perhaps in the X chromosome, with the development of the parietal lobes, and the parietal lobes with the capacities of the Number Module. And this is what we are currently working on in my lab. With luck, we should have an answer within the next five years.

NUMBERS AND THE DEVELOPING BRAIN

One of the most unexpected recent findings in neuroscience is that the brain turns out to be quite flexible—the technical term is 'plastic'—in how jobs are assigned to different areas. These findings support the importance of practice, but they offer no comfort for those who believe in innate talent.

The Musician's Hand and the Braille Reader's Fingers

Musicians, pianists, and violinists develop manual skills requiring great accuracy and precise timing of hand movements. We now know that to program the intricate dance of fingers and thumbs, the brain assigns extra brain cells to the job, just as your computer assigns more memory for powerful software. The motor cortex—the region that controls hand and finger movements—of the brains of professional keyboard and string players has been measured using very accurate imaging techniques. This area turns out to be much bigger in the musicians than it is in the brains of otherwise similar non-musicians. And it is not only the motor cortices in each hemisphere that are bigger, but also the white matter that connects them together. The defenders of innate talent might say, 'Aha, the people who ended up as professional musicians started out with brains that were bigger (better) in the relevant respects!', but that would be to ignore one further finding: the size of the motor cortex is related to the age at which the musician began training. The earlier their training started, the bigger their motor cortex.

Similarly, Braille readers use their fingers where we use our eyes. Many Braille readers feel the letters with just one finger. It has been found that after years of reading with their index finger, the representation in the brain of this finger was larger than that of the non-reading index finger. That is to say, the brain of Braille readers assigns more nerve cells to interpreting what this finger feels. Practice doesn't make the fingertips more sensitive. Rather, when the fingers are reading Braille, the patterns the tips feel have a meaning beyond raised dots: they stand for letters and words. As a consequence, cells in the brain need to be dedicated to handling this extension of the normal output from the nerves leading in from the fingertips.[54]

These long-term adaptations depend on short-term practice effects. Like the text you are now reading, Braille texts need to be proofread before they are published. And Braille proofreaders work about 6 hours a day. Alvaro Pascual-Leone and his colleagues mapped the brain regions controlling the fingers of the reading hand of a Braille proofreader after a working day, and also after a day off from work. The resulting maps were clearly bigger after 6 hours of hard work. The brain recruits more cells to do a job, but when the job is over the cells are re-assigned.[55]

In the long term, repeated practice at a skill will increase the number of neurons the brain assigns to that skill on a more or less permanent basis, though it seems that if you stop altogether the neurons that are no longer in employment will become available for other tasks. Long-lasting structural changes in the brain are dependent on practice.[56] Use it or lose it!

VICIOUS AND VIRTUOUS CIRCLES

If deliberate practice is critical, particularly practice directed to understanding the basic principles of numbers, then it easy to see why some people get left behind by the educational system, and therefore end up both incompetent and anxious about their incompetence. They don't do enough practice. But it's important to understand how this comes about, and why it has particularly disastrous effects where mathematical skills are concerned.

Maths, like music and many other skills, is progressive and cumulative. If you slip behind you will get worse, incurring unwanted reactions from peers, teachers, and parents: disappointment or worse—even anger or ridicule. This will lower your own confidence and your enjoyment of maths tasks. A likely consequence is avoidance, as far as possible, of anxiety-inducing, self-esteem-lowering maths tasks. And that means not practising. The gap will continually widen between understanding the ideas needed to keep up with the class and ideas that you have a confident grasp of. And as the 'chasm of incomprehension' gets wider, class performance will get worse, anxiety will increase, and practice will be avoided even more: a vicious circle (Figure 7.3).

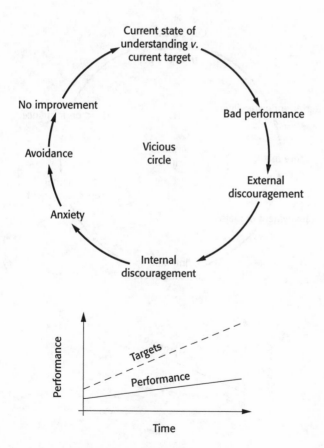

Figure 7.3 A vicious circle: poor understanding leads to avoidance and to falling further behind targets set in school.

On the other hand, it is also easy to see how maths abilities can be improved: more deliberate practice. When the grasp of current concepts is sure, and performance on current tasks is good, teachers and peers are encouraging, confidence rises, enjoyment of numbers increases, practice increases. New concepts are acquired, and you can keep up with or even exceed current conceptual demands. The result: a virtuous circle (Figure 7.4). One can imagine the virtuous circle rotating fastest in prodigies. The degree to which they exceed current expectations becomes greater very quickly. The rewards of excelling at mental arithmetic are, in fact, considerable. The twentieth-century prodigy Hans Eberstark lists the external rewards it offers: 'Making

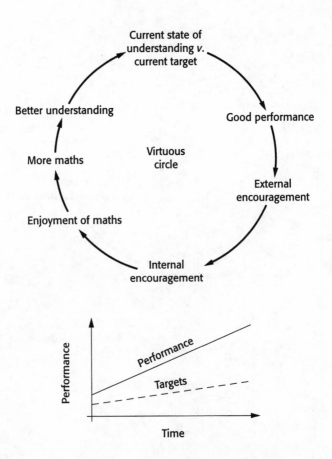

Figure 7.4 A virtuous circle: good understanding leads to more maths work, better understanding, and exceeding targets set in school.

friends, making money, showing off, and giving pleasure.' But there are even greater, internal rewards: 'Mastery, dependability, transformation, insight.' This is how Eberstark explains them:

Mastery. There are few areas of knowledge in which you can make faster progress. What was inconceivable yesterday is within your grasp today and an effortless achievement tomorrow. If ever you are plagued by doubts about your capacity to cope, here is a powerful boost to your ego and self confidence.

Dependability. Life in this irrational world is chaotic, confusing, unfair. The response to love is contempt; backbreaking efforts go unrewarded; results seem to bear little relation to input. In the world of numbers, all comes out right in the end. Figures never fail you . . .

Transformation. Like [a] Magician you wield your wand and your numbers evolve. What moves is more interesting than what is set, just as a kaleidoscope is more riveting than a fixed pattern . . .

Insight. . . . One way of catching a glimpse of the harmony of the Universe . . . is to delve into the mystery of numbers.[57]

This may help to explain the fascination numbers have for idiot savants. Here's one thing they can be good at, indeed better than their parents and peers. Their feats will be greeted with admiration, even astonishment, rather than condescension and frustration. They will also feel in control, rather than at a loss. No wonder they are willing to spend so much time memorizing tables and calendars. And the more time they spend at it, the better they get and the more positive the rewards, both external and internal.

Upper Bounds

Sir Francis Galton knew that 'zeal' and 'very laborious work' were essential to eminence in any field, including mathematics. He also believed that differences in our innate intellectual abilities, which went beyond differences in innate capacity for hard work and innate interests and passions, put an upper bound on our potential achievements, on the likelihood of what he called 'eminence'. We have seen good evidence—statistical, biographical, psychological, and historical—for the contribution of hard work. There is evidence for zeal (a plausible cause of hard work) from the biographies of prodigies. What is lacking is any evidence for differences in intellectual ability that *precede* zeal and hard work in mathematics. We have found no warrant for the Will Hunting story. A real-life case like Will, who really didn't work abnormally hard at maths, would be a counter-example to my thesis.

There is no evidence for individual differences in upper bounds to achievement that cannot be explained in terms of training, the best predictor of achievement (in music, at least) being simply the number of hours of solitary deliberate practice. Of course, the type of practice, the programme of learning, and the inspiration of the teacher are all likely to be important (as I discuss in the next chapter).

It remains a theoretical possibility that some innate intellectual capacity for numbers will predispose a child to apply zeal and hard work to that field, rather than some other; but again there is no evidence that this is so. This intellectual capacity, if it existed, could not be something like general intelligence, since many prodigies score only average, or even well below average, on the relevant tests. This capacity would therefore have to be specific to numbers. What would such a capacity look like? One possibility, and it is only a possibility, is that the Number Module is variable in its capacity at birth. For example, infants' subitizing capacity could vary, say, from 3 to 6, rather than being fixed at 4, as is currently believed. If variations in this capacity predict later mathematical skill, then there would be a case for difference in specific innate number abilities.

I have also discussed people—like Julie and Charles—who never get the hang of numbers, despite hard work and good teaching. These are the developmental dyscalculics. I attribute this to the abnormal development of the Number Module in the brain. Without properly functioning brain circuits for numerosity, the upper bound to numerical abilities is very low: roughly what they count out on their fingers. Most of us are born to count, but beyond that the only established limits to mathematical achievement are, in Galton's words, zeal and very laborious work.

8

HOME, STREET, AND SCHOOL

MATHEMATICS

The advancement and perfection of mathematics are ultimately
connected with the prosperity of the state.

NAPOLÉON BONAPARTE

Few subjects in the school curriculum are as important to the future
of the nation as mathematics; and few have been the subject of
more comment and criticism in recent years.

KEITH JOSEPH (SECRETARY OF STATE FOR
EDUCATION AND SCIENCE), 1982

THE CHASM OF INCOMPREHENSION

Many people hate maths. You may be one of them. You may have the
sense that numbers are mysterious, difficult; they may make you feel
confused and uncertain. You lack confidence that you've carried out a
calculation correctly. It is as if there is an unbridgeable gap between
what you *think* you understand and what you think you *ought* to
understand. This 'chasm of incomprehension' is a direct result of your
schooling. The curriculum has been designed to build, stage by stage,
from basic concepts and techniques to more advanced ones. If your
understanding—this side of the chasm—does not advance, but what
you need to understand to keep up with the curriculum does
advance—the other side—the chasm will get wider and wider.

There's no alternative to the stage-by-stage approach of starting
with basic concepts and building more advanced ones onto them. You
cannot teach children calculus before they have mastered basic arithmetic and geometry, any more than you would start young pianists on

Rachmaninov's Third before they can play 'Twinkle, Twinkle'. Also most of mathematics is interconnected: algebra can serve arithmetic, while being able to add, subtract, and multiply is of use in trigonometry. This means that losing your grip on any one idea or technique could have repercussions elsewhere in your mathematical repertoire.

In the attainment of goals set by a school for its pupils, maths more than any other subject is sensitive to earlier failures to understand. How well children understand depends on how well they learn at each stage, and this in turn depends on how well the curriculum is designed and the teaching is carried out. Both curriculum and teacher will have an impact on the two factors that make the difference between being good or bad at numbers: Galton's 'zeal' and 'very laborious work'. Zeal makes for work; work is needed to keep abreast of each new conceptual target set by the curriculum. I don't mean working long hours, but working reflectively: thinking about what you're doing and making sure you really understand it.

In the last chapter I described the virtuous circle that keeps people working hard at their mathematical understanding, and also the vicious circle that creates avoidance and widens the chasm of incomprehension. Avoiding this chasm is, in my view, fundamental to an effective education.

STREET MATHEMATICS

Not all number skills are learned in school. As we saw in Chapters 2 and 3, everyone counts. Children start developing number skills before school, and even without much instruction from their parents. There is now a growing body of evidence that surprisingly good calculational skills can be found among people who have learned their maths outside the school as well as, or instead of, inside school. Here's one example, from the work of Terezinha Nunes and her colleagues in northeast Brazil. The customer (actually the investigator) asks 'M', a twelve-year-old boy who trades in a street market and is in Third Grade (8–9 years) at school, about the price of coconuts. How much is one, she asks? M answers 'Thirty-five'.

CUSTOMER: I'd like ten. How much is that?

M (*Pause*): Three will be one hundred and five; with three more, that will be two hundred and ten. (*Pause*) I need four more. That is ... (*Pause*) three hundred and fifteen ... I think it is three hundred and fifty.[1]

This is very different from the method M—or we—would have learned in school. M's street method involves solving the following steps:

Step 1. 35 × 3 (which he may have known already)

Step 2. 105 + 105

Step 3. 210 + 105

Step 4. 315 + 35.

He decomposed the multiplier 10 into 3 + 3 + 3 + 1, keeping track of this sequence while carrying out the calculations. So clearly M has considerable arithmetical skills. But when he was tested formally in a school setting with '35 × 4', he was not only inaccurate, but was so in a very interesting way. This is how he explains what he was doing: 'Four times five is twenty, carry the two; two plus three is five, times four is twenty.' And he wrote down 200! That is, he started like this:

$$\begin{array}{r} {}^{2}35 \\ \times\,4 \\ \hline 0 \end{array}$$

and continued as follows:

$$\begin{array}{r} (2+3)5 \\ \times\,4 \\ \hline 200 \end{array}$$

Now, he has already solved this problem correctly as part of his more complex solution to the price of ten coconuts. M, like most of the other children tested, was significantly worse using school methods than street methods. Not only that, the kinds of mistake were different. While each step of his own calculation represents an operation of real objects, this is not true of the school maths procedure. What would 'carry two' mean in the world of coconuts? To M, it is meaningless, and he treats it accordingly. What indeed does putting down the first zero mean? Even our standard procedure of adding a zero to 35 to get the solution to 35×10 has no obvious meaning in the world of coconuts.

M's school solution, 200, is way out, and he doesn't seem to realize it. He was not carrying out the same kind of check as he was when selling coconuts. Is this because real money—eating or not eating—is involved? No doubt. But there is another reason. His method is very closely tied to the ideas of collections and numerosities of (number of things in) collections. These ideas, I have argued, are built into the Number Module of our Mathematical Brains and are the foundations of the rest of our arithmetic.

For this reason, as Nunes and her colleagues note, 'children rely upon calculations that are closely linked to the quantities [numerosities] being dealt with,'[2] which may be why they prefer to use successive addition to solve multiplication problems. In the formal test, on the other hand, they rely blindly on a procedure that is divorced from the quantities. This would be fine if the procedure were correct, but in M's case the carrying part of the procedure is wrong. Divorcing the procedure from the numerosity meaning of the numbers leads you into making mistakes that are an order of magnitude wrong without your noticing it.

Research in Brazil shows that street maths doesn't stop at addition and subtraction. Quite sophisticated methods can be acquired through apprenticeships. For example, carpenters have to carry out complicated multiplication and division to know how much wood, in standard plank sizes, will be needed to make a piece of furniture specified in a drawing. Because carpenters' margins are so small, errors—buying too many planks, or too few so that the piece cannot be finished in time—could wipe out their tiny profit—the week's food money. Professional carpenters are almost always accurate, and almost always calculate in their heads rather than on paper, using invented procedures mixed with the occasional school algorithm. The apprentices start off by using school algorithms, and usually get the wrong answers.

Without any schooling at all, fairly advanced mathematical ideas can be mastered. Some of the most intriguing examples come from radical agronomists working with subsistence farmers in Africa and India. The idea is to hand the planning initiative to local people, rather than send in troubleshooters from the World Bank, say, to sort things out in a single visit. Problems change, and so will solutions. The first step is to get the farmers to quantify what they are doing. Gordon Conway and his team at the University of Sussex's Institute of Development Studies have found that farmers, usually with very little schooling or none at all, are well able to represent the amount of rainfall going back 10 years, or the distribution, yield, and income of their various crops, or even to map the relative degradation of different parts of the local forest. They don't use Excel spreadsheets, they don't even use written words or numerals; instead they use seeds of varying colours to represent, say, days of rainfall or crop yields, arranged in matrices to represent years, or on maps drawn in the sand to show the geographical distribution of crops and their yields. Sometimes they will redraw these diagrams from nature's sketchpad onto real paper to protect the data from marauding hens.[3] These representations can be used to model past agricultural performance and to forecast, and plan for, the future, just as our spreadsheets (invented just a few years ago) now can do for us. Handling numerical distributions is by no means straightforward, as we shall see in Chapter 9.

These are examples of what is sometimes called 'situated learning':[4] learning in a familiar and meaningful situation. It is clear that oral arithmetic, say for a problem with decimals, will be less prone to ludicrous errors than a written problem, especially if the units themselves have a meaning. So, for example, 12.45 plus 13.7 presented orally as a problem with money, would be spoken out loud and thought of, as 'twelve pounds forty-five pence plus thirteen pounds seventy pence', and it would be extremely unlikely that an answer will differ by more than one pound from the correct answer. On the other hand, one can imagine a child writing

$$\begin{array}{r} 12.45 \\ \underline{13.7} \\ 2.615 \end{array}$$

not having properly mastered where to put the decimal point. Even when the algorithm is performed correctly, the answer still needs to be interpreted. Here's a problem that was put to 45,000 US thirteen-year-olds: 'An army bus holds 36 soldiers. If 1,128 soldiers are being bussed to their training site, how many buses are needed?' Reassuringly, 70% performed the long division correctly, but 29% gave the answer as '31, remainder 12', and 18% gave the answer '31 [buses]'; only 23% gave the right interpretation of the answer as 32 buses.[5]

One of the advantages of street mathematics is that it is easy to imagine, or what educationalists call 'model', the situation, and this can help. The US pupils may have done better imagining the more familiar situation of people seated at tables, rather than soldiers in buses. On the other hand, imagining a real-life situation can be very misleading. 'There are ten birds in a tree. A hunter shoots two of them. How many are left in the tree?' Well, none, obviously. Certainly, being able to see the point of doing a calculation correctly in the first place will encourage you do it accurately—especially if getting the answer wrong is likely to be costly. Repeated practice with the same kinds of problem, as with the carpenters, will improve your skills in doing them. Also, the calculation procedures will in many cases have been invented by the user rather than learned from a teacher, and this may help to fix them in the memory.

However, the point about multiplication and division—indeed about number manipulations generally—is that they are not bound by their context, their situation, but apply equally to planks of wood, to pots of paint, or to the length of radio waves. Learners must be aware of this if they are to grasp the abstract nature of numbers. Formal schooling is an opportunity to go beyond the 'street situation', but at the same time it is itself a situation—the school situation. M applied the school procedure in the school situation and the street procedure when selling coconuts. The main objective is to get learners to understand the abstractness and the unity of arithmetic.

ZEAL AND ANXIETY

Number work provokes strong reactions. Many people don't like it at all. Surprisingly, relatively few fourteen-year-olds in England have strongly negative feelings towards it, 1% according to the latest international survey, and 80% of this sample liked it or liked it a lot.[6]

Not surprisingly, people who like maths a lot score better on maths tests than those who dislike it a lot: those who said they liked it a lot were some 15% better than those who disliked it a lot for each of the countries sampled. This is not surprising. But in general we cannot tell just from these correlations whether those who liked maths became good at it, or those who were good at it came to like it.[7] Both could be true—creating the virtuous and vicious circles I described in the last chapter. Being good leads to zeal, which in turn leads to more work, and so on. Being bad leads to anxiety and hence to avoidance.

In one of the few studies to look at students' enjoyment of maths lessons, Jo Boaler, a maths teacher, described in detail some of the causes and effects of a lack of enjoyment over a three-year period.[8] One of the secondary schools she researched, called 'Amber Hill', used the traditional, 'transmission model' of maths teaching favoured by the previous Conservative Government in the UK. Classes follow standard coursebooks, those from the widely used and recommended Secondary Mathematics Project, with the teacher and the books transmitting knowledge of facts and procedures to the student. Most lessons begin with an exposition by the teacher, after which the student carries out exercises. There is whole-class teaching, still a politically favoured option, with classes ranked by mathematical ability. Here's what one sixteen-year-old student from the top class said: 'Normally, there's a set way of doing it and you have to do it that way. You can't work out your own way'. When another student was asked whether a particular method made sense, she said, 'Not as much as my own'.[9] Although the classroom atmosphere is friendly and non-authoritarian, students are pressured to work fast so that teachers can get through the syllabus.

Students didn't enjoy this method of teaching. One said, 'I don't think we should work on boring textbooks all the time.' Another said, 'Maths would be more interesting if there were more projects to do.' This conflict between projects and working through textbooks is at the heart of the current educational debate—more accurately, the political debate about education. 'Amber Hill' students, who had experienced projects in their previous school, though they did little project work here, clearly enjoyed them more: 'Coursework was better because you could spend time on that and get involved with it, and you worked because you wanted to.' At the core of the students' criticism was that they weren't understanding the concepts. 'The way sir teaches, it's like he just wants us to remember it, when you don't really understand things.'[10] These bored students did significantly less well in their GCSE exams (public examinations for 16-year-olds) than a student at a comparison school which used more project-based methods. I'll say more about other methods in a moment.

How do we get children to enjoy their maths (or, more modestly, get some of them to hate it less)? Educational pundits—including our own politicians—neglect this aspect of maths education. In *Numeracy Matters*, the report of the UK Government's Numeracy Task Force, there is almost nothing about having fun or even avoiding anxiety. Not only does there seem to be very little official regard to this issue, there is very little research to guide us. We don't really understand what it is that makes maths unpleasant to some people and fun for others.

In the last chapter I quoted the rewards that one mathematical prodigy, Hans Eberstark, got from being good at arithmetic. He divided the rewards into two sorts: external and internal. The external rewards were 'Making friends, making money, showing off, and giving pleasure,' to which the schoolchild might add the following special cases of showing off: pleasing teachers and parents, impressing fellow pupils, doing well in exams. But, Eberstark, went on, there are even greater, internal rewards: 'Mastery, dependability, transformation, insight.'[11] You can get on top of the one system that guarantees its answers and allows you to feel in control of an enormous range of situations. This feeling of control is often missing in school maths. Instead, children suffer anxiety and lack of confidence because they have no way of telling that they have found the right answer, except when the teacher tells them.

Children naturally develop sophisticated numerical ideas and methods at home and in the street. These, as we have seen, are based on the idea of numerosity, and the methods and principles that can be derived from this idea. School often undermines children's confidence in these street and home methods. A leading US educational authority, Lauren Resnick of the Learning Research and Development Center at the University of Pittsburgh, wrote that:

The failure of much of our present teaching to make a cognitive connection between children's own math-related knowledge and the school's version of math feeds a view held by many children that what they know does not count as mathematics. This devaluing of their own knowledge is especially exaggerated among children from families that are traditionally alienated from schools, ones in which parents did not fare well in school and do not expect—however much they desire—their children to do well, either. In the eyes of these children, math is what is taught in school.[12]

How does this make children *feel* about maths? Occasionally, there is transfer of school knowledge to non-school situations, for example, when children use school algorithms to prove to their parents that the new designer trainers really are affordable. But most of the time, Resnick finds, children seldom see the point of mathematical activity. It can seem just a collection of unrelated facts and procedures, useful only in the context of schoolwork.

Having Fun
Hearing your own ideas devalued, lacking confidence in your skills, and not seeing the point of mathematical activity are not conducive to fun. Applying a procedure learned by rote, even where it is efficient and leads to a degree of mastery, is less fun than inventing a procedure for yourself. Inventing a procedure provides those internal rewards that Hans Eberstark spoke of: transformation, seeing how to turn one thing into another—a kind of magic; insight, because you now understand the relationship brought about by the transformation; dependability, 'figures never fail you'; and a sense of mastery because not only can you do it, but you know you can do it.

For teachers of maths there is, all too often, a right way and a wrong way: the teacher's way is the right way, the student's way is the wrong way. No doubt the teacher's way will usually be more efficient and more elegant than the student's, but one of the absolutely fundamental points about arithmetic is that there are many equivalent ways of reaching a goal, and understanding their equivalence is a key to understanding the concepts and the principles of arithmetic. M, the Brazilian coconut-seller described earlier, used his own procedure for working out the price of ten coconuts at 35 cruzeiros each. It involved adding the price of three coconuts, 105, three times, and adding an extra one. Clearly this is less efficient than just putting a zero after 35 to get 350. M's method wasn't wrong, and it had three important virtues. First, it exemplified the relationship of multiplication to successive addition; second, it exploited the idea of 'additive composition' (numbers are composed of other numbers, in this case 10 is composed of 3 + 3 + 3 + 1); third, it was an arithmetically meaningful procedure. 'Adding' 0 is not meaningful (at least, not straightforwardly). It makes sense only in the context of our decimal number system. You cannot, for example, carry out this procedure with words.

Here's another example, this time from a second-grade classroom; the children had had a year and quarter of schooling:[13]

> **Problem:** Monique told her friend TaRae that she would give her 95 barrettes. Monique had 4 bags of barrettes'[hairslides] and each bag had 9 barrettes. Does Monique have enough barrettes?

> The class were encouraged to first develop an **estimated** answer. They were asked, 'How many more does she need?' The solutions were generated by different class groups [seated around separate tables].

> Group 1 first decomposed 4×9 into 2×9 plus 2×9, which they could solve by addition. Then they set up a **missing addend** problem, $36 + \underline{\quad} = 95$, which they solved by a combination of estimation and correction.

$$36 + 60^* = 96$$
$$96 - 1 = 95$$
$$60 - 1 = 59$$
$$^*\text{means an estimate}$$

> Group 2 set up a **subtraction equation** and then developed a solution that used a negative partial result.

$$90 - 30 = 60$$
$$5 - 6 = -1$$
$$60 - 1 = 59$$

> Group 4 began with the total number of barrettes needed and **subtracted** out **successive** bags of 9.

$$95 - 9 = 86$$
$$86 - 9 = 77$$
$$77 - 9 = 68$$
$$68 - 9 = 59$$

All the solutions were right, and all the methods valid. One has to ask whether figuring this out in a group setting, and then seeing how other children solved it, would be more or less fun than applying a teacher-prescribed procedure for solving this kind of problem.

This example comes from Pittsburgh teacher Victoria Bill, who is working with Lauren Resnick to improve primary maths education. Their approach, which they call 'Math math', gets children to draw on their own informal knowledge, and to develop their trust in it, because many pupils believe that 'home-acquired knowledge does not count in school'. This approach builds confidence, and it confronts directly the problem of integrating the school and the non-school situations.

At a slightly more advanced level, think about finding the square of 47. You could do this by applying the normal procedure for long multiplication:

$$
\begin{array}{r}
47 \\
47 \\
\hline
329 \\
1880 \\
\hline
2209
\end{array}
$$

But there's another way, which probably isn't quicker on paper, but it is in your head. It also makes use of a deep property of numbers, and this in itself encourages insight. This can be very exciting, as indeed it was for Alexander Aitken, one of the greatest calculating prodigies (as well as being a major mathematician), as I described in Chapter 7. To recap: he had not been much interested in mathematics until the age of 13, when his teacher showed how to find the value of 47^2 by means of the equation

$$a^2 = (a + b) \times (a - b) + b^2$$

Taking $b = 3$, the teacher showed how to make the calculation much easier:

$$47^2 = (47 + 3) \times (47 - 3) = 9$$
$$47^2 = (50 \times 44) + 9 = 2209$$

With the insight Aitken gained from this transformation, he never looked back.

To have fun with arithmetic, and with maths generally, is to see the relations among different facts, different procedures, different ways of thinking. This how the greatest mathematicians make advances.[14] But it is also how the rest of us can have fun: by seeing how to transform one kind of thing into another kind of thing, by seeing how things fit together. By being inventive.

This connectivity isn't fancy maths. It is absolutely fundamental to the way even simple, whole-number maths, the maths of numerosities, works. If children don't see this, then they have failed to grasp its essential nature. It is vital to understand the complementarity of procedures: adding 3 to 5 to get 8 is a complement of taking 5 away from 8 to get 3. Dividing by 75 is the same as multiplying by 1⅓ (and adjusting the decimal point). Multiplying 8 by 3 is equivalent to adding 8 and 8 and 8. Multiplying 25 by 39 is the same as $(25 \times 40) - (25 \times 1)$. The interconnectedness of facts and procedures is what distinguishes maths from school subjects that really do need a lot of memorization, such as history with, for example, the sequence of the kings and queens of England.

Teacher Victoria Bill uses group discussions, encouraging different solution strategies and acknowledging pupils' own intuitions and knowledge to stimulate inventiveness in the classroom.[15] Bill's inventive pupils were not from middle-class families, where educational expectations (as opposed to hopes) are high, but from families 70% of whom were eligible for free or subsidized school lunch, and almost all were African-American. In the very first year of operating her programme, the median first-grade class percentile rankings on the school district's standardized tests went from the 30th percentile to above the 80th (i.e. her class was better than 80% of the classes in the school district). Even the worst-performing child was at the 66th percentile.[16]

Similar ideas seem to work at a more advanced level as well. In 'Phoenix Park', the other UK secondary school studied by Jo Boaler, thirteen- to sixteen-year-olds spent most of their time on projects and activities, which they enjoyed.

> VICKY: I thought the activities were really interesting because you had to work out for yourself what was going on, and you had to use your own ideas.
> BOALER: How does that compare to the SMP [Secondary Mathematics Project] you used to do in middle school?
> VICKY: Boring, it was boring doing stuff out of books.[17]

One immediate, practical effect of students finding maths more fun and more interesting, was better examination results than 'Amber Hill', the traditional school described above. But this is not the main point. For students to see the connections between different methods and concepts, and to be able to apply them in new situations, not only must their own ideas and techniques be acknowledged, as Bill and Resnick stress, but ideas and techniques learned in the classroom must be seen to be applicable in other situations.

Avoiding Anxiety

The converse of having fun with numbers is being anxious about them. Many sufferers of mathematics anxiety meet the standard criteria for genuine phobia: it's a learned fear, specific to the situation (doing maths), and accompanied by physiological signs such as increased heart rate, sweating, and so on. Students diagnosed as sufferers do a lot worse on maths tests, and, of course, avoid taking maths courses where they can.[18] A key question is this: are they anxious because they do badly, or do they do badly because they are anxious? Both may be true if we think in terms of the vicious circle described in Chapter 7. Doing badly causes anxiety, anxiety causes avoidance of maths, avoidance causes poor performance, which in turn causes more anxiety, and so on.

Anxiety appears to be greater in schools which use traditional 'exposition and practice' teaching, such as 'Amber Hill'. This is, at least in part, due to a well-founded fear of falling into the chasm of incomprehension. Here's how it felt to Karen, sixteen:

> I mean she's rushing through, and she's going, 'We've got to finish this chapter by today,' but I'm still on C4 [a textbook exercise] and I don't know what the hell she's chatting about and I haven't done any of it, because I don't know it. She hasn't explained it properly. She just says, 'Take this off, take that off,' and she puts the answers up and like—what? I don't know what she's doing.

It's easy to see how this kind of response could lead to avoidance. As Helen, a sixteen-year-old from the top maths set, puts it, 'I don't mind maths, but when he goes ahead and you're left behind, that's when I start dreading going to maths lessons.'[19] From here it is but a short step into the downward spiral of the vicious circle.

Mark Ashcraft, an authority on the mental processes of arithmetic, and his colleagues at Cleveland State University, have pioneered the study of the causal role of maths anxiety. Their starting point is the Mathematics Anxiety Rating Scale, a standardized questionnaire. It asks subjects to rate from 1 (not at all) to 5 (very much) how much they would be made anxious by various everyday occurrences. There are ninety-eight items in all. Here are a few examples:

1. Deciding how much change you should get back from buying several items.

9. Having to figure out how much it will cost to buy a product on credit (figuring in the interest rates).

10. Adding up a bill for a meal when you think you have been overcharged.

45. Raising your hand in a maths class to ask a question about something you do not understand.

53. Taking an examination (quiz) in a maths course.[20]

Using this questionnaire, people can be classified in terms of their anxiety, from Low Anxious to High Anxious. High Anxious subjects report all kinds of intrusive and worrying thoughts when they contemplate doing maths. They get confused. When the High Anxious subjects were studied in more detail, heart rate—a good measure of anxiety—increased as maths questions got harder, but only the maths questions. It wasn't that they got anxious just because they were attempting a harder task. On a hard anagram task, their heart rates were just the same as for Low Anxious subjects.

High Anxiety correlated with slow and error-prone answers even for university students presented with arithmetical tasks so simple that most ten-year-olds would have mastered them. This convinced Ashcraft that anxiety caused poor performance, rather than low ability causing anxiety. Of course, avoidance has been found to lead to avoidance, less practice, and hence weaker skills.

FACTS, PROCEDURES, AND UNDERSTANDING: THE THREE SIDES OF THE ARITHMETICAL COIN

Arithmetical facts and arithmetical procedures are profoundly interconnected, both logically and practically. In addition, for example, we have seen (in Chapter 3) how children progress from solving 5 + 3 by counting procedures to recalling the answer from long-term memory. Very often they will start by 'counting all', both the 5 and then the 3 on their fingers, and then both together. Later they will 'count on' from the 5, at some point, not using their fingers at all, but only the counting words. Later still, some of the results of counting will stick in memory and can be reused when the problem is encountered again.

Procedures themselves are interrelated. Many people, not just children, tackle subtraction by counting on from the subtrahend (the number to be subtracted), so that 13 − 8 is transformed into a missing addend problem: what must be added to 8 to make 13? Multiplication results can be achieved by successive addition. Problems can be transformed into more easily solved problems, for example, by turning 9 + 6 into 10 + 5. Division can be approached by transforming it into a missing multiplicand problem: for instance $72 \div 6 = ?$ becomes $6 \times ? = 72$. More complex procedures are learned for more advanced arithmetical problems: carrying in addition, borrowing in subtraction, applying the same transformation to both sides of an equation, simplifying using common factors, and so on.

Procedures, as we have seen, are learned in the classroom, but they are also invented by all users of numbers. They follow directly from our understanding of numerosity, from the way collections can be combined and subdivided. Procedures learned or invented can be stored in our memory, and it is part of the task of the classroom to make sure they are. We also learn facts. Sometimes the learning is incidental to and a result of solving problems, as happens with addition, subtraction, and division facts, at least in England. Other educational systems, the French for example, teach these facts explicitly. In England, learning by rote—by simple repetition of the words—is confined to multiplication tables. The facts learned both intentionally and incidentally are stored in long-term memory.

Despite the inevitable integration of facts and procedures in the practice of arithmetic, the memory structures for them in the brain seem to be distinct. We can see this when brain damage affects facts but not procedures, or procedures but not facts. We saw in Chapter 4, 'Numbers in the Brain', how some patients, for example Dr Constable, had great difficulty recalling even simple number facts, but still knew procedures and could apply them correctly. Even more spectacularly, Signor Bellini had almost completely lost his multiplication tables, but applied complex and efficient procedures to find answers to multiplication problems. On the other hand, some patients could still retrieve facts but something had gone seriously awry with their procedures. Signor Tiziano, for instance, consistently made the following mistake in subtraction: he always took the smaller number away from the larger, whatever the problem. Other patients had forgotten how to carry or borrow, though their memory for simple facts was still functioning.

As well as the separation of facts and procedures in the brain, our studies of neurological patients such as Signor Bellini show that, provided one has a good understanding of the idea of numerosity and the laws that follow from it, then it is possible to invent procedures and apply them appropriately. For example, although he had lost his memory for the product of 8 and 7, Signor Bellini could apply the law that distributed multiplication over subtraction to find the answer:

$$8 \times 7 = (10 \times 7) - (2 \times 7)$$

10×7 can be solved by using the rule of 0 to give 70, and $2 \times 7 = 7 + 7$, which Signor Bellini can work out by his retained ability to add. Margarete Delazer and her colleagues were able to restore Signor Bellini's tables through training.[21] However, they found it impossible to retrain people whose brain damage has left them unable to understand numerosities, like Frau Huber.

Facts: The Pleasures of Strict Discipline?
Arithmetic is more than facts and procedures: it's understanding. Nevertheless, the California Education Board and successive British Secretaries of State for Education have believed it is a matter of simple common sense that learning the multiplication tables by heart, for example, must be a good thing. But common sense is not the same as the results of properly conducted research, and there is a history of research into the value of rote learning going back to the 1920s. In 1922, the American psychologist Edward L. Thorndike published a small but highly influential book, *The Psychology of Arithmetic.*[22] He argued that the key to learning any skill was the 'formation of associative bonds'—in the case of arithmetic, the bonds between problems and solutions, such as the bond between '3 + 3' and '6'. The problem bonded with its solution is an arithmetical fact, and the learning of facts was the focus of Thorndike's approach.

His approach was based on extensive research, not with children in school, but with animals. He had found that rats, monkeys, and pigeons could learn 'associations' by reinforcing the bond between the stimulus and the desired response. He inferred that the same principles of reinforcing the right bonds would work just as well with humans. Thorndike realized that arithmetic was more complex than anything animals could be taught, and that the design of stimuli, the order in which they are presented to children, and the relationship between one bond and another was by no means straightforward. Each bond, each new skill, had to take its place in an 'organized co-operating system of bonds', in the same way that a soldier fighting in an army cooperates with others to achieve a goal. Reinforcing bonds meant rewards. Just as his animals had to be given a food reward for producing the response the experimenter wanted, children had to be rewarded for producing the right answer to the question.

In 1928, six years after Thorndike's book, William Brownell went on the counter-attack in *The Development of Children's Number Ideas in Primary Grades:* 'The child who can promptly give the answer 12 to 7 + 5 has by no means demonstrated that he knows the combination. He does not "know" the combination until he understands something of the reason 7 and 5 is 12.'[23] The child may come home from school and tell his dad, 'Today I learned that seven and five is twelve.' After a pause he asks, 'What's "twelve", daddy?' If 7 + 5 is learned separately from 5 + 7 it may indeed stand in the way of the child seeing the relationship between the two; not to mention the relationship of 7 + 5 to 7 + 15 and 7 + 25.

In the late 1920s and the 1930s there was a great deal of research testing the virtues of drill against Brownell's meaning-based approach. Overwhelmingly, meaningful learning was found to be demonstrably superior, especially when it came to dealing with new problems. Even modern versions of the drill approach, using computers to schedule and mark the drills, show that children who start with poor understanding do not catch up with children who start with better understanding.[24]

Brownell found that children who used numerosity-based strategies, such as counting on their fingers to solve addition problems, did better than children who simply learned by rote. What is more, the rote-learners tended to stick longer with 'immature' approaches to problems. All this has been known for sixty years or more. One wonders why the authorities, at least in Britain, seem to ignore it. To ignore this history is to be condemned to repeat it.

Tables

Of all the myriad kinds of arithmetical fact, multiplication tables are especially beloved of educational pundits. Here, there is one thing we can learn from Thorndike: the importance of making even rote learning rewarding—that is, enjoyable. For readers who have forgotten how tables are learned, or who went to a school where they were not drilled in them, here's a description of what actually happens. Children begin by reciting the words of the two times table: 'Once two is two; two twos are four; three twos are six; four twos are eight' and so on. When they can recite this table perfectly, they generally go on to the three times table (though in some schools they go next to the five times table, since this is held to be easier than the three or four times tables). The idea is that by some age, usually eight or nine, they will be able to recite faultlessly the tables up to ten, though in my schooldays we needed to go up to twelve since there were twelve pence to a shilling.

One child I quizzed about his tables correctly recited his two times table, but was a bit shaky when I asked him what six twos were. Being able to recite the sequence did not mean that he understood what the components of the sequence meant. Another child I asked about tables could recite both her two and three times tables, and could answer my question 'What are five threes?' A little later I asked her, 'What are three fives?' She looked at me with a severe reprimand in her eyes, and admonished, 'We haven't learned the five times table yet.' No doubt she learned to answer both in time. But it is possible—though I have no direct evidence of this—that her understanding of the commutativity of multiplication was delayed by being forced to learn $3 \times 5 = 15$ and $5 \times 3 = 15$ as quite separate facts.

However, there is some indirect evidence. In international comparisons of mathematics ability, the Chinese—in the People's Republic, Taiwan, and Singapore—are the best by far. In one recent study, the average performance on standardized tests of US twelve-year-olds was at the 11th percentile of the Shanghai sample. This means that 89% of the Shanghai children were better than the average American. In fact, the Shanghai twelve-year-olds performed as well as US seventeen-year-olds.[25] Of course, these tests involve more than just multiplication, but it is worth seeing how the relatively successful Chinese educational system deals with multiplication. Do they force children to recite the words to eighty-one multiplication facts? No, they do not. To start with, children do not have to learn 'once times' anything. Second, they do not learn both 3×5 and 5×3. They learn 5×3 in their three times table, but their five times table begins with 5×5, which, of course, doesn't come into the two, three, or four times tables (see box on pages 309–10).[26] Not only does this method reduce the memory load from eighty-one to thirty-six facts, it helps children see that 3×5 and 5×3 are equivalent. It is therefore no wonder that when Jo-Anne LeFevre and J. Liu, psychologists at Carleton University in Ottawa, compared the adult multiplication skills of Chinese and Canadian students, the Chinese were found to be faster and more accurate.[27]

It may be that rote learning of the three times table and the eight times table will lead to an understanding that $8 \times 3 = 3 \times 8$. It could serve as a ladder to reach up to comprehension, and when there the ladder can be thrown away. But why not start by ensuring that all the steps in learning are meaningful?

How Are Facts Stored in the Brain?

Since so much of our early experience of number facts is verbal, not just reciting tables, it has seemed plausible to many researchers and many educational pundits that they are represented in the brain as words. Indeed, two influential theories of number processing assume just that. Stanislas Dehaene in *The Number Sense*[28] claims that facts are stored as words, just as words; Jamie Campbell of the University of Saskatchewan argues that all the numerical representations we experience are stored in a vast and intricate network—words, numerals, magnitudes, and so on.[29]

If number facts are stored as words, then they should be organized in a verbal way. Words are, of course, stored verbally, and we can tell a lot about their organization in memory by the kinds of problems speakers suffer when trying to find the right word. All of us have been in the 'tip-of-the-tongue state'. There has been so much research on this topic recently that the term has become reduced to an acronym—TOT. In the experimental elicitation of TOTs, subjects are given a definition to which the right word must be found, for example, 'a navigational instrument used for measuring distances, especially the altitude of the sun, moon, and stars at sea'. For some people the right word just pops out, while others have no idea at all. A third group know they know it, but can't quite get it out. They are the ones in the TOT state. But, and this is what makes the phenomenon so intriguing, they do know something about the word they are looking for. They usually know how long it is, and what the first sound is. Often they come up with a word they know to be wrong, such as *sextet*, *sexton*, or *secant*, instead of *sextant*. The most widely accepted explanation is that the target word is for some reason blocked, but you can still get to a near neighbour. Since the neighbours are similar in sound but not in meaning, it has been inferred that the organization of words is in terms of their sounds. This organization shows up in mistakes we make in fluent speech, too, as in 'We need a few laughs to break up the monogamy.' The error has the same number of syllables, the same pattern of stress, and the same initial sounds as the target, 'monotony'. Words similar in sound are stored in neighbouring locations in the mental lexicon. A small addressing error in going from the meaning of the word you want to its form will lead you to a similar-sounding word.[30]

When people make mistakes in simple arithmetic, do they come up with answers that sound similar to the right answer? Actually, it's hard to tell, because the words for numbers sound so different, and where they start with the same sound, they are also similar in magnitude—four/five, six/seven. What we do know is that they make errors that are related in terms of *numerosity*. In single-digit addition and subtraction, people tend to be within 1, or at most 2, of the right answer. These are called 'close errors', suggesting that the answers are arranged in memory in terms of their numerical size.

Another piece of evidence for size ordering is the 'problem-size effect': the larger the sum, the longer it takes you to come up with the answer. You are slower to solve 9 + 8 than 3 + 2. One possible explanation is that this information is organized in memory as a kind of mental matrix (again, see box on pages 309–10). Several years ago, Mark Ashcraft and his colleagues suggested that whenever we search for an addition answer (as opposed to calculating it), our mental pointers for each number are set to zero, and we move them 'up' and 'across' until the co-ordinates fit the problem. The answer is in the square defined by the coordinates.[31] In this scheme, memory organization is built on numerosity. Notice that the commuted pairs are both in this matrix. We saw in Chapter 4 that brain damage can selectively impair a memory for the facts of a single operation, including addition, leaving the facts of the other operations intact. This suggests that the brain has sorted these facts into separate circuits—an addition circuit and a multiplication circuit. Subtraction and division depend more on procedures than on fact retrieval, often making use of previously learned addition and multiplication facts. However, there is little direct evidence to support the idea that the adult brain contains the complete matrix. But there is evidence that facts are ordered by size.

Now, if we are presented with the problem as '8 + 9', it does not mean that we leave it that way. Jo-Anne LeFevre and her colleagues asked subjects what they did when they carried out a simple addition, after they had done each problem. She recorded both their answer and the time they took to find it. What she found was that they often transformed one problem into an easier one: 9 + 8 into 10 + 7, for example. The ones they transformed took longer to solve, as the process of transformation was itself time-consuming. Now we are not talking minutes, or even seconds, here. The problems that subjects 'just knew' or said they retrieved from memory took 0.65 of a second to about 0.8 of a second to solve, while the transformed problems took 0.3 to 0.5 of a second longer than that. Since large problems tend to be transformed more than small problems, this is at least part of the explanation for the problem size effect. But the important point here is that this explanation depends on subjects recoding the problem in terms of the size—the numerosity—of the numbers and not treating them simply as words associated with the answer word. Even in the problems that subjects said they had recalled from memory, large sums took longer to find than small sums.[32] This again suggests organization in terms of number size.

Let me now return to the notorious case of multiplication tables. I do not deny that our brains contain the tables in verbal form. How could it be otherwise after all that dreary drill? In Chapter 4 we saw that, following damage to the critical left parietal area of the brain, the patient Frau Huber was still able to recite her tables and to answer simple multiplication questions, but she was unable to add or subtract, or indeed do almost anything else numerical.

Our responses to single-digit multiplication problems show the signature of size ordering (rather than verbal ordering) in our memory for these facts—the problem size effect. Larger problems take longer to solve. The kinds of multiplication error people make are rather different from addition errors. Close miss errors are rare: few people would say 'nine fours are thirty-seven', for example. Typically, people make 'operand errors', selecting a wrong answer from the same table as the correct answer: for example, 'seven eights are forty-eight.' Rarely do answers come from outside the table. This suggests that not only are there brain circuits specialized for multiplication facts, but that these circuits function in terms of operands—all the products with, say, 8 as a factor, rather like tables, in fact. Occasionally, people give an answer which is not from the same table as the correct answer. There was one well-publicized occasion in 1998, when the British Education Minister,

MENTAL MATRICES OF ADDITIONS AND MULTIPLICATIONS

According to the complete matrix model, the sums of the left- and right-hand numbers in a problem are organized as a matrix in the brain. Two pointers move outward from the origin, **0**, to the row and column values corresponding to the numbers in the problem. For 7 + 4, the pointers would move to row 7 and column 4, and the cell at the intersection of the row and the column provides the sum of the two numbers, **11**:

Right-hand number

0	1	2	3	4	5	6	7	8	9
1	2	3	4	5	6	7	8	9	10
2	3	4	5	6	7	8	9	10	11
3	4	5	6	7	8	9	10	11	12
4	5	6	7	8	9	10	11	12	13
5	6	7	8	9	10	11	12	13	14
6	7	8	9	10	11	12	13	14	15
7	8	9	10	11	12	13	14	15	16
8	9	10	11	12	13	14	15	16	17
9	10	11	12	13	14	15	16	17	18

But there would be just as much information if the numbers weren't coded left and right, but larger and smaller instead.

Smaller number

0	1	2	3	4	5	6	7	8	9
1	2								
2	3	4							
3	4	5	6						
4	5	6	7	8					
5	6	7	8	9	10				
6	7	8	9	10	11	12			
7	8	9	10	11	12	13	14		
8	9	10	11	12	13	14	15	16	
9	10	11	12	13	14	15	16	17	18

The same applies to multiplication, but multiplications by 1 (or by 0) don't need to be stored in memory. Instead of trying to remember eighty-one multiplications, which is what British children are taught at school, only thirty-six are needed. 4×7 (or 7×4) in the multiplication matrix is located thus:

Smaller number

0	2	3	4	5	6	7	8	9
2	4							
3	6	9						
4	8	12	16					
5	10	15	20	25				
6	12	18	24	30	36			
7	14	21	28	35	42	49		
8	16	24	32	40	48	56	64	
9	18	27	36	45	54	63	72	81

Stephen Byers, talking to the press about his Department's new numeracy programme, was asked to give the answer to 'Seven eights', he said, 'fifty-four'. Even so, 54 is the answer to a table problem (6×9 or 9×6). On the basis of research findings, he would almost never have given 53 or 57 as an answer, because errors nevertheless come just from the products in the tables up to ten,[33] again suggesting that there are brain circuits specialized for multiplication.

Procedures

Of course, teachers, and even politicians, are well aware that there is more to number skills than learning facts. Mixed in with learning facts is learning the different kinds of procedure needed to solve problems that are beyond the reach of simple memory. Once we are confronted with multi-digit problems, we need to know how to carry and borrow, how to simplify and rearrange numbers, along with a bag of specialized tricks of the trade. Many of these procedures, can, as we have seen, be invented on the spot for the task at hand, but they have to conform to basic arithmetical principles. These have first to be understood.

Often they are not. The result is that children who have acquired a lot of facts, perhaps through drill, and have the self-discipline to follow procedures, end up following the wrong procedure because they do not understand what the procedure does in terms of numerosities. Here's a nice example from psychologists and educationalists Lauren Resnick and Wendy Ford.[34] What is happening in this pupil's set of addition solutions?

7	9	17	87	365	679	923	27,493
+8	+5	+8	+93	+574	+794	+481	+1,509
15	14	25	11	819	111	114	28,991

This boy certainly appeared to know some addition facts, for he got the first three problems correct. But notice how many 1's there are. In the fourth problem he adds 7 and 3 and then writes 1, then he adds 9 and 8 and again writes 1. In the next problem he adds 5 and 4 correctly, but when he comes to add 6 and 7 he again writes 1. What seems to be happening is that he adds the column correctly, but when there is a carry he writes down the number to be carried, in these cases the number 1.

In fact, this student made exactly the same error when multiplying:

68	734	543
×46	×37	×206
24	792	141

In the first problem, he seems to find the correct product of 8 and 6, 48, but writes the carry, 4, rather than the 8. In the second column, he again seems to multiply correctly, but again writes the carry. In all these addition and multiplication problems, the procedure is executed correctly: it's just that it's the *wrong* procedure. And it is hard to see why he should be doing it if he really understood what he was doing. Somehow, in the process of learning, the procedure became divorced from what it meant, and without understanding there was no way for him to check that his answers were absurd.

Sometimes brain damage throws procedures into sharp relief. Signor Tiziano, whom we met in Chapter 4, had a 'bug' in his subtraction procedure; he always took away the smaller from the larger. He had an understanding of what he was doing, but it was the wrong understanding. 'Three take away four is impossible, so it must be four take away three.' Given a problem like

$$\begin{array}{r} 23 \\ -17 \\ \hline \end{array}$$

he would have given the answer '14'. But there was one exception. When he was subtracting a one-digit number from a two-digit number, or a two-digit number from a three-digit number, he treated the two leftmost digits in the top line as a single number. So here he gets the right answer:[35]

$$\begin{array}{r} 13 \\ -7 \\ \hline 6 \end{array}$$

The reason why learners make these glaring mistakes in applying procedures is that they do not understand what the procedures do. In particular, the learners seem to need help thinking about the procedures in terms of operations on collections and numerosities, ideas that they can grasp much more easily than the meaning of carrying, or finding the lowest common denominator.

LESSONS FOR TEACHERS AND PARENTS

On one side of the arithmetical coin are facts you have learned, sometimes at school, sometimes at home, and sometimes you have worked them out for yourself. On the other side are the procedures you have learned again at home, on the street, or at school. Facts and procedures are part of our intellectual heritage: ideas and techniques that some of our most able ancestors invented, often after years of very laborious work. Of course, we need to learn them. We don't want to have to reinvent them for ourselves, even if we could. But these two sides of the coin do not exist in the abstract—they have to be imprinted on something. By preference, this should be understanding. Understanding allows us to make the appropriate connections between the facts and the procedures.

It is usually not possible for us experimenters to randomly assign facts and procedures to different groups of subjects in order to test the effectiveness of teaching methods, as we might assign laboratory rats at random to different experimental conditions. Even if we could, it would not be clear which aspect of the most successful teaching method was responsible for its success. I have shown how Victoria Bill's method has raised the performance of children in her Pittsburgh school, but which aspect of her method is the vital ingredient? Is it giving children ownership of their procedures? Is it allowing a diversity of solution strategies? Is it group problem-solving? Is it Bill's personality? Is it just that the kids are getting more attention from the teacher? Is it all these things?

The criterion I have used to identify good educational practice is this: is it supported by psychological research? The value of reflective practice and enjoyment is supported by the study of expertise (see Chapter 7). My own area of research in the neuropsychology of number processing shows that the brain is built to represent numbers in terms of collections of things and their numerosities. For most non-mathematicians, understanding means being able to transform the core of a problem into collections and numerosities, and the various solution strategies implied in these representations. My suggestion is that teachers, and parents, can help children understand what they are doing by showing them how to transform arithmetical problems into collections and numerosities.

It cannot be necessary to be able to recall instantly that 8×7 is 56, even if you are an education minister. You can always look up the answer, use a calculator, ask someone else, or—best of all—figure it out. In itself, knowing this fact does not promote understanding, especially if you have to learn it as a fact quite separate from $7 \times 8 = 56$. It is far more important to understand that 8×7 is equivalent to $(4 + 4) \times 7$, or to $(2 + 2 + 2 + 2) \times 7$, or to $(5 + 3) \times 7$, and so on. If you can see this, then you understand additive composition (numbers are composed of other numbers), and the distributivity of multiplication over addition. You can multiply each of the 2's by the 7 and add the results together. This could be the basis for understanding the equivalent law of subtraction, and for the more abstract algebraic principle

$$a(b_1 + b_2 + b_3 + \cdots + b_n) = ab_1 + ab_2 + ab_3 + \cdots + ab_n.$$

Laws like this express fundamental properties of numbers. Failing to understand them could leave you teetering on the brink of the chasm.

You will have difficulty learning new ideas that depend on them. On the other hand, not being able to recite 'eight sevens are fifty-six' is easy to rectify, and the fact in itself doesn't form the conceptual basis for anything else you will have to understand.

Great mathematicians, even great number theorists, are not always good calculators. Some don't even know their tables. There is a story that Ernst Kummer, the nineteenth-century number theorist, was standing at a blackboard trying to calculate 9×7, and found the product as follows: 'It can't be 61 because that's a prime; it cannot be 65 because that's a multiple of 5; 67 is another prime and 69 is too big. Therefore it must be 63.'[36] Without being able to remember what most nine-year-olds can remember, he could nevertheless arrive at the answer from first principles.

Once you can understand multiplication concepts, you can see that there are many ways to arrive at the same answer. This enables you to check your work. Being drilled to rely on table recitation can leave you stranded when you forget what '$N \times N$' is, or when you think you know, but are wrong. Understanding breeds confidence. Lack of understanding breeds anxiety, avoidance, and the vicious circle that can leave you spiralling down into the chasm as the rest of the class moves on. Ever since psychologists and educationalists began to research this in the 1920s, it has been clear that understanding-based learning is more effective than drill and practice. This is because understanding has to be based on representations of numbers, and operations on numbers, that are abstracted away from the mode of presentation. That is, your Mathematical Brain will be representing the concepts and facts, not as words, not as numerals, but as numerosities and concepts derived from the idea of numerosity.

Drill and Prejudice

The battle for the Mathematical Brains of our children continues around the world. Despite the investment of large sums of money and effort in finding better ways of getting children to understand mathematical concepts, drill is making a comeback. The California Board of Education recently voted 10 to 0 (one abstention) for rote learning of the tables by the end of the Third Grade (age eight), and calculators were banned from state tests and discouraged before Grade Six (age eleven). In England, the Government's Numeracy Task Force recommends lots of drill and practice, so that children 'know by heart number facts such as number bonds, multiplication tables, doubles and halves'.[37] The idea is that when these facts are known by heart then they can form the basis of 'figuring out' new facts.[38]

The Task Force was forbidden to recommend the use of calculators. The authors of the report say that 'DfEE [Department for Education and Employment] Ministers have recently asked the QCA [Qualification and Curriculum Authority] to develop guidance for teachers on the use of mental calculation methods at Key Stages 1 and 2 [primary school], discouraging as far as possible the use of calculators at those key stages'.[39] We are not told why. It is not that new technology is generally discouraged. It can be used for drill and practice. 'Programs to "teach" a particular number skill have been used successfully for practice and reinforcement with young children at home and school.'[40]

In his Foreword to the Government's Report, the Chairman of the Numeracy Task Force writes, with irony, one hopes, 'We have deliberately set out to be evidence-based, rather than adopt any particular "faiths" about numeracy and numeracy teaching.'[41] And yet the report reflects the Ministers' faith in drill, especially drill carried out by the whole class, and in no calculators. So when evidence is described, the conflict with faith leads, as it always will, to wonderful—though depressing—contradictions. Children should be differentiated into smaller groups according to attainment,[42] even though groups 'give particularly good results when [they] are mixed in attainment'.[43]

Apart from one sentence about teachers' correcting errors and misconceptions,[44] I could find nothing in the Government's Report on how to ensure that children *understand* what they are doing. In England it looks as though it will be up to parents to help their children understand basic numerical concepts and principles. And England, alas, is not alone in its stress on drill.

Fun

Martin Gardner, the doyen of popular mathematical writing, has consistently advocated the value of fun in maths teaching. He introduced a collection of essays thus:

A teacher of mathematics, no matter how much he loves his subject and how strong his desire to communicate, is perpetually faced with one overwhelming difficulty: How can he keep his students awake? . . . The best way, it has always seemed to me, to make mathematics interesting to students and laymen is to approach it in a spirit of play . . . Surely the best way to wake up a student is to present him with an intriguing mathematical game, puzzle, magic trick, joke, paradox, model, limerick, or any of a score of other things that dull teachers tend to avoid because they seem frivolous.[45]

Good teachers, I am sure, have been turning to Gardner's regular *Scientific American* columns for inspiration for more than three decades. Alas, systematic scientific research on the value of fun in maths is nonexistent.

Looking across the whole range of expertise, the key to being good at something is reflective practice—hours, days, years of it. Whether you are a musician or a arithmetician, by far and away the most predictive factor, and indeed usually the only predictive factor, is the amount of time spent in reflective practice. We saw in Chapter 7 that the best young violinists at the Berlin Academy, the ones most likely to go on to a performing career, practised on their own for 24 hours a week, while those probably destined only to be music teachers practised alone for just 9 hours a week. Full-time professional concert musicians continued to put in 24 hours a week of solitary practice. The best way to keep someone, especially a young someone, at reflective practice is to make sure they enjoy it. Feeling anxious and insecure about what they are doing, not to mention bored with it, will not help.

Building Bridges Across the Chasm:
Reflective Practice and Confidence
In the last chapter I described the vicious and the virtuous circles that students of mathematics of all ages and levels can fall into. The key to being in the virtuous circle is understanding what you are doing, and this implies seeing how specific procedures relate to each other and to wider principles. The teacher can help students to reflect on their use of procedures. Just telling students they are right or wrong is often

insufficient. This is what Diana Laurillard, who is educational technologist at the Open University, calls 'extrinsic feedback'. Usually students will benefit more from 'intrinsic feedback', where the teacher gives them detailed information to help them adapt their actions, including their thinking, in specific and appropriate ways. Imagine testing the seasoning of the soup you are making. Extrinsic feedback is a celebrity cook like Delia Smith telling you that you've got it wrong. Intrinsic feedback is tasting it: then you can tell whether there is too much seasoning, or too little. Even if Delia tells you it's OK, you still won't *know* what the correct saltiness is without tasting it.

In the box on pages 318–19, adapted from Diana's book *Rethinking University Teaching*, we can see how the teacher can use both extrinsic and intrinsic feedback to help a student understand a basic mathematical idea.[46] Notice how the teacher gets the student to create a mental model of the problem in terms of collections and numerosities. As this student moves from one level of understanding to the next, he is rethinking the situation he is trying to represent mathematically. In this example, the student was helped by the teacher's getting him first to think about a cancellation problem, formulated algebraically, in terms of collections and numerosities: sharing out a collection of apples and a collection of bananas among a collection of people. This was enough to get the student thinking along the right lines. The teacher then prompted him to reflect on another sharing problem that was more closely analogous to the problem set, express it mathematically, and solve it both mathematically and in terms of sharing apples and bananas. This led, here at least, to an 'Aha!' experience, and understanding. Each stage of the solution was meaningful because of its link with the ideas of collections and numerosities.

Lack of understanding leads to confusion, confusion to anxiety, avoidance, and no further learning. For people to enjoy mathematical activities, understanding is the key. This does not mean that mathematical tasks need always be easy. Hard problems won't put people off. After all, newspapers and magazines carry regular columns posing horrendously hard mathematical brain-teasers, which people evidently enjoy. Henry Dudeney and Sam Loyd became rich and famous

HELPING A STUDENT ACROSS THE CHASM

Topic goal: to represent correctly the cancellation of algebraic quotients.

Task goal: to simplify $(ca + b)/c$.

Student	(writes)	Action on task
	$$\frac{ca + b}{c} = a + b$$	
Teacher	Can we just look at this bit again? Let's turn this into a real problem.	*Extrinsic feedback on action*
	Suppose you've got six apples and six bananas and you divide them among six people, what does each person get?	*Model the abstract as a situated task in collections and numerosities*
Student	One apple and one banana.	*Implicit intrinsic feedback from imagining the action operating on collections and numerosities*
Teacher	OK,	*Extrinsic feedback;*
	and we can write 'six a's plus six b's shared among six' as $(6a + 6b)/6$, and that comes to $a + b$.	*Asks student to think about his action as a mathematical representation*
	OK?	*Checks this rethinking is shared*
Student	Yes.	*Agrees the rethinking*
Teacher	Now can you write down something similar for dividing four apples and one banana among four people?	*Checks if principle is understood by getting the student to formulate its application to another problem, one more similar to the task goal, but maintaining the link to the situated task*

Student	(4a + 1b)/4	**Reflects** on new problem and presents it in his own mathematical terms
	Is that it?	Checks with teacher on this representation
Teacher	Yes, terrific.	Extrinsic feedback;
	So, four apples and a banana, what would they get each?	Asks for application of mathematical representation to imagined collections and numerosities.
Student	One apple and a quarter of a banana . . .	Applies mathematical representation to imagined collections and numerosities
	. . . Ahh.	'Aha!' experience: understanding
Teacher	Right. Can you write that down? Write down the whole thing.	Adapts topic goal to check that student and teacher share the mathematical representation
Student	(writes) $= a + \dfrac{b}{4}$	Own mathematical representation of action
Teacher	Good,	Extrinsic feedback;
	so you can't just cancel one of them. The four divides both the terms on the top line.	Teacher reformulates student's representation in general terms

by inventing hard mathematical puzzles for the average reader, and Martin Gardner has used the puzzle form brilliantly to proselytize mathematical ideas in his immensely popular *Scientific American* pieces and his books. As long as the problem-solvers are confident, they will understand the principles by which a solution is reached, and will be content. If an apparently simple problem about prime numbers entails using the Taniyama–Shimura conjecture—a fantastically advanced mathematical idea about 'module forms', unimaginable objects that exist in hyperbolic (four-dimensional) space—then the average Sunday paper reader will be understandably annoyed.[47]

The best puzzles show you surprising applications of ideas you already understand, or make surprising connections between ideas. This is why people enjoy them. They would not enjoy solving long multiplication problems.

There is nothing intrinsically dull or hateful about mathematics. It will be, and can be, fun, as long as children understand what they are doing and feel pride of ownership in mathematical ideas.

9

HARD NUMBERS

AND EASY NUMBERS

There are some mathematical ideas that just seem harder to grasp than others, without any obvious reason why. These ideas include the various kinds of number, outlined in Chapter 1. The reason for this is that we do not think about the hard numbers in the way that seems most natural to us: as numerosities. (Of course, I except professional mathematicians from all that follows, as they are quite happy thinking about objects which are abstractions away from numerosities— distributions, probabilities, infinities, groups, functions, and so on.) It is often possible, however, to reconfigure the way we think about these hard numbers so as to make them easier: to make them, in fact, more like the familiar numerosities.

I have argued that we are born with a brain specially equipped with a Number Module designed by evolution to detect and recognize numerosities in the world about us. These tend to be small numerosities— less than 5—but the basic idea is there. We have needed, and developed, a range of conceptual tools, as well as tools you can touch and see, to get us beyond 5. These include fingers, the number words, the numerals, counting-boards, tallying on walls, sticks, making marks in the sand, the abacus, the computer, and the pocket calculator. Historically, the first main use of these tools was to extend the size of numerosities we could reach, think about, and manipulate. Perhaps the most important tools of all are the techniques of calculation invented by mathematicians down the ages. However, as these techniques become more advanced, they get further and further away from collections and numerosities.

NEGATIVE NUMBERS

Quickly now, which is larger: $-6 + 1$ or $-2 - 4$?[1] Why are negative numbers hard? One reason may be that they are not easy to map onto numerosities. What kind of collection has a negative numerosity? How do you take away a larger collection from a smaller one? How, indeed, do you combine two collections with negative numerosities? It boggles our idea of numerosities. Children are taught negative numbers with the help of a number line, partitioned by zero into positive and negative numbers:

```
     −5  −4  −3  −2  −1   0   1   2   3   4   5
.... |___|___|___|___|___|___|___|___|___|___| ....
```

Larger positive numbers are further to the right, while larger negative numbers are further to the left. This is a natural, and historically very early, way of thinking about negative numbers. But it contains a conceptual conflict. The number 5 is bigger than 3 (it denotes a bigger numerosity) while −5 is smaller than −3. The bigger the negative number, the smaller it is. The number line representation does not in itself explain what happens when you add or subtract a negative number. Which way do you travel along the line? Is it the same way as when you add or subtract a positive number? Is subtracting a negative number from a negative number the same as subtracting it from a positive one?

The difficulty we have in learning about negative numbers recapitulates history: negative numbers came late in our own personal development, and also in the historical development of the idea of numbers. As far as is known, the idea of negative numbers depended on the invention of zero,[2] and had its origin in the Indus Valley around AD 500–600. Positive whole numbers, as we saw in Chapter 2, had by then been written down for perhaps 10,000 years, and carved on cave walls and bones for very much longer. So it is not just you and me, as individuals, who find negative numbers difficult: it has taken people many millennia to arrive at the idea. The Hindu poet-astronomers to whom we owe these inventions envisaged each negative as the counterpart to a positive number: –1 to +1, –2 to +2, and so on. This was the relational basis, rather than a numerosity one. The Hindus, and later European mathematicians such as Fibonacci, talked about negative numbers in terms of bookkeeping. For each positive number credit entry, there could be a negative number debit entry. Debt arose when the debit number was larger than the credit number. By the sixteenth century, it was accepted that equations could have negative roots, that is, the value of the unknown could be negative. For example, in $9 + x = 6$ and in $9x = -27$, x has the value -3. However, they were usually termed 'false' roots, and the idea of an absolute negative magnitude as a genuine number was resisted by many mathematicians until the beginning of the nineteenth century.

Even with the intuition that every positive number can have a corresponding negative, translating this into ideas of numerosity is not completely obvious. The negative number (of pounds you owe) is the numerosity of that collection of pounds needed to balance the books. This way of thinking about it will keep you solvent. Debts can be added together. If we go out together and I pay for your theatre ticket, you owe me £20 for that; and then I pay for dinner too, so you owe me for your share, £25. You can settle up by adding the two debts together and giving me a cheque for £45. Debts can be subtracted. If you pay for the theatre, but I pay for dinner, then you owe me just £5. So far, so simple. But it is likely to be mathematically misleading. For example, how can a debt be multiplied by another debt to yield a credit? Talking about negative numbers in terms of debts, or even in terms of 'taking away', leaves children and adults with the conceptual problem of understanding why $5 \times -2 = -10$, while $-5 \times -2 = 10$. It is usually explained in terms of the change of direction of movement along the number line. So, 5×2, where both numbers are positive, would be moving to the right from 0 five steps of size two; a negative on one of the numbers would mean changing direction and moving to the left five steps of size two; and with two negatives, you change direction twice: to the left, and then again back to the right.

The difficulty with negative numbers is that once they are introduced into a problem, each number will have both a size and a direction (as we saw on the number line), whereas numerosities have just a size. Surprisingly little is known about adults' troubles with negative numbers, or how children learn, or fail to learn, about them. One can only speculate that they are hard precisely because they are hard to think about in terms of numerosities.

FRACTIONS

A year or so ago my daughter Anna, then ten, was learning about fractions. She seemed to have no trouble at all with what were called in my school 'proper fractions', which were fractions less than or equal to 1. She understood that $\frac{3}{3}$, $\frac{10}{10}$, $\frac{1500}{1500}$ were all equal to $\frac{1}{1}$. The difference between a numerator and the denominator was clear to her. The larger the denominator the smaller the number, so that ½ is bigger than ¼. At the same time she knew that ¾ was larger than ¼. Perhaps more surprisingly she understood that ⅝ might not be bigger than ¾, even though both numbers were larger. A few months later she was able to find the lowest common denominator, and actually work out that ¾ was larger because it was equivalent to ⅝. But she completely failed to understand 'improper' fractions, those bigger than 1, and denied that they made any sense at all.

The way Anna was thinking about fractions was based on her idea of numerosity, and in her terms it was perfectly sensible. A fraction was a part of a whole. She could take a whole and divide it up into any number of equal parts. The parts formed a collection with a numerosity. Fractions with the denominator 4 were sub-collections of collections of four members; fractions with the denominator 1,000,000 were subcollections of a collection with a million members. This way of thinking made it easy to see that the larger the denominator, the smaller the value of the fraction. It was also easy to see that from this collection of parts you could form sub-collections whose numerosity was given by the numerator. A sub-collection of two quarters was going to be bigger than just one quarter. From this way of thinking about how fractions differ, it was clear that when the denominators of two fractions differ, their relative size was going to be problematic. You couldn't immediately tell whether two-fifths was bigger or smaller than one quarter: you had to do some calculating.

Anna stuck to this way of thinking about fractions because it built upon her well-developed concept of numerosity. She understood fractions, and could even manipulate them quite effectively. But it limited her to fractions that could be expressed as parts of a whole.

Naturally, as a professional father and an amateur maths teacher, I tried to encourage her to see that fractions bigger than 1 behaved exactly like proper fractions. She just said, 'You can't have four thirds, you can only have three thirds.' End of story. In due course her professional teacher achieved what I had failed to do, and now, at eleven, she is just as happy calculating with improper fractions as with proper fractions. She still thinks of them as collections with numerosities, but now she is willing to acknowledge that there can be collections of collections. So ⁴⁄₃ is all the parts of one collection with three equal parts, plus one part of a second collection with three equal parts.

I use Anna's achievements and failures as an illustration of how numbers that can be thought of straightforwardly in terms of collections with numerosities are easy to grasp, while those that need to go beyond a collection with a numerosity, even when it is a matter of thinking of two collections, can be hard, at least to begin with. Fractions are another example of individual development recapitulating history. Ideas that hard for the child to grasp have been hard for adults too. The ancient Egyptians, who were formidable mathematicians, only used unit fractions—fractions with a numerator of 1 (with the exception of ⅔). A papyrus written by the scribe Ahmes in 1650 BC (the Rhind Papyrus), and probably copied from older documents, lists the translations of fractions $2/n$ into sums of unit fractions.[3] It is not known why the Egyptians, the Greeks, and the Romans preferred unit fractions, but one possibility is that in this way they were always able to think of fractions in terms of simple collections, sub-collections, and their numerosities.

PROBABILITIES

Probabilities are notoriously hard to grasp. History shows us that even very elementary mathematical concepts of probability arrived very late on the scene, two thousand years after the foundations of geometry and number theory had been laid by the Greeks. Of course, if probabilities were easy to understand then we'd be richer because lotteries, bookmakers, and insurance companies would be poorer.

Let me start with a really easy problem. You know that Mr and Mrs Smith have two children; you also know that one of the children is male. What is the chance that the other one is female, given this knowledge? Was your answer '50%' or 'One-half'? You were wrong. The correct probability is two-thirds (assuming no twins). Let me ask you another very simple, almost identical question. You know that Mr and Mrs Smith have two children; you also know that the *older* child is male. What is the chance that the other child is female? Was your answer 'Two-thirds'? Wrong again! The correct answer is 'One-half'. How can that be?

The four possibilities for two children, assuming no twins, triplets, etc. and that male and female children are equally likely, are given in Table 9.1.

First child	Second child
M	M
M	F
F	M
F	F

Table 9.1 The four possible combinations of two children.

In the first problem, we can rule out FF, which leaves three possible arrangements of pairs of children: MM, MF, and FM. So in two out of three cases, the other child will be female. In the second problem, we can rule out the two possibilities where the first child is female. Of the remaining two possibilities, one has M for the second child, the other F. So the probability is one-half. The key step is to lay out the collection of all possibilities, and then to think of each situation as a sub-collection of these possibilities. When problems arise it is because this key step is not taken.

Here's a slightly more difficult problem. A test for breast cancer gives a positive reading for 80% of the women who have the disease. Miss

Smith is told by her doctor that, alas, her test is positive. What's the chance that she has the disease? Actually, one cannot say, because the base rate (in this case, the proportion of all tests, positive and negative, that are accurate) of test accuracy is not given. The rate of positive tests in those cases where the patient actually has the disease is not sufficient: you also need to know what the accuracy of the test is for patients who do *not* have the disease. Even where the base rate is given, most people practice 'base-rate neglect', and don't take it into account, at least not properly. This can be serious. The same problem is posed in the box below. When it is given with base-rate information and framed in terms of probabilities, I am willing to bet that most of you still get it wrong. Doctors did: 95 of 100 doctors gave answers between 70 and 80%. However, when the same problem is expressed in terms of numerosities, then about half get it right. Try it for yourself (the answer is in the Notes section).

If you got this probability problem wrong, you are in very good company—and I don't mean just doctors. Even though the mathemat-

DIAGNOSIS PROBLEMS[4]

Version 1: Probabilities

In routine screening, the probability of breast cancer is 1% for a woman at the age of forty (all figures are invented). If a woman has breast cancer, the probability is 80% that her test will show positive. If a woman does not have cancer, the probability is 10% that her test will also show positive.

A woman's test shows positive. What is the probability that she has breast cancer?

Answer: ____%

Version 2: Numerosities

In routine screening, 10 out of 1,000 women have breast cancer at the age of forty. Of the 10 who take the test, 8 show a positive result. Of the 990 women without breast cancer, 100 will test positive.

In a new sample of 100 women with a positive test, how many do you expect actually to have breast cancer?

Answer: ____ out of ____

ics of probability is generally very simple, the concepts are really hard. Almost nothing sensible was written about it until the great mathematician (and gambler) Girolamo Cardano started to write *Liber de ludo aleae* ('Book on Games of Chance') in 1525. He kept working on it until his death, and it wasn't published until 1663. He regarded this book as his greatest achievement, since he had discovered the *reasons* (the theories, that is) behind the facts known to any skilled gambler.

Any poker player who is still reasonably solvent knows that drawing to an inside straight is a good way to become insolvent. That is, putting up good money to draw an 8 to a hand with 6, 7, 9, 10 is almost always a very poor bet. Now, not many solvent poker players can tell you how to calculate the correct odds on drawing the 8; it is nearly 11 to 1 (the four 8's out of the forty-seven cards you haven't yet seen). Still fewer could work out the odds on being dealt a straight in the first place; fewer still, the odds on making a straight with a one-card draw. After a few years of Saturday night poker, most players will have a good intuitive sense of the likelihood of these outcomes and will bet accordingly. What they will not have, with rare exceptions, are the mathematical *reasons* for these probabilities. This is why Cardano was so excited by his results. But even he failed to calculate correctly the odds on throwing a 1 or a 2 with two dice.[5]

It took two of the greatest minds of European history working together to put probability on firm mathematical footing: the philosopher and mathematician Blaise Pascal, and Pierre de Fermat (of the famous Last Theorem), whom Pascal described as 'a man so outstanding in intellect ... [that his works] will make him supreme among the geomasters of Europe'.[6] It was not as though the idea of probability, of chance, was unknown. As the author of Ecclesiastes wrote, 'The race is not to the swift, nor the battle to the strong, neither yet bread to the wise, nor yet riches to men of understanding, nor yet favour to men of skill; but time and chance happeneth to them all.'[7] But betting against the swift is an excellent way to lose money. The key is to know the odds at which it is sensible to risk your money on the swift. In his fascinating history of risk management, *Against the Gods*, Peter Bernstein reminds us of its importance. 'The ability to define what may happen in the future and to choose among alternatives lies at the heart of contemporary societies. Risk management guides us over a vast range of decision-making, from allocating wealth to safeguarding public health, from waging war to planning a family, from paying insurance premiums to wearing a seatbelt, from planting corn to marketing cornflakes.'[8] There is also our 'casino culture', both literally and metaphorically. I am one of only 5% of British adults never to have placed a bet on our National Lottery. I take the view that the directors of Camelot, the operating company, are rich enough without a contribution from me.

Investing in stocks and shares, or in interest-bearing bank accounts; buying life insurance, or taking out a pension; these are personal gambles on the future. Again, one can ask why stockbrokers, abitrageurs, bankers, and directors of insurance companies are rich, while the average punter in these activities is relatively poor. One reason is that they employ experts to work out the odds for them; we don't.

Straightforward gambling is ancient. Roman soldiers cast lots at the foot of the Cross. Estimating risk has a long history, too; for example, it lies at the centre of Shakespeare's *The Merchant of Venice*. Antonio, who stands as surety for Bassanio's three-thousand-ducat loan from Shylock, says that his 'ventures are not in one bottom trusted';[9] that is, he has spread his risk among several 'bottoms'— ships. Shylock, however, is less sure. It is true Antonio 'hath an argosy bound to Tripolis, another to the Indies; I understand moreover upon the Rialto, he hath a third at Mexico, a fourth for England . . . But [and for Shylock this is a very big 'but'] ships are but boards, sailors but men; there be land-rats and water-rats, land-thieves and water-thieves, I mean pirates; and then there is the peril of waters, winds and rocks.'[10] He therefore demands further assurance from Antonio against the possibility that none of these ventures pays off within the three-month period of the loan.

The business of insurance didn't exist until the eighteenth century, when laws of probability became better understood and actuarial statistics began to be collected. However, there was one insurance practice that Antonio may have used, called 'bottomry'. This is, to quote the *Encyclopaedia Britannica*, 'a maritime contract by which a ship (or bottom) is hypothecated in security for money borrowed for expenses incurred in the course of a voyage, under the condition that if she arrive at her destination the ship shall be liable for repayment of the loan, together with such premium as may have been agreed for'.[11] If the ship is lost, then the borrower owes no money. Doubtless the premium would reflect the risk of the ship's going down, though it would have been calculated by some rule of thumb. So although Antonio owed Shylock his pound of flesh, and he'd lost all the money tied up in his ships, their failure would not have exposed him to further debts.

There's a moral to all this. If you don't want to expose your wealth and income to the predations of loan sharks, insurance schemes, or lottery organizers, it's a good idea to make sure you understand probabilities. And the way to do this is to turn them into more manageable concepts based on numerosity.

THE CALCULUS OF HAPPINESS IN AN UNCERTAIN WORLD

We live in an uncertain world: everything about it is uncertain except death and the taxman. From the day we are born, we are constantly making decisions about outcomes that are uncertain. I leave home in the morning, and catch a tube to work. If the tube is working more or less normally, then I can make my first appointment. If it is not, then I will be late. London tubes are far from certain, and over the years I suppose I must have developed an estimate of how likely I am to be late. If I leave home earlier than usual then I will have a better chance of making the appointment, but against that I lose a little sleep or miss some breakfast. Most days I am willing to take the chance because being late is not too costly. There will be days with important meetings—for example where allocation of space in my department is decided, or where relative strangers will form a view about me—then I'll leave home earlier.

Now, the importance of the appointment affects my decision even though my estimate of the probability of tube delays has not. Conversely, if I hear that the rail workers' trade union will be taking industrial action that may disrupt the service, I will leave earlier even though my being late won't be a disaster. Here my estimate of the possibility of arriving late, given my usual departure time, is changed, though the cost of being late has not. If there is a service disruption on the day of a vital meeting, I will leave earlier still.

This set of circumstances can be described in terms of a concept called *expected value*. This is simply the probability multiplied by the value of the outcomes:

Expected value = Probability × Value

One could use a cost—say the adverse consequences of being late for a meeting—rather than a benefit. An example of an expected-value problem, adapted from the kind used in experiments by two of the leading authorities, psychologists Amos Tversky and Daniel Kahneman,[12] is presented in the box that follows—try it (the answer is in the Notes section).

LOTTERIES[13]

Which would you prefer?:

    A. A sure gain of £75, or

    B. A lottery in which there is a 75% chance of winning £100 and a 25% chance of winning nothing?

Now, which of the following choices would you prefer?:

    C. A sure loss of £75, or

    D. A lottery in which there is a 75% chance of losing £100 and a 25% chance of losing nothing?

If you had trouble with these problems, then young children should do even worse. Expected values and utilities are surely far too advanced for young children to understand. Yet they seem to understand them as well as adults. This was beautifully demonstrated by my colleague at University College London, Anne Schlottmann, and by Norman Anderson from the University of California at San Diego.[14] The task that Schlottmann and Anderson gave children from five to ten years old was this. There was a two-coloured sealed tube with a ball in it. The proportion of each colour could be varied, so that when the tube was shaken up the probability of the ball landing in the red or blue section would depend on the relative lengths of these two sections: lots of red, equal red and blue, lots of blue. In this way they could experimentally manipulate the probability variable. In one version of the experiment there were the two prizes, the large prize for the red section and the small prize for the blue section. The children, after some instruction and practice, were asked to mark on a scale how happy a doll, Hilda, would be at the different outcomes. They had no trouble understanding what to do, and their results were really quite similar to what they would have found had they multiplied probability by expected value, but not quite. The results suggested to Schlottmann and Anderson that the children weren't really using the multiplication rule, but were relying on a kind of adding rule. Hilda would be a little happier with the large prize than the small, and also a little happier when the probability of the large prize was better.

In terms of collections and numerosities, children (and adults) would create a collection of 'units of happiness'. They would add units according to the value of the outcome, and for the estimated likelihoods of favourable outcomes. Even small children can judge expected values, provided they can reconfigure the situation in terms they understand.

DISTRIBUTIONS

Most of us are now accustomed to thinking about some aspects of distribution, in particular, 'averages'. We all know that an average (mathematically, the *mean*) is the total of the samples divided by the number of samples. A batsman's average is the total number of runs made divided by the number of innings completed. The average income of citizens of a country is the total gross domestic product divided by the number of citizens. But averages can be very misleading if other aspects of the distribution being averaged are ignored. The example of average income is perhaps the most important. How is this income shared out? Are there a few very rich citizens and lots of very poor ones? Although most of us are well aware of this kind of issue, it is not always properly understood. In the box that follows there is a distribution problem for you to try (the answer is in the Notes section).

FINITE MEANS, INFINITE ENDS

So far, this book has focused almost exclusively on whole numbers. Even though they are so basic and so simple, they are extraordinary and

WAITING TIMES[15]

You know that the average interval between buses is half an hour, but you don't know the schedule. When you arrive at the bus stop, how long is your wait likely to be?

    A. 15 minutes
    B. At least 15 minutes, probably more
    C. At most 15 minutes, probably less
    D. Can't tell.

You may like to think about this problem in another way. Imagine a thousand travellers in your position, or even a million. They all arrive at the bus stop throughout the day and night without knowing the schedule. What will their average waiting time be?

There's a third way of thinking about it. You arrive at a particular time at the station, say 12 noon, but the buses arrive at random (which is certainly how it usually seems to me). However, the average interval is half an hour.

deeply mysterious, perhaps the most extraordinary and mysterious objects we can imagine. If we start with just 1 and a single operation, addition, which we have recently discovered newborn babies can manage (see Chapter 3), we can construct the whole sequence of numerosities:

$$1$$
$$1 + 1$$
$$1 + 1 + 1$$
$$1 + 1 + 1 + 1$$
$$\cdots$$

From these finite means we can reach a number larger than the number of grains of sand on Brighton beach or, as Archimedes demonstrated in *The Sand-Reckoner*, larger than the number of grains of sand needed to fill the entire universe.

He had taken the best data then available, and the boldest contemporary hypothesis about the size of the universe, proposed by Aristarchus of Samos in the third century BC. Aristarchus, like Copernicus nearly 2,000 years after him, argued that the earth went round the sun.

However, if the earth moves, the apparent positions of stars should change as a result of parallax. That is, the nearer stars should appear to move in front of the more distant stars as the earth moves in its orbit, just as street lights appear to be displaced relative to more distant lights when we drive past them at night. But the stars are not displaced, but appear fixed relative to one another. The theory can be saved only if the stars are so far away that the movement of the earth in relation to them is so tiny that parallax is undetectable, in the same way that a tree on a distant mountain will not appear to move relative to the summit if we, as observers, only move a few feet to the left or to the right. And this indeed was Aristarchus's defence. Archimedes calculated the number of grains of sand in Aristarchus's universe to be fewer than 10^{63}.

Without a place-value notation, and neat devices for expressing powers, he had to invent a way of writing down these big numbers. All the numbers up to a myriad (10,000) he called the first order of numbers; the numbers from 10,000 to a myriad myriads ($10,000^2$ or 10^8) were numbers of the second order; and so on. His estimate of the number of grains of sand in the Aristarchan universe was ten million units of the eighth order. The eighth order is the seventh power of a myriad myriads: $(10^8)^7$, which is 10^{56}. Multiplying this by 10,000,000 (10^7) gives 10^{63}. Having made this spectacular demonstration, Archimedes went on to show that he could create even bigger numbers by raising a myriad myriads to the power of a myriad myriads, a number that would need 800,000,000 Greek letters to write down. This number was just the beginning of the first 'period'. In this system, one could continue to count through to the 10^8th period. This is just one reason why he is regarded as the greatest mathematician of antiquity.

The Greeks were well aware that there is no largest whole number; the number series went on forever, as we can read in Aristotle's *Physics*. The largest prime number found at the time of writing is the Mersenne prime, 2 to the power of 3,021,377 minus 1—a 909,526-digit number— so called because the French mathematician and philosopher Marin Mersenne proposed in 1644 that numbers of the form $2^n - 1$ are always prime, when n is prime. All the prime values of n that Mersenne tested did indeed yield primes, and he conjectured that $2^{67} - 1$ was therefore also a prime. This was something that was extremely hard to check before the advent of computers, and although no proof could be found of the proposal, no mathematician disputed that here was a mechanism for generating primes. That was until 1903, when Frank Cole of Columbia University went to the blackboard at a meeting of the American Mathematical Society and wrote

$$2^{67} - 1 = 147,573,952,589,676,412,927$$

followed by

$$193,707,721 \times 761,838,275,287 = 147,573,952,589,676,412,927$$

and then sat down to a standing ovation.[16] That was the end of Mersenne's conjecture, and no one has yet come up with a formula guaranteed to generate primes, let alone all the primes.

REACHING TO INFINITY

Even these very big numbers are small compared with infinity, and one can create infinity just by adding 1, infinitely often. The philosopher René Descartes, a very sophisticated and original mathematician, worried that we could not understand God because God was infinite whereas Man is finite. The great mathematician Hermann Weyl called mathematics '*the science of the infinite*, its goal the symbolic comprehension of the infinite with human, that is finite, means' (his italics).[17] Indeed, one cannot get far in mathematics without infinities. Even the sequence of counting numbers (or *natural numbers*) 1, 2, 3, . . . has infinity implied in the 'dot, dot, dot'. We all understand this. As children we know that we can always add one to any number to get a bigger number. Provided we have a procedure by which we can construct a series, then we can understand the infinite collection of things in that series.[18] The procedure of adding one enables us to see that any number can be understood as just a collection of 1's added together. It is also easy to see that the collection of these collections—the collection of all natural numbers—cannot be counted in any finite time, because at the end of any finite interval there will be the last number counted plus one still to count.

What worried mathematicians and philosophers, from at least the time of the ancient Greeks, was whether the collection of all whole numbers really existed—existed in something like the sense in which the collection of numbers between 90 and 100 exists. The problem was that this collection—or, to use standard terminology, this set—had paradoxical properties. For example, there was Galileo's paradox: there are as many square numbers (1, 4, 9, 16 . . .) as there are natural numbers. And there was the paradox that if you add 1 or even 1,000,000 to the infinite collection, it doesn't get any bigger. In modern terminology the *cardinality* (numerosity) of this set is $\aleph_0$ (pronounced 'aleph nought' in the UK, 'aleph null' in the USA). It has many counter-intuitive properties, for example:

$$\aleph_0 + 1 = \aleph_0$$
$$\aleph_0 + 1,000,000 = \aleph_0$$
$$\aleph_0 + \aleph_0 = \aleph_0$$

Many of us find such paradoxes hard to grasp precisely because they violate our natural idea of numerosities, of finite numerosities, where a subset has fewer members than the whole set that it's part of, and where adding together two sets, each with at least one member, gives a set bigger than the sets you started with.

Let's start with something easy. Two collections have the same numerosity if their members can be put into one-to-one correspondence. For example, my collection of children has the same numerosity as my collection of cats because I can pair daughter Amy with cat Fudge, and daughter Anna with cat Snuggles. Let us now take the collection of all the natural numbers in the range 1 to 10 inclusive, and the collection of all the square numbers in the range 1 to 10, and try to pair them up in the same way:

```
1   2   3   4   5   6   7   8   9   10  ...
|   |   |   |   |   |   |   |   |   |
1   4   9
```

It can't be done: there are numbers that are not paired up from the first collection. We may conclude that there are more natural numbers than square numbers in the collection of numbers up to 10. Exactly the same would be true for collections of numbers up to any number you choose. But are there more natural numbers than square numbers if you consider the entire set of natural numbers—the infinite set?

Let's apply our pairing procedure:

1	2	3	4	5	6	7	8	9	10	...
|	|	|	|	|	|	|	|	|	|	
1	4	9	16	25	36	49	64	81	100	...

We have a procedure for constructing a square number to go with every natural number, so there would never be a natural number in the first row that doesn't have a square number to go with it, and likewise no square number that cannot be paired with a natural number (as any natural number n may be paired with the corresponding square number, n^2).[19] Therefore there are the same number of square numbers as natural numbers.

The situation seems even odder for prime numbers. We do not have any procedure for constructing prime numbers. Essentially, all we can do is to check whether a given number is prime by looking for factors. The Greek mathematician Eratosthenes invented a famous short cut, known now as the 'sieve of Eratosthenes', but this doesn't actually reduce the sheer trial and error of testing by very much. We do know that the proportion of primes in a sequence of numbers gets smaller as the numbers get larger: there are four primes in the first ten numbers (40%), twenty-five primes in the first hundred (25%), and one hundred and sixty-eight in the first thousand (16.8%), but only 78,498 in the first million (7.8%). We also know, courtesy of a proof by Euclid, that there is no largest prime number. So, are there more natural numbers than prime numbers? Let's try our pairing procedure:

1	2	3	4	5	6	7	8	9	10	...
|	|	|	|	|	|	|	|	|	|	
2	3	5	7	11	13	17	19	23	29	...

For the next natural number in the sequence, we can always find a prime. So, there are as many primes as there are natural numbers. When this demonstration was first shown to me I felt that there must be a trick somewhere. From one point of view it's obvious that there must be fewer primes, because primes are a subset of the set of all natural numbers, but this reasoning just doesn't apply when it comes to infinite sets.

One of the reasons why infinite numerosities are sometimes hard to grasp is that aspects of our familiar concept of numerosity are in conflict: one-to-one correspondence between sets can be used to establish relative numerosity, but the set–subset relation doesn't hold. In fact, the characteristic of infinite sets is that an infinite set can be put into one-to-one correspondence with any subset that is neither the whole set nor the empty set (the set equivalent of zero).

We are still left with the problem of whether an infinite set such as $\aleph_0$, which is, of course, but one of infinitely many different infinite sets, really exists. When thinking about this, it is worth bearing in mind that the collection of all the atoms in the universe is infinitely smaller than the collection of all the natural numbers (or all the squares, or all the primes). In their book *The Mathematical Experience*, mathematicians Philip Davis and Reuben Hersh, like Descartes, compare the infinite set to God:

> Mathematics, then, asks us to believe in an infinite set. What does it mean that an infinite set exists? Why should one believe it? In formal presentation this request is insitutionalized by axiomatization. Thus in *Introduction to Set Theory*, by Hrbacek and Jech, we read on page 54:
>
> 'The Axiom of Infinity. An inductive (i.e. infinite) set exists.'
>
> Compare this against the axiom of God as presented by Maimonides (Mishneh Torah, Book 1, Chapter 1):
>
> 'The basic principle of all basic principles and the pillar of all sciences is to realize that there is a First Being who brought every existing thing into being.'

Davis and Hersh then ask, 'Which is mathematics and which is theology?'[20]

The answer is that the mathematics is the mathematics: the problem arises because perfectly comprehensible finite procedures, like adding one, give rise to infinite collections. We have seen that one of the infinite sub-collections of the collection of natural numbers is the collection of prime numbers. Even though we still have no sure-fire way of generating prime numbers, we still know that there are infinitely many of them. The sceptical reader will by now be asking for a proof. And there is one: a beautiful proof, over two thousand years old, due to Euclid—who, in the words of the American poet Edna St Vincent Millay, 'alone has looked on Beauty bare'.

Imagine that the opposite is true (a favourite trick of Euclid's): that there is a greatest prime, call it P. Imagine also a number larger than P, call it Q, constructed from all the primes up to P and P itself, plus 1: $Q = (2 \times 3 \times 5 \times 7 \times \ldots \times P) + 1$. Now, Q cannot be divided by any prime factors, including P, since it would always leave the remainder 1. So if it is not a prime then it must be divisible by a prime greater than P, in which case there is a prime greater than P. If it cannot be divided by any prime, then it is itself a prime, and one larger than P.

We can now show that there are as many prime numbers as natural numbers. The way to establish the number of a collection relative to another collection is to put the members of the first collection in one-to-one correspondence with those of the other. We can show that it is possible to do this with collections of the natural numbers and prime numbers, since there is no largest prime.

Now, if you think that an infinity of whole numbers, or prime numbers, is big, you may be surprised to discover that it's actually the smallest of all the infinities. Any collection that can be put into one-to-one correspondence with the natural numbers, 1, 2, 3, $\ldots$, is a collection with a numerosity $\aleph_0$, aleph with a subscript 0 to show that it is but the first in a series. This is what is called a *countable* infinity. That is not to say that one can count its members in a finite time, but that in principle it would be possible to count them one after another. Any collection which can be put into one-to-one correspondence with the natural numbers is also countably infinite. But not all infinities are countable: the number of points on a straight line, for example, is not countable. You cannot count them because there is no next point: between any two points there are infinitely many points. It is like the decimal numbers; between any two there are infinitely many, so, unlike the natural numbers, there is no next decimal. For example, there is no next decimal after 0.5. If you were to say that it's 0.6, I'd reply that you've missed out 0.51; if you had said 0.51 in the first place, I'd have countered with 0.511, and so on.

Towards the end of the nineteenth century the German mathematician Georg Cantor constructed several ingenious arguments to show that there are infinitely many infinite numerosities. Here is one. He showed that no set could be paired up with the set of all its subsets, and that therefore the set of subsets had more members than the set itself. This is easy to see when you consider a finite set, for example $\{1, 2, 3\}$ (in mathematical notation, the members of a set are enclosed by curly brackets). This has eight subsets ($\{1\}$, $\{2\}$, $\{3\}$, $\{1, 2\}$, $\{2, 3\}$, $\{1, 3\}$, $\{1, 2, 3\}$, and the empty set $\{\ \}$), and we cannot therefore pair them up with the numbers 1, 2, 3. Let us apply this idea to the infinite set of natural numbers $\{0, 1, 2, 3, \ldots\}$ which we'll call N. N has fewer members than the set N^* of all the subsets of N. Cantor showed that N^* has the same numerosity as the set of infinite decimals, and of points on the line. We can go on to make a set of the subsets of the subsets: $\{\{1\}, \{2\}\}$, $\{\{1\}, \{1, 2\}\}$, $\{\{1\}, \{1, 2, 3\}\}$, and so on. This, by the same argument, will have a larger numerosity than the set of subsets. We can apply this idea to N^* to get the set of all subsets of N^*, which we can call N^{**}, which in turn has fewer members than N^{***}, and so on ad infinitum. Each of the numerosities of the collections, N^*, N^{**}, N^{***} is an infinity larger than the last.

It turns out that there is a very deep mystery here. Is the next biggest infinity after $\aleph_0$, called $\aleph_1$, the same as the number of points on the line, N^*, which has the numerosity $2^{\aleph_0}$? Cantor believed that

$$\aleph_1 = 2^{\aleph_0}$$

This is called Cantor's continuum hypothesis. Neither he, nor anyone since, has been able to prove that it's true; nor has anyone been able to prove that it's false. Indeed, Kurt Gödel (about whom more in a moment) and Paul Cohen showed that it is undecidable in relation to our current understanding of numbers.[21]

Astounding Patterns

Numbers form themselves into the most extraordinary patterns, but one of the most intriguing and the most important is built from the simplest bricks with the simplest mortar—addition. It is usually known as Pascal's triangle, because the seventeenth-century mathematician and philosopher Blaise Pascal studied it intensively. However, it was described three hundred and fifty years earlier by Chinese mathematician Zhu Shijie in his book *Siyuan yujian* ('The Jade Mirror of the Four Unknowns'). It is believed that Omar Khayyam wrote about it also, though his text appears to have been lost.

Pascal's interest was inspired by Pierre de Fermat, who hoped to interest him in number theory. He sent Pascal a statement of one of his remarkable and beautiful theorems, which was to remain unproved until the nineteenth century:

> Every integer is composed of one, two, or three triangular numbers; of one, two, three, or four squares; of one, two, three, four, or five pentagons; of one, two, three, four, five, or six hexagons; and thus to infinity.[22]

In Pascal's triangle (see Figure 9.1a) the first diagonal, starting at the top 1, gives a sequence of 1's from which all else is constructed:

$$1, 1, 1, 1, 1, 1, 1, 1, \ldots$$

The next diagonal gives the counting numbers

$$1, 2, 3, 4, 5, 6, 7, 8, 9, \ldots$$

The third diagonal gives the *triangular numbers*:

$$1, 3, 6, 10, 15, 21, 28, \ldots$$

The fourth diagonal contains the *tetrahedral numbers*, those that make up a tetrahedron—a triangular pyramid. They are therefore formed by adding the triangular numbers thus: $1 + 3$, $1 + 3 + 6$, $1 + 3 + 6 + 10$, $1 + 3 + 6 + 10 + 15$, $\ldots$ to give:

$$1, 4, 10, 20, 35, 56, \ldots$$

And you can add the tetrahedral numbers to give pentatope numbers (the pentatope is the simplest regular figure in four dimensions). Numbers formed in this way are known collectively as *figurate numbers* (Figure 9.2).

There's more. When the numbers are rearranged slightly to make the process clearer (Figure 9.1 b), taking sums along lines in an oblique direction gives the *Fibonacci* sequence:

$$1, 1, 2, 3, 5, 8, 13, 21, \ldots$$

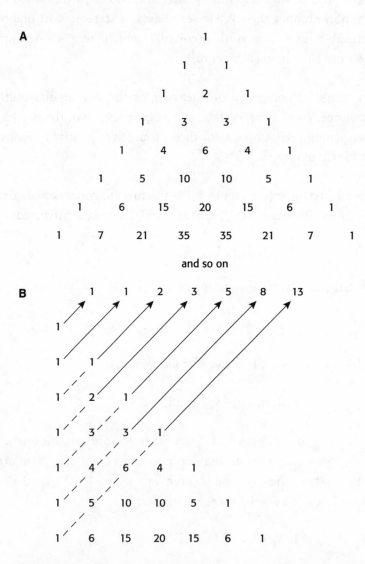

Figure 9.1 Pascal's triangle. (a) The triangle is constructed very simply: each number (with the exception of the 1 at the apex) is formed by adding together the two numbers immediately to its left and right in the row above. (b) The Fibonacci sequence is generated by summing oblique diagonals in Pascal's triangle, shown here slightly rearranged for clarity.

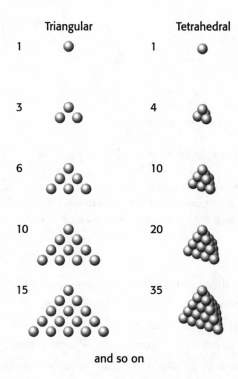

Triangular   Tetrahedral

Figure 9.2 Numbers that can be represented by an array in the form of a regular geo-metric figure are called figurate numbers. The square numbers are the most familiar sequence; the triangular and tetrahedral numbers are examples of figurate numbers that correspond to arrays in two and three dimensions, respectively.

This sequence was discovered by Fibonacci of Pisa and published in his popular book *Liber abaci* at the beginning of the thirteenth century (see Chapter 2). He introduced the sequence to solve the follow-ing problem: 'How many pairs of rabbits will be produced in a year, beginning with a single pair, if in every second month each pair bears a new pair which become productive from the second month on?'[23] Summing the rows in Figure 9.1 gives the sequence

$$1, 2, 4, 8, 16, 32, 64, \ldots \quad \text{or} \quad 2^0, 2^1, 2^2, 2^3, 2^4, 2^5, 2^6, \ldots$$

The rows themselves give the coefficients of the binomial expansion, a formula for finding the powers of the sum of a pair of numbers a and b. It was known to Omar Khayyam in the eleventh century that the coefficients of the terms in the expansion (i.e. the multiplying-out)

$(a + b)^0 =$	1			1			
$(a + b)^1 =$	$a + b$			1	1		
$(a + b)^2 =$	$a^2 + 2ab + b^2$		1	2	1		
$(a + b)^3 =$	$a^3 + 3a^2b + 3ab^2 + b^3$	1	3	3	1	
$(a + b)^4 =$	$a^4 + 4a^3b + 6a^2b^2 + 4ab^3 + b^4$	1	4	6	4	1

Figure 9.3 The coefficients of the binomial expansion, i.e. the numerical coefficients in the multiplying-out of an expression of the form $(a + b)^n$, are given by the nth row of Pascal's triangle (counting the 1 at the apex as the 'zeroth' row).

of $(a + b)^n$ were as shown in the left-hand column of Figure 9.3. It was Pascal who, six hundred years later, demonstrated how these coefficients related to choice and chance.

There is another way of generating Pascal's triangle: from the choice numbers formed by calculating the number of choices, r, from a collection of n things. This is given by the general formula

$$\binom{n}{r} = \frac{n!}{r!(n-r)!}$$

where $n!$ (pronounced 'n factorial') means $n \times (n-1) \times (n-2) \times \ldots \times 1$. For example, the number of ways of choosing 2 things from a collection of 4 things can be found if we replace r with 2 and n with 4:

$$\binom{4}{2} = \frac{4 \times 3 \times 2 \times 1}{(2 \times 1)(4-2)}$$

Figure 9.4 shows the successive binomial choices: the number of ways of choosing r things from a collection of n. It starts at the top with $n = 0$ and $r = 0$. In the next row are $n = 1$ and $r = 0$, and $n = 1$ and $r = 1$; the third row begins with $n = 2$ and $r = 0$; and so on. When the number of choices is calculated, these numbers form Pascal's triangle. In the last line shown in Figure 9.4, for sets of three things, there is just 1 way of choosing nothing, 3 ways of choosing 1 thing, 3 ways of

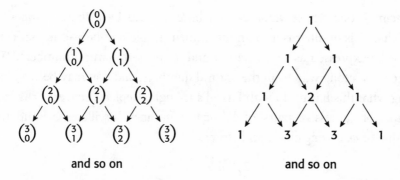

and so on   and so on

Figure 9.4 Choice numbers indicate the number of ways you can choose r things (the bottom number in the brackets) from a collection of n things (top number). For example, take a collections of $n = 3$ things, A, B, and C. There is $r = 1$ way to choose no things from it; there are $r = 3$ ways to choose one thing, choose A or choose B or choose C; $r = 3$ ways to choose two things, A and B, A and C, or B and C; and only $r = 1$ way to choose all of them. This sequence of numbers—1, 3, 3, 1—is the bottom line in the Pascal's triangle shown on the right. Both triangles can, of course, be extended indefinitely.

choosing 2 things, and just 1 way of choosing 3 things. Think of it in terms of numerosities. If the three things are A, B, and C, then for choosing just one, you could pick A, B, or C (three ways); for choosing pairs you could pick A and B, B and C, or A and C; and for choosing three there is just the whole set.

I haven't even begun to exhaust the resources of Pascal's triangle. But one further thing is worth mentioning. It has a wonderful property that links the ancient Greeks, Fibonacci, and the great astronomer Johannes Kepler. There was a certain proportion that was thought to be so aesthetically pleasing that it was called the *golden section*, or even the 'divine proportion'. There is a ratio obtained by dividing a line into two parts:

A   C   B

such that the proportion of the whole line to the greater part is the same as the proportion of the greater part to the smaller part. In other words,

$$AB : AC = AC : CB$$

This ratio, given the symbol ϕ, has a value of 1.618 . . .: a non-repeating decimal, one whose value cannot be expressed by a finite number of digits. This number is also an incommensurable number—one that cannot be expressed as p/q, where p and q are both natural numbers. We are now a long way from the natural numbers, and you may be wondering what this has to do with Pascal's triangle. Kepler discovered that the ratio of successive pairs of Fibonacci numbers oscillates around the value of ϕ, getting closer and closer:

$$2:1 = 2$$
$$3:2 = 1.5$$
$$5:3 = 1.666\ldots$$
$$8:5 = 1.6$$
$$13:8 = 1.625$$
$$21:13 = 1.615\,38\ldots$$

And all this from adding 1 to 1: sequences of numbers that turn out to describe sets of choices, beautiful proportions, . . .

DEEP MYSTERIES

Many of these number patterns have surprised their discoverers. There is a whole branch of mathematics, called number theory, devoted to these patterns in the whole numbers. You may think that by now, after more than two thousand years of investigation by some of the best minds in human history, all the simple properties of the number sequences are known, and it just remains to look for the more obscure patterns. But this is far from the case. Even some of the simplest properties of numbers, the ones that depend on arithmetical operations familiar to every eight-year-old, are not known—and may never be known.

One of the simplest and most famous mysteries about numbers was conjectured in 1742 by the German mathematician Christian Goldbach in a letter to Leonhard Euler, though it is believed that Descartes thought of it even earlier. If we take the sequence of even numbers above 2, we notice that they share an interesting property. They are all sums of two prime numbers:

$$4 = 2 + 2$$
$$6 = 3 + 3$$

$$8 = 5 + 3$$
$$10 = 5 + 5$$
$$12 = 5 + 7$$
$$14 = 7 + 7 \ldots$$

To date, no one has been able to show that this applies to all even numbers. So Goldbach's conjecture remains exactly that—a conjecture.

Another mystery about addition and multiplication goes back to the ancient Greeks. Take the divisors of a number and add them up. For example, the divisors of 4 are 1 and 2, which add up to 3; the divisors of 10 are 1, 2, and 5, which add up to 7. Now, consider the factors of 6: they are 1, 2, and 3, which add up to 6. Pythagoras and his followers regarded these numbers as *perfect* because their divisors added up to the number itself. They knew of three other numbers which were perfect: 28 (divisors 1, 2, 4, 7, and 14), 496, and 8,128. One reason they didn't know of any more is because the fifth perfect number is 33,550,336! We still know of only thirty-seven of them. And they are all even numbers. The Greeks wondered whether all perfect numbers are even. We still cannot be sure that the next perfect number we discover will not be odd, which makes this the oldest unsolved problem in the theory of numbers.

Deeper Mysteries

Whether Goldbach's conjecture or the perfect number conjecture turn out to be true or not, the deepest mystery of all concerns the 'truth' of mathematical statements. We know from Fibonacci that one rabbit plus another rabbit will, in the end, add up to more than two rabbits. But we also know that shooting at two birds in a tree in which there are ten birds is not going to leave eight birds in the tree. The world doesn't straightforwardly obey the laws of arithmetic. And the collection of natural numbers is infinite, while the number of things in the universe is finite, which means that we cannot test any interesting mathematical truth by examining the real world. So how do we *know* that $1 + 1 = 2$?

The approach that mathematicians favour is to see if they can find a *proof*. The ancient Greeks, starting with Pythagoras, were the first to appreciate the need to prove mathematical statements. The Babylonians and the Egyptians had known hundreds of years before Pythagoras that the square on the hypotenuse equals the sum of the square on the other two sides, and they calculated tables of these squares. But they didn't try to show that this relationship held for *all* sizes of right-angled triangle. Without a proof, they were in the same position as we were for Fermat's Last Theorem before Andrew Wiles came up with a proof.[24] In the equation

$$a^n = b^n + c^n$$

we couldn't be sure that there wasn't some value of n greater than 2, and some values of a, b, and c, that made that equation true. We knew only that it didn't hold for the numbers we'd tested.

Now, a proof in mathematics is not like a proof in a court of law, where 'highly probable' or 'highly improbable' is sufficient. In most scientific studies, it is enough to establish a plausible causal connection if the odds that the connection could have occurred by chance are greater than 100 to 1, and sometimes only 20 to 1. For mathematicians, this would not be remotely good enough: they have to be absolutely sure that there will never be a counter-example. Remember the Mersenne primes: it was 250 years before a value of n was found where $2^n - 1$ did not yield a prime, but find it Professor Cole did.

The Greeks demanded an unassailable argument, such as the one Euclid produced to show there was no largest prime. Euclid's *Elements* contained another type of proof, one that can get you from one statement you know to be true to another true statement. Euclid started with definitions and five postulates, or *axioms*, from which he derived by strict logic all the remaining theorems of his geometry. Essentially he was saying, 'If you accept my axioms, then all else follows.' And he was right. No one in over two thousand years has found a significant error in his reasoning. (However, people have worked with other postulates, for example, by rejecting the so-called parallel postulate to create what are now known as non-Euclidean geometries.) Euclid *axiomatized* geometry.

Strangely, the axiomization of whole-number arithmetic turned out to be much more difficult. No one tried to *prove* $1 + 1 = 2$ until the end of the nineteenth century. The English logicians Alfred Whitehead and Bertrand Russell offered a proof for this 'occasionally useful proposition' as the one numbered *110.643 in Volume 2 of their axiomatization, *Principia mathematica*.[25] It turned out that Russell and Whitehead were wrong, deeply wrong. But it takes a special kind of genius to make an absolutely fundamental error. Theirs was to think they could start with the idea of a collection and build the concept of numerosity and arithmetic securely on these foundations. So their Proposition *110.643 was, they believed, derived from the axioms that no false propositions could be derived from the axioms (in technical terms, the axioms were 'consistent'), and that all the true propositions of arithmetic could be derived from the axioms (the axioms were 'complete').

In one of the most profound, unexpected, and ingenious pieces of work in all of mathematics, a young German logician, Kurt Gödel, showed definitively that axiomatizations were not what they seemed to be. There would always be arithmetical truths that any axiomatization would fail to capture. We are all still reeling from his short paper, published in 1931 with the innocuous-sounding title, 'On formally undecidable propositions of *Principia mathematica* and related systems'.[26] It's such a wonderfully intricate piece of reasoning, and packs so much into the argument. Attempts to popularize it are bound to lose something of its style or substance. Many who have tried to do so end up with a caricature paraphrase of the famous unprovable Gödel sentence, 'This sentence is unprovable.' Putting it this way makes it sound like some kind of trick or, at best, like the liar paradox. (In its classical form: ' "All Cretans are liars," said a Cretan.' Was he [or she] telling the truth? If he was, then as a Cretan he's lying; if he's lying, and Cretans are in fact truth-tellers, then he's telling the truth.) It also obscures what it has to do with the axiomatization of arithmetic. In the Appendix, I have tried to give you an idea of Gödel's proof.

Gödel proved two fundamental properties of arithmetic. First, in any consistent system of axioms (containing a certain minimum of arithmetic[27]) there will be some truths you cannot prove within that system. In short, no axiomatic system will give you the truth, the whole truth, and nothing but the truth about arithmetic. Second, given any consistent system of axioms (containing that certain minimum of arithmetic) you will not be able to prove the consistency of that system within the system itself. In short, no system of axioms for arithmetic carries within itself a guarantee that it is free of internal contradictions. This is no idle worry. Gottlob Frege proposed an axiom system for arithmetic which was the forerunner of the approach Russell and Whitehead were to take in *Principia Mathematica*. But in 1901, quite unexpectedly, Russell discovered a contradiction in the idea of a set that Frege—and other mathematicians—had been using.

Essentially, what Russell demonstrated was that to 'prove' the consistency of an axiomatic system of arithmetic one would have to use means whose consistency is no less doubtful than the system being considered. So, 1 + 1 = 2 is true, if, and only if, the axioms on which it is based are true; but we cannot prove that the axioms are true within arithmetic. This means we have to base the proof on something outside arithmetic—but what on earth can provide a more reliable basis than arithmetic itself? Gödel thus showed that consistency is not genuinely provable. It is with this profound mystery that logicians and philosophers have been wrestling ever since.

The Evolution of the Number Module

On one mathematician's wall hangs a sign that reads, 'Anyone who cannot cope with mathematics is not fully human. At best he is a tolerable subhuman who has learned to wear shoes, bathe, and does not make messes in the house.'[28] To be human today is to be numerate; to be unskilled at arithmetic is a severe handicap. In fact, recent research suggests that poor numeracy is more handicapping than poor literacy in getting post-school education, getting a job, and even in getting promotion.[29]

The basis of mathematics, aside from geometry, is our sense of numerosity, and this does not depend on modern education. It doesn't depend on education at all, but on circuits in our brain that have evolved for the specialized purpose of recognizing numerosities in the world. Our fully human *Homo sapiens* ancestors had this ability, as they demonstrated in the paintings and scratchings on the walls of their cave dwellings, from Europe to Australia, and at least as far back in time as 30,000 years ago.

It is possible that our cousins *Homo sapiens neanderthalensis*, and even our more distant ancestors, *Homo erectus*, possessed it too, but the archaeological record is not conclusive. The capacity to learn to recognize small numerosities in the laboratory has been demonstrated in the great apes, in parrots and ravens, and in rats, though what they do with this capacity in the wild is not well understood. It is clearly useful to know that there are more berries in this patch than that, how many nestlings you will be able to feed, or that your troop is outnumbered and you should flee not fight.

Many perceptual systems have evolved to pick out individual things in the world: individual objects as tasty or noxious; individual animals as friends, foes, or possible mates; and so on. I have argued that some avian and mammalian brains, including our own, have gone one further: they have evolved to pick out collections of individuals and to recognize their numerosity. We now know that the human brain has evolved specialized circuits to exploit the fact that much of the perceptible world is countable. This is why neurological damage can affect numbers and nothing else, and why people are born dyscalculic. But we have two abilities that make us fundamentally different from other species.

First, we are able not just to discriminate the numerosity of a collection of four things from a collection of three, we are able to experience the 'fourness of four' and to reflect on this conscious experience. This ability may be necessary to build distinct mental representations for each numerosity so that we can talk about them and write them down. Second, we can count. This enables us to enumerate beyond four. Counting words are the most familiar tool we use for counting, but we know that many cultures can enumerate without specialized words. Some use the names of body parts, others build piles of stones, to represent numbers.

The combination of our innate sense of numerosity and these two abilities are the foundation on which the great edifice of modern mathematics has been erected. Next time you leave your home, get into your car, and drive down the road to the shopping centre, reflect on this: none of it would be there had we been unable to use numbers. Trade, architecture, road building, complex manufacturing, money—all depend on numbers. Numbers are the language of science, and yet thinking about the world in terms of numbers is as natural and as human as talking. To understand the world, and our place in it, we need to understand our innate gift for numbers.

APPENDIX

GÖDEL'S PROOF

A proof is piece of mathematics. The statement that there is a proof for some proposition, e.g., $a + b = b + a$, is a piece of *metamathematics*—a statement *about* mathematics. Think for a moment about the loosely analogous case in language. We can use language, but we can also talk about language. A French–English dictionary would describe the French word *chaise* as meaning something like the English word '*chair*'. This is not using the word *chaise* as a French-speaker would, it is talking *about* the word. The *metalanguage* in which we are talking about French words is not itself French.

Now, if a statement that 'There is a proof of proposition such-and-such' is metamathematics, so is the statement 'There is *no* proof of the proposition such-and-such'. For there to be a proof of a proposition, it must be possible to reason in a sequence of strictly logical steps from the axioms to the theorem, just as Euclid did. To say there is no proof is to say that there is no sequence of logically valid steps from the axioms to the theorem.

Metamathematics can itself be a piece of mathematics, just as the language in which the meaning is described, English, is itself a language. And indeed English can be and is used to talk about the meaning of English words, as is demonstrated by the *Oxford English Dictionary* or *Webster's*.

The first really clever part of Gödel's proof was to arithmetize the metamathematics, so that it was expressed in the same way as arithmetic. Now, this is arithmetic that has been axiomatized. To give you a flavour of what such an axiomatization might look like, here's a version of the first axiomatization by the Italian mathematician, Guiseppe Peano, in 1889:

Axiom 1   0 is a natural number

Axiom 2   If x is a natural number, there is another natural number denoted by x' (and called the *successor* of x)

Axiom 3 $0 \neq x'$ for any natural number x

Axiom 4   If $x' = y'$, then $x = y$

Axiom 5   If P is a property of 0, and if, whenever P is a property of the number x, then P is also a property of x', then P is a property of all natural numbers (this is called the principle of induction)

Now, if you think this is stating the obvious at unnecessary length, let me tell you that it isn't nearly formal enough. Here's an expanded version which includes definitions of addition (+) and multiplication ($\cdot$). I shall call this system of axioms **A**. The numbers are now denoted by x with a subscript to distinguish them; thus x_1 and x_2 denote numbers that may be different. I also use three logical symbols: '$A \supset B$' to mean 'if A, then B'; '$\forall x$' to mean 'all x'; and 'NOT A' to mean 'negation of A'—that is, NOT A is true when A is false. My explanations in square brackets are not part of the system of axioms **A**.

Axiom 1 $x_1 = x_2 \supset (x_1 = x_3 \supset x_2 = x_3)$
[roughly, two numbers are equal if each of them is equal to a third number]

Axiom 2 $x_1 = x_2 \supset x_1' = x_2'$
[roughly, if two numbers are equal then their successors are equal too]

Axiom 3 $0 \neq (x_1)'$
[0 is not the successor of any number]

Axiom 4 $x_1' = x_2' \supset x_1 = x_2$
[if the successors are equal, then so are the numbers they are the successors of]

Axiom 5 $x_1 + 0 = x_1$
[any number to which 0 is added remains unchanged]

Axiom 6 $x_1 + x_2' = (x_1 + x_2)'$
[a number added to the successor of another number equals the successor of the two numbers added together]

Axiom 7 $x_1 \cdot 0 = 0$
[any number times 0 is 0]

Axiom 8 $x_1 \cdot (x_2') = (x_1 \cdot x_2) + x_1$
[any number times the successor of another number is the product of those two numbers plus the original number]

Axiom 9   For any $P(x)$, $P(0) \supset (\forall x \, (P(x) \supset P\,(x'))) \supset \forall x \, P(x)$
[very roughly, if P is a property of 0, x, and x' then it is a property of all numbers]

It's fairly straightforward to use these axioms to prove all the familiar arithmetical laws such as $a + b = b + a$, $a + (b + c) = (a + b) + c$, $a \cdot b = b \cdot a$, and so on.[1]

Here's how the commutativity of addition is proved. I assume that a few other obvious but necessary steps have already been proved; and some of the mechanics necessary to convince logicians have been eliminated. The idea is to show that $x + y = y + x$ holds where $y = 0$, and if it holds for y, then it also holds for the successor of y, y'.

(1) $x + 0 = x$ Axiom 5

(2) $0 + x = x$ previously proved

(3) $x + 0 = 0 + x$ from (1) and (2) [This establishes the property for the number 0; now we go on to establish it for x and for its successor, x']

(4) $x + y = y + x$ by hypothesis

(5) $x + y' = (x + y)'$ by Axiom 6 [e.g. $4'$ [i.e. 5] + 2 = $(4 + 2)'$ [i.e. 7]]

(6) $y' + x = (y + x)'$ by a previous proof

(7) $(x + y)' = (y + x)'$ from (4) and by Axiom 2

(8) $x + y' = (y + x)'$ from (5) and (7), by Axiom 1

(9) $x + y' = y' + x$ from (6) and (8)

(10) $(x + y = y + x) \supset$ From (9), so we no longer need hypothesis 4

$(x + y' = y' + x)$ [that is, if the property of commutativity applies to y, then it applies to its successor, y']

(11) $(\forall x \, \forall y) \, x + y = y + x$ from (3) and (10), by Axiom 9, the principle of induction

We can therefore conclude that this applies to all numbers. The sequence of 1 to 10 takes you in small, completely logical steps from the axioms to the theorem in step 11. At the metamathematical level we can say that there is a proof for 11 in the axiom system **A** defined by Axioms 1 to 9. Now, there are lots of propositions that we cannot prove in this axiom system: for example, there is no sequence of steps from the axioms to the proposition that the commutativity law can be negated.

The metamathematical statements about whether proofs do or do not exist have been made from a standpoint outside the system defined by our axioms. What is this standpoint? Is it common sense, logic, or what? If we want to be sure about metamathematical statements, what standpoint could be more secure than arithmetic itself? The next step Gödel took was to show how statements about a system like **A** could be made in the language of **A** itself, rather in the way that the *Oxford English Dictionary* uses English words to talk about English words. It's obvious when the metalanguage for English is English, but how can we be sure that the metalanguage for talking about arithmetic is the language of arithmetic? Here's where his next really neat and novel move came in—*Gödel numbering*, as it now universally known.

Each of the symbols in **A** is given a number:

0	+	=	(	)	′	⊃	·	∀	NOT
↓	↓	↓	↓	↓	↓	↓	↓	↓	↓
2	3	4	5	6	7	8	9	10	12

The variables, such as x and y, are denoted by powers of a prime:

$$x \quad y \quad \ldots$$
$$\downarrow \quad \downarrow$$
$$11^1 \quad 11^2 \quad \ldots$$

The expression $x + y$ thus corresponds to the sequence 11^1 3 11^2. We now want to make a whole proposition, by which I mean a sequence of symbols forming a well-formed sentence in the formal language, correspond uniquely to a number. Gödel did this by defining the proposition as the sequence of prime numbers raised to the powers of each symbol, all multiplied together. For example, the proposition numbered (4) above becomes

$$2^{11} \cdot 3^3 \cdot 5^{11^2} \cdot 7^4 \cdot 11^{11^2} \cdot 13^3 \cdot 17^{11} \qquad \text{(G4)}$$

An enormous and unwieldy number, but with one essential virtue: every number has a unique prime factorization. The point is that we can recover the proposition by factorizing the number, and there is no way two propositions can have the same Gödel number. I have called the Gödel number of proposition (4) in the proof 'G4'. Now, we can assign numbers in exactly the same way to each of the other propositions in the proof sequence, from G1 to G11. Not only that, we can assign the whole proof sequence an enormous Gödel number, by taking the sequence of primes again and raising them to the powers G1 to G11:

$$2^{G1} \cdot 3^{G3} \cdot 5^{G4} \cdot 7^{G5} \cdot 11^{G6} \cdot 13^{G7} \cdot 17^{G8} \cdot 19^{G9} \cdot 23^{G10} \cdot 29^{G11} \quad \text{(P1)}$$

This gives each proof sequence a unique number, and again, prime factorization can give you back the propositions in their original order. I have called this proof sequence 'P1'. Functions of variables are represented by powers of another prime. I'll be using only one, B, which will have the Gödel number 13^1. $B(x, y)$ will mean that y is the Gödel number of the proof sequence for the proposition with the Gödel number x.

Using Gödel's numbering, we can now talk about proofs by talking about numbers. To say that there *is* a proof for Proposition (11) $((\forall x\ \forall y)\ x + y = y + x)$ is to say that there is a number that can be unpacked as a proof sequence that will get you from the axioms of **A** to the proposition. Let me introduce now another, and final, symbol, $\exists$, which means simply 'there is', while NOT $\exists$ means 'there is not'. Thus $(\exists n)\ n > 1$ means simply that there is a number n, greater than 1, which can be derived from **A**. (Incidentally, the symbol $\exists$ isn't strictly necessary. I could have used $\forall$ and NOT: I could have written NOT $(\forall n)$.NOT$(n>1)$, which means 'It's not the case that all n are not greater than 1'. Now you can see why I introduced the existence symbol, $\exists$.)

Now we can write things such as $(\exists y)\ B(x, y)$, which means there is a Gödel number proof sequence y which is a proof sequence for the proposition with Gödel number x. If there is no such proof sequence, I would write NOT$(\exists y)\ B(x, y)$. These formulae are just functions of numbers. If I had defined a function 'L' meaning 'larger than', then I could have written a formula of exactly the same form, $(\exists y)\ L(x, y)$, meaning that there is a number y that is larger than the number x.

In this way, Gödel was able to map the metamathematics of an axiom system like **A** onto **A** itself (that is to say, each symbol of the metamathematics—the language we are using to describe **A**—corresponds systematically to elements of **A**). This was a crucial step because it made the metamathematics as formal as the mathematics it was describing. It also showed what could be proved within the system, within **A**. You don't have to stand outside on even shakier ground.

The first question was this. Could the axioms of **A** be used to prove all true arithmetical propositions? In technical terms, is axiomatized arithmetic 'complete'? Of course, there are a lot of true propositions that cannot be proved within **A**, for example the true proposition that Monet painted water lilies. The critical point concerned true propositions that were statable in the formalism of **A**—just using the terms I have already defined, and numbers. Being a mathematician, Gödel wasn't interested just in **A**, but in any conceivable axiomatization of arithmetic. So although I am asking you to think in terms of a particular axiom system, the proof is actually completely generalizable and applicable to any axiom system that contains a certain minimum amount of arithmetic.

The following Proposition (1) will have a Gödel number. Let us call it g. The proposition states that there is no proof for the proposition with the Gödel number x.

$$(1) \quad \text{NOT}(\exists y) \, B(x, y)$$

Using a substitution function, we can substitute for x the proposition with Gödel number g, to give

$$(2) \quad \text{NOT}(\exists y) \, B(g, y)$$

The proposition now states that there is no proof for g; that is, that it is itself unprovable.

If (2) is provable, then it proves that it is unprovable. Assuming that **A** is consistent, then contradictory propositions cannot both be proved in it. If **A** is consistent, then there is at least one proposition, the one labelled (2), which is both true and unprovable. We have to go outside the system **A** to see that (2) is true, but it is constructed entirely according to the rules of **A**.

I have assumed that **A** is consistent, but can I prove it? Being consistent means that a proposition and its opposite cannot both be proved. Gödel showed us how to formulate this metamathematical statement in mathematical terms. Essentially, this means saying that you cannot find proof sequences for both x and its negation. Can you prove that these proof sequences cannot be found? Well, we have already assumed consistency to show that (2) is unprovable. Let us call consistency of **A** 'Con' and say (you'll have to take my word for it) that Con is stable in the formalism of **A**. Then

$$\text{Con} \supset \text{NOT}(\exists y) \, B(g, y)$$

Thus, if Con were provable, then so would be $\text{NOT}(\exists y) \, B(g, y)$. Since we have shown that it is not provable, then neither is Con. Here I am talking about provability within **A**. The informal argument given above proves (2), but not within **A**.

Thus a consistent system of axioms containing a certain minimum amount of arithmetic, such as **A**, is not complete: there will be truths that it cannot capture. And we cannot prove within the system itself that it's consistent. Notice that the proof did not depend on any special features of **A**, and in fact it applies to any consistent axiomatic system that contains enough whole-number arithmetic.

NOTES AND REFERENCES

Chapter 1. Thinking by Numbers

1. Cited by Murray (1978), p. 141.
2. E.g. Kline (1990); Struik (1954).
3. Cited by G. A. Miller (1969).
4. *Encyclopaedia Britannica*, 11th edn, vol. 11, p. 444.
5. The standard measure of loudness, the decibel, is a proportional value, so that the energy in 'one decibel' actually varies according to whether it is, say, the one decibel greater than 90 decibels or the one decibel greater than 10 decibels. This is because more energy is needed to make a noticeable difference to the loudness of a 90 dB sound than of a 10 dB sound.
6. Invented by Paul Eisler, a little-known shaper of the twentieth century. See Eisler (1989) for a fascinating insight into the problems of the inventor.
7. Seidenberg (1960) argued for this position: invented once by an unknown Einstein somewhere in the Fertile Crescent, whence it was diffused to the rest of the world on the back of a Creation myth. See Chapter 2 for more details.
8. Diamond (1997a).
9. Fodor (1983).
10. Dehaene (1997).
11. Numerosities are essentially what are traditionally called 'cardinal numbers'. My treatment of numerosities in this section and hereafter follows closely the treatment proposed by the philosopher of mathematics Marcus Giaquinto (1995).
12. The developmental psychologist Jean Piaget tried to reduce the child's understanding of numerosities to an understanding of sets, operations on

them, and reasoning about them. He failed, as we shall see, because children, even infants, seem to have a sense of numerosity even before they can reason about sets in the way Piaget required.

13. Whorf (1956), pp. 139–40.
14. I am grateful to Professor Deborah Howard, historian of Venetian architecture, for referring me to this fascinating work.
15. My account follows that of Menninger (1969), pp. 16–21.
16. Zaslavsky (1973), p. 85.
17. Strohm (1996), from whom both these passages are taken. I am grateful to Peggy Laurillard for drawing them to my attention.
18. Gelman & Gallistel (1986), p. 240.
19. Reeve & Pattison (1996).

Chapter 2. Everybody Counts

Recommended Reading

Karl Menninger's magisterial *Number Words and Number* combines immense Germanic scholarship with verve, fascinating detail, and strong opinions. The first edition appeared in 1934; the English translation of the revised (1958) edition was published in 1969, alas without footnotes or references of any kind, which is a profound disservice to it. Graham Flegg's *Numbers Through the Ages* is a useful distillation of Menninger, along with some new and very interesting material. It is very clear and well organized, as one might expect for an Open University coursebook. For Sumerian and Babylonian numbers, Denise Schmandt-Besserat summarizes her main argument in her *Scientific American* article of 1978, which is republished in C. C. Lamborg-Karlovsky's collection of *Scientific American* readings, *Hunters, Farmers, and Civilizations*. This collection also contains relevant articles by Jöran Friberg and the great historian of Palaeolithic art, André Leroi-Gourhan. Claudia Zaslavsky's excellent scholarly polemic *Africa Counts* demonstrates the presence of numerical skills in that continent from the earliest times. Robert J. Sharer's massive and masterly *The Ancient Maya* is the authoritative and up-to-date account of their history and culture. As well as describing their number words and numeral system, it shows very clearly how obsessively the Maya wove their numerals and mathematics into the fabric of their religion, trade, and astronomy.

There is no book on the prehistory of numbers, but there is much good background material for thinking about what life was like in the Palaeolithic. *Journey Through the Ice Age* is a balanced and accessible introduction to prehistoric art and symbolism by one of the leading experts, Paul Bahn, with wonderful photographs by Jean Vertut. Alexander Marshack's *The Roots of Civilization* is ground-breaking and provocative, and lays out the arguments for notational systems in the Palaeolithic. It should be read in conjunction

with the work of Francesco d'Errico (see e.g. d'Errico 1992; d'Errico &
Cacho 1994), who has used scanning electron microscopy to differentiate
likely notations from accidental and decorative marks. Two books on the
French Upper Palaeolithic provide intriguing details of two key sites. The first
is *Les Cavernes de Niaux*, by Jean Clottes, the doyen of modern French Palaeolithic archaeology. The second, *Chauvet Cave*, describes the cave's discovery
in 1994 and is written by the discoverers themselves: Jean-Marie Chauvet, Eli-
ette Brunel Deschamps, and Christian Hillaire; there is a scene-setting foreword by Bahn, and a technical and interpretative epilogue by Clottes.

For body-counting systems in New Guinea, David Lancy's *Cross-Cultural Studies in Cognition and Mathematics* summarizes the work of a long-
term, large-scale project designed not just to collect anthropological data but
also to guide the Papua New Guinea Education Department. Yupno body-
part counting comes from a later study (Wassmann & Dasen 1994) by Wassmann and Pierre Dasen, a student of Piaget who has spent a lifetime testing
Piaget's ideas in non-European cultures.

The introduction of Arabic numerals into Europe, and the resistance to
their use, are described in great detail in Alexander Murray's fascinating
Reason and Society in the Middle Ages. A translation of the Treviso Arithmetic, the first printed text for teaching what was the 'new maths' of its day,
has been published as *Capitalism and Arithmetic*, with an excellent introduction Frank Swetz.

For the history of numbers and calculation in science that goes well
beyond what is treated in this chapter, Dirk Struik's *Concise History of
Mathematics*, which first appeared in 1954, is still hard to beat. Morris
Kline's justly celebrated *Mathematics in Western Culture* is still in print. I
very much enjoyed Ivor Grattan-Guinness's *The Fontana History of the
Mathematical Sciences*, which came out in 1997.

1. Le Guin (1975), p. 36. I am grateful to George Mandler for drawing my
   attention to this story.
2. Le Guin (1975), p. 40.
3. Although Europeans first found out about these numerals from Arab
   traders, they were in fact invented by Hindus in the sixth century AD, as
   we shall see in the next section.
4. Friberg (1984), p. 80.
5. Friberg (1984), p. 83.
6. Falkenstein (1936).
7. Schmandt-Besserat (1978), p. 44.
8. Schmandt-Besserat (1987), p. 48.
9. Seidenberg (1960). For a more accessible account of Seidenberg's theory,
   see Flegg (1989), pp. 7–12.

10. The number words in Gumulgal, Bakairi, and Bushman are from Flegg (1989, p. 9); the Kiwai number words are from Lancy (1983, p. 104).
11. Seidenberg (1962).
12. E.g. Mithen (1996), pp. 140–46.
13. Bahn & Vertut (1997), p. 203.
14. Ucko & Rosenfeld (1969), p. 211.
15. Leroi-Gourhan (1968).
16. See Ucko & Rosenfeld (1969), especially chapter 4, for a discussion.
17. Rhys Jones (1997, personal communication) and Brian D. Lee and Steven Tresize (1996, personal communication) mention the same system being used by people in the far north of Queensland.
18. Clottes (1996), pp. 159–60.
19. Clottes (1995), plate 177.
20. de Heinzelin (1962).
21. de Heinzelin (1962).
22. Marshack (1991), p. 28.
23. Maynard & Edwards (1971).
24. Marshack (1991), p. 51.
25. Marshack (1991), p. 50.
26. d'Errico & Cacho (1994), p. 194.
27. I am grateful to Dr Dorothy Einon of University College London, and Professor David Howard of the University of Newcastle, for helping me see sense on this matter.
28. Marshack (1991), p. 288.
29. Clottes (1995), p. 126.
30. Chauvet et al. (1995), p. 27.
31. Quoted by Flegg (1989), p. 37–38.
32. Fullagar et al. (1996), though their dating has been questioned.
33. Marshack (1991) p. 349, figure 209.
34. Gore (1997).
35. Morwood et al. (1998).
36. This and subsequent quotes are from Locke (1961), book II, chapter XVI.
37. Dixon (1980), p. 108. However, Kendon's (1988) review of Australian sign languages devotes half of one page (168) to number signs. He gives North Central Desert Signs for 1, 2, 3, and 'many', adding that the fingers are 'instantiations of the number concepts', but he does not say whether there are more signs than these.
38. Wilkins (1989).
39. Diamond (1997b).
40. Lancy (1983).
41. Wassmann & Dasen (1994).

42. Lancy (1983), p. 109.
43. Saxe (1981).
44. Lancy (1983), pp. 102–4.
45. Lancy (1983), p. 104.
46. Zaslavsky (1973), p. 47.
47. Menninger (1969), p. 100.
48. Adapted from Menninger (1969), pp. 92–97.
49. Menninger (1969), p. 107.
50. See Winter (1991) for a discussion of this idea, and other aspects of IE number words.
51. Flegg (1989), p. 71.
52. Flegg (1989), p. 71.
53. Flegg (1989), pp. 73–74.
54. Winter (1991), p. 25.
55. Winter (1991).
56. Menninger (1969), pp. 147–48.
57. Menninger (1969), pp. 148–49.
58. The linguist Zdenek Salzmann (1950) talks about the vocabulary as the 'frame pattern', and the base as the 'cyclic pattern' of repeating elements; there is also the 'operative pattern' for combining number terms—multiplying, adding, and, as we shall see later in this section, subtracting.
59. Salzmann (1950).
60. Neugebauer (1962). p. 81.
61. Menninger (1969), p. 66.
62. Menninger (1969), p. 165.
63. Menninger (1969), p. 69.
64. Flegg (1989), p. 48.
65. Cited by Flegg (1989), p. 48.
66. Cited by Menninger (1969), p. 141.
67. Flegg (1989) pp. 106–16.
68. Flegg (1989), p. 106.
69. Menninger (1969), pp. 299–303.
70. Datta & Singh (1935), part I, p. 59.
71. Flegg (1989), p. 117.
72. Quoted by Sharer (1994), p. 599.
73. R. J. Sharer (1997), personal communication.
74. Sharer (1994), p. 558.
75. Struik (1954), p. 24.
76. Struik (1954), page 22.
77. Sharer (1994), p. 568.
78. Murray (1978), p. 144.
79. Quoted by Murray (1978), p. 146.

80. Flegg (1989), p. 176.
81. Murray (1978), p. 163.
82. Murray (1978), p. 167.
83. Murray (1978), p. 190.
84. Quoted by Murray (1978), p. 170.
85. Swetz (1987), p. 10.
86. Menninger (1969), p. 428.
87. Murray (1978), p. 177.
88. Adapted from Flegg (1989), p. 114.

Chapter 3. Born to Count

Recommended Reading

Two particularly good, accessible reviews of infant and child mathematics have recently been published: Terezinha Nunes and Peter Bryant's *Children Doing Mathematics*, and David Geary's *Children's Mathematical Development*. The three classics describing the seminal experiments are Piaget's *The Child's Conception of Number;* Rochel Gelman and C. R. Gallistel's *The Child's Understanding of Number*, and Karen Fuson's *Children's Counting and Concepts of Number*. These are, however, hard going. There is no general review of animal number abilities. Hank Davis and Rachelle Pérusse's (1988) technical article 'Numerical competence in animals', with peer commentary, has been influential. W. H. Thorpe's classic *Learning and Instinct in Animals* contains beautifully written accounts of the research up to the early 1960s; it is superb on Thorpe's own speciality, birds, and includes one of the few detailed descriptions in English of the work of Otto Koehler. *The Development of Numerical Competence*, edited by Sarah Boysen and John Capaldi, contains excellent papers by all the leading groups researching animal abilities in the lab, but there is almost nothing about animal uses of numbers in the wild. This applies also to the sections on number in C. R. Gallistel's massive *The Organization of Learning*.

1. Piaget (1952), p. viii.
2. Kitcher (1984), p. 108.
3. This is a description of part of an experiment carried out in 1983 by two infant psychologists at the University of Maryland, Sue Ellen Antell and Daniel Keating.
4. Eimas *et al.* (1971).
5. On colour see Bornstein *et al.* (1976); on shape see McGurk (1972).
6. Starkey *et al.* (1990). Actually, in this experiment they tried it with four dots changing to six, or six dots changing to four, but found no increased looking after the change.

7. This idea was suggested by George Mandler (Mandler & Shebo 1982) as an explanation for 'subitizing'—the ability in both adults and children to take in up to four objects at a glance. See Chapter 7 for further discussion of subitizing in adults.
8. Van Loosbroek & Smitsman (1990).
9. Wynn (1995).
10. Mandler & Shebo (1982); Atkinson *et al.* (1976a,b).
11. Dehaene & Changeux (1993).
12. You will not, however, infer that the laws of addition, on which your expectations were based, have ceased to hold, or that they are simply a rough approximation (like the Law of Librarians—they all wear brown socks). You will infer that I have used some trick to magic one of the dolls away.
13. Wynn (1992).
14. Simon *et al.* (1995).
15. I am grateful to Marcus Giaquinto for this point.
16. These practical skills are three of Gelman & Gallistel's (1978, chapter 8) 'how-to-count principles'.
17. Fuson (1992).
18. Gelman & Gallistel (1986), p. 93.
19. Fuson (1992).
20. Potter & Levy (1968).
21. Gelman & Meck (1983).
22. Gelman & Gallistel (1986), p. 112.
23. Gelman & Gallistel (1986), pp. 79–80.
24. Wynn (1990).
25. Gelman & Gallistel (1986), p. 82.
26. Wynn (1990).
27. Fuson (1992).
28. Or indeed, research on the reasoning of highly educated post-teenage adults. Peter Wason discovered that even philosophers have difficulty with apparently very simple abstract reasoning problems which, according to Piaget, all adults should be able to manage easily. Here is the classical version of the problem from Wason (1966).

    There are four cards, face down on a table, each with a letter on one face and a number on the other. You can see the following faces: A, 3, B, 4. The question is, which cards do you *need* to turn over to tell whether the following statement is true of the cards: 'Every card with a vowel on one side has an even number on the other.' (Answer at the end of the notes to this chapter.)
29. Frydman & Bryant (1988).
30. Piaget (1952), chapter III.
31. Brissiaud (1992).

32. Miller & Stigler (1987).
33. Described by Nunes & Bryant (1996), pp. 62–63.
34. Nunes & Bryant (1996), pp. 71–74.
35. Power & dal Martello (1990).
36. Quoted in the Cockcroft report (1982), appendix A2 by Miss H. B. Shuard.
37. Cockcroft report (1982), p. 273.
38. Wertheim (1997), p. 191.
39. Geary (1996).
40. See e.g. Keys et al. (1996).
41. Adapted from Keys et al. (1996), pp. 23–24.
42. Bright (1998).
43. Geary (1996).
44. Leakey (1994).
45. This account is based on Davis (1993).
46. Davis (1993), p. 119.
47. Fouts & Mills (1997).
48. Cited by Rilling (1993).
49. C. B. Ferster, cited by Rumbaugh & Washburn (1993).
50. Matsuzawa (1985, 1996).
51. Boysen (1993).
52. Boysen (1993).
53. Boysen (1993).
54. Boysen (1993).
55. Boysen (1993).
56. Rumbaugh & Washburn (1993).
57. Rumbaugh & Washburn (1993).
58. Rumbaugh & Washburn (1993).
59. In 1990, C. R. Gallistel made only one reference to Koehler in his massive review of animal cognition, *The Organization of Learning*, even though he devotes a long section to animal number skills. As recently as 1993, an important collection of papers on animal numbers edited by Sarah Boysen and John Capaldi made few references to Koehler and offered no serious discussion of either his ideas or his experiments, except in a historical introduction by Mark Rilling (1993).
60. Thorpe (1963), pp. 389 and 390, figures 60 and 61.
61. Thorpe (1963), p. 391.
62. Pepperberg (1987); see also comments in Davis & Pérusse (1988), p. 571.
63. See Reiss et al. (1997) for a recent review of dolphin cognition.
64. The genotypic advantage may, for example, be located on a chromosome near genes that do provide an advantage. Selective pressures will favour phenotypes with chromosomes containing the advantageous genes, and the 'number genes' will piggyback a ride into the species' genotypic future.

65. Gallistel (1990).
66. The celebrated work of Nobel laureate Karl von Frisch.
67. Seibt (1988).
68. Thorpe (1963), p. 385.
69. Thorpe (1963), p. 419.
70. Seibt (1988).
71. Hauser *et al.* (1996).
72. McComb *et al.* (1994).
73. Boesch (1996).
74. Boesch (1996).
75. Davis (1993).
76. Skuse *et al.* (1997).
77. Rovet *et al.* (1994).

Answer to Wason's task: A and 3. Consider what happens when you turn over each of the cards. If A has an odd number on the reverse, then the statement is false; if 3 has a vowel on the reverse, then again the statement is false. However, whether 4 has a vowel or a consonant on the other side will not affect the truth of the statement, since it is not being claimed that every even number has a vowel on the other side. The number on the other side of the consonant B is also irrelevant.

Chapter 4. Numbers in the Brain

Recommended Reading
There are no good reference works for the anatomy and physiology of numerical processes. Most neuropsychology and neuroscience textbooks contain next to nothing, or nothing at all, on deficits of number processing. One exception is Rosaleen McCarthy and Elizabeth Warrington's *Cognitive Neuropsychology*, published in 1990. An excellent recent popular account, with a somewhat different perspective from my own, is Stanislas Dehaene's *The Number Sense*. He provides neat summaries of his own researches in this area, and much else.

1. All the patients described in this chapter are real, and their case reports have been published in learned journals. In each case, I provide the reference in a note. The names and some other personal details have been changed to protect the patients' anonymity. 'Signora Gaddi' was published as 'patient C.G.' in the journal *Brain* (Cipolotti *et al.* 1991).
2. Henschen (1920).
3. This idea was inspired by the 'Logicist programme' of Bertrand Russell and Alfred North Whitehead who, in their massive *Principia mathematica*,

tried to prove that all concepts and truths of arithmetic could be derived from the concepts and truths of logic. See Chapter 9 for an explanation of why this is, in principle, impossible.

4. E.g. Bloom (1994).

5. E.g. Gallistel & Gelman (1992); Dehaene (1997).

6. E.g. Kahn & Whitaker (1991).

7. Tragically, her stroke left her unable to read or write words, or even letters. Imagine how it would be if newspapers, books, advertisements were as incomprehensible as Chinese characters; if you couldn't leave a note for your family saying when you'd be back, or write a shopping list. This was even more distressing for her than her loss of numbers. Paradoxically, she could read the numbers from 1 to 4. She also showed the symptoms of Gerstmann's syndrome (see note 11 below, and Chapter 5).

8. For non-Italians the correct answer is a *tonnellata*, which is 1000 kilograms.

9. The British businessman Ernest Saunders escaped prosecution and conviction when it was claimed by his lawyer that he was suffering from Alzheimer's disease. After his release, he became a management consultant.

10. Rossor *et al.* (1995).

11. Rossor *et al.* (1995).

12. However, she showed the symptoms of the mysterious Gerstmann's syndrome, which I discuss in detail in Chapter 5. She was left unable to write words at all, and was very bad at writing or even copying single letters. Paradoxically, she could write even four-digit numerals to dictation very accurately. Her spatial skills were also affected: she had trouble distinguishing left from right, and she couldn't tell which finger was being touched when she was prevented from seeing her hands.

13. Delazer & Benke (1997).

14. Delazer & Bencke (1997).

15. Dehaene & Cohen (1995); see also Dehaene (1997), chapter 5.

16. Delazer *et al.* (1996).

17. Rémond-Besuchet *et al.* (1998).

18. Jackson and Warrington (1986), for example, found a correlation of 0.6 between digit span and simple arithmetic (addition and subtraction) in 100 normal adults.

19. Hulme & Mackenzie (1992), p. 21.

20. Holmes (1871), p. 33.

21. Butterworth *et al.* (1996); Cipolotti *et al.* (1996).

22. This account is taken from Warrington (1982). Recently, Elizabeth Warrington kindly showed me a video of part of her testing of Dr Constable. His personality shone through and was confirmed by Elizabeth's own memory of the case.

23. Warrington (1982).

24. The case of Dr Constable is important from another point of view. It has been claimed for more than 25 years that representations of numbers as analogue magnitudes—as continuous quantities—are used to compute additions. He seemed to have no problem with numbers as analogue magnitudes, since he was easily able to estimate the correct answers. So a defective sense of number size cannot be at the root of his problem. Warrington concludes that, 'to account for normal calculation in terms of analogue processing would be insufficient . . . for not merely *accurate* calculations but *rapid* calculations'.
25. Caramazza & McCloskey (1987).
26. Caramazza & McCloskey (1987).
27. Girelli & Delazer (1996).
28. Girelli & Delazer (1996).
29. Pesenti *et al.* (1995).
30. Hittmair-Delazer *et al.* (1994).
31. Cipolotti & Costello (1995).
32. Unpublished internal report, 1996.
33. Adapted from Hittmair-Delazer *et al.* (1994).
34. Adapted from Hittmair-Delazer *et al.* (1994).
35. Sokol *et al.* (1991).
36. Cipolotti (1995).
37. Cipolotti *et al.* (1995).
38. Anderson *et al.* (1990).
39. Anderson *et al.* (1990).
40. Power & dal Martello (1990).
41. This, by the way, is an informal implication of McCloskey's influential 'abstract-modular' model.
42. Cipolotti & Butterworth (1995).
43. I have borrowed this title from a brilliant neuropsychological study of a man with aphasia and dyslexia, *Missing the Meaning?*, by David Howard and Sue Franklin.
44. The full case report can be found in Delazer & Butterworth (1997).
45. Delazer & Butterworth (1997).
46. Fuson (1992).
47. By Moyer & Landauer (1967).
48. The comparison times would be averaged over starting from the smaller and starting from the larger. (There was no way of telling which was which: introspection is a poor guide to what people actually do, as opposed to what they think they do.)
49. Jackson & Warrington (1986).
50. Warrington & James (1967).
51. Grafman *et al.* (1989).
52. Cohen & Dehaene (1996).

Chapter 5. Hand, Space, and Brain

There is no good general reference for the subject-matter of this chapter.

1. See Zeki (1993) for an excellent account of the human visual system. He also explains why the nerves from the eye end up here rather than somewhere else in the course of evolution—the answer to a further 'why?'.
2. Butterworth (1994).
3. Miceli *et al.* (1983).
4. For a useful summary, see McCarthy & Warrington (1990), chapter 1.
5. Seron *et al.* (1992).
6. Dantzig (1962), p. 9.
7. Barrow (1992), p. 26.
8. Juvenal, *Satires*, X, 248–49.
9. In part because he was the first historian to attempt a numerical chronology of the events he described.
10. Menninger (1969).
11. Menninger (1969), p. 203.
12. Quoted by Menninger (1969), pp. 206–8.
13. Barrow (1992), p. 47.
14. Menninger (1969), p. 204.
15. Dantzig (1962), p. 11.
16. Quoted by Menninger (1969), p. 218.
17. Critchley (1939, p. 77) reports the identical method used by gypsies.
18. Pascual-Leone & Torres (1993).
19. Brissiaud (1992), pp. 46–47.
20. Psychologists often test home-produced subjects. There is one big advantage: the subject is almost always available (and you don't have to pay them). I've done it myself. I used my three-week-old daughter to see if she could discriminate displays of two rectangles from displays of three. Against the advice of Prentice Starkey, a pioneer in infant number abilities, I used a sucking habituation technique rather than looking habituation as Starkey had done. Babies suck less and less as they get bored, and suck more when they see something that is new for them. After running half the trials, with very promising results, my child refused to suck on the teat any more. Since I had had no experience of running infant experiments, I couldn't expect other people to lend me their three-week-old children (not so easy to come by in any case). So, end of experiment. That's the problem with relying on one home-produced subject. *(Postscript:* There seem to have been no long-term ill-effects on her. She does well at maths at school. But it had a bad effect on her father. He gave up number experiments for six years, and then worked only with adults, for whom sucking habituation is not usually the technique of choice.)

21. Girelli (1998).
22. Neuman (1987), p. 186.
23. Neuman (1987), p. 103.
24. Neuman (1987), p. 189.
25. Fuson & Kwon (1992).
26. Galton (1880).
27. Zangwill was the son of the novelist Israel Zangwill *(Children of the Ghetto)*, and the first person to offer me an academic position.
28. Spalding & Zangwill (1950).
29. Spalding & Zangwill (1950).
30. Spalding & Zangwill (1950).
31. Gelman & Gallistel (1986).
32. Seron *et al.* (1992).
33. Dehaene et al. (1993).
34. Seron *et al.* (1992).
35. Though in Signor Strozzi's case the area that shows up most clearly on brain scans is in the frontal lobe.
36. Gerstmann (1940); Critchley (1953, chapter VII) offers a good summary and critique.
37. Critchley (1953, p. 209) gives a tabulation of the older cases showing this.
38. Kinsbourne & Warrington (1962).
39. Critchley (1953).
40. Kinsbourne & Warrington (1963), p. 499.
41. Rourke (1993).
42. Ta'ir *et al.* (1997).
43. Penfield & Rasmussen (1952).
44. Penfield & Rasmussen (1952), p. 57.
45. Jeannerod *et al.* (1995).
46. Jeannerod *et al.* (1995).
47. Pascual-Leone & Torres (1993).
48. Warrington and James (1967) have shown that damage to the right parietal lobe in adults leads to impairments in subitizing—estimating the number of dots in an array. See also Chapter 4.

Chapter 6. Bigger and Smaller

In this chapter I have drawn extensively on research done in my own lab. There is no general review of number research yet written.

1. Fodor (1983).
2. Pinker (1994).
3. Butterworth *et al.* (1999a).

4. The data is from Butterworth *et al.* (1999a).
5. The first such study of children was by Sekuler & Mierkiewicz (1977).
6. Washburn & Rumbaugh (1991).
7. Brannon & Terrace (1998).
8. Stroop (1935).
9. MacLeod (1991); MacLeod & Dunbar (1988).
10. Foltz *et al.* (1984).
11. Girelli *et al.* (1999b).
12. Dehaene *et al.* (1998).
13. Girelli *et al.* (1999b).
14. Girelli *et al.* (1999b).
15. Girelli *et al.* (1999b).
16. Duncan & MacFarland (1980).
17. Mandler & Shebo (1982).
18. Critchley (1953), p. 365.
19. Delazer & Butterworth (1997).
20. Girelli *et al.* (1999b).

Chapter 7. Good and Bad at Numbers

There are many excellent books on how to improve your number skills. But there are no published systematic accounts of why some of us are good at numbers, and others bad. I have found considerable enlightenment reading about prodigies, especially in Stephen Smith's *Great Mental Calculators* and Robert Kanigel's biography of Ramanujan, *The Man Who Knew Infinity*.

1. This version of the tale is from Cambridge mathematician Tom Körner (1998).
2. When estimating the normal variation of abilities it would be misleading to include dyscalculics, in the same way that it would be misleading to include dyslexic performance in deriving the range of normal reading. I also exclude a proportion that could be assumed to be chronically anxious or sick during exams. For statistical reasons, I exclude the bottom (and top) 5% of scores from these estimates.
3. Third International Mathematics and Science Study, First National Report, Part 1 (Keys *et al.* 1996).
4. Bright (1998), reporting a survey of public exam (GCSE) performance of sixteen-year-olds in England.
5. Butterworth *et al.* (1999c).
6. Baroody & Gannon (1984).
7. Siegler & Shrager (1984).

8. Butterworth *et al.* (1999b).
9. LeFevre *et al.* (1996).
10. Girelli *et al.* (1999a).
11. Galton (1979), p. 37.
12. *A Mathematician's Apology* (Hardy 1967), p. 148.
13. From C. P. Snow's foreword to *A Mathematician's Apology* (p. 27), which in my view is the best and certainly the most moving piece Snow ever wrote. Perceptively, he notes that the *Apology* 'for all its high spirits is a book of desperate sadness', the work of a creative man who had lost the power and the will to create.
14. I am told that the baseball equivalent is Babe Ruth.
15. Quoted by Robert Kanigel (1991) in his brilliant biography of Ramanujan, *The Man Who Knew Infinity*, p. 159.
16. C. P. Snow, foreword to Hardy (1967), pp. 30–31.
17. Kanigel (1991), p. 39.
18. Kanigel (1991), p. 44.
19. Kanigel (1991), p. 45.
20. Kanigel (1991), p. 93.
21. Kanigel (1991), p. 97.
22. Hardy (1967), p. 68. He also noted: 'If a man is in any sense a real mathematician, then it is a hundred to one that his mathematics will be far better than anything else he can do ... Newton made a quite competent Master of the Mint (when he was not quarrelling with anybody). Painlevé was a not very successful Premier of France. Laplace's political career was highly discreditable, but he is hardly a fair instance since he was dishonest rather than incompetent ... It is very hard to find an instance of a first-rate mathematician who has abandoned mathematics and attained first-rate distinction in any other field'. (pp. 70–72)
23. C. P. Snow, foreword to Hardy (1967), p. 37.
24. Ericsson *et al.* (1993), p. 366.
25. Hunter (1962), p. 254.
26. Hunter (1962), p. 252.
27. Smith (1983), p. 129.
28. Hunter (1962), p. 252.
29. Gardner (1990), pp. 74–75.
30. A letter from Glasgow mathematician Thomas O'Beirne, quoted by Gardner (1990), p. 75.
31. Sacks (1986), pp. 197–98.
32. Ericsson *et al.* (1993).
33. Dehaene (1997), p. 165.
34. Hermelin & O'Connor (1990).
35. Smith (1983), p. 49.

36. Hunter (1962).
37. Adapted from Smith (1983).
38. Defries *et al.* (1976).
39. See Mandler (1997, pp. 34–39) for an interesting discussion of these issues.
40. Smith (1983).
41. Davidson *et al.* (1996).
42. These figures apply only to children learning to read English. Other languages and other orthographies pose different challenges to the learner, so that reading disabilities are likely to be less prevalent.
43. Campbell & Butterworth (1985).
44. A very good review of developmental dyscalculia can be found in a textbook by one of the area's pioneers, Christine Temple of the University of Essex (Temple 1997). The English study was by Lewis *et al.* (1994); the US by Kosc (1974); the Israeli by Gross-Tur *et al.* (1996).
45. Dehaene's excellent book *The Number Sense* is called in the French original, *La Bosse de calcule*—'The Maths Bump'—and contains a nice discussion of phrenology.
46. Quoted by Temple (1997), p. 256.
47. Geary (1994), especially chapter 4.
48. Girelli & Butterworth (1995).
49. Mandler & Shebo (1982).
50. Kinsbourne & Warrington (1963).
51. Rourke (1993).
52. Five of Kinsbourne and Warrington's seven patients were reported to have perinatal trauma; Ta'ir *et al.'s* (1997) patient Y.K. apparently had normal pregnancy and birth, and reported no relevant childhood diseases or injuries.
53. Rovet *et al.* (1994).
54. Pascual-Leone & Torres (1993).
55. Pascual-Leone & Torres (1993).
56. Schlaug *et al.* (1995a,b); Amunts *et al.* (1997).
57. Eberstark, 'Introductory Comment' to Smith (1983), pp xiii–xiv.

Chapter 8. Home, Street, and School Mathematics

Recommended Reading

I am happy to acknowledge that a key influence on my thinking about education has been the work of Lauren Resnick, of the University of Pittsburgh's Learning Research and Development Center. Her approach combines rigorous experimentation, open-mindedness, and a serious concern for children's experience of school, in the context of their own lives. Readers could do worse than start with *The Psychology of Mathematics for Instruction*, written in 1981 with Wendy Ford. Thinking about statistics nearly every day in my own work makes me particularly gripped by the *Third International Mathematics and Science Study*, which is full of statistics. The results appear in various guises in different countries (e.g. Keys *et al.* 1996 in the UK; Beaton *et al.* 1996 in the USA).

Street Mathematics and School Mathematics by Terezinha Nunes at London's Institute of Education, and her colleagues in Brazil, contains a fascinating series of studies about the mathematical skills outside the classroom. Its title inspired my own chapter title.

1. Nunes *et al.* (1993), pp. 18–19.
2. Nunes *et al.* (1993), p. 23.
3. Conway (1988); Lamb (1993).
4. Brown *et al.* (1989); Lave & Wenger (1991).
5. Schoenfeld (1988).
6. TIMSS (Beaton *et al.* 1996, p. 126).
7. TIMSS (Beaton *et al.* 1996, p. 128).
8. Boaler (1997).
9. Boaler (1997), p. 30.
10. Boaler (1997), pp. 35–7 and chapter 7.
11. Eberstark, 'Introductory Comment' to Smith (1983).
12. Resnick (1995), p. 82.
13. Resnick (1995), p. 84.
14. Andrew Wiles found the proof to Fermat's Last Theorem by bringing together quite different domains of mathematics. See the gripping *Fermat's Last Theorem* by Simon Singh (1997, chapters 6–8).
15. Resnick (1995).
16. Resnick (1995), p. 82.
17. Boaler (1997), p. 51.
18. Ashcraft (1995).
19. Boaler (1997), p. 128.
20. From Richardson & Suinn (1972), quoted by Faust *et al.* (1996).
21. Hittmair-Delazer *et al.* (1994).
22. Thorndike (1922).
23. Brownell (1928).
24. Resnick & Ford (1981), p. 29.
25. Geary *et al.* (1997).
26. I am grateful to Dr Yin Wengang of the Chinese Academy of Science for this information.
27. LeFevre & Liu (1997).

28. And more formally in Dehaene & Cohen (1995).
29. Campbell (1995).
30. Butterworth (1981, 1989).
31. E.g. Ashcraft & Battaglia (1978).
32. LeFevre *et al.* (1996).
33. See e.g. Campbell (1995) for a typology of errors and their significance.
34. Resnick & Ford (1981), p. 87.
35. Girelli & Delazer (1996).
36. Hoffman (1998), pp. 192–3. Kummer was one of the leading number theorists of the last century. He showed that Fermat's Last Theorem—that there are no values of $n > 2$ for which $x^n = y^n + z^n$ is true—holds for an infinitely large class of primes, called 'regular primes', but not for all n.
37. DfEE (1997), paragraph 11.
38. DfEE (1997), paragraph 35.
39. DfEE (1997), paragraph 58.
40. DfEE (1997), paragraph 54.
41. DfEE (1997), foreword.
42. DfEE (1997), paragraph 45.
43. DfEE (1997), paragraph 46.
44. DfEE (1997), paragraph 73.
45. Gardner (1990), pp. ix–x.
46. This is adapted from Laurillard (1993), pp. 100–102. I have allowed myself some liberties in interpreting the interaction, but the interaction itself is as published. The Teacher, incidentally, is Laurillard herself. She writes, 'This is not, I'm afraid, another excursion to the primary class-room. It is an edited extract of a remedial maths session for UK undergraduate technology students.'
47. Andrew Wiles needed to prove this conjecture as part of his proof of Fermat's Last Theorem about whole, essentially prime, numbers (Singh 1997, pp. 209–15).

Chapter 9. Hard Numbers and Easy Numbers

Recommended Reading

Almost all of the mathematics in this chapter is entirely standard and may be found in any of numerous textbooks. Some of the history of number theory and some of the most intriguing results are presented clearly and very entertainingly in Paul Hoffman's life of the great number theorist, Paul Erdös, *The Man Who Loved Only Numbers*. I also recommend Robert Kanigel's life of the Indian number theorist, Ramanujan, *The Man Who Knew Infinity*, which explains the key problems and their solutions really well.

There are many general histories of mathematics with good sections on number theory. The ones I find myself relying on most often are Dirk Struik's *A Concise History of Mathematics*, Ivor Grattan-Guinness's *The Fontana History of the Mathematical Sciences*, and Carl Boyer and Uta Merzbach's *A History of Mathematics*. Both Bertrand Russell and A. N. Whitehead wrote popular books about mathematics and its foundations, which are still very readable (e.g. Russell 1956; Whitehead 1948).

For astounding number patterns, *The Book of Numbers* by John Conway and Richard Guy is a wonderful source. To get the most out of it you will need good high-school maths, or to be willing to put in some work figuring out what some of the equations mean. (I am very grateful to Dr John McCarthy for drawing my attention to this book, and indeed for lending it to me.)

Peter Bernstein's *Against the Gods* is the gripping and surprising tale of the development of ideas of probability and their application. l am grateful to Lady Kristen Daniel for recommending, and indeed lending me, this book (I will return it eventually). *Inevitable Illusions* by Massimo Piatelli-Palmerini is a lucid and entertaining introduction to some of the biases that infect our reasoning about probabilities, especially about expected value. These two books are important sources for my section on probabilities, and my approach to making probabilities easier to understand has been influenced by the work of Gerd Gigerenzer and his colleagues.

Ideas of infinity are magically evoked in German poet Hans Magnus Enzensberger's book *The Number Devil*, which I hope will soon find a UK publisher. I am grateful to Phillip Blom, formerly of Harvill Press, for sending me the manuscript of the English translation. My eleven-year-old daughter was gripped by it, as indeed was I.

1. Just in case you weren't sure, the answer is $-6 + 1$, which is -5, while $-2 - 4$ is -6.
2. Kline (1990), p. 115.
3. It can be shown that any fraction is the sum of unit fractions in infinitely many ways. There is a modern proof that makes use of an identity already known to Fibonacci in 1202:

$$1/a = 1/(a + 1) + 1/a(a + 1)$$

for example

$$1/2 = 1/(2 + 1) + 1/2(2 + 1) = 1/3 + 1/6$$

See Boyer & Merzbach (1991, p. 255); Hoffman (1998, p. 154).
4. After Chase *et al.* (1998). The right answer to 'Diagnosis Problems' is:

about 7 out of 100. If you don't see why, you might try thinking about it like this:

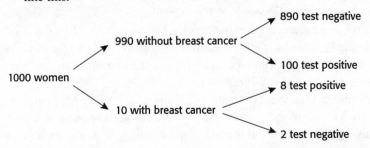

So there were 108 women altogether who showed a positive test, but only 8 of these actually had the disease: that is, only 8/108 or 7.4%, roughly 7 out of 100.

5. Cardano knew that the chance of throwing 1 or 2 with one die is ⅓, and assumed that the chance of throwing it with two would be twice as great (⅔), but he had failed to notice that there is a ⅙ chance that 1 or 2 will be thrown on both dice at once, and this probability has to be subtracted from ⅔ to give the correct probability, ⅚. See Bernstein (1996), p. 51.

6. Quoted by Bernstein (1996), p. 67.

7. Ecclesiastes 9: 11.

8. Bernstein (1996), p. 2.

9. *The Merchant of Venice*, I. i. 42.

10. *The Merchant of Venice*, I. iii. 17–24.

11. *Encyclopaedia Brittanica*, 11th edn, vol. 4, pp. 310–11.

12. An excellent non-technical, but sophisticated, presentation of this work can be found in Piatelli-Palmerini (1994), chapter 4.

13. The answer will give you a 'rationality check'. The expected value for choices A and B is the same:

A. £75 × 1 = £75

B. 100 × 0.75 = £75

Similarly, C and D have the same expected values. Therefore we shouldn't care which we chose. Most people however choose a certain gain over an uncertain one. This is not surprising since the difference between winning nothing at all and £75 is subjectively, psychologically greater than the difference between £75 and £100, which is what constitutes the gamble. Technically, this is what distinguishes 'expected utility' from expected value. The utility of an extra £1 to a beggar is greater than to a millionaire because it represents a greater proportional increase in wealth. On these grounds it is not irrational to choose A over B. It would be irrational then to choose D over C, since the proportional loss is greater for the £75. Is this what you did? Then you are in the same leaky boat as most of the rest of us.

14. Schlottmann & Anderson (1994).
15. The answer to 'Waiting Times' is B: at least 15 minutes, probably longer. The reason is very simple. If the intervals are all exactly half an hour, then the average waiting time will indeed be 15 minutes. But, if the intervals vary in length, some long and some short, then you are more likely to arrive during a long interval than during a short interval.

    Think about the extreme case, where the buses all come along one immediately after another, so that all 48 a day arrive during a single hour, with an interval between them of about 1 minute. There will be one enormous interval of over 23 hours, and that, alas, is the interval during which you are far and away the most likely to arrive. What's critical is the distribution of interval durations.
16. Based on Hoffman (1998), pp. 34–35.
17. Quoted by Davis & Hersh (1983), p. 108.
18. This point is beautifully illustrated by Enzensberger (1998).
19. I am grateful to Marcus Giaquinto for pointing this out.
20. Davis & Hersh (1983), pp. 154–55.
21. I am very grateful to Marcus Giaquinto for discussions on Cantorian issues.
22. Letter of 1654, quoted by Boyer & Merzbach (1991), p. 364.
23. Boyer & Merzbach (1991), pp. 255–56.
24. Singh (1997).
25. Quoted by Grattan-Guinness (1997), p. 724; Russell & Whitehead (1910–13).
26. Gödel (1962).
27. The minimum of arithmetic is known as 'primitive recursive arithmetic'. The axiom system presented in the Appendix provides this minimum. Gödel actually proved something very slightly weaker than this, but the full-strength version soon followed his proof.
28. Hoffman (1998), p. 16.
29. Bynner & Parsons (1997).

Appendix

Recommended Reading

I am probably alone in thinking that Kurt Gödel's original paper (in translation: Gödel 1962) is the clearest statement of his position. For anyone with some training in logic or mathematics, it's hard work but immensely rewarding to go through his proof step by step, for you can see how one of the great geniuses of our time constructed one of the most important results of modern thought. He also puts the theorems and the method of proof into the context of the philosophical debates of the time.

1. These proofs are laid out very formally, but very clearly, in Elliott Mendelson's classic *Introduction to Mathematical Logic* (1964, pp. 102–7). I follow his proof for $x + y = y + x$.

BIBLIOGRAPHY

Amunts, K., Schlaug, G., Jancke, L., Steinmetz, H., Schleicher, A., Dabring-haus, A., & Zilles, K. (1997). Motor cortex and hand motor skills: Structural compliance in the human brain. *Human Brain Mapping*, *5*, 206–15.

Anderson, S. W., Damasio, A. R., & Damasio, H. (1990). Troubled letters but not numbers: Domain specific cognitive impairments following focal damage in frontal cortex. *Brain*, *113*, 749–66.

Antell, S. E., & Keating, D. P. (1983). Perception of numerical invariance in neonates. *Child Development*, *54*, 695–701.

Ashcraft, M. (1995). Cognitive psychology and simple arithmetic: A review and summary of new directions. *Mathematical Cognition*, *1*, 3–34.

Ashcraft, M., & Battaglia, J. (1978). Cognitive arithmetic: Evidence for retrieval and decision in processes in mental addition. *Journal of Experimental Psychology: Human Learning and Memory*, *4*, 527–38.

Atkinson, J., Campbell, F., & Francis, M. (1976a). The magic number 4 ± 0: A new look at visual numerosity judgements. *Perception*, *5*, 327–34.

Atkinson, J., Francis, M., & Campbell, F. (1976b). The dependence of the visual numerosity limit on orientation, colour, and grouping in the stimulus. *Perception*, *5*, 335–42.

Bahn, P. G., & Vertut, J. (1997). *Journey Through the Ice Age*. London: Weidenfeld & Nicolson.

Baroody, A. J., & Gannon, K. B. (1984). The development of the commutativity principle and economic addition strategies. *Cognition and Instruction*, 1, 321–39.

Barrow, J. D. (1992). *Pi in the Sky: Counting, Thinking, and Being*. Oxford: Clarendon Press.

Beaton, A. E., Martin, M. O., Mullis, I. V. S., Gonzales, B. J., Smith, T. A., & Kelly, D. L. (1996). *Mathematics Achievement in the Middle School Years: IEA's Third International Mathematics and Science Survey (TIMSS)*. Boston: Boston College.

Bernstein, P. L. (1996). *Against the Gods: The Remarkable Story of Risk*. New York: John Wiley & Sons.

Bloom, P. (1994). Generativity within language and other cognitive domains. *Cognition*, 51, 177–89.

Boaler, J. (1997). *Experiencing School Mathematics*. Buckingham: Open University Press.

Boesch, C. (1996). The emergence of cultures among wild chimpanzees. *Proceedings of the British Academy*, 88, 251–68.

Bornstein, M., Kessen, W., & Weisskopf, S. (1976). Colour vision and hue categorization in human infants. *Journal of Experimental Psychology: Human Perception and Performance*, 2, 115–29.

Boyer, C. B., & Merzbach, U. C. (1991). *A History of Mathematics*, 2nd edn. New York: John Wiley & Sons.

Boysen, S. T. (1993). Counting in chimpanzees: Nonhuman principles and emergent properties of number. In S. T. Boysen & B. J. Capaldi (Eds), *The Development of Numerical Competence: Animal and Human Models*. Hillsdale, NJ: Lawrence Erlbaum.

Boysen, S. T., & Capaldi, B. J. (Eds) (1993). *The Development of Numerical Competence: Animal and Human Models*. Hillsdale, NJ: Lawrence Erlbaum.

Brannon, E. M., & Terrace, H. S. (1998). Ordering of the numerosities 1 to 9 by monkeys. *Science*, 282, 746–49.

Bright, M. (1998). Boys performing badly. *Observer*, 4 January, p. 13.

Brissiaud, R. (1992). A toll for number construction: Finger symbol sets. In J. Bideaud, C. Meljac, & J.-P. Fischer (Eds), *Pathways to Number: Children's Developing Numerical Abilities*. Hillsdale, NJ: Lawrence Erlbaum.

Brown, J. S., Collins, A., & Duguid, P. (1989). Situated cognition and the culture of learning. *Educational Researcher, 18,* 32–42.

Brownell, W. (1928). *The Development of Children's Number Ideas in Primary Grades.* Chicago, IL: University of Chicago Press.

Butterworth, B. (1981). Speech errors: Old data in search of new theories. *Linguistics, 19,* 627–62.

Butterworth, B. (1989). Lexical access in speech production. In W. Marslen-Wilson (Ed.), *Lexical Representation and Process.* Cambridge, MA: MIT Press.

Butterworth, B. (1994). Disorders of sentence production. *Philosophical Transactions of the Royal Society, Series B, 346,* 55–61.

Butterworth, B., Cipolotti, L., & Warrington, B. K. (1996). Short-term memory impairments and arithmetical ability. *Quarterly Journal of Experimental Psychology, 49A,* 251–62.

Butterworth, B., Girelli, L., Zorzi, M., & Jonckheere, A. R. (1999a). Organisation of addition facts in memory (to be published).

Butterworth, B., Zorzi, M., Girelli, L., & Jonckheere, A. R. (1999b). Addition and comparison (to be published).

Butterworth, B., Marchesini, N., & Girelli, L. (1999c). Organisation of multiplication facts in memory: Developmental trends. In A. Baroody & A. Dowker (Eds), *The Development of Arithmetical Concepts and Skills.* Mahwah, NJ: Lawrence Erlbaum (to be published).

Bynner, J., & Parsons, S. (1997). *Does Numeracy Matter?* London: The Basic Skills Agency.

Campbell, J. I. D. (1995). Mechanisms of simple addition and multiplication: A modified network interference theory and simulation. *Mathematical Cognition, 1,* 121–64.

Campbell, R., & Butterworth, B. (1985). Phonological dyslexia and dysgraphia in a highly literate subject: A developmental case with associated deficits of phonemic processing and awareness. *Quarterly Journal of Experimental Psychology, 37A,* 435–75.

Caramazza, A., & McCloskey, M. (1987). Dissociations of calculation processes. In G. Deloche & X. Seron (Eds), *Mathematical Disabilities: A Cognitive Neuropsychological Perspective.* Hillsdale, NJ: Lawrence Erlbaum.

Chase, V. M., Hertwig, R., & Gigerenzer, G. (1998). Visions of rationality. *Trends in Cognitive Science, 2,* 206–14.

Chauvet, J.-M., Deschamps, B. B., & Hillaire, C. (1996). *Chauvet Cave: The Discovery of the World's Oldest Paintings*. London: Thames & Hudson.

Cipolotti, L. (1995). Multiple routes for reading words, why not numbers? Evidence from a case of Arabic numeral dyslexia. *Cognitive Neuropsychology, 12*, 313–42.

Cipolotti, L., & Butterworth, B. (1995). Toward a multiroute model of number processing: Impaired number transcoding with preserved calculation skills. *Journal of Experimental Psychology: General, 124*, 375–90.

Cipolotti, L., Butterworth, B., & Denes, G. (1991). A specific deficit for numbers in a case of dense acalculia. *Brain, 114*, 2619–37.

Cipolotti, L., Butterworth, B., & Warrington, E. K. (1996). From "One thousand nine hundred and forty-five" to *1000, 945*. *Neuropsychologia, 32*, 503–9.

Cipolotti, L., & Costello, A. d. L. (1995). Selective impairment for simple division. *Cortex, 31*, 433–49.

Cipolotti, L., Warrington, E. K., & Butterworth, B. (1995). Selective impairment in manipulating Arabic numerals. *Cortex, 31*, 73–86.

Clottes, J. (1995). *Les Cavernes de Niaux*. Paris: Editions du Seuil.

Clottes, J. (1996). Epilogue: The Chauvet Cave today. In J.-M. Chauvet, E. B. Deschamps, & C. Hillaire, *Chauvet Cave: The Discovery of the World's Oldest Paintings*. London: Thames & Hudson.

Cockcroft, W. H. (1982). *Mathematics Counts: Report of the Committee of Inquiry into the Teaching of Mathematics in Schools under the Chairmanship of Dr W H Cockcroft*. London: HMSO.

Cohen, L., & Dehaene, S. (1996). Cerebral networks for number processing: Evidence from a case of posterior callosal lesion. *Neurocase, 2*, 155–74.

Conway, G. (1988). Rainbow over Wollo. *New Scientist*, 5 May, p. 70.

Conway, J. H., & Guy, R. K. (1996). *The Book of Numbers*. New York: Copernicus.

Critchley, M. (1939). *The Language of Gesture*. London: Arnold.

Critchley, M. (1953). *The Parietal Lobes*. London: Edward Arnold.

d'Errico, F. (1992). Technology, motion and the meaning of epipalaeolithic art. *Current Anthropology, 33*, 94–109.

d'Errico, F., & Cacho, C. (1994). Notation versus decoration in the Upper

Palaeolithic: a case-study from Tossal de la Roca, Alicante, Spain. *Journal of Archaeological Science*, *21*, 185–200.

Dantzig, T. (1962). *Number: The Language of Science*, 4th edn. London: George Allen & Unwin.

Datta, B., & Singh, A. N. (1935/1938). *History of Hindu Mathematics. A Source Book*, Parts I and II. Bombay: Asia Publishing House.

Davidson, J. W., Howe, M. J. A., Moore, D. G., & Sloboda, J. A. (1996). The role of parental influences in the development of musical performance. *British Journal of Developmental Psychology*, *14*, 399–412.

Davis, H. (1993). Numerical competence in animals: Life beyond Clever Hans. In S. T. Boysen & E. J. Capaldi (Eds), *The Development of Numerical Competence: Animal and Human Models*. Hillsdale, NJ: Lawrence Erlbaum.

Davis, H., & Pérusse, R. (1988). Numerical competence in animals: Definitional issues, current evidence and a new research agenda. *Behavioral and Brain Sciences*, *11*, 561–79.

Davis, P. J., & Hersch, R. (1983). *The Mathematical Experience*. London: Penguin.

DeFries, J. C., Vandenberg, S. G., & McClearn, G. E. (1976). Genetics of specific cognitive abilities. *Annual Review of Genetics*, *10*, 179–207.

Dehaene, S. (1997). *The Number Sense: How the Mind Creates Mathematics*. New York: Oxford University Press.

Dehaene, S., Bossini, S., & Giraux, P. (1993). The mental representation of parity and numerical magnitude. *Journal of Experimental Psychology: General*, *122*, 371–96.

Dehaene, S., & Changeux, J.-P. (1993). Development of elementary numerical abilities: A neuronal model. *Journal of Cognitive Neuroscience*, *5*, 390–407.

Dehaene, S., & Cohen, L. (1995). Towards an anatomical and functional model of number processing. *Mathematical Cognition*, *1*, 83–120.

Dehaene, S., Naccache, L., Le Clerc, H, G., Koechlin, E., Mueller, M., Dehaene-Lambertz, G., van de Moortele, P.-F., & Le Bihan, D. (1998). Imaging unconscious semantic priming. *Nature*, *395*, 597–600.

Delazer, M., & Benke, T. (1997). Arithmetic facts without meaning. *Cortex*, *33*, 697–710.

Delazer, M., & Butterworth, B. (1997). A dissociation of number meanings. *Cognitive Neuropsychology, 14,* 613–36.

Delazer, M., Ewen, P., Butterworth, B., & Benke, T. (1996). Implicit memory and arithmetic. Paper presented at International Conference on Memory, Abano Terme, Italy.

DfEE (1998). *Numeracy Matters: The Preliminary Report of the Numeracy Task Force (1998).* London: Department for Education and Employment.

Diamond, J. (1997a). *Guns, Germs and Steel: The Fates of Human Societies.* London: Jonathan Cape.

Diamond, J. (1997b). The language steamrollers. *Nature, 389,* 544–46.

Dixon, R. M. W. (1980). *The Languages of Australia.* Cambridge: Cambridge University Press.

Duncan, E., & MacFarland, C. (1980). Isolating the effects of symbolic distance and semantic congruity in comparative judgments: An additive factors analysis. *Memory and Cognition, 8,* 612–22.

Eimas, P., Siqueland, E. R., Jusczyk, P., & Vigorito, J. (1971). Speech perception in infants. *Science, 171,* 303–6.

Eisler, P. (1989). *My Life with the Printed Circuit.* London: Associated University Presses.

Enzensberger, H. M. (1998). *The Number Devil: A Mathematical Adventure* (M. H. Heim, Trans.). New York: Metropolitan Books.

Ericsson, K. A., Krampe, R. T., & Tesch-Römer, C. (1993). The role of deliberate practice in the acquisition of expert performance. *Psychological Review, 100,* 363–406.

Falkenstein, A. (1936). *Archaische Texte aus Uruk.* Berlin: Kommissions-Verlag Harrassowitz.

Faust, M. W., Ashcraft, M. H., & Fleck, D. E. (1996). Mathematics anxiety effects in simple and complex addition. *Mathematical Cognition, 2(1),* 25–62.

Flegg, G. (Ed.) (1989). *Numbers Through the Ages.* London: Macmillan in association with the Open University.

Fodor, J. A. (1983). *Modularity of Mind.* Cambridge, MA: MIT Press.

Foltz, G. S., Poltrock, S. E., & Potts, G. R. (1984). Mental comparison of size and magnitude: Size congruity effects. *Journal of Experimental Psychology: Learning, Memory, and Cognition, 10,* 442–53.

Fouts, R., & Mills, S. (1997). *Next of Kin*. London: Michael Joseph.

Friberg, J. (1984). Numbers and measures in the earliest written records. *Scientific American*, February, 78–85.

Frydman, O., & Bryant, P. E. (1988). Sharing and the understanding of number equivalence by young children. *Cognitive Development, 3*, 323–39.

Fullagar, R. L. K., Price, D. M., & Head, L. M. (1996). Early human occupation of Australia: Archaeology and thermoluminescence dating of Jinmium rock-shelter, Northern Territory. *Antiquity, 70*, 751–73.

Fuson, K. C. (1988). *Children's Counting and Concepts of Number*. New York: Springer-Verlag.

Fuson, K. C. (1992). Relationships between counting and cardinality from age 2 to 8. In J. Bideaud, C. Meljac, & J. P. Fisher (Eds.), *Pathways to Number: Children's Developing Numerical Abilities*. Hillsdale, NJ: Lawrence Erlbaum.

Fuson, K. C., & Kwon, Y. (1992). Subtraction: Effects of number words and other cultural tools. In J. Bideaud, C. Meljac, & J. P. Fisher (Eds.), *Pathways to Number: Children's Developing Numerical Abilities*. Hillsdale, NJ: Lawrence Erlbaum.

Gallistel, C. R. (1990). *The Organization of Learning*. Cambridge, MA: MIT Press.

Gallistel, C. R., & Gelman, R. (1992). Preverbal and verbal counting and computation. *Cognition, 44*, 43–74.

Galton, F. (1880). Visualised numerals. *Nature, 21*, 252–56.

Galton, F. (1979). *Hereditary Genius: An Inquiry into its Laws and Consequences*. London: Julian Friedman. [1st ed. 1869.]

Gardner, M. (1990). *Mathematical Carnival*. London: Penguin.

Geary, D. C. (1994). *Children's Mathematical Development*. Washington, DC: American Psychological Association.

Geary, D. C. (1996). Sexual selection and sex differences in mathematical abilities. *Behavioral and Brain Sciences, 19*, 229 et seq. [With peer commentary.]

Geary, D., Hamson, C. O., Chen, G.-P., Fan, L., Hoard, M. K., & Salthouse, T. A. (1997). Computational and reasoning abilities in arithmetic: Cross generational change in China and the United States. *Psychonomic Bulletin & Review, 4*, 425–30.

Gelman, R., & Gallistel, C. R. (1986). *The Child's Understanding of Number*. Cambridge, MA: Harvard University Press. [1st ed. 1978.]

Gelman, R., & Meck, E. (1983). Preschoolers counting: Principles before skill. *Cognition, 13*, 343–59.

Gerstmann, J. (1940). Syndrome of Finger Agnosia: Disorientation for right and left, agraphia and acalculia. *Archives of Neurology and Psychiatry, 44*, 398–408.

Giaquinto, M. (1995). Concepts and calculation. *Mathematical Cognition, 1*, 61–81.

Girelli, L. (1998). Accessing number meaning in children and adults. Ph.D. thesis, University College, London.

Girelli, L., & Butterworth, B. (1995). Finger counting in adulthood. Paper presented at conference on Language and Mathematical Thinking, London.

Girelli, L., & Delazer, M. (1996). Subtraction bugs in an acalculic patient. *Cortex, 32*, 547–55.

Girelli, L., Delazer, M., Guadagni, C., & Butterworth, B. (1999a). Applying conceptual knowledge of arithmetic (to be published).

Girelli, L., Lucangeli, D., & Butterworth, B. (1999b). The development of automaticity in accessing number magnitude. *Journal of Experimental Child Psychology* (to be published).

Gödel, K. (1962). *On Formally Undecidable Propositions of* Principia mathematica *and Related Systems* (B. Meltzer, Trans.). Edinburgh: Oliver & Boyd.

Gore, R. (1997). The dawn of humans: The first Europeans. *National Geographic*, January, pp. 96–113.

Grafman, J., Kampen, D., Rosenberg, J., Salazar, A., & Boller, F. (1989). Calculation abilities in a patient with a virtual left hemispherectomy. *Behavioral Neurology, 2*, 183–94.

Grattan-Guinness, I. (1997). *The Fontana History of the Mathematical Sciences*. London: Fontana.

Gross-Tur, V., Manor, O., & Shalev, R. S. (1996). Developmental dyscalculia: Prevalence and demographic features. *Developmental Medicine and Child Neurology, 38*, 25–33.

Hardy, G. H. (1967). *A Mathematician's Apology*. Cambridge: Cambridge University Press. [1st edn 1940.]

Hauser, M., MacNeilage, P., & Ware, M. (1996). Numerical representations in primates. *Proceedings of the National Academy of Sciences, USA, 93*, 1514–17.

Heinzelin, J. de (1962). Ishango. *Scientific American*, June, pp. 105–14.

Henschen, S. E. (1920). *Klinische und Anatomische Beitrage zu Pathologie des Gehirns*. Stockholm: Nordiska Bokhandeln.

Hermelin, B., & O'Connor, N. (1990). Factors and primes: A specific numerical ability. *Psychological Medicine*, 20, 163–69.

Hittmair-Delazer, M., Semenza, C., & Denes, G. (1994). Concepts and facts in calculation. *Brain*, 117, 715–28.

Hoffman, P. (1998). *The Man Who Loved Only Numbers*. London: Fourth Estate.

Holmes, O. W. (1871). *Mechanism in Thought and Morals*. Boston, MA: Osgood.

Howard, D., & Franklin, S. (1988). *Missing the Meaning? A Cognitive Neuropsychological Analysis of Single Word Processing in an Aphasic Patient*. Cambridge, MA: MIT Press.

Hulme, C., & Mackenzie, S. (1992). *Working Memory and Severe Learning Difficulties*. Hove: Lawrence Erlbaum.

Hunter, I. M. L. (1962). An exceptional talent for calculative thinking. *British Journal of Psychology*, 53, 243–80.

Jackson, M., & Warrington, E. K. (1986). Arithmetic skills in patients with unilateral cerebral lesions. *Cortex*, 22, 611–20.

Jeannerod, M., Arbib, M. A., Rizzolatti, G., & Sakata, H. (1995). Grasping objects: the cortical mechanisms of visuomotor transformation. *Trends in Neuroscience*, 18, 314–20.

Kahn, H. J., & Whitaker, H. A. (1991). Acalculia: An historical review of localization. *Brain & Cognition*, 17, 102–15.

Kanigel, R. (1991). *The Man Who Knew Infinity: A Life of the Genius Ramanujan*. London: Abacus.

Kendon, A. (1988). *Sign Languages of Aboriginal Australia: Cultural, Semiotic and Communicative Perspectives*. Cambridge: Cambridge University Press.

Keys, W., Harris, S., & Fernandes, C. (1996). *Third International Mathematics and Science Study. First National Report*, Part 1. Slough: National Foundation for Educational Research.

Kinsbourne, M., & Warrington, E. K. (1962). A study of finger agnosia. *Brain*, 85, 47–66.

Kinsbourne, M., & Warrington, E. K. (1963). The developmental Gerstmann Syndrome. *Annals of Neurology*, 8, 490–501.

Kitcher, P. (1984). *The Nature of Mathematical Knowledge.* Oxford: Oxford University Press.

Kline, M. (1990). *Mathematics in Western Culture.* London: Penguin. [1st UK ed. 1954, London: George Allen & Unwin.]

Körner, T. (1998). Pi in the sky. *Guardian,* 21 April, Education Guardian section, p. 4.

Kosc, L. (1974). Developmental dyscalculia. *Journal of Learning Disabilities,* 7, 159–62.

Lamb, R. (1993). Designs on life. *New Scientist,* 30 October, pp. 37–40.

Lamberg-Karlovsky, C. C. (Ed.). (1978). *Hunters, Farmers and Civilizations. Old World Archaeology.* San Francisco: W. H. Freeman.

Lancy, D. F. (1983). *Cross-Cultural Studies in Cognition and Mathematics.* New York: Academic Press.

Laurillard, D. (1993). *Rethinking University Teaching: A Framework for the Effective Use of Educational Technology.* London: Routledge.

Lave, J., & Wenger, E. (1991). *Situated Learning.* Cambridge: Cambridge University Press.

Leakey, R. (1994). *The Origin of Humankind.* London: Weidenfeld & Nicolson.

LeFevre, J., & Liu, J. (1997). The role of experience in numerical skill: Multiplication performance in adults from Canada and China. *Mathematical Cognition,* 3, 31–62.

LeFevre, J.-A., Sadesky, G. S., & Bisanz, J. (1996). Selection of procedures in mental addition: Reassessing the problem size effect in adults. *Journal of Experimental Psychology: Learning, Memory, and Cognition,* 22, 216–30.

Le Guin, U. K. (1975). The Masters. In *The Wind's Twelve Quarters.* New York: Harper & Row.

Leroi-Gourhan, A. (February 1968). The evolution of paleolithic art. *Scientific American.*

Lewis, C., Hitch, G., & Walker, P. (1994). The prevalence of specific arithmetic difficulties and specific reading difficulties in 9- and 10-year-old boys and girls. *Journal of Child Psychology and Psychiatry,* 35, 283–92.

Locke, J. (1961). *Essay Concerning Human Understanding* (J. W. Yolton, Ed.). London: J. M. Dent [1st ed. 1690.]

McCarthy, R. A., & Warrington, E. K. (1990). *Cognitive Neuropsychology: A Clinical Introduction.* London: Academic Press.

McCloskey, M., & Caramazza, A. (1987). Dissociations of calculation processes. In G. Deloche & X. Seron (Eds.), *Mathematical Disabilities: A Cognitive Neuropsychological Perspective.* Hillsdale, NJ: Lawrence Erlbaum.

McComb, K., Packer, C., & Pusey, A. (1994). Roaring and numerical assessment in contests between groups of female lions, *Panthera leo. Animal Behaviour, 47,* 379–87.

McGurk, H. (1972). Infant discrimination of orientation. *Journal of Experimental Child Psychology, 14,* 151–164.

MacLeod, C. M. (1991). Half a century of research on the Stroop effect: An integrative review. *Psychological Bulletin, 109,* 163–203.

MacLeod, C. M., & Dunbar, K. (1988). Training and Stroop-like interference: Evidence for a continuum of automaticity. *Journal of Experimental Psychology: Learning, Memory, and Cognition, 14,* 126–35.

Mandler, G. (1997). *Human Nature Explored.* New York: Oxford University Press.

Mandler, G., & Shebo, B. J. (1982). Subitizing: An analysis of its component processes. *Journal of Experimental Psychology: General, 11,* 1–22.

Marshack, A. (1991). *The Roots of Civilization,* 2nd ed. London: Moyer Bell.

Matsuzawa, T. (1985). Use of numbers by a chimpanzee. *Nature, 315,* 57–59.

Matsuzawa, T. (1996). Chimpanzee intelligence in nature and captivity: Isomorphism of symbol and tool use. In W. C. McGrew, L. F. Marchant, & T. Nishida (Eds.), *Great Ape Societies.* Cambridge University Press.

Maynard, L., & Edwards, R. (1971). Wall markings. In R. V. S. Wright (Ed.), *Archaeology of the Gallus Site, Koonalda Cave.* Australian Aboriginal Studies No. 26. Canberra: Australian Institute of Aboriginal Studies.

Mendelson, E. (1964). *Introduction to Mathematical Logic.* Princeton, NJ: Van Nostrand.

Menninger, K. (1969). *Number Words and Number Symbols: A Cultural History of Numbers.* (P. Broneer, Trans.). Cambridge, MA: MIT Press.

Miceli, G., Mazzuchi, A., Menn, L., & Goodglass, H. (1983). Contrasting cases of Italian agrammatic aphasia without comprehension disorder. *Brain & Language, 19,* 65–97.

Miller, G. A. (1969). *Psychology: The Science of Mental Life.* London: Pelican. [1st ed. 1962, London: Hutchinson.]

Miller, K. F., & Stigler, J. W. (1987). Counting in Chinese: Cultural variation in a basic skill. *Cognitive Development, 2,* 279–305.

Mithen, S. (1996). *The Prehistory of the Mind*. London: Thames & Hudson.

Morwood, M. J., O Sullivan, P. B., Aziz, F., & Raza, A. (1998). Fission track ages of stone tools and fossils on the east Indonesian island of Flores. *Nature, 392*, 173–76.

Moyer, R. S., & Landauer, T. K. (1967). Time required for judgements of numerical inequality. *Nature, 215*, 1519–20.

Murray, A. (1978). *Reason and Society in the Middle Ages*. Oxford: Clarendon Press.

Neugebauer, O. (1962). *The Exact Sciences in Antiquity*, 2nd edn. New York: Harper Torchbooks.

Neuman, D. (1987). The Origin of Arithmetic Skills: A Phenomenographic Approach. Ph.D. thesis, Göteborg.

Nunes, T., & Bryant, P. (1996). *Children Doing Mathematics*. Oxford: Blackwell.

Nunes, T., Schliemann, A. D., & Carraher, D. W. (1993). *Street Mathematics and School Mathematics*. Cambridge: Cambridge University Press.

Pascual-Leone, A., & Torres, F. (1993). Plasticity of the sensorimotor cortex representation of the reading finger in Braille readers. *Brain, 116*, 39–52.

Penfield, W., & Rasmussen, T. (1952). *The Cerebral Cortex of Man*. New York: The Macmillan Company.

Pepperberg, I. M. (1987). Evidence for conceptual quantitative abilities in the African Grey parrot: Labelling of cardinal sets. *Ethology, 75*, 37–61.

Pesenti, M., Seron, X., & Van Der Linden, M. (1995). Selective impairment as evidence for mental organisation of arithmetical facts: BB, a case of preserved subtraction? *Cortex, 31*, 661–72.

Piaget, J. (1952). *The Child's Conception of Number*. London: Routledge & Kegan Paul.

Piatelli-Palmerini, M. (1994). *Inevitable Illusions: How Mistakes of Reason Rule our Minds*. New York: John Wiley & Sons.

Pinker, S. (1994). *The Language Instinct*. London: Allen Lane.

Potter, M. C., & Levy, E. I. (1968). Spatial enumeration without counting. *Child Development, 39*, 265–72.

Power, R. J. D., & dal Martello, M. F. (1990). The dictation of Italian numerals. *Language and Cognitive Processes, 5*, 237–54.

Reeve, R. A., & Pattison, P. E. (1996). The referential adequacy of students' visual analogies. *Mathematical Cognition, 2,* 137–70.

Reiss, D., McCowan, B., & Marino, L. (1997). Communicative and other cognitive characteristics of bottlenose dolphins. *Trends in Cognitive Sciences, 1,* 140–45.

Rémond-Besuchet, C., Noel, M.-P., Seron, X., Thioux, M., Brun, M., & Aspe, X. (1998). Selective preservation of exceptional arithmetical knowledge in a demented patient. *Mathematical Cognition.*

Resnick, L. B. (1995). Inventing arithmetic: Making children's intuition work at school. In C. A. Nelson (Ed.), *Basic and Applied Perspectives on Learning, Cognition, and Development.* Mahwah, NJ: Lawrence Erlbaum.

Resnick, L. B., & Ford, W. W. (1981). *The Psychology of Mathematics for Instruction.* Hillsdale, NJ: Lawrence Erlbaum.

Richardson, F. C., & Suinn, R. M. (1972). The Mathematics Anxiety Rating Scale. *Journal of Counseling Psychology, 19,* 551–54.

Rilling, M. (1993). Invisible counting animals: A history of contributions from comparative psychology, ethology, and learning theory. In S. T. Boysen & E. J. Capaldi (Eds.), *The Development of Numerical Competence: Animal and Human Models.* Hillsdale, NJ: Lawrence Erlbaum.

Rossor, M. N., Warrington, E. K., & Cipolotti, L. (1995). The isolation of calculation skills. *Journal of Neurology, 242,* 78–81.

Rourke, B. P. (1993). Arithmetic disabilities, specific and otherwise: A neuropsychological perspective. *Journal of Learning Disabilities, 26,* 214–26.

Rovet, J., Szekely, C., & Hockenberry, M.-N. (1994). Specific arithmetic calculation deficits in children with Turner syndrome. *Journal of Clinical and Experimental Neuropsychology, 16,* 820–39.

Rumbaugh, D. M., & Washburn, D. A. (1993). Counting by chimpanzees and ordinality judgments by macaques in video-formatted tasks. In S. T. Boysen & E. J. Capaldi (Eds.), *The Development of Numerical Competence: Animal and Human Models.* Hillsdale, NJ: Lawrence Erlbaum.

Russell, B. (1956). *Introduction to Mathematical Philosophy.* London: George Allen & Unwin [1st ed. 1919.]

Russell, B., & Whitehead, A. N. (1910–13). *Principia mathematica.* Cambridge: Cambridge University Press.

Sacks, O. (1986). *The Man Who Mistook His Wife for a Hat.* London: Picador.

Salzmann, Z. (1950). A method for analyzing numerical systems. *Word, 6,* 78–83.

Saxe, G. B. (1981). *The Changing Form of Numerical Reasoning Among the Oksapmin.* Port Moresby, Papua New Guinea: UNESCO/Education.

Schlaug, G., Jancke, L., Huang, Y. X., Staiger, J. F., & Steinmetz, H. (1995a). Increased corpus callosum size in musicians. *Neuropsychologia, 33,* 1047–55.

Schlaug, G., Jancke, L., Huang, Y. X., & Steinmetz, H. (1995b). In-vivo evidence of structural brain asymmetry in musicians. *Science, 267,* 699–701.

Schlottmann, A., & Anderson, N. H. (1994). Children's judgements of expected value. *Developmental Psychology, 30,* 56–66.

Schmandt-Besserat, D. (1978). The earliest precursor of writing. *Scientific American,* June, 50–59.

Schmandt-Besserat, D. (1987). Oneness, twoness, threeness: How ancient accountants invented numbers. *The Sciences, 27*(4), 44–48.

Schoenfeld, A. H. (1988). When good teaching leads to bad results: The disasters of well taught mathematics courses. *Educational Psychologist, 23,* 145–66.

Seibt, U. (1988). Are animals naturally attuned to number? *Behavioral and Brain Sciences, 11,* 597–98.

Seidenberg, A. (1960). The diffusion of counting practices. *University of California Publications in Mathematics, 3*(4), 215–99.

Seidenberg, A. (1962). Ritual origin of counting. *Archive for the History of Exact Sciences, 2,* 1–40.

Sekuler, R., & Mierkiewicz, D. (1977). Children's judgements of numerical inequality. *Child Development, 48,* 630–33.

Seron, X., Pesenti, M., Noël, M.-P., Deloche, G., & Cornet, J.-A. (1992). Images of numbers, or "When 98 is upper left and 6 sky blue". *Cognition, 44,* 159–96.

Sharer, R. J. (1994). *The Ancient Maya,* 5th ed. Stanford, CA: Stanford University Press.

Siegler, R. S., & Shrager, J. (1984). Strategy choices in addition and subtraction: How do children know what to do? In C. Sophian (Ed.), *Origins of Cognitive Skills.* Hillsdale, NJ: Lawrence Erlbaum.

Simon, T. J., Hespos, S. J., & Rochat, P. (1995). Do infants understand simple arithmetic? A replication of Wynn (1992). *Cognitive Development*, 10, 253–69.

Singh, S. (1997). *Fermat's Last Theorem*. London: Fourth Estate.

Skuse, D. H., James, R. S., Bishop, D. V. M., Coppin, B., Dalton, P., Aamodt-Leeper, G., Bacarese-Hamilton, M., Creswell, C., McGurk, R., & Jacobs, P. A. (1997). Evidence from Turner's syndrome of an imprinted X-linked locus affecting cognitive function. *Nature*, 387, 705–8.

Smith, S. B. (1983). *The Great Mental Calculators*. New York: Columbia University Press.

Sokol, S. M., McCloskey, M., Cohen, N. J., & Aliminosa, D. (1991). Cognitive representations and processes in arithmetic: Inferences from the performance of brain-damaged subjects. *Journal of Experimental Psychology: Learning, Memory, and Cognition*, 17, 355–76.

Spalding, J. M. K., & Zangwill, O. L. (1950). Disturbance of number-form in a case of brain injury. *Journal of Neurology, Neurosurgery and Psychiatry*, 13, 24–29.

Starkey, P., Spelke, E. S., & Gelman, R. (1990). Numerical abstraction by human infants. *Cognition*, 36, 97–128.

Strohm, P. (1996). The 1390s: The empty throne. In A. Briggs & D. Snowman (Eds), *Fins de Siècle: How Centuries End*. New Haven, CT: Yale University Press.

Stroop, J. R. (1935). Studies of interference in serial verbal reactions. *Journal of Experimental Psychology*, 18, 643–62.

Struik, D. J. (1954). *A Concise History of Mathematics*. London: G. Bell & Sons.

Swetz, F. J. (1987). *Capitalism and Arithmetic: The New Math of the 15th Century*. La Salle, IL: Open Court.

Ta'ir, J., Brezner, A., & Ariel, R. (1997). Profound developmental dyscalculia: Evidence for a cardinal/ordinal skills acquisition device. *Brain and Cognition*, 35, 184–206.

Temple, C. (1997). *Developmental Cognitive Neuropsychology*. Hove: Psychology Press.

Thorndike, E. L. (1922). *The Psychology of Arithmetic*. New York: Macmillan.

Thorpe, W. H. (1963). *Learning and Instinct in Animals*, 2nd ed. London: Methuen.

Ucko, P. J., & Rosenfeld, A. (1969). *Palaeolithic Cave Art*. London: Weidenfeld & Nicolson.

Van Loosbroek, E., & Smitsman, A. W. (1990). Visual perception of numerosity in infancy. *Developmental Psychology, 26,* 916–22.

Warrington, E. (1982). The fractionation of arithmetical skills: A single case study. *Quarterly Journal of Experimental Psychology, 34A,* 31–51.

Warrington, E. K., & James, M. (1967). Tachistoscopic number estimation in patients with unilateral lesions. *Journal of Neurology, Neurosurgery and Psychiatry, 30,* 468–74.

Washburn, D. A., & Rumbaugh, D. M. (1991). Ordinal judgments of numerical symbols by macaques *(Macaca mulatta)*. *Psychological Science, 2,* 190–93.

Wason, P. C. (1966). Reasoning. In B. M. Foss (Ed.), *New Horizons in Psychology*. London: Penguin.

Wassmann, J., & Dasen, P. R. (1994). Yupno number system and counting. *Journal of Cross-Cultural Psychology, 25*(1), 78–94.

Wertheim, M. (1997). *Pythagoras' Trousers*. London: Fourth Estate.

Whitehead, A. N. (1948). *An Introduction to Mathematics*. London: Oxford University Press. [1st ed. 1911.]

Whorf, B. L. (1956). *Language, Thought and Reality*. Cambridge, MA: MIT Press.

Wilkins, D. P. (1989). Mparntwe Arrernte: Studies in the Structure and Semantics of Grammar. Ph.D. thesis, Australian National University.

Winter, W. (1991). Some thoughts about Indo-European numerals. In J. Gvozdanovic (Ed.), *Indo-European Numerals*. Berlin: Mouton de Gruyter.

Wynn, K. (1990). Children's understanding of counting. *Cognition, 36,* 155–93.

Wynn, K. (1992). Addition and subtraction by human infants. *Nature, 358,* 749–51.

Wynn, K. (1995). The origins of numerical knowledge. *Mathematical Cognition, 1,* 35–60.

Zaslavsky, C. (1973). *Africa Counts: Number and Pattern in African Culture*. Boston, MA: Prindle, Weber & Schmidt.

Zeki, S. (1993). *A Vision of the Brain*. Oxford: Blackwell Scientific.

INDEX

Abacus, 88–89, 93
Abel (rhesus monkey), 231–32
Abelard, Peter, 90
Abilities in mathematics. *See* Numerical and mathematical abilities
Aborigines, xii–xiii, 49–50
Absolon, Karl, 46
Absolute numerosity, 144
'Abstract-modular' model, 371n41
Abstract reasoning. *See* Reasoning
Abstractness principle of counting, 112
Acalculia, 149–52, 163, 164, 170, 174, 190, 218–20, 240–41
Access deficit, 170
Accounts and bookkeeping, 68–75, 323
Accumulator, 6–7
Adding composition principle, 70–71
Addition: animals' training in, 131–32, 135; by Signor Bellini, 173–75; commutativity law of, 254–55, 355–56; counting used in, 253; and developmental dyscalculia, 278; by Dr. Constable, 168–70; and finger arithmetic, 204–205, 304;
impact of stroke/brain damage on, 168–70, 171, 173–75, 185, 187; mental matrices of, 309–10; mistakes in procedures, 311; multiplication as distributive over, 255; mysteries about, 346–47; and number line, 217; stages in children's learning, 253–54; and street mathematics, 288–92, 295–96; transformation in problem solving, 307–308
Additive composition, 10, 57, 117–18, 156, 296
Africa, 30, 31, 36–39, 46, 55–56, 142–43, 291, 362
African Grey parrot, 127, 138
Agni-Purana, 80
Agraphia, 218, 219
Agriculture, 26–32, 290–91
Ahmes, 325
Ai (chimpanzee), 129
Ainu language, 66, 67, 117
Aitken, Alexander, 263–64, 297–98
Aleph nought/null, 336
Alex (African Grey parrot), 127, 138
Alexandria, 77, 78
Algebra, 318–19
Algorithm, etymology of, 76

Warrington, Elizabeth K., 154, 161–62, 168, 170, 174, 191, 219–21, 279–80, 369, 370n18, 370n22, 371n24, 373n48, 376n52

Washburn, David, 134, 135, 231–32

Wason, Peter, 367n28

Wassmann, J., 363

Weber, Ernst, 3, 230–31

Weights and measures, 91–92

Wernicke, Carl, 154, 198

Wernicke's aphasia, 198

Wernicke's area, 154, 198

Wertheim, Margaret, 123

West Africa, 142–43

Weyl, Hermann, 124, 335

Whitehead, Alfred North, 348–49, 350, 369–70n3, 379

Whole numbers, Kronecker on, 16

Wiles, Andrew, 348, 377n14, 378n47

Wilkins, David, 50

Williams, Serena, 269

Williams, Venus, 269

Woods, Tiger, 269

Words. *See* Language; Number words

Working memory. *See* Short-term memory

Working Memory and Severe Learning Difficulties (Hulme and Mackenzie), 161

Writing of numerals versus letters, 181–85

Writing system, 83

Wynn, Karen, 103, 106, 111–12, 141

Y.K., 376n52

Yard measurement, 15

Yerkes Primate Research Center, 129, 134–35, 231–32

Yupno, 51–52, 200, 205, 363

Zangwill, Israel, 373n27

Zangwill, Oliver L., 214–16, 373n27

Zaslavsky, Claudia, 362

Zeal: for mathematics, 288, 292–99; of prodigies, 258–62, 285–86, 297–98

Zeki, S., 372n1

Zero: evolution of words for, 76, 77; of Hindus, 76–81; history of, 75–84; and Maya, 82–84; and negative numbers, 322

Zulu, 55–56, 94